THE
DON

ALSO BY WILLIAM BRASHLER

The Bingo Long Traveling All-Stars
and Motor Kings

City Dogs

The DON

The Life and Death of Sam Giancana

William Brashler

HARPER & ROW, PUBLISHERS
New York, Hagerstown
San Francisco, London

For Julie Fallowfield, cheers

Portions of this book have appeared in slightly different form in *New York* magazine.

THE DON: THE LIFE AND DEATH OF SAM GIANCANA. Copyright © 1977 by William Brashler. All rights reserved. Printed in the United States of America. No part of this book may be used or reproduced in any manner whatsoever without written permission except in the case of brief quotations embodied in critical articles and reviews. For information address Harper & Row, Publishers, Inc., 10 East 53rd Street, New York, N.Y. 10022. Published simultaneously in Canada by Fitzhenry & Whiteside Limited, Toronto.

Designed by Dorothy Schmiderer

Library of Congress Cataloging in Publication Data

Brashler, William.
    The don.

    1. Giancana, Sam, 1908–1975. 2. Crime and criminals
—United States—Biography. 3. Mafia. I. Title.
HV6248.G48B72 1977   364.1′092′4 [B]   76–5113
ISBN 0–06–010447–3

77 78 79 80 10 9 8 7 6 5 4 3 2

Contents

A section of photographs
follows page 150.

Preface

DURING THE WRITING of this book I spoke with a woman who had just returned from a trip to Sicily with her 80-year-old Italian aunt. While on the island, she said, her aunt looked up into the hills and said in her Old World tongue, "They're up there." The woman asked who, "Who's up there, auntie?" But the old woman would only reply, "Them." She was coaxed to explain, but she would say no more, not even the *word*. To her generation, those who remember life in Sicily so well, *mafia* is still a dreaded concept, something known but not discussed.

That feeling has been diluted through the years, but I sensed it strongly in certain stages of my research. I was told that it was useless to dig too deeply, not necessarily for the sake of my own safety, but because the specter of a gangster like Sam Giancana, even in death, is enough to keep those who knew him afraid to talk. Fortunately, I was on many occasions able to break through the silence, and though most wished to remain anonymous, I'm grateful to them for the information and insights they provided me.

A much different problem also arose, however, one perhaps more difficult for many people to deal with than the existence of organized crime. Sam Giancana was a Sicilian, as were many but not all of the major crime figures in this country. It should not be necessary to add that all Sicilians and Italian-Americans are not criminals, or that crime is not inherent to that community. But the question of bias invariably arises and often manages to obscure more important issues. If, in reading the first portion of this book especially, the reader comes away with the assumption that the author believes all Italian immigrants and their children became hoodlums, then he has missed the point. It seemed useless to me to qualify every negative reference to Italian-Americans, just as the reverse would have been true had I chosen to write a biography of an Italian-American brain surgeon.

But the charge will no doubt arise; the study of the ethnic origins of anyone with so grisly a life as Sam Giancana will scratch thin skins, and unnecessarily arouse rational people. While I sympathize, I cannot apologize in order to pacify that kind of sensitivity.

I do apologize for not talking to everybody. Sam Giancana got around, and I fully believe I could have spent the rest of my life tracking him. I was lucky to have the cooperation of many who did, especially those in the various police agencies. No hoodlum anywhere at any time underwent tighter surveillance during his salad days than Giancana, a fact that sharply enhances this book. I am deeply grateful to the many individuals who've spent years working against organized crime and who were kind enough to share their insights into it with me. In a time when various police agencies are less than favorably portrayed, these men struck me as impressive professionals.

There were many others, all of whom illumined some aspect of my research and deserve much gratitude:

David Schippers, former Assistant U.S. Attorney; Peter Vaira and Doug Roller of the U.S. Justice Department's Organized Crime Strike Force;

Emmett Dedmon and the library staff of the Chicago *Sun-Times* and *Daily News;* Jack Mabley of the Chicago *Tribune;* Art Petacque of the *Sun-Times;* Dorothy Storck of the Philadelphia *Inquirer;* Sandy Smith of *Time* magazine;

Myke Novotnak of the Chicago Crime Commission and Charles Siragusa of the Illinois Legislative Investigating Commission, both of whom gave me access to their voluminous files;

The staffs of the Chicago Public Library; the Chicago Historical Society; and the Joseph Regenstein Library of the University of Chicago;

Judge George N. Leighton; Don Ricker; Stephen and Marion Malato; Jack Star;

Corrado DeSylvester, one-time assistant of the late John Landesco, who helped research and write the unpublished manuscript "The Forty-Two Gang: A Study of a Neighborhood Criminal Group," and who shared with me his own research papers as well as his expertise on Chicago's Near West Side Italian community.

Finally, there are two people whose help was immeasurable: my agent, Julie Fallowfield, who saw from the beginning; and my wife Cindy, who has always made the difference.

WILLIAM BRASHLER
Chicago
June 1976

THEY WERE TOUGH, bull-necked Italian kids, just out of their teens, scarred where acne screamed across their shoulders and necks. But they looked old, mean, and all because of their hair. It was air-brushed up and straight back, no part, dry and natural like the commercials but slicked over their ears like old-time grease-balls. It was immaculate, macho, but old.

Eight of them ran madly around the parking lot of the Mont-clair Funeral Home on West Belmont. It was 92 degrees on a Monday afternoon, sticky Chicago heat, yet these Italian kids were wearing long-sleeved $18 Qiana shirts. Open to mid-chest, marked by gold chains or beaded necklaces, the Qianas tapered to flared pants, then thick-heeled platform shoes that clopped over the pavement.

It was "us against them" for the Italian kids, them being the leering pack of reporters and cameramen, sound crews, photographers, columnists, federal agents, police intelligence officers, neighbors—all of them spilling onto Belmont Avenue and pushing onto the funeral parlor's parking lot trying to get a better look. It was all the Italian kids could do to push them back. They did it by scurrying around like a junior corps of the Secret Service, pushing television cameramen off balance, shoving Nikons into noses, cursing, blocking lenses, threatening anyone who dared come too close.

It was all for Uncle Mo, nothing but a perimeter defense around the wake of a skinny, beak-nosed, hollow-eyed man these kids never knew. Had he been alive he probably would have told them to go away and grow up.

But Sam was laid out, the object of three-inch headlines, and these razor-cut nephews and cousins decided that his remains were to be protected. It didn't matter that none of them understood the mechanics of why he was murdered, and why they themselves were added insult.

They ran to shield guests who got out of compact cars and stationwagons. There weren't many: a couple of hundred—women in wigs and curled, dyed hair, middle-aged men in black suits who perspired and pushed the elbows of their wives, occasionally ducking heads from a camera or shielding already shaded eyes.

But there was almost nothing reminiscent of Sam Giancana and the crowd he kept. No pink Cadillacs, no leased Continentals, not a single front-page hood familiar to the cameras and the mob writers, the federal agents and their tripod-supported field glasses.

Only Keely Smith and Phyllis McGuire showed, Keely looking older but just as ravishing, the Keely Smith who sang with Louis Prima and whose toothy, autographed picture once hung in Giancana's office, and Phyllis, the treetop of Arthur Godfrey's McGuire Sisters, whose affectionately signed portrait Giancana kept in his home.

Both kept their heads down and pushed into the chapel along with Giancana's three wan-faced daughters, Antoinette, Bonnie, and Francine. Phyllis wore a wig and got by so quickly that the reporters missed her completely. Keely was spotted, but with the shoving and pushing, the punks with the hair who thought nothing of cuffing a couple hundred bucks' worth of telephoto lens, she wasn't worth the effort.

Once the glass doors closed, with not a single reporter or agent allowed inside, the Italian kids fell back. Barely a half hour passed before the doors reopened. The guests stepped back into the parking lot as furtively as they had come in. Again, the open-shirted punks went into action, this time with more spit and rancor because the $8,000 casket of Giancana was coming out. And no reporters were going to get close to it.

The Cadillacs pulled up, the pallbearers came into view, and suddenly there was a crush of activity. The Italian kids went wild, running between flanks, pushing, waving their hands in front of cameras, cursing, shoving anyone who made an advance on the relatives, the daughters, Keely and Phyllis.

When the silver casket came out there was no way to hide it or keep the cameras out. They snapped and whirred as the pallbearers bumped it into the hearse, pallbearers who included not one high-ranking friend or associate of Giancana, not one notable except for Butch Blasi, the longtime bodyguard and chauffeur. Butch, who was like a brother.

Even that was lost on the scrambling punks. The fact that they were doing what they were doing at such a funeral was lost on them: the comedown, the lack of class, the very idea that a guy like Giancana would go out under a phalanx of coiffed kids who talked little or no Italian, who wouldn't know Sicily from the old neighborhood, yet who thought they had to muscle people in Giancana's honor. It was an embarrassment no one would have thought possible a few years ago. But this hot and agitated funeral was not a few years ago, not the old days.

Finally the hearse moved away, headed for Mount Carmel Cemetery. The Qiana kids ran alongside the car with their hands over the roof, a final awkward attempt to conceal what everyone knew was inside. They stumbled laterally, looking foolish even to the members of the procession. It was embarrassing to watch as they gave the finger to the cameramen, the finger if one could believe it, not even an authentic Italian gesture. But it was what was expected from this bunch: frantic, stupid, and looking so old. The hair.

The visitor had waited all afternoon for her to return home. He'd inquired of her dark-haired sons about her arrival, but they were evasive and close-mouthed, having acquired through the years a natural suspicion of strangers in sportcoats and ties. So he sat in his car idly surveying the rolling subdivision of the far western Chicago suburb, where kids rode bikes in the middle of the roads and cats chased bugs in the grass.

Finally she greeted him and asked him inside the colonial-style house. She was his daughter, and immediately the lines of Giancana could be seen in her face and her expressions. She offered the visitor a glass of wine. "If you're going to spend time with Italians you better get a taste for red wine," she said. The room was quiet, darkened from the outside light by drapes. Standing in a corner was a picture taken years before of her and her two sisters and their mother. Near it was one of her, head bowed, at first communion. And still another of Sam, a soft, pastel-colored portrait of years back when his face was full, a slight smile on closed lips.

She quickly finished her wine, then scolded a son who was noisily toying with the family's miniature greyhounds. The son refused to leave; he was around eleven, a chunky, moist-mouthed kid with black hair that hung over his forehead. But he was more friendly and curious than his brothers.

"What do you do for a living?" he asked while bending his head and trying to read the documents the visitor had under his arm.

"I'm self-employed," the visitor said.

The boy looked crookedly at him.

"No you're not," he said. "My grandfather was self-employed."

Though most of them have long since moved to nondescript suburbs into large homes with private lots that all but cut them off from their neighbors and one another, the wives and daughters of hoods still congregate at markets and bakeries from time to time and talk as they did years back on stoops in the old neighborhood. Shopowners and managers soon get to know them, or recognize who they are, and can't help but overhear them. Most of their talk is gossip about family or other mundane matters, but occasionally they will talk about the business of the underworld. They have even been known to cancel health and beauty appointments on short notice, thereby giving signal of mob doings explosive enough so that they will have to leave town with their husbands.

Such activity occurred after the death of Giancana. In a particular market in a western Chicago suburb, the wife and daughter of a prominent hood chatted openly about the murder, discussing why it was ordered and the details of how it happened. They laughed about newspaper accounts of hoods leaving town after the murder, knowing that nobody had gone anywhere. One mentioned a newspaper story that described the age and height of a particular suspect, and she added, "They couldn't be further from the truth."

They were joined shortly by another relative, and after exchanging small talk, they resumed talking about the murder. One said that the word had gone out from the top that no outfit members were to attend the funeral unless they could get there without being tailed by the FBI. It was enough, they said, to keep everybody away. Other events of the week were casually mentioned, a subject broached like anything else in the women's daily routines. Finally one shook her head and said matter-of-factly, "I don't know why they didn't kill him a long time ago."

Then they parted and proceeded to go about their day's shopping.

Where his parents walked with uncertainty and not a little fear, he roamed with brazen self-assurance. He was a dago, the son of an illiterate Sicilian who had come to Chicago at the turn of the century and filtered into the Near West Side, a place of tenements and open fields and peddlers known as the "Patch." In his home, the family spoke thick Italian, but on the streets, on Taylor Street, he spoke English, a slick street jargon that he and his buddies had invented and of which, to their delight, their parents, whom they referred to as greaseballs, had no comprehension.

They also dumped their clumsy Italian first names in favor of nicknames—Teets, Chudaback, Archie, Mibs. His was Mooney, a tag taken from his unpredictability, a guy who was at times crazy —just a little mooney. But he was mooney like a fox, quickly building a reputation on the street for being a "smart head," a big guy in the block gangs that thrived in the Patch. He dressed swell and talked tough.

As wise and hard as he thought he was, Mooney Giancana was still a neighborhood kid, one who could barely read or write after dropping out of the eighth grade, who strutted and flaunted his stuff in the Patch but who was lost when he left it. He and his buddies played checkers and softball, or shot craps on the sidewalk, hung out in shacks and kept an eye out for the coppers. For money they went after peanut machines, smashing the glass, scooping up the pennies, then sprinting off into the alleys. With the pennies they went to the delicatessens or the Nuti Bakery for its sandwiches piled high with Italian beef, or to the Jewish delis, where they bought corned beef, or they ambled over to the sweet shops and bought watermelon, the sugary lemon ice, or corn on the cob for a penny, which they ate with the melted butter running down their arms.

But his tastes gradually changed. Smashing peanut machines for pennies gave way to swiping clothes from lines, grabbing goods from department stores, or better yet, stripping cars of their tires, fender skirts, or the elaborate motor meters on the hoods. Those goods could be sold for dollars, fast money that bought smart clothes like the big-time gangsters wore and steaks like they ate in restaurants. The money also carried risks, and Mooney began packing a "heater" and watching for cops who had to be paid off or they would chase him and throw slugs at him. And such money bought him a car, a jalopy, something Mooney's father never thought anyone could be rich enough to own, but which Mooney had as a teenager and which he drove like no other kid in the Patch. He was a wheelman supreme. And to keep his jalopy safe from like-minded thieves he lined the underside of the fender skirts with razor blades, so that when the punks came to pull them off they left with fingers sliced and bloody.

But his tastes would change even more, like the times, the faces, the ambitions. He was still Mooney to his friends, but now he traveled in cars driven for him, smoked imported cigars and enjoyed fine whiskeys, and collected exquisite German porcelain. The porcelain was a special love, and he spent hours admiring groupings and delicate, hand-painted figurines, then paying top prices for them. He prized a piece of four white horses and a carriage with four attendants and two figures inside; a Dresden group of three musicians and a dancing couple; a seventeen-piece porcelain monkey band; a figurine of a girl with a basket of flowers and a lamb. He collected others: horses and carriages, cherubs, mermaids, Leda and the swan, flowers, fruit, beggars, lovers. He complemented them with paintings, pedestals, urns, a Louis XV mahogany piano, a complete set of fine German Meissen china.

His pieces numbered in the hundreds and still Mooney sought out more, buying antique credenzas and glass cases to hold them. His wife and housekeepers often profaned his name as they cleaned and dusted the collection. Still, he brought home more and better objects, tufted chairs and hand-painted porcelain lamps to match, and he basked in them, believing that the collection was a kind of legacy. "When I die," he said to his daughters, "at least you'll have something."

In his mind he convinced himself that he had come a long way from the days of Taylor Street and the Patch, the times of Nuti sandwiches and jalopies. Few would argue. There had been many years, many changes, many lives in between.

PART ONE

From Taylor Street to Leavenworth: 1908–1939

1

By the time the train pulled into the Polk Street station they had begun to have second thoughts. They had retched and heaved throughout the weeks on the ocean liner, most in the cramped, steerage sections, then waded through the lines and English-speaking clerks on Ellis Island. It had been a chaotic, confusing time of questions and checkups, of cramped rooms and communal toilets. The puff of pride that hit them as they passed the statue in the harbor had passed quickly, lapsing into fear that for some reason—sickness, improper papers—they'd be sent back. So, when they finally boarded a train for Illinois, another trip they endured because of friends or relatives already there, they were eager to get on with it, settle down, eat a meal—some pasta, some sausage—and find out if this place was all it was cracked up to be, this Chicago, which they couldn't imagine and couldn't pronounce.

Most were men, young and strong, from southern Italy, the provinces of Campania, Basilicata, Abruzzi. Many others were from Sicily, with dark eyes and olive skin, bushy hair roughly cut with scissors, and they looked out from beneath heavy sacks full of the belongings and the few necessities they had brought with them from the island. Though it was spring—most came in the spring—they wore two and three layers of clothing out of fear of the storms and blizzards they had been told about. Most of the women had stayed behind, the wives and mothers, even the children and the old men, because this land, this Chicago, had to be conquered, at least in part, before the rest of the family, those prone to catch pneumonia or cholera, could come over.

He didn't feel like a conqueror as much as a survivor. His name was Antonino Giangana, and in this year of 1905 he was 24 years old, skinny, small, but strong and tough. Among the bodies that poured into the Polk Street station, smelling from days on the train and the disinfectant of Ellis Island, Antonino was just another dark-eyed greaseball, a dago among dagos.

There had been fewer than a thousand of them in Chicago in 1870, a year Italy suffered another of its revolutions. It and hard times in Europe drove more than 5000 Italians to America by 1890. The idea caught on, and in the next ten years the number of Italian immigrants tripled. They poured out of the barren provinces of southern Italy and Sicily, where crops were more rocks than anything else, where life held promise of little money, little opportunity, and no change. Antonino Giangana came with them, a peddler in his Sicilian town of Castelvetrano, but one who couldn't resist the urge to do something better for himself and his wife, Antonia. She was a slight, beautiful girl of 19, pregnant with their first child, a village girl he had courted as Antonia DiSimone. With her thin, almost gaunt face, and its high, soft cheekbones, her long dark hair, which she usually pulled up on her head, she was a stunningly attractive girl. He had promised her that he would take her to America, that she would see the Statue of Liberty, and that their lives would be changed.

He settled in a tenement house near the railroad station. Some Italians went north, to Kinzie Avenue and Wells, but he knew none of those people and stuck by friends from his village and neighboring villages, who in turn knew friends who'd come years before. They found flats along Clark Street, Federal, and LaSalle in an area that was then Chinatown and bordered the Levee, Chicago's brawling brothel district. Four and five Italian immigrants packed basement rooms and flats beneath stores and supply houses, or the whorehouses, gambling rooms, and saloons. Most, like Antonino, whom they called Tony, spoke broken English or none at all, and knew nothing about this city but the names of friends, *paesani.*

They also knew a *padrone.* He was little more than a middleman, an agent, but one who at the turn of the century held overwhelming power among the rural, mostly illiterate immigrants who came to him for help. He was their meal ticket, for he owned contracts with railroads, mining firms, manufacturers, and slaughterhouses, which called for the services of hundreds of immigrants. It was a buyer's market: a demand for unskilled labor and the limited skills of the immigrants (the majority of them were *contadini,* rural laborers and fieldhands, stonecutters, and stone statuette peddlers) made the *padrone* a busy man. He played his role for everything he could. He served as an interpreter, relying however unscrupulously on the fears of wary immigrants who understood little of proper English and next to nothing of the language mumbled by Chicagoans. He also set up a company store and benefited enormously from labor contracts that said the immigrant had to buy from him even if he did sell macaroni and bread for two and three times the price charged on the street. He was also a landlord to hundreds of Italians who didn't have *paesani* to move in with and who were forced to bunk down in his dank, barren flats with scores of their compatriots.

Antonino had other friends, relatives, other contacts, and he was able to peddle fruit as he had done in Sicily. He quickly learned the routines of the markets and bought a watermelon cart of his own. For him, the first steps of his dream came quickly. Among his own people, in his own tongue, he worked the alleys and the streets selling melons and fruits for pennies. Enough of them to send for his wife.

She came over in late December, 1906, his beautiful Antonia, now the mother of a baby girl born in Sicily a few months earlier. To Antonino she was Lena, Lena who was as pretty as ever, Lena who was a resolute, strong woman even young as she was, so serious that relatives used to tell her to smile more often. She did, she told them, especially at the sight of her baby girl. They named her Lena also.

Though it was the new world, Antonino Giangana had little to offer his wife and baby but a crowded ghetto of tenements stuffed between factories and manufacturing plants. The air was clogged with soot and smoke; it was noisy, crowded, and above all confusing. In southern Italy and Sicily there wasn't a dime to be made, but at least there one could bask in the sun along with one's poverty. In Chicago, this dirty city, the skies were gray and cold, and nothing introduced the wolf at the door better than the cold, the damp, the wind that came off the lake most Italians also could not pronounce. It was not by chance that the neighborhoods were called not only Little Italy, or Little Sicily, but also Little Hell, the Valley, or the Patch.

Women like Antonia DiSimone Giangana also came over in the spring when fickle weather made adjustment most difficult. Many soon suffered rheumatic and respiratory diseases, bronchitis, pleurisy, even pneumonia. There were few ways to avoid such maladies, for the immigrants were used to the tough rural routines of Italy, not the inactive tenement living of the city. The change was crippling, and Italian women also came down with dyspepsia, dysmenorrhea, and chlorosis. Their children fared worse. Infant mortality rates soared because of insufficient or incompetent medical attention at childbirth. Part of it was due to simple poverty, much of it due to the old-country practice of relying almost completely on midwives at birth because for centuries Italians had held a prejudice against males, hence most doctors, being present during delivery.

The ill-health was compounded by the fact that the tenements in the Little Italys were often dark and unheated, with little or no plumbing. Kids ate poorly and maintained uneven, insufficient diets that did not prevent tuberculosis and rickets. Their resistance to disease was almost nonexistent. In winter they caught pneumonia and bronchitis; in summer they vomited from gastroenteritis and infant cholera, which was often fatal. At the turn of the century, Italians lost many of their skinny, dark-skinned children before they made it past their fifth birthdays; they were placed in graves without markers.

To combat the odds, they lived that much harder. They clung to each other and their families, even settled blocks with neighbors from the same villages. They built churches and camped around them—from *campanilismo,* the desire to live in the shadow of the church tower—but they weren't "crazy Catholics" like the Polish or French. They went to church, the women more regularly than the men, but they didn't support them well, mainly because in Italy the state paid for the church. The church was simply the final ingredient in the family, ruled by a *pater familias* and populated by an obedient, prolific wife and clamoring children. Life was blood: relatives, family, and if you were a dago you'd do anything to help a relative and considered it a personal attack if an outsider did him harm. Old people were respected, even revered, and babies were adored. A good wife considered a yearly child a privilege as well as a duty, and each birth was cause for celebration, a feast to be followed by other feasts such as baptisms, communions, marriages, even deaths.

That is why shortly after she arrived in Chicago at the Polk Street station, after she had relived with Antonino the thrill of seeing the statue in the harbor, Lena Giangana went about her privilege and became pregnant. In late 1907, they were three of close to 30,000 Italians in Chicago, many of them Sicilians, a number that swelled to 40,000 by 1910. Lena's second baby would be one more, due sometime in May.

They lived in a walkup flat at 223 South Aberdeen, an area west of the Loop dotted with small factories. But the noise and foul air of the neighborhood wasn't as much a hazard to Italians like the Gianganas as was the fact that the area was heavily Irish. That promised nothing but grief, for Chicago's ethnics fought for their territories, fought to settle them and to keep them. The Italians, who arrived generally after the Irish, the Jews, the Bohemians, and the French, had to fight for every block. In 1905 few Italians lived west of Halsted Street even though they overflowed the dark, dirty tenement houses between Taylor and Mather streets. If they went across Halsted they risked abuse or full-scale attacks. Street wars were not uncommon, usually between the Italians and the Irish, also with the Jews, Bohemians, and later the Greeks. Most of the skirmishes were hit-and-run fist fights, but occasionally bottles, pipes, and baseball bats were used to bloody and bash one another. The police, most of whom were Irish or Polish, made few attempts to break up the street wars. They seldom paid attention to complaints or crime reports from non-English-speaking Italians, especially if the incident involved an Irishman. Instead, the police were feared by the immigrants because they often came into the neighborhoods and arbitrarily enforced quarantine laws, which kept the father, the wage earner, from going out and earning his family's keep. The Italians in the Patch soon turned to their own resources, regarding police as the enemy, to be bargained with only to buy a relative out of jail. When an incident arose severe enough to bring police around, the Italians moved off the stoops, closed the doors and shutters, and replied to questions with a sudden loss of any English. *"No capisch. No capisch."*

On the 24th of May, 1908, Lena Giangana went into labor in the bedroom of their flat on Aberdeen. Antonino called in a neighbor, Alesantrina Vitale, to be midwife, and shortly after the Gianganas' first son was born. A week later, Alesantrina Vitale filled out a birth report in her own handwriting, and in her best phonetic spelling wrote Aberdeen Street first as "Ebeten," then as "Abeten," and the name of the baby boy, as best she could remember it: "Gilormo Giangona." But the infant was called Salvatore by his parents, Salvatore Giangana, and they celebrated the appearance of his thin face and his blazing eyes, the second child but the firstborn son. In an Italian household, no mortal was more prized.

The family was still virtually penniless, but Antonino was able to support it with his fruit peddling. Shortly after the birth of Salvatore, they moved to a bigger, cleaner apartment a few blocks away at 1127 West Van Buren. It was then still an Irish area, but in 1908 families learned of apartment vacancies from friends and seldom moved very far away. Van Buren would soon be a part of the Italian ghetto expanding outward from Taylor Street, and that meant mud and garbage and wooden sidewalks so treacherous that people walked in the streets. City refuse collectors seldom entered the district until it became politically more powerful. Peddlers and their horse-drawn cars added to the mess as did the dripping water from the ice wagons, the butter-and-egg carts, the waste from the fruit and vegetable peddlers, and the constant heaps of steaming horse droppings.

Even the horses themselves were a problem. When they died they often lay where they fell. City workers with flatbed wagons eighteen inches off the ground were detailed to take away the carcasses, but often the crews didn't show up for days and the horses rotted and stank, providing carrion for stray dogs and cats, and in summer for blankets of flies.

Still, the world of little Salvatore wasn't all sickness and poverty and dead horses. The Italians yearned for the smells and the tastes of Italy and they brought them to the streets in the Patch. People lived in the streets, on stoops, on the corners, in the shops, the saloons, anywhere where there were other voices and sounds. Peddlers like Antonino turned the Patch into a bazaar, catering to the Italians' passion for *frutta e verdura,* the fruits and vegetables that grew cheaply in Italy and Sicily. They provided a constant supply of vegetables to be eaten with pasta. Meat was a luxury indulged in maybe once or twice a week, and in the meantime, the table steamed with beans, cauliflower, zucchini, lentils, kohlrabi, broccoli, and peas.

In the streets, the peddlers were inspired performers, singing their wares, slapping their horses, bantering with the kids and the housewives. Those that didn't sell something to eat collected rags and iron, or coal in bushels to sell to families that couldn't afford bigger loads. But mostly they peddled food. The pizza man in a white coat sold pans of pizzas ten to twelve deep; another sold candy apples and popcorn.

The *passatempo* vendor, meaning literally to "pass the time," pushed a cart with *lupini* beans, the giant Italian bean soaking in salt water, *ceci* beans, pumpkin seeds, and dozens of other beans and nuts roasted and warm. The families, the mothers and kids, the men sitting and standing in groups, ate them on warm nights and drank homemade wine. They told stories in Italian about relatives. They told of scrapes on the job, fights with the Irish, arguments with the Jewish store owners on Halsted Street. They got drunk and wandered into ice-cream shops and lemon-ice shops and bought slices of watermelon or hot corn on the cob. They drank their wine, dark red wine they'd learned to make in the Old Country and which they made now in stills in back rooms. With it came the smell of yeast and the heavy, sodden smell of fermentation, which seeped from the houses and hung over the neighborhood, telling anyone who ventured close by, who may not have understood a word of Italian or read any of the signs in the stores, that this was the Patch.

As animated as street life was, however, it did not hide the hard times indoors. Life was subsistence, a struggle against sickness and the ways of a new city, and no member of the family felt it more than the immigrant wife. She was the other parent, stifled by Italian *pater familias,* responsible to cook and clean, to shop and wash clothes, but most of all to bear more Italians. Antonino Giangana expected a child every two years, an expectation he was to see fulfilled beginning with his daughter in 1906 and ending sixteen years later.

But it was not to come about without casualties. In March of

1910, Lena Giangana came down with excruciating abdominal pains and vaginal bleeding. Her condition was so severe that on March 7 she was admitted to Mary Thompson Hospital on Ashland Avenue just a few blocks from the Giangana apartment. Given the frequency with which they bore children, it wasn't uncommon for women like Lena to have severe gynecological problems. Infections of the vagina and uterus were common and dangerous because of the lack of antibiotics, or, in many cases, the lack of any professional medical care whatsoever. Bleeding like that Lena suffered was brought about by hosts of causes: tuberculin bacteria, gonorrhea, crude pessaries women often inserted into the vagina or cervix to act as contraceptives, even the existence of old placentas from recent childbirths. Complications from self-induced abortions were also not unknown, even in this staunchly Roman Catholic society. Women used a stick called "slippery elm," which they inserted into the uterus because it absorbed water and was believed to cause the cervix to dilate and abort the fetus.

Lena Giangana's bleeding was diagnosed as acute septic endometreitis, a bleeding of the lining of the uterus. The causes could have been many, but a common one, and one which fits with the child-bearing history of the Giangana family, was a miscarriage.

Seven days later, at 6:20 A.M. on March 14, one day after the frail and beautiful Lena turned 24 years old, she died on her hospital bed. With doctors powerless to do much for her condition, she simply bled to death. No autopsy was performed, and it would have taken one to discover the specific cause of the condition. All Antonino Giangana knew was that in the spring of 1910 he was not feasting the birth of another child, but lowering his wife into a cemetery plot.

Life in the Patch and the Giangana house went on as surely as peddlers appeared on the streets every day. Antonino was soon remarried, this time to Mary Leonardi, a 25-year-old woman who had come to Chicago in 1906 from Partanna, Sicily, a small town just six miles away from Antonino's home town of Castelvetrano. Mary Leonardi, with her dark hair and drooping eyelids, had none of the good looks of Lena Giangana, but she was a resolute woman and suitable wife for Antonino. In March of 1912, two years after Lena's death, she was pregnant with his third child. She delivered on Christmas Eve, another girl, named Antoinette. Every two years during the next ten she would conceive and bear another of Antonino's children—three more girls and two boys—until the Giangana brood totaled eight.

They were part of an Italian population in Chicago that grew to more than 45,000 in 1910, 27,000 of whom were native Chicagoans with both parents born in Italy. That year Our Lady of Pompeii Catholic Church was built in order to take some of the load from Holy Guardian Angel Church, the church that first ministered to the Patch's Italians and in which the oldest Giangana children, including Salvatore, were baptized.

Although Our Lady of Pompeii was at 1225 West Lexington, it wasn't until 1915 that the Italians moved across Racine Avenue. That area was Irish and French, groups still hostile toward the Italians. Greeks were separated from them by Harrison Street to the north of the Patch; Jews lived east around Halsted; and Bohemians lived north of the Taylor Street car line. None was receptive to the close-knit, fierce-eyed Italians, but there was no containing the westward push of the Patch. Year by year the Italian peddlers found more and more countrymen on heretofore forbidden blocks: west on Taylor Street to Vernon Park, Racine, then Ashland. Once there, the *paesani* would stay.

2

HE WAS A STOCKY, pug-nosed kid with a barrel chest and thick arms that reminded people of Babe Ruth's. So, for as long as he could remember, Joey Colaro was called Babe Ruth, "Root" as the kids in the Patch said it, the same kids who considered him as mean and as fearsome as the real Babe. In 1925 he was 19 and considered a "smart head," an older boy who knew his way around, wore the clothes, drove a car, bought the cops, and beat the raps. Before then, when he and Vito Pelletieri, Louis Pargoni, and Mibs Fillichio were in Rees Elementary School, they used to bum from school and strip clotheslines. They usually did it outside the Patch, in German or Jewish neighborhoods, or in places like Oak Park, where lines held expensive shirts that could be sold for a buck back in the neighborhood. They seldom stole much from those on their own block, but they always sold their stolen goods there because immigrants would blindly buy anything. Most Italians simply never considered it illegal to buy goods from anyone on the street, without asking questions, be it from neighbors or relatives or a total stranger.

When Babe Ruth and his buddies weren't doing that they were shooting dice around Throop and Elburn streets. By staying out of school they accumulated street smarts, which generally consisted of an eye for rackets. Babe Ruth's specialty was stealing tires, a racket he stumbled on when a neighbor asked him if he

could pick up a spare. It was so easy, so painless, and so lucrative
—a set of tires could fetch $6 to $10—that Babe Ruth realized his
calling.

He quickly graduated to other accessories. Picking a car, a
"short" they called it, he and a companion could strip the tires,
fender skirts, engine parts, and most often, the prized motor meter, the sculpted hood ornament and radiator cap. To recruit
others, Babe began making his presence known in the Patch as
an organizer, taking any kid old enough to wear pants who had
a touch of larceny in his heart. From block to block he commis-
sioned boys in their early teens, loosely organizing them into
gangs, or mobs, and setting up their jobs.

In 1923, there was no lack of recruits to choose from, for the
American sons of Italian immigrants had the run of the streets.
Or at least many of them did. A substantial percentage resisted
the pull, or were severely disciplined by parents who refused to
let them leave school and fall in with the gangs. It became a
cliché in the Patch that kids became saints or hoods, cops or cop
killers. Those who went straight, however, lived in the shadow
of those who did not, and they sustained an uneasy association
that would be an object of concern throughout the years.

But the undeniable fact of the immigrant Italian family was
that tradition provided its sons with the utmost freedom (the
girls were for the most part jealously protected from worldly
vices and immediately ostracized if they got into trouble) and
many used it to become sharper, quicker, more brazen, more
contemptuous of punishment or the possibility of getting caught
than their fathers ever imagined. In fact, while many fathers
were working twelve-hour days peddling or digging sewer lines
or cleaning vats in slaughterhouses, their sons were too often
bumming from school and running the streets in an eighteen-
hour day of petty crime. It was simply difficult to avoid if they
lived on Taylor, or Bishop, or Throop, or Laflin, difficult to resist
the pull of friends or brothers who made big money stealing,
stripping clotheslines, shoplifting, stripping cars, jackrolling
winos, or selling stolen copper and iron.

There was nothing like life in the Patch. A kid who yielded to
the temptation started by stealing from his mother, pennies just
for dough to spend on the corner. Then he hung out, at pool halls

or sweet shops, and mixed in with kids who constantly topped each other's exploits. If it wasn't petty robberies, it was sex. The Patch kid was always proving himself and his prowess. By their early teens they were "banging," usually with Irish girls, Poles, Jews, and even occasionally with an Italian girl from the neighborhood. Contrary to the long-held belief about the Italian male's respect for his own women, many neighborhood girls accommodated as many boys as were interested, even if such a practice, if it became known, quickly earned the girl the label of tramp and all but lost her her home. Even though the violation of an Italian daughter, sister, or wife was traditionally legitimate cause to kill the violator, it didn't always prevent Italian boys from making advances to the girl next door. Years in America wore sacred mores thin, and as Italian girls became more and more Americanized, their double standards also faded. By the 1930's, many Italian girls engaged in illicit sex and boasted that they didn't regret it.

By the time a boy was 17 in the Patch, he not only had lost his virginity but he probably had been arrested at least once for rape, a charge that then meant only that he was guilty of having had sex with a girl under 18. More than likely he had also taken part in innumerable gang rapes, called by the boys "gang shags." Although they continually went to prison for it, a gang shag was as common an outing among kids in the Patch as was gate crashing a theater. It happened so often in a garage near the corner of Paulina and Flournoy that the intersection was known as Gang Shag Corner.

Apart from the banging, the frequent trips to can (whore) houses, the gang shags, young Patch boys, usually from age eight to around fifteen, experimented widely and frequently with each other. Sodomy and masturbation were casually practiced. It aroused no horror, no shame, in fact, no more notice than heterosexual conquests. One kid had a nickname in Italian which meant simply "Bang me."

It was not uncommon for a block gang to congregate in a cellar or a garage for intergang shags. They had masturbation contests, "pulling," as they called it, in which at a starting signal they saw who could ejaculate first. The winner of a contest got to choose any boy he wished to bang. Most gave as well as received. "I get banged. All the boys bang me," one revealed to a University of

Chicago sociologist. "I bang them too. . . . My brother bangs me a lot of times." And the brother agreed. "Bang? Sure, I always bang my brother many times a week and he asks me to bang him. I bang a lot of these kids. We have contests and I always win."

The banging among the younger boys usually stopped when they reached middle to late teens, or when they got interested in girls. But it wasn't uncommon for them to brag of banging girls in the same breath in which they talked of banging their buddies. "I banged a little girl that lived in our building. We were playing in the basement. So I asked her. She didn't say anything. I banged her every day. Then my brother banged her and her sister. One day they came up to my house while my mother was in the store and we banged them."

Alone, the kids occasionally pulled, but were more sheepish about admitting to it. Pulling bordered on the practice of fellatio, or "sucking off" another gang member. That was generally not done, and boys often had arguments about whether or not a guy was insane if he sucked off.

The parents were generally oblivious of such exploits. Sex wasn't a thing talked about in an Italian household, but something a man and a woman did to procreate as the Roman Catholic Church demanded. Although they raised their daughters in this strict tradition, it was lost on their sons to the degree that they tried to have sex with any and every neighborhood girl who would comply. "When I was twelve years old I tried to bang a girl named Mary," one said. "She went and told her father and he kicked me all over the street. Then there was another girl and I banged her. She never said anything. She used to like it. . . . We were playing in an empty lot and there were a lot of girls. So we started playing hide-and-seek. So one girl went to hide herself and I ran after her. She was in a basement. So I banged her. . . ."

With indiscriminate sex came venereal diseases. Taylor Street kids got them early and often. They talked about their continuing fight with a "dose." "I didn't know what it was that burned me. . . . I went to a doctor. He told me he thought it was a light case. He told me not to drink, smoke, or eat tomatoes or anything like it. He told me not to bang. . . . Then I went to see Jimmy. He told me, 'Now that's only the first. Wait until you get five or six doses, then you start using brains and rubbers.' . . . After a month of the clap I lost fifteen pounds. My family was worried over me but I told them I was working too hard. My parents never mentioned anything to me about sex. The doctor told me after a month that I was cured. He warned me I was heading for my grave. The doctor even told me to quit banging so much. . . . But that night all the guys picked up somebody in this place and I picked this French coat checker. I laid up with her all night. The following morning I gave her $20. A few days later on a nice cold morning I discovered what I paid $20 for and it nearly knocked me out. I told Jimmy about it and Jimmy, spitting on the floor and slapping my shoulder, said, 'Learn how to take it, boy. You'll be having an all-year-round clap, like a lot of the guys around here. You're one of the guys that won't learn. Can't you use 606 G or rubbers? Go to the doctor, he'll give you a shot.' So I went up to the doctor. 'Well,' he said, 'I bet you got another clap. . . .' "

Though it was generally the boys who ran the streets, the boys who slept into the late afternoons and then stayed out all night, the boys who stripped cars and stole everything in sight, the girls of the Patch weren't totally pure and protected. Many neighborhood Italian girls idolized the block thugs and not only acceded to them sexually in vacant garages and basements, but also went so far as to steal with them and become their "gun girls." Mostly that involved acting as lookouts or drivers, keeping guns, and sometimes even participating in a burglary or a stickup. Eventually, gun girls hung out together and pulled off "rackets" themselves, mostly shoplifting, or, if they were interested in big money, con games. A common con consisted of one of the girls being dropped off in another section of town, where she would make eyes at passing men and then give them a hard-luck story. Most gave her money thinking it would lead to sex, an angle the con girls played heavily. But the game seldom if ever led to relations; marks were simply talked out of their money.

Life for the gang—the boys and girls—when times were good meant big cars, clothes, nightly dancing and visits to roadhouses. Yet most of their time and attention went into pulling more jobs, more heists. They often signed on to make liquor runs for the big bootleggers in town. Twenty to thirty cases of liquor were packed into a single car, with room left over only for the boy and his girl. Runs went to Springfield, Rockford, Aurora, Freeport—all over the state—and usually meant $75 for the girl and two to three times that for the boy.

Liquor runs were precisely planned affairs. The cars, after being filled with booze, were often stacked with furniture, a baby carriage or a sofa, anything to make it look as if the couple were moving. The driver was then given a chart that detailed the route and the time to be taken between various checkpoints along the road. Lookouts were stationed at the checkpoints, and if the car didn't pass within a 15-minute time span dictated by the schedule, the gang would consider it hijacked and send a crew after it. Usually the trips went off smoothly. The cars traveled at a wild 60 to 70 miles per hour as demanded by the chart. If the cops stopped the car, the boy and his girl would play dumb. If the liquor was discovered, they wouldn't say anything at all.

After a few liquor runs, heists, stickups, and nights on the town with the boys, the gun girls, all supposedly protected virginal daughters of first-generation American Italians, were totally committed to crime and their criminal friends. And most of them didn't apologize for it. As one boasted to a Chicago sociologist:

"I am an Italian. Damn proud of it. Say, the Italians are great people, not like the Jews, Irish, or Germans. The wops are the greatest people. Look who we got. Al Capone, the world's biggest bootlegger; Jack McGurn, the best machine gunner of the town; Marino, the best daring boy of '42.' Then, say, listen at that music. That's a wop too from the Edgewater Beach Hotel. We got the best singers—Schipa, Ruffo, and a lot more. We got the best lovers. Say, how about Valentino? Say, when he kissed you, you stayed kissed. He kissed on the lips, not wash your face. Boy, how he made love. That's why I am proud I'm a wop."

It took somebody like Joey Colaro, "Babe Ruth," to organize them. In 1923, 16-year-old Augusto Russo lay wounded on a hospital bed and gave an example of how the Babe did it. Russo told police he and Louis Guerero had been talked into stealing a car by Babe's description of the easy money that would come of it. Babe was not only a talker, but he was so persistent that in a matter of minutes he could cause kids like Russo and Guerero to drool over their potential wealth. Usually the Babe planned the operation and located the car, the "short," to be stripped or stolen, accompanied his boys to the scene, then took off. For him it was foolproof: a cut of the take and none of the risk.

On a December night, Russo said, Babe drove Guerero and him

to the short but left before Chicago policeman George Mills showed up. Mills spotted the theft and chased the two boys before taking out his .45 and shooting Guerero through the head, killing him instantly, and wounding Russo in the back. Mills's conduct was standard procedure at the time, and not questioned. Police constantly chased car thieves or robbery suspects through the streets, often as not shooting as they went. Gang members soon considered it a routine hazard of the trade, that if the coppers showed up, they took a "lam" and expected them "to start throwing slugs."

But the risks were not great enough to scare the Italian kids, and Babe found himself with many young joiners. At first they hung out in small groups—a brother, neighbor, a fellow's cousin —until small gangs of five and eight boys formed. In 1925, Bonfiglio's poolroom opened at Elburn and Loomis, and small mobs began to hang out there. Babe saw the opportunity and began consolidating them, not only using his reputation as a smart head but also shaking down the rackets of smaller, younger boys and forcing them to fork over a cut of their takes.

Babe was only one of the smart heads, though he was considered the smoothest, the best talker. Another was Babe's friend and boyhood companion Vito Pelletieri. If Babe Ruth was the organizer and diplomat of the street, Pelletieri was the operating head. The smart heads hung out at Vito's house when they weren't at Bonfiglio's, and Vito's word was considered law. He and Babe both drove "legit" cars, called jalopies, and they were usually expensive and fast.

The smart heads continued to set up gang recruits, first with the promise of a fin ($5) to steal tires; if the newcomer passed that test, he had to steal an entire machine. They sometimes gave the recruit a stolen or forged car key and then took him to the car. Then the young thief drove the short away while Vito and Babe followed to look out for the cops, even cutting them off if necessary. Once the short was inside the Patch, Vito and Babe paid off the recruit and drove the car off themselves, either to strip it for parts or sell the complete machine.

By 1925, Vito and Babe were the foremost smart heads of the Patch, but close behind them, wearing chesterfield coats and expensive clothes, duds that mimicked the best worn by the beer barons in town, were Sharkey Icola; a kid known only as Salvi;

Pete "Mibs" Fillichio; Patsy Pargoni, the toughest of four Pargoni brothers; and a short, skinny kid who lived on Taylor Street at Loomis known as "Sam Gagiano," or simply Mooney. Though he often lived up to his nickname, causing others to wonder if he was all there, Mooney was nevertheless regarded as one of the toughest of the smart heads. His real name was Salvatore Giancana, Antonino Giangana's oldest son, a hard "c" now permanently placed in his last name.

Most of the time Mooney and the smart heads could be found at Bonfiglio's or at a barbershop at Taylor and Loomis, a wash station for autos at Elburn and Loomis, or a delicatessen at Laflin and Taylor. Finding them wasn't hard, for owing to Babe Ruth's recruiting the gang got bigger and bigger, incorporating smaller mobs around certain smart heads.

But it wasn't until mid-1925 when the gang took up around Mary's, a restaurant at Bishop and Taylor, that the total mob came together. One night Patsy Pargoni related the story of "Ali Baba and the Forty Thieves" to the gang and totally fascinated his audience. It was immediately decided that they would go Ali Baba two better. They would call themselves the "42's," the "42 Gang."

The gang gained or lost any number of members through the years, depending on who told the stories of its exploits. But the original 42 Gang, according to a roll call taken in 1925 by one of the members, numbered only 24.

Apart from the smart heads, the 18 other members consisted of Hank and Jit Pargoni, Fat Riccio, Ned Rooney, Red O'Brien, John Bolton (three Irish originals whose families were holdovers in the Patch), Joe Roberti, Katsy Catrina, Monk Pupillo, Nick Muscato, Louis "Cadoodles" DeChristoforo, Mibs Fillichio's brother Frank, the DeMilio brothers, the two Schiulo brothers, Fat Campanelli, and Frank "Chudaback" DeLuca.

They were the originals, the older smarter kids who knew the Patch and knew each other. They attracted the younger kids, the pimply, unkempt Patch teenagers who idolized their every move. They became synonymous with the Patch, putting it into the newspapers and on the lips of residents. There were few things in the life of the Italian kids on Taylor Street more alluring than a 42. His style, his swagger, the way he stood against a street post with his hands in his pockets jiggling his privates—all combined to make him daring and exciting. It was the gang that Joey Colaro—Babe Ruth—with his smooth tongue and persuasive style, had put together. In the years to follow, it would grow in number and notoriety, finally far surpassing him.

3

IN 1925 HE WAS 18 and a smart head of the 42's, now living with his family at 1422 West Taylor in the very heart of the Patch. But Sam "Mooney" Giancana, Sam "Gagiano," "Gincanna," had no real identity of his own apart from what he was in the 42's. And the 42's, as they grew more and more infamous in the daily papers, had no identity apart from the neighborhood, the culture of the Near West Side Patch that had spawned them.

To an outsider, the Patch was the "Spaghetti Belt," a No-Man's Land of greaseballs who suspected anyone who didn't speak their language. Irish fought with them, then begrudgingly gave them block after block. The Jews, French, and Bohemians avoided them, fearing their reputations, spreading stories of the blood that they spilled.

But among the *paesani* life was a scratching, vicious existence. From the moment an immigrant got off the train his life was in the hands of the *padrone,* the countryman who took him for what he could, who cheated him and gouged him until he learned the ropes. It was painful, somewhat insidious, for he was being beaten in his own tongue by something and someone he thought he could trust. Though he hated the *padroni,* he learned from them that a person had to offer a bribe to get a better job or a better flat. He stole to eat, he sold stolen goods to feed his children. He lived by a code of survival that had little to do with so-called American law and justice, but everything to do with dago instinct and guile.

It was no coincidence that the neighborhood's most accomplished and durable fences were recent immigrants who saw nothing wrong in buying and selling stolen goods to get by. They didn't understand American laws, and wouldn't abide by them. The strange law called Prohibition was an example, for how could something like wine and beer, things they had drunk like water in their homeland because they were safer than water, be prohibited? And "alky" cooking. Done in primitive household stills, it was as common a practice in the Patch as was preparing daily pasta, not only because it brought in a few dollars but because, like winemaking, it was an age-old skill. Why should it matter that it was against the law, or that it was collected each day in five-gallon pails by the Genna Brothers, the "Terrible Gennas"—Sam, Angelo, Pete, Tony, and Jim—who ran with the Capone gang and were known for their vicious killings? It was simply alky and alky was a part of everyday life. So, from every second house in the Patch, regardless of what block or what generation *paesani* lived there, the dull smell of sour mash hung over the streets like a fog.

It didn't take an immigrant long to know that in Chicago he was a greaseball, not only among *paesani* (and from them he could take the insult because Italians said it with a tinge of empathy) but, most bitterly, among non-Italians, many of them first-generation Americans who had come to the country just as impoverished and ignorant. It was thrown at him when he tried to get a job, when he tried to enroll his kids in school, when he tried to get a political or police favor. It was pushed in his face by the newspapers, which identified individuals in front-page crime stories as "Sicilian," or "Italian," as if the ethnic description somehow explained the crime.

Hence, when fellow greaseballs like the Gennas, or the Capone gang hoods, made their marks, when they strutted in their fine clothes and expensive cars, the community revered them. It didn't matter how they made their money or what they had to do to get it, because every dago knew the odds. Jack McGurn, né Vincenzo DeMora, Capone's notorious machine gunner, was raised in the Patch. So were Frankie Pape; Lawrence Mangano; Anselmo Scalisi, another close Capone hoodlum; and "Diamond

Joe" Esposito, the area's most powerful beer runner. And they were honored for it.

"I remember these men in large cars, with boys and girls of the neighborhood standing on the running boards. I saw them come into the neighborhood in splendor as heroes. Many times they showered handfuls of silver to the youngsters who waited to get a glance at them—heroes—because they had just made the headlines in the newspapers," a Patch resident remembered.

Immigrant parents were not about to diminish the gangsters' appeal, for in many cases they considered the beer barons and the alky runners of the neighborhood not criminals but businessmen. What could be wrong with operating a business that put households to work cooking alky, or supplying beer and wine and liquor to people who wanted it and who drank it as naturally as they breathed? And in many cases the hoods lived private, gentle lives within the neighborhood. Angelo Genna, who was known as "Bloody Angelo" because of the brutal assassinations he was believed to have participated in, was a prince to the neighbors. On the streets of the Patch he walked like a gentleman and approached friends with a warm, affectionate Sicilian greeting, patting their arms and saying, "Let us kiss our hands." He was an animal only in the newspapers, not in the Patch.

Yet, if there was any one person who taught first- and second-generation Italians what power in the neighborhood was really all about, it was the cop. Chicago's force in the 1920's was made up mostly of Irish and Polish, all beneficiaries of a relative or a friend with enough political clout to get him on the payroll. Even if a copper's salary was abysmally low, a city job meant security and all the money you could steal, and nobody knew it better than the policeman. In the Patch, where crime was a casual, constant phenomenon, a cop had little trouble acting as judge, jury, and, with few exceptions, clerk of the court.

To the 42's, dealing with cops was a skill on a par with stripping fender skirts or tripping ignitions. Getting caught was referred to merely as a "jam," and getting out of a jam was learning merely how to put in the "fix." Generally, that meant a straight cash payoff. "I learned that when you are picked up and you have money in your pocket you can fix the copper," one young 42 said quite matter-of-factly to a sociologist.

At first, it was Babe Ruth who dealt with the cops and he alone who had the reputation for being able to fix anything. When he was in the process of consolidating the little mobs, he often established his authority by putting in the fix when jobs were botched and the young hoods pinched. Babe and other smart heads even came around once a month and collected money from gang members for payoff money. The running rate was $10 to $15 a month from younger gang members. For the smart heads, getting in a jam meant coming up with much more, not enough to break them (to pay off a fix with a copper most 42's pulled off another job) but enough to make the cost of payoffs a major operating expense. And cops on the take were always around, always ravenous. "When we were making so much, we thought the police were scums, shysters. They could be bought for so little; they were money hungry," one 42 said.

When a 42 was pinched, he usually had enough money on him to get out of the jam before he ever got to the police station or in front of a judge. If he didn't, the price went up considerably, as high as $400 to $500 just to get the case quashed. That kind of money often came from the boy's parents, from loans from relatives, even mortgages on their homes. It was all done in a ritual of tradition and trust. From the parents' point of view, tradition called for any measures to defend one's son, and most parents went to any expense. As far as the American-born sons were concerned, most accepted such help (some even went to lengths to repay it) and did so with an almost demonic glee over once again cheating the cops and beating a rap.

But the game was not in the fix as much as it was in the "lam," in getting away from the "heat," even if it meant turning the Patch into a drag strip. Again, a lam was a part of their obsession with their jalopies. They became incredible "wheelmen," able to turn a flivver into a getaway car. They prided themselves on their hot cars, either souped up or powerful stock models, usually Chrysler 70's. It didn't matter that oftentimes a wheelman was barely able to see over the steering wheel. What counted was that they considered their jalopies to be extensions of themselves, hands feeling past the steering wheel into the drive shaft and transmission, legs straining for speed from the accelerator, smoking the tires and laying rubber. Most of the 42 jobs were spontaneous, hit-and-run sprees that involved little planning, a lot of guts, and a wild getaway. They were jobs that earned them the label "crazy boys."

In the early years of the gang, Babe Ruth calmly scouted shorts and planned things ahead of time, but later on mobs of two and three 42's would simply say, "Hey, I got something," and take off. Stealing cars led to crashing, the Babe Ruth–inspired caper of driving up to a store, hitting the gas, and crashing through the front display window so four or five gang members could hop in and grab everything in sight, then peeling off.

To do any and all of his jobs, a crazy boy had to know how to wheel. The gang practiced daily on the streets, accelerating, swerving, cutting down alleys, and "whipping." Perhaps no word was more common to the boys of the Patch when the 42's ruled. Whipping meant taking a corner as fast as possible, usually on two wheels to the car's limit of equilibrium without turning over. Good whippers were the best wheelmen and they practiced the skill as often as a shortstop practices the double play or a swimmer his turns. Kids on Taylor Street were told once and only once to clear a corner when a whipper was coming. Seconds later the whine of the engine and the squeal of tires exploded a whipper around Taylor onto Laflin, or Garibaldi, or Loomis. The neighborhood kids didn't mind, for they considered the 42's the barons of the street, and whipping a magnificent skill. Youngsters practiced whipping on their bikes and tricycles, or they tried to flip handmade wooden carts by whipping them in the alleys. They even helped the 42's set up trash barrels as obstacle courses in the alleys, a practice employed for keeps when the heat chased the gang.

Police chases in the Patch, with all the noise and speed and danger, were as common as its vendors. Younger kids looked forward to them, and ran to the streets to watch, even though their mothers cringed in terror. It was common for a squad car to come across a gang of 42's stripping a car or robbing a butter-and-egg truck and give chase with heads out windows and guns blazing. What was comic in the movies was frightening in the calm of the afternoon or the dead of night, for the old Marmon squad cars, with gongs and gun mounts, charged after the 42's regardless of the crime. The 42's most often fled because they didn't have the cash to put in the fix, but sometimes because it was a chance to practice their beloved whipping.

Their cars, they knew, were faster and lighter than the bigger, heavier squad cars the cops drove. Babe Ruth perfected a gadget that flipped the license plates horizontal, making them impossible to read, if the cops got too close. Because the 42's knew the neighborhood and the gridwork of alleys so precisely, they usually outdistanced the coppers. They were smug and cocky about it, even if the heat was "throwing lead," and trying to shoot out their tires, their back windows, or the backs of their heads.

It was a daily game of cops and robbers to where the gang's exploits soon dominated much of the newspapers' crime news. Beginning in 1925, when the 42 Gang was first mentioned in the press, the gang was front page. Still, the daily papers seldom captured the fury of the 42's, for outsiders, anyone not living along the thoroughfares of the Patch, wouldn't have believed it.

"We moved on a Saturday during the summer," one newcomer remembered. "Sunday night the family sat at the top of the stairs; none of us dared leave the door. Cars were speeding down the street at fifty or sixty miles an hour even though the streets were filled with children playing, and people standing and sitting along the sidewalk. We lived near the corner and cars turned the corner at great speed with a screeching of brakes. All at once a police squad car came down the street chasing another car and shooting. My family was in an uproar; we were excited and held on to each other. The people on the next stair just laughed and told us we hadn't seen nothing yet. But that was enough for us, and we all went to bed at 9:30 that night, trembling. I had never heard or saw the likes of it. It was just hell to me. I sat in the living room looking out at the street from the closed window, watching those cars speeding around the corner. I never knew a car could speed like that around a corner and yet keep on going. After about ten minutes I went to bed but I couldn't sleep. I just kept hearing the squealing of brakes all night.

"About two o'clock I heard some shooting, and all the family was up at the front windows. It was a police car chasing another car down the street. The police car had cracked against a tree across the street from our house. The policemen were not hurt, but the car was cracked. All at once we heard sirens of other cars coming down the street. It was another chase. It surprised me how the gang's cars could outdistance the big squad cars. But it wasn't long before I knew why. . . ."

As much as whipping and racing by the 42's were great fun for the kids along Taylor Street, they were an annoyance and a terror to their parents. Since an Italian kid played in the streets as soon as he could walk, the chances for tragedy were overwhelming. It happened in early October, 1926, as the kids and vendors and the old men weaved among each other in the sun along Taylor near Loomis. In front of 1422 Taylor, a four-year-old boy named Charley ran about the sidewalk and the stoops chasing a cat, then stopping and running after a playmate. His mother, Mary, a 41-year-old housewife with six children and two stepchildren, kept an eye on Charley as she went about her housework. She was a stern-looking, thin-faced woman, whose life in America had been little but childbearing and unceasing housework.

It was sheer coincidence that she spotted the Cadillac and her four-year-old son when she did. She hurtled off the stoop and ran into Taylor Street, desperately hoping to grab Charley and push him out of the way of the car. In an instant of confusion and screeching tires the car hit her as she grabbed her son, knocked her and the child to the pavement, then ran over her with a single wheel in an attempt to swerve out of the way.

In fright, the driver sped off, leaving the woman, Mary Leonardi Giancana, Antonino Giancana's second wife and the mother of six of his children, lying unconscious in the street. The shield of her body protected her son, and he wailed in terror.

In minutes an ambulance arrived and carried Mary Giancana to Mother Cabrini Hospital. Neighbors gave the license number of the Cadillac to police, and its driver, Raymond Sansonetti, who lived only a few blocks away on Blue Island Avenue, was arrested a short time later. But Mrs. Giancana, suffering from shock and internal hemorrhaging, never regained consciousness and died the next day. Her son Charles was fine, and present when the family buried its mother in Mount Carmel Cemetery three days later. Also there was the family's oldest son, Salvatore, who was now 18, a smart head in the 42 Gang, soon to be considered one of its premier wheelmen, a street whipper with no equal.

What was occurring with the rise of the 42's and their escapades with the police in the middle 1920's was more than just a reckless cops-and-robbers routine on a neighborhood scale. The 42's came to realize that the police were not the objective, impersonal arm of the law, and that justice was not the blind lady with balanced scales. The police were coppers, heat, to be bought and sold on a par with any commodity the gang needed. The routine was more than simple graft, more than an occasional pass for an under-the-table sum, but rather a way of life, that any criminal charge no matter how severe, no matter what happened to the victims, could be beaten with a payoff. And if things had to go further than the police, they went to politicians and even to the courts.

What had started with the smooth arrangements of Babe Ruth greasing the palms of a few neighborhood squads soon became matter of course. The police were the enemy, but one that could be fixed. A politician was as much an ally as a getaway car. Of greater help was the clout of a big-time gangster, a Capone ideally, or one of the Gennas, or Diamond Joe Esposito, the Patch's beer boss. Joe Roberti, one of the later members of the 42's, secured a chauffeur job with Esposito that gave him a pull with police that proved most powerful. Once, Roberti and others were calmly checking out their gun supply in preparation for a hunting trip. Guns were scattered all over, on a table, chairs, a daybed, when a squad of uniformed police walked through the front of their hangout, a flower shop, and barged in on them. Instead of making a break for it, Roberti grabbed a shotgun and pointed it at the coppers. "What right have you got coming in here without any questions?" he shouted. "Go see Diamond Joe or Angelo and they'll set you straight." Roberti then routed the squad from the hangout, and he and his buddies continued to work over their arsenal.

Without such connections (and any clout the 42's had with the big-time gangsters was rare) the 42's were at the whim of the police. Political clout was also difficult to come by, not only for the gang, but for most of the Italians in the Patch, because the neighborhood was still under the control of the Irish. Irish also ran the labor unions and found the unskilled Southern Italian and Sicilian immigrants easy to keep in line.

At the turn of the century the Patch was part of the Nineteenth Ward, the "bloody Nineteenth" because of election-day beatings and bombings. When Italians began to move west of the Chicago River, into the area politicians referred to as "Kansas and Nebraska," they were little threat to the political organization there or to its alderman, John Powers. In the streets he was "Johnny DePow," a freewheeling Democrat who made no bones about his power, his ability to win elections and make deals.

In 1905 Powers was charged by an election opponent with intimidation, vote stealing, threats, even the shooting of a relative of his opponent in a Taylor Street saloon. But the charges did nothing to dent Powers' overwhelming victory margin. That same year he was charged with receiving a $50,000 bribe from a telegraph company, and earlier with taking $20,000 from a cigarette company in exchange for killing a proposed city ordinance banning the sale of cigarettes. But those charges had no effect on his standing and his power in the Nineteenth, and he kept it in the face of the hordes of Italians pouring into the district during the next 15 years.

In the neighborhood, Johnny Powers worked his political, quasi-social organization to perfection. In the tradition of all of Chicago's powerful aldermen, he scrupulously attended to the mundane, day-to-day needs of his largely immigrant constituents, those at least who posed no threat to him, and generally intimidated or terrorized those who did. With a handful of Italian lieutenants, he gave out what jobs he wanted to (reserving most of them for Irish who lived in the fringes of the district or outside of it altogether) and played heavily on his role of benefactor. In hard times he put many Italian families on welfare lists, which meant money and food. He also provided food for hosts of newly arrived immigrants, thus giving them a start and establishing an immediate IOU. Italian families living around Johnny Pow were practically fed by him. All he asked in return was total power and the freedom to turn his lucrative backroom deals.

At no time did Johnny Powers fail to grasp the need for muscle to keep his Irish hands on his increasingly Italian ward. To do it he not only employed his own enforcers to strongarm and intimidate, but he often called upon the services of the neighborhood Black Hand hoods.

Few elements of the Italian-Sicilian tradition in America have been more misrepresented than the existence of the Black Hand. A common belief is that Black Hand, *La Mano Nera,* was the precursor of the Sicilian mafia in this country and the prototype for organized crime. Actually, there was no society or organization of the Black Hand among Italian immigrants. The term instead applied to a general system of terror, the specter of kidnapping and extortion.

Among Italian immigrants in New York and Chicago at the

turn of the century, the practice of Black Hand, especially the use of Black Hand notes, became as common as holdups and petty thefts. It amounted to a vicious albeit amateurish attempt at extortion by a neighbor, a relative, or the block hoodlum, and it was aimed at anyone who had come into some money and could pay off. The implicit threat was always abduction and murder, and persuasion was in the form of midnight sluggings or bombings, the latter usually a Molotov cocktail lobbed into the entrance of a house or store, which blew out windows and doors, and which managed to awaken and petrify everyone nearby.

In the Patch, Black Hand extortionists became so active that a group of moneyed Italian businessmen formed a White Hand Society to combat them. Though White Hand hired detectives and aided prosecutors in winning convictions, theirs was an uphill battle. Most families terrorized by Black Hand were gripped by a horror that had its roots in the Old Country, and they trusted neither White Hand nor the police. Police, in fact, generally considered Black Hand threats a "Sicilian" matter and seldom investigated. Hence, Black Hand victims often looked to big-time hoodlums for help, believing they were the ultimate dispensers of justice. In the Patch that meant Tony Lombardo, a top Capone gang hoodlum whose word was law on the streets and who had the power to regulate and mediate extortion attempts.

Lombardo's power came into play in early September, 1928, in one of the Patch's most notorious Black Hand cases. Billy Ranieri, a thin, dark-faced ten-year-old, was walking home from school one afternoon when he was approached by an auto carrying four men. Before he knew what was happening, he was lifted off his feet and driven to a small house in Bourbonnais, Illinois, a village just south of Chicago near Kankakee. Then, in typical Black Hand fashion, his abductors sent a scribbled note to his father demanding $60,000.

These Black Handers, however, were not dealing with an impoverished immigrant with horrors of Sicilian secret societies lingering in his head. A. Frank Ranieri was a prosperous sewer contractor, an intense, gaunt-faced Italian who had long since moved from the Patch and its poverty. He responded to the note by offering his boy's kidnappers a mere $5,000. They said they would take $7,000. While they waited, Ranieri contacted Angelo Scalzetti, a relative and fellow contractor, who still lived in the

Patch and who was active in the White Hand Society. Scalzetti was a swarthy, strong man with a handlebar mustache, heavy eyebrows, and a passion for becoming "Americanized." By that time, he'd even legally changed his name to Ole Scully, a name he considered more American. His hatred for Black Handers came from his belief that they were among the curses of the Patch, a vicious holdover of the Old World that had to be eradicated if Italians were going to have a chance in America. Scully was also Billy Ranieri's second cousin and his godfather.

When told of the abduction, Scully first attempted to seek out Tony Lombardo. But on September 7, the day after Billy's kidnapping, as Lombardo walked out of his Loop office building with two associates, he was approached from behind and shot twice in the head, dying before he even hit the sidewalk. The Lombardo assassination had nothing to do with the Ranieri abduction, but it was cruelly coincidental. Scully had to resort to bolder tactics. He immediately fingered a neighborhood Black Hander by the name of Angelo Petitti, a heavy-set bull of a thug, whom Scully had implicated in other Black Hand extortions.

With Petitti, he took on one of the most vicious men in Chicago. Petitti was an ignorant, ruthless man, built like a fireplug and known to every Italian in the Patch. The message sent to the Ranieris after Billy's abduction had said that if they didn't comply with demands, the boy's head would be cut off and sent to the parents "in a nice little package." To Ole Scully, such a threat could only come from Angelo Petitti.

Scully approached Judge Frank Commerford of the circuit court and asked him for help in the Ranieri kidnapping. Commerford's response was one even Scully didn't expect. He ordered police to pick up Angelo Petitti and hold him until Billy Ranieri was released. They promptly did that, arresting Petitti at his ice-cream parlor at 1737 West Polk.

The move worked. Within two weeks Billy was released, unharmed and unhurt, and shortly after, Petitti and his confederate, Andrew Cappellano, in whose house Billy had been kept, and Cappellano's son Tony, were indicted for extortion and kidnapping. Chief witnesses for the prosecution would be the Ranieris and the dour-faced Ole Scully.

The trial was scheduled to begin in mid-December of that year. Though the rest of Chicago was generally oblivious, it generated overwhelming interest in Italian neighborhoods because it was another significant legal action against the dreaded doings of the Black Handers.

The night before the opening of the trial, Ole Scully got together at a restaurant in the Patch, as he had done frequently, with five friends. As they talked, as they discussed the Cappellanos and Angelo Petitti—Petitti with his thick neck and glowering smile and a sense that he was untouchable—they spat out Sicilian obscenities. The six of them sat in the front of the restaurant, unaware that they were being observed by a dishwasher named Julio Romano. Romano sent word out from the restaurant that Scully and his friends were there, and a short time later five men burst into the front door and herded Scully and the rest into a back room. Then one of the men asked who owned the Willys-Knight automobile parked out front. Ole Scully sensed the setup and who the five men were after. He made a lunge for the back door, but as he did he was cut down with two blasts from a shotgun. He was hit in the head and the back. Because of the size of the wounds, Scully's killers didn't even check back to see if he was dead. They instead turned on the five others and beat them with baseball bats. Two of them suffered broken arms, three others fractured skulls, but their assailants left them alive. Ole Scully's corpse was the only one they wanted.

The murder made headlines and ignited tempers in the courtroom the next morning. Judge Commerford assigned 50 Chicago policemen to guard the Ranieri family, and even the two prosecutors in the case, around the clock. Even then, with the trial commanding front-page attention and the murder of Ole Scully going unsolved, the Ranieris received more Black Hand threats. One letter, scrawled in capital letters in handwriting like that of a schoolboy, was exhibited in the courtroom.

> You better save the money and do not be crazy. And if you do not do it and let Angelo alone you won't see the end of the trial. If you want trouble we give it to you. We see you every day and you get it soon. Last chance remember the boys.

But Ranieri and his son Billy stuck to their stories and refused to be intimidated. In sensational proceedings, Billy Ranieri, with his wide-eyed expression, his neatly pressed suit and hair combed across his head but clipped short of his big ears, his feet not reaching the floor as he sat in the witness chair, repeated loudly in his thin tenor voice the events of his abduction. His father followed. Articulately, without a trace of emotion, he outlined the Black Hand attempts to extort money in exchange for Billy's release.

Little time was wasted. Petitti and the elder Cappellano were both convicted; Andrew Cappellano's son Tony was acquitted. A few days later Petitti and Cappellano were sentenced to twenty-five years in prison. But even then they emerged from the courtroom smiling. Petitti said he was relieved not to be given the death sentence. And the city's most feared Black Hander went off to serve his time, leaving a wife and four children and his ice-cream shop behind.

Ole Scully was buried with due ceremony. He left a wife and three children—Bert, 20, Lawrence, 19, and Lydia, 17. All of them, along with the Ranieri family, would continue to have police guard around the clock.

Although the Ranieri case brought attention to the Black Hand scourge among Italian immigrants, it did little to discourage the practice. With the fading of the White Hand Society, the fight was left to individuals. Ultimately, federal laws were applied to the use of mails to send Black Hand letters, and that did much to reduce the activity. But forms of extortion, even if not in *La Mano Nera* traditions, continued to flourish, most commonly through the appearance of bombings.

"Pineapples," as the gangsters called them, were the muscle behind a threat, and they were used at will in the Patch to intimidate union leaders, politicians, businessmen, even the small shopkeepers. The motives varied, from revenge to power struggles to simple demands for money. No one was exempt, and bombs went off so often that those who grew up in the Patch considered bombings as extraordinary as rainstorms, and remembered few of them.

Two, however, occurring in the very week following the Ranieri kidnapping were unforgettable to Antonino Giancana. In September of 1928 he was operating an ice-cream and lemonade store at 1510 West Taylor in partnership with Anthony Gremilda. It was a small but prosperous shop that had grown out of Giancana's fruit and vegetable peddling; its stock consisting of groceries, fruits, vegetables. But Antonino also made ice cream and Italian lemon ice, the rich, sugary snow made with the juice of squeezed lemons and chips of lemon peel, and the kids ate it like candy.

On the night of September 16, neighbors of the shop were awakened by an explosion that blew out the front window of the building. It was a typical pineapple bombing, and the damage was repaired in the next few days. But 11 days later, a second blast occurred, this one at 2 A.M., and so powerful that it was heard as far away as the Loop. Residents of the block were shaken to the point of panic, and even in their relative familiarity with bombings, they streamed out into the street. The explosion ripped the front of the building apart, shattering the entrance and blowing a hole in the floor, and breaking windows for half a block either way.

Antonino, who lived a few blocks away at 818 South Hermitage, rushed to the scene, but he told the police who investigated the bombing nothing. It was rumored that Antonino had ignored extortion attempts against him and his partner. That story gained credence the following night when he and Gremilda were shot and beaten as they emerged from the battered shop. Gremilda was shot three times but not seriously and Antonino was pistol whipped about the head. Though they were severely injured, neither revealed anything about extortion or any other circumstances surrounding the bombings and the attack.

That led police to speculate on one other possibility, that the father was being dealt with for the sins of his son. In this case, Salvatore Sam "Mooney" Giancana, Antonino's eldest, was now 20 and well known to the detectives. He was no longer the mean-eyed punk who tied the tails of cats together and swung them against buildings while his 42 Gang friends watched and laughed, or the punk who broke into peddlers' stables and stole from the carts or killed the horses, then hacked off the hind legs to sell for horsemeat. Mooney Giancana was now into bigger things, jobs and accomplices who operated in manners every bit compatible with bombings and beatings of the degree experienced by the elder Giancana and his partner. And, though Antonino Giancana would say nothing, and Mooney less (on the evening of the second bombing of the ice-cream store he was sitting in a cell at the Maxwell District station on an auto-theft investigation), the detectives had their hunches.

4

HIS FIRST ARREST and conviction came in September, 1925, when he was only 18 but known well in the neighborhood and to police as a smart head of the 42's. The arrest was for simple auto theft, appropriately enough since stealing or stripping shorts was the gang's biggest enterprise at the time. He was known to the police then as Sam Gincana, a short—five-foot-eight-inch—thin-faced kid with a shorter temper and a peerless reputation for wheeling.

The conviction put him away for 30 days in the state penitentiary at Joliet. It was a place he and a lot of other 42's would get to know well, for as the gang's reputation grew penalties and sentences became stiffer. They were no longer considered wayward boys worthy of the juvenile home at St. Charles, but hardened, tough hoods who had to be sent away. Likewise, on the street, coppers went out of their way to push the 42's. They couldn't loiter on a street corner for long before a squad or a beat cop would come and tell them to move, shoving them, often as not cracking a few skulls with a night stick or a gun butt. To those police not on the dole, the 42's were the enemy, and one to make a reputation on.

Only a few days after Mooney went to Joliet, police raided a garage at 621 South Paulina and found what they termed a major storage spot for the 42 Gang's stolen loot. The raid was led by Sergeant John Leyendecker, a Marquette District cop who was to go out of his way to pinch the gang and make considerable news doing it. Leyendecker said the garage held $11,500 worth of sample merchandise stolen from salesmen, most of it silk shirts, hosiery, sweaters, coats, and hats. At least a half-dozen salesmen showed up to claim the goods from a caper that would have ordinarily seemed minor but that was played up in the press as evidence that the 42 Gang was no longer a mob of neighborhood car thieves.

The papers followed quickly with more of the gang's exploits, now naming the offenders and summing up their intentions by identifying them as 42's. Few if any of the incidents were invented; it was simply that the papers began paying attention and police obliged them by naming almost any pinch with an address in the Patch as a 42.

And the 42's did their best to provide the stories. In March of 1926 Pete Nicastro and Paul Ricco led police on a two-mile chase through the Patch and fielded twelve shots from the cops before they and the stolen auto they were driving were curbed. Two days later, seventeen 42's were arrested in a pool hall after they tried but failed to burglarize a boxcar full of silk.

Mooney, after his 30 days in Joliet, added to the activity. He was picked up on a traffic charge in January of 1926, then pinched again in May by detectives investigating a burglary. He was released without charge that night, but his luck held for only a short time. On the night of July 3, he, Dominic Caruso, and Joey Sypher drove up to the North Side and hit a dress shop at 2663 North Clark. Amidst the silence of the early morning, they broke into the shop and grabbed 50 dresses, expensive numbers valued at about $35 apiece. They loaded up their jalopy but were spotted by a cruising squad car as they drove out of the alley. With Mooney at the wheel, the chase was on until he lost control and crashed the car. He managed to swing the door open and sprint off, losing the cops and leaving Sypher and Caruso behind to take the rap. They fingered him, however, and detectives came to the Giancana house the next morning and made the arrest.

He was charged with burglary and bond was set, and in a routine that would follow for many years to come, Antonino Giancana, the immigrant grocer and father of eight, came down to the station house with cash to bail out his oldest son. That, and money to pay off cops, lawyers, politicians, and judges, all on behalf of his son, kept him and his family impoverished.

Mooney left the Patch in the days that followed, no doubt after some severe discipline from his father, and headed south. He had little money and got by mainly by begging and stealing until he was picked up on a charge of vagrancy by police in Louisville, Kentucky. He was released and quickly got back to Taylor Street, the Patch, where the cops knew him and gunned for him, but where he was still a smart head.

But police had more to keep up with than just young Giancana. Two close friends and fellow 42's, Ralph Orlando and Sam De-Stefano, the latter being known then by his nickname, "Jack Napoleon," were charged on September 18, 1927, with four others, with raping a 17-year-old girl from Taylor Springs, Illinois, as she walked near Halsted and Forquer streets with a boyfriend. The gang dragged the girl off after beating up her escort. Police broke up the attack when they heard the girl screaming and arrested DeStefano and Orlando. Orlando at the time was free on bond on a charge of robbing a can company. In preliminary hearings, Judge John Bugee freed both boys on grounds that the girl's story was vague and that she couldn't identify her attackers. He also said that it was his impression that the girl, who was hysterical when rescued by police, was "very vacant-minded and looked like a psychopathic case."

Police and public prosecutors had other ideas about who was psychopathic and reindicted Orlando and DeStefano, vowing that if they won convictions they would ask for life imprisonment. Two months later the pair were tried before a jury and details of the gang shag came out. They were convicted and sentenced, ten years for Orlando, three for DeStefano. Orlando, before being taken away, screamed at the presiding judge, "This town will see a couple of murders when I get out," indicating the police sergeant who had arrested him and the prosecutor who had pressed the case.

But the convictions didn't tone down other 42's, and clusters of them were arrested for gang shags and abductions. Most were sent off to prison, but others, particularly first offenders and younger gang members, were sent to the boys reformatory at St. Charles. In early 1928, after a number of 42's had been sent there, the head of the reformatory, Major William J. Butler, received a long-distance phone call from Chicago. "This is the 42 Gang," the caller said. "Unless you let our pals go we'll come down there and kill everybody we see. We've got plenty of men and some machine guns."

Major Butler at first laughed off the threat but was told by Chicago police that the 42's probably meant it, that the gang would do anything. Butler then ordered the state militia to guard the school. He himself carried a pistol. A few nights later three 42's were stopped as they drove near the school, among them Patsy Steffanelli, a gang member well known on Taylor Street for his wild, unpredictable antics. Crazy Patsy was once pinched for driving about the Patch shining a flashlight in the eyes of oncoming cops. At St. Charles, he admitted to harboring ideas of springing fellow 42's from the reformatory. With him was Johnny Colash, a young hood who had been in St. Charles seven times and at the time was being sought for allegedly killing a jailer in Iowa and for a robbery in Galena, Illinois.

The incident fired a controversy between Major Butler and Cook County judges, with Butler stating they had no right to send hardened criminals like the 42's to St. Charles, a place supposedly meant for wayward young boys. Judges generally agreed with Butler, but one added that it was almost impossible to separate criminals by age, since many of the 42's were irredeemable thugs while still in their teens. The Chicago *Tribune* attempted to simplify the problem by stating that the 42's were in a criminal class by themselves, and should be sent to higher institutions such as "Joliet or the electric chair."

As quick as law-enforcement officials were to denounce the gang in the press, they were also eager to sound the death knell of the gang. The 42's themselves referred to such statements, by cops, prosecutors, or politically ambitious judges, as "swan songs," and they ridiculed them. A swan song usually appeared after the conviction of a big-name 42. The state's attorney's office said it after Patsy Pargoni got 25 years on a rape conviction. "The 42 Gang has virtually passed into oblivion," a press release claimed. It seemed a safer statement just two weeks later when Patsy Pargoni's brother Jerry was killed in a shootout with Oak Park police in the middle of a dress-shop robbery. Jerry escaped police—being hustled off by three companions, although he was fatally wounded. To the 42's it was a hard and fast rule that all gang members had to be carried off, no matter how severe the wounds. In most cases, the wounded accomplice was taken to a hospital or doctor's office, and left there for treatment. Nobody talked—even the wounded 42 seldom identified his comrades— and police usually watched him die, or recover and go to the penitentiary, without naming his pals. Jerry Pargoni died at St. Anthony Hospital, where he'd been taken by three men and two women. He insisted to the end that he didn't know who was with him, or who shot him.

But perhaps no death or imprisonment of a 42 brought about a bigger swan song than an incident in November, 1927. The notorious Babe Ruth was, by this time, enjoying the fruits of his power. He bought and sold police, set up shorts for other 42's, continually brought new, younger kids into the gang, and generally established himself as the man to see in the 42's. He was making a lot of money and dressing the part, hanging out on corners or at Vito Pelletieri's house. To the surprise of many, he bought himself a "legit" car, instead of appropriating a short. "Riding in a hot car is advertising to the coppers to come and get you," he told his buddies. Riding in Babe's new jalopy was a pleasure, for the flivver had overhead valves and special carburetors, which made it the fastest, if not the hottest, car in the Patch.

His position in the gang was unchallenged, and he continued to make new rules and devise new hits. One of the rules forbade girls, for Babe was wary of women. "They're all squawkers," he sneered. Another prohibited drugs, and still another suggested that 42's go on jobs without guns because Babe reasoned that if one was caught without a gun, punishment would be lighter. Despite Babe's influence, most 42's ignored his rules, and guns and women were as common among them as stolen tires and motor meters.

But the gang never failed to take Babe's lead on new jobs. He circulated around town, visiting various retail clothing shops, and lined up owners who would buy stolen merchandise from him. Once he had sufficient demand, he would find another shop with the goods and simply "crash" it, using the tested practice of smashing the front window and grabbing what was needed.

Babe Ruth seldom took on much of the risk himself, but occasionally he did go on a job in person, usually because he couldn't find young suckers to do his bidding. His relations with police became strained. Not only was he unable to buy them all off, but as the exploits of the 42's gained the public's attention, coppers became more and more antagonistic. Those who did deal with him complained that he was becoming too abusive for his own good and even accused him of not splitting takes and gang payoff money as had been arranged. The combination of circumstances made Babe's rope a thin one, his risks greater.

In the fall of 1927 Babe's predicament became such that he was unable to find anyone to lift a set of tires he needed for his jalopy. On impulse, because he had never really outgrown the style and mentality of the 42's, he found a car like his and in broad daylight began to work on the rims. Minutes later a squad car from the Maxwell Street station spotted him. Officer Ben Bowman took a shot at Babe when he started running. He ran a half block, with Bowman and his partner shooting as he went, until Bowman nailed him. The Babe was taken to Mother Cabrini Hospital. He lived for three hours.

Bowman's superiors at the Maxwell station couldn't get the news to the papers fast enough. Feature spreads on the Babe and the 42's appeared the next day. The *Tribune* ran an editorial which stated that it was hoped Babe Ruth's death would be a lesson to his followers and any other young men who might be persuaded to run afoul of the law.

But the death of Babe Ruth did little except whet the appetites of the police and make the gang, which sent flowers to Babe's wake, that much more wary of the heat. It did not make them any wiser. They were still crazy boys, bred in the Patch and consolidated by Babe Ruth, and they would do anything at any time as long as someone said, "Hey, I got something." And, anyway, there were plenty of smart heads to take over from the Babe.

Gone were the elegant brothels. Gone were the madams like the Everleigh sisters, who invited clients into mahogany- and walnut-paneled sitting rooms and sold them their pleasures amidst brocaded draperies and gold-plated spittoons. Gone was Big Jim Colosimo and his highrolling café at 2126 South Wabash, where politicians, industrialists, and gangsters had wiped foam from their lips next to velvet wall coverings, tapestries, and gold chandeliers. By late summer, 1926, most of the splendor of the infamous Levee had faded, the best and bawdiest establishments raided or boarded up by vigilant police commissioners, state's attorneys, or reform-minded politicians. But, even as many of its brightest lights darkened, the Levee's reputation hung on. In the 1920's it was still the place visitors and conventioneers, or Chicagoans timid of the Black and Tan district further south, wanted to go. Taxis did a good all-night business in the area, and small shops and clubs stayed awake.

One of them was a small cigar shop at 1834 South Dearborn, and on the night of September 13, with the warmth of summer still in the air, taxicabs attending to the Levee swarmed around it. Two were parked nearby at 3 A.M. when a light-colored Chrysler pulled up and parked out front. Two men got out. The driver stayed behind the wheel, the motor running.

Inside the shop, a 55-year-old clerk named William Girard, a barber moonlighting to support his wife and two children, took little notice of the men. Both were well dressed, in suits and hats. They walked slowly in, one stopping at the door, the other, a short man with a deep-olive complexion typical of the hordes of Sicilian immigrants who poured out of the Dearborn station down the street, approached Girard as he stood behind the counter. He was Diego Ricco, and in one motion he pulled out a pistol and told Girard to put his hands up. Although there was but $35 in the till, Girard resisted and went for a gun he had under the counter. As he did, the man standing at the door opened fire. He was Joe Pape, a well-known member of the 42's, and his three shots hit Girard in the thigh and the right side of his chest.

The sound of the shots drew the taxicab drivers to the shop. As they approached, the driver of the Chrysler standing out front, a thin-faced, tight-lipped kid not yet out of his teens, roared away, but not before he looked into the faces of the startled cabbies and they into his.

One of the cab drivers, William Jones, took his pistol from under the front seat of his cab and began firing at the two men as they emerged from the cigar store. Both Ricco and Pape shot wildly back at Jones, then sprinted down an adjoining alley. Three other cabbies ran after them. Ricco lost them; Pape ran into a building on Archer Avenue, threw his gun down on a landing, then disappeared in a winding hallway. But, from blotches of blood along the way, his pursuers were certain he had been hit.

A few blocks away, Ricco emerged from the buildings and

flagged down a DeLuxe cab driven by Alex Burba, 25, who was moonlighting from his job as a grocer. Ricco excitedly jumped into the cab and told Burba to step on it, to drive him to the 900 block of South Loomis. When they approached the area, Ricco leaned forward and again told Burba to drive on, this time to Polk and Racine. There Ricco again pulled his gun.

"Give up what ya got," he ordered Burba.

Burba pulled his pockets inside out and give Ricco $9.50.

Ricco took $9 then tossed the remaining coins back at Burba.

"Keep fifty cents for gas," he said, then swung out of the cab and ran into the street.

As he did, a Chrysler sedan squealed next to him. Ricco eyed the driver and hopped inside. Burba watched it all; then, instead of lamenting his loss, he drove back to where he had picked up his jackroller.

Within blocks of the cigar store he spotted the squad cars. His intuitions were correct, and he told detectives of the man he had picked up. Through mug shots he positively identified Ricco, and his identification was added to that of the other cabbies, who'd also fingered Pape and the driver of the Chrysler, Sam Giancana.

The three of them were rounded up the next day and held on $25,000 bond on charges of robbery and assault to kill. The latter charge was changed to murder when William Girard died in St. Luke's Hospital that day.

In custody the three were surly and uncommunicative, answering police questioning with inventive stories of their own.

Ricco said he had been sleeping at the time of the robbery and had awakened at 4:15 in the morning. "I got up early. I fried some pancakes. Had some coffee. I went downstairs. I was going over to the restaurant."

He had also stopped at a drugstore and bought some bandages and adhesive tape. "I always keep some around," he explained.

Pape, who had been severely wounded in the left shoulder and would ultimately lose the arm, had an even more interesting tale. He said he lived with his parents at 1645 Taylor and worked as a laborer for his uncle. The night before he'd watched a movie at the Broadway-Strand Theater at Roosevelt and Paulina, then he'd gone out driving in his uncle's car.

"How long were you driving?" a detective asked.

"About forty-five minutes."

"Why did you stop riding?"

"I stopped because I was shot."

"Where were you when you were shot?"

"In the machine."

"Who shot you?"

"I don't know."

"Where did you go after you were shot?"

"I don't know."

"Why?"

"I was unconscious."

He added that he didn't know how he got to the hospital until the cops came, but that he thought he had staggered out of his car and fallen unconscious. He wasn't really sure.

The detectives decided to backtrack a bit.

"What was the name of the show you went to?"

"I don't remember," Pape said.

With that he refused to say anything more. Both he and Ricco refused to sign their statements.

Mooney Giancana didn't talk at all.

Again the arrest forced Antonino Giancana to come up with cash to get his son out of jail. It was money he couldn't afford, for not only did his seven other kids press his earnings, but other costs came up. In only two weeks his second wife, Mary Leonardi, would be struck and killed in her effort to save their youngest son, and Antonino would have to finance her funeral.

Once out on bond, Mooney stayed out of trouble and managed even to get a break. In December of that year his burglary charge for the Clark Street dress-shop job went to trial. Sam steadfastly refused to admit any involvement in the burglary, and for want of evidence, his case was dropped. Joey Sypher, whom the coppers had caught with Dominic Caruso when the getaway car crashed, was convicted and sentenced to a jail term of one to ten years. Caruso, however, was acquitted.

The reprieve was only temporary for Mooney. As the months passed, the trial for the murder of William Girard began to hang heavily over the heads of Mooney, Pape, and Ricco. To offset it, they went to devices best known to the 42's.

The trial was scheduled for April, 1927, and in the weeks preceding it, Ricco, Pape, and Mooney contacted Alex Burba and asked if he had had second thoughts about testifying. Burba had

since quit his taxi driving to work full time in his grocery store
on West Pershing Road. He operated it with a partner and lived
upstairs with his wife of 15 months, Sophia, a four-month-old
baby, and his father. It was hard work and the many calls from
the three Italians didn't make things easier. Yet Burba resisted,
though the strain on him began to tell. He worried constantly,
seldom smiling, yet denying any problems by saying what he had
eaten had disagreed with him.

By April the calls came more frequently, each time the exchange being the same. Burba held out. At first he was offered
bribes, a simple cash payment in exchange for a sudden loss of
memory. The offers increased until one day Diego Ricco and
Giancana appeared at the grocery store and in a hushed back-
room conference offered Burba $2,000 in cash. That was the kind
of money Burba had never seen before, money that would take
his family and his business out from under the day-by-day worry
of meeting expenses. Still he refused, and his visitors left the
small grocery with grim faces, pushing aside the door and roaring off in their machine.

On April 20, they called the store once again. This time Burba
was not in and the call was taken by his partner Charles Ralce.
That afternoon Ricco, Pape, and Giancana came by once again
and had another backroom conference with Burba. As they left,
Burba pointed them out to Ralce, and though he knew Alex had
not acceded to their demands, Ralce noticed that they seemed to
be on good terms with him. What he did not realize was that the
seeming good cheer on the part of the three visitors was probably
due to the fact that they had finally made up their minds about
what they were going to do.

That night, just before the grocery was to close, one of the three
men returned to the store. He was stocky, short, wearing a dark
suit and a light brown cap. As he entered he noticed one customer inside, a 17-year-old girl named Betty Klenchuk, so he sat
down at the store's small soda fountain and asked Burba for a
drink. Alex told him he had nothing to drink and the man asked
instead for an ice-cream soda.

As Burba prepared the soda, his wife Sophia came down the
back stairs. She noticed the late-model blue Chevrolet coupe
parked out front and asked whose it was.

"Never mind, lady," the man at the soda fountain said. "That's
my car."

Then, hardly touching his ice cream, the man asked Alex if he would talk with him outside. It was after 8:30 and dark, but Alex agreed and the two of them walked out. In a moment two shots rang out. Sophia Burba screamed and ran to the door, then turned and shouted to Betty Klenchuk to fetch her father from upstairs. Outside she found Alex lying face down against a fireplug, blood pouring from him. She turned him over and saw that he had been shot once in the shoulder and once in the back of the head.

The blasts brought neighbors into the street, and one of them, John Donlon, helped Sophia carry her husband into the store. Burba's assailant had sprinted off; the blue coupe parked out front had gone. But a couple walking on South Francisco heard the shots and spotted the man in the dark suit and light hat running down the street. They got a good look at him, his build, his dark complexion, before he jumped inside the blue Chevrolet.

Inside the grocery store, Alex Burba lay dying. Police called for a wagon to take him to a hospital, but both the Fifteenth District police wagons were out and officers asked a passing motorist who had stopped out of curiosity to take Burba and his wife away. As he did, loading Burba, who was unconscious and bleeding profusely, into the auto, Betty Klenchuk held the couple's baby girl. Tears coursed down Betty's cheeks. The baby cried wildly.

An hour later Burba died in People's Hospital. Though he was conscious for a short time, Sophia said she couldn't understand his reply when she asked him who killed him. It was part of the story she stuck with in the shock and grief of her husband's murder. Initially she told detectives it was Diego Ricco who had come into the store that night, and descriptions from witnesses who saw the man running from the grocery matched that of Ricco. But Sophia Burba later recanted that statement and insisted she couldn't identify anybody. She refused at first even to go downtown to the Bureau of Investigation to identify Ricco, Pape, and Giancana. A few days later she viewed a line-up consisting of Giancana and five other men but said she didn't recognize any of them. She said the same when she was shown mug shots of Ricco and Pape. She simply wanted nothing more to do with investigations of any kind. She requested her husband's clothing, and took it home in a shoebox.

Police also received the same reception from other witnesses.

Betty Klenchuk said she didn't get a good look at the killer. Charles Ralce said only, "I could not identify them by picture and I am not sure I could identify them in person as the store was dark and I did not take a good look at them."

The Burba murder investigation became a brick wall for detectives. The 42's had effectively accomplished their goal, for not only had they intimidated any witnesses to the Burba murder, but they had wiped out the only witness against them in the Girard rap. The state had no choice ten days later but to drop the charges against the three 42 Gang defendants. This outraged the police and press to such an extent that Chief of Police Hughes asked detectives to find new witnesses to the Girard murder.

But news of the Burba slaying reached those witnesses faster than the detectives. Gus Nordstrom, a cabbie who had chased Joe Pape into a nearby building, was nowhere to be found. William Jones, the cab driver who had shot and wounded Pape, had moved three times since the murder. Detectives finally found him in an apartment on West 22nd, but they had to kick the door down to get inside. Jones said he had lost all memory of the incident and adamantly refused to identify anybody.

A third driver and eyewitness, Richard Pankratz, was last seen on his way to California.

The 42's thrived on such victories. They became that much bolder, that much cockier, ready to take on any job. They had a supreme confidence in their abilities to beat a rap, harboring feelings of invincibility, and always, always likening themselves to the big-time gangsters like Capone, Moran, Zuta—and none of those guys ever got caught. It didn't matter that 42's were being thrown into jail every month on rape charges, auto thefts, petty larcenies, for a single case of beating a rap as Ricco, Pape, and Mooney had done was enough to make them forget the falls that other gang members were taking. More than that, such capers in their eyes increased their stature before the big-timers. And that was the real goal of the 42's. They constantly attempted to give the impression that they were highrollers, buying expensive clothes and cars and dropping hundreds of dollars in nightclubs. The club routine was big with them, for they felt that if the big-time hoodlums saw them drop wads and live high, they would be impressed enough to take them on. But big bootleggers seldom seriously considered the 42's even though they occasionally put them to work as beer runners or drivers. The 42's were still "those crazy boys."

Louis Romano, a Capone and Frank Nitti lieutenant, said of them, "Nearly every one of them had been in and out of prisons and jails since they were kids. Most of these boys were eighteen, nineteen, twenty-one years old. They didn't hang around with the older gangsters because they called them punks or screwy kids. These kids would pick fights with the cops. They would pull off daring robberies. They were usually the headliners. Some of these kids one night visited a nightclub and during the robbery one of them banged a girl on a table."

In all, the 42's succeeded in making names among nobody but the police and themselves. The gang lacked any cohesion and flailed in all directions, with little or no discipline and only the presence of a few smart heads to organize a job. Their strength came not from any power they had as a "gang," but rather from traditional instincts: an intimate knowledge of the neighborhood, childhood ties, a mutual confidence, trust, instant communication, and a common enemy in the police. Apart from those, 42's were on their own.

In the days following the Burba killing, Mooney's luck with the law held. He was pinched in May for auto theft, but that charge was dropped in June for lack of evidence. Meanwhile, he and other 42's got into other lines of work. They were of particular help to politicians around election time, especially during the Republican primary in April of 1928. Known as the "Pineapple Primary" because of the numerous bombings that preceded it, the election was a bloody power struggle between incumbent Mayor William Hale Thompson and his state's attorney Robert E. Crowe, and the forces of reformer Senator Charles Deneen. In Little Italy, Thompson's Twentieth Ward committeeman Morris Eller was challenged by a Negro attorney, Octavius Granady, the first black ever to attempt to gain office in Chicago and one of the few people who dared challenge Eller's supremacy.

When election day came around, the 42's were widely used by the Eller forces as vote "floaters," which meant that they did nothing all day but travel from precinct to precinct to vote over and over again. To extend the parlance, many were even "stingers," which meant that not only did they float, but they carried guns and used them if any election judge challenged them.

In their home ward, Mooney and fellow 42's worked feverishly for Eller. They even performed the ultimate service. At the close of the day, challenger Granady was shot at as he stood outside a polling place. He ran for his car and attempted to escape, but the car from which the first shot had been fired doubled back and chased him, its occupants shooting as they went. Granady finally lost control and crashed into a tree, and his assassins finished the job by shooting him more than a dozen times.

A furious grand-jury probe attempted to discover Granady's killers and subpoenaed dozens of West Side gangsters, politicians, and bootleggers. Mooney Giancana, dubbed in the press the "generalissimo" of the notorious 42 Gang, was duly subpoenaed but was quickly released and not implicated.

From vote floating and election-day terrorism, the 42's went on to work in union fights. The Master Barbers' union in the summer of 1928 hired them to coerce barbers into joining the union and conforming to its rules. Gang members received $2,000 to wreck the shops of recalcitrant barbers, which they did with late-night pineapple raids. Mooney was never implicated for those, even though an official of the Master Barbers' union was later indicted for the terror tactics. But in the summer of 1928 Mooney, who had just passed his twentieth birthday, was involved in another murder case.

On the night of August 7, Barney Clamage, who ran a soft-drink parlor at 736 South Paulina, was counting up the night's receipts when someone began pounding on the front door. It was 3 A.M. and Clamage had long since closed the place, but he opened the door anyway and let in a frantic regular he knew as Dibbets. His name was Eddie Divis, and he was a small-time gambler in the Patch. But Clamage knew him better as an oft-times unruly customer given to throwing steins at the wall when he was loaded.

But that night Divis was frantic, and no sooner had Clamage opened the door to him than it was kicked open by three men. At the first gunshot blast Clamage dove behind the bar. He stayed there amidst the roar of a half-dozen shots, and then waited twenty minutes more just to be sure.

When he came out he found Divis dead from wounds in the chest, stomach, jaw, the left side of his neck, and one of his fingers. Clamage decided he was in no mood to hang around, and he took a blanket from a rear room and covered Divis. Then, without reporting the killing to police, he left.

The next morning, after Clamage finally notified detectives, the investigation of Divis' murder began. His common-law wife told police that he had gotten a telephone call around midnight and left saying that he had to see someone. Then she told detectives that the key to the killing probably lay with Divis' new girlfriend, Mildred Mollinari.

Miss Mollinari painted a vivid picture of Divis, not only as a small-time hood but as a lover. He was seeing her behind the back of her current boyfriend, Dominic "Dunk" Caruso, a prominent 42 and accomplice of Mooney Giancana in the Clark Street dress-shop burglary. Caruso was furious at Divis' attentions to Mildred, even more so the night of August 8 when he called and discovered that Dibbets was there at the time. He ranted at her, calling her a tramp and a whore, then said he would get even with her and Divis.

That night, according to Miss Mollinari, Divis had come over with Mooney Giancana. Both of them were drunk, and Mooney continued to drink from a bottle he had on him. When Caruso called, Divis and Mooney revealed their contempt for him. Mooney recalled the burglary he'd pulled with him and said Caruso owed him money. Divis was simply sick of Dunk's threats concerning his relationship with Mildred. The two of them vowed to get Caruso and put the word out around Halsted and Taylor streets. It quickly got to Caruso.

Mildred told detectives that was typical of Divis. When he was threatened he quickly turned the tables and threatened back. He had been around, in prison, with arrests for burglary and larceny, and now, at age 29, he was as reckless as ever.

"Divis wasn't afraid of anybody, he told everybody that," Mildred said. "He told me he would lick any fella I went out with."

But she, like most others involved in Patch murders, claimed to know nothing of his killer. "I read it in the paper, and while reading it you guys came. Divis said he had a lot of enemies, but that he would never die of a bullet, that he had been shot at but none of them had guts enough to get him. He liked trouble and always wanted to be in a fight."

Which is what he got from the three men who crashed through

the door of Barney Clamage's saloon. Detectives were certain that his hoodlum friends got him before he could get them. The case went no further than that.

The only eyewitness, Clamage, who had a reputation with police for questionable activities in his saloon, told police what they expected.

Could he identify the killers?

Barney answered tartly, "Only if I was tired of living."

A few weeks later Mooney's father's ice-cream store was bombed twice in eleven days. And, though Antonino and his business partner were severely beaten the night after the second bombing in what many police believed was an extortion attempt, other investigators refused to separate the bombings from the Divis killing, believing that somehow Mooney had either turned the tables and allied himself with Caruso, or that Divis' friends had no idea who did what and simply struck out at both men. None of those theories was ever resolved.

After the heat of the murder and bombing investigations passed, Mooney went about his old routines of making a buck. In November, he, Ralph Orlando, and Tumpa Russo, pulled one of the 42 Gang's favorite capers. For years they had preyed on delivery trucks, the butter-and-eggs trucks, ice vans, and other delivery wagons that came into the neighborhood. Mostly they pulled hit-and-run thefts, a holdover from the days when they stole from peddlers and ran into the alleys. But on this afternoon, Mooney, Russo, and Orlando decided they would steal not just the van's goods, but the van itself.

They drove the West Side until they spotted one. The driver, Joe Cardose, had left the truck with the door open while making a delivery and Ralph Orlando jumped inside, shoved it into gear, and took off, with Mooney and Russo in Mooney's Chrysler providing rear escort. Cardose came out as his truck was being taken, and in an auto he commandeered from a passerby he gave chase.

For blocks he stayed on the heels of his truck and Mooney's Chrysler, but he was unable to curb the truck because Mooney kept cutting him off and running him into the curb. But Cardose kept at it, honking madly and finally attracting the attention of a squad car. The police pulled them all over, collared Mooney and Russo, who tried to run, and arrested them all for auto theft.

The caper was similar to those of other 42's. As the months passed, the gang got into more and more scrapes, some of them laughably inept, others daring and vicious. In an attempt to steal turkeys from a peddler, Joey DeCorrado was shot and wounded, and found later in an alley, where his companions had left him to bleed to death. Six other 42's were arrested for raping an 18-year-old woman. Sam Domico, on a lam from police, ran over a pedestrian, and though he stopped and took the man to a hospital, it wasn't enough to save him. Domico fled from the hospital but was arrested and charged with manslaughter. Six 42's, after being ejected from the Smart Set Taxi Dance Hall on West Lake in the Loop, turned on the bouncer and shot him. Ameda Perna, a 42 whose wife Mary was suing him for divorce and custody of her two-year-old, kidnapped the child, then demanded $95 for his return.

The incidents continued day after day. Antagonism between the gang and police escalated. Frank "Duke" Battaglia, the youngest of four Battaglia brothers but the only one officially listed as a member of the 42 Gang, was constantly in the station house, and in the process incurred several beatings from police impatient with his lack of cooperation. In 1930, Battaglia was one of four men riding in a car that police said had fled from where a 49-year-old Berwyn woman had been shot and killed after she resisted a purse snatching. Although conviction never resulted, police claimed that the woman's purse was thrown from the 42's' car as they gave chase.

Battaglia's downfall came when he was trapped in a basement in the Patch by police. Sergeant Leyendecker said Battaglia aimed a pistol at him and attempted to shoot it out, but the gun failed to fire. Battaglia was later given a year in prison on a concealed-weapons charge, and as he was being taken from court he snarled at Leyendecker, "I'll kill you when I get out. I'll get you for this." Leyendecker snarled back, "I'll kill *you*, you hoodlum. The first time I catch you up to anything I'm going to let you have it." Judge John Lyle witnessed the exchange, and contrary to his usual stern demeanor, he smiled.

Frank's brother Sam, a big good-looking kid with the nickname "Teets" because of his muscular chest, hit the news even more prominently in the fall of 1930 when he was arrested and charged with robbing the mayor's wife, Mrs. William Hale Thompson, of jewelry valued at $15,500. Her policeman chauffeur, Peter J. O'Malley, stood at gunpoint as the thieves took his gun and his shield.

A few days later Battaglia was arrested, but no positive identification was made. To reporters and editorial writers, the arrest appeared to be the result of a political maneuver by Judge Lyle, who was anxious to become mayor and who was also angry with Acting Police Commissioner John Alcock for demoting some of Lyle's friends. Teets Battaglia was the goat of it all. He was later released for lack of evidence.

If the 42's weren't the victims of police or politicians' wrath, they were their own worst enemies. When Pete "The Ape" Nicastro was suspected of hijacking alcohol stills he was shot in the head and dumped out of a jalopy onto South Canal Street at 1 A.M. His fate matched that of another wild 42, Hank Petitto. Though only 17, Petitto ran as one of the toughest, gutsiest 42's around. As a freelancer he was robbing neighborhood stills, basements, stores, and flats, and even committed a few muggings. He drove a Chrysler "80" Imperial, had it painted black, and soon it earned the label "The Black Coffin." But Hank also got a reputation as being untrustworthy, and after one con too many among fellow 42's, he was taken for a ride. His body was found in the mud of a ditch near McCook, Illinois. He had been shot 15 times. In his hands police found a nickel. It was the gang's symbol for a double-crosser, and also an estimate of what it felt Hank Petitto's life was worth.

Because the 42's took life one job at a time, few of them had much of a future. If they weren't killed by the police, or other gang members, they were pinched in bungled burglaries or car thefts and given stiff jail sentences. At the beginning of the Depression, with the repeal of Prohibition drastically changing the enterprises of the lowliest alky cookers and the biggest bootleggers, the original 42's, the smart heads, had suffered badly. In 1931, University of Chicago sociologists took an informal roll call, and the results were staggering.

Babe Ruth was dead, shot by police after his tire theft attempt. Vito Pelletieri was still in the Patch, but his role as a smart head had diminished and he did not align himself with the bigtime gangsters. Patsy Pargoni was in jail under a 25-year sentence on a rape conviction. His brothers Jerry and Louis had both been killed in shootouts with police. Salvi was killed in an automobile crash.

Among other 42's, crazy Patsy Steffanelli was killed when he provoked one too many confrontations with the cops. Police chased Patsy's car after spotting it at Kedzie and Ogden. A shootout resulted and Steffanelli was killed by Patrolman James Doherty. Patsy, who had amassed a staggering record of arrests, including that for his planned machine-gun attack on the St. Charles Reformatory, was 23. Another smart head, Patsy Tardi, was shot and killed by two men in January, 1931, as he walked near Miller and Polk in the Patch.

The list went on. Mibs Fillichio and his brother Frank both married and moved on to other enterprises. But George Schiulo, Angie Russo, and Joe Leopold went to Leavenworth on a postal robbery conviction. Two Gun Pepe and Archie Capozzi each got one year to life for a jewel robbery in St. Louis. Chickie Lombardo got one year to life for a robbery rap. Tony and Carlo Torrisello; Baba and Johnson Orlando; Tony the Giant—all went to prison on various felony convictions. Willie Doody made headlines when he shot and killed a cop in Cicero in 1929. He was sentenced to the electric chair.

Many 42's who weren't in prison could hardly walk straight. Vito Mascini, though married and "legit," was disabled from a gunshot wound. Vito Fosco was also permanently disabled from a wound. Joe Pape, though he, Mooney, and Diego Ricco beat the Girard murder charges, had his left arm amputated because of the wounds he received in the robbery.

And Frank Battaglia. By 1931 he had been beaten up so much by police under the guise of "questioning," that he was maimed for life. Fellow 42's considered him "queer," punch drunk and undependable. After his year in prison for the shooting attempt on Sergeant Leyendecker, Frank had a mania for confronting police. But as mooney as Frank was, he was better off than his older brother Augie, who was shot to death in 1931. Augie's death came before the death of the Battaglia boys' father in September of that year. Frank and brother Sam were at their father's funeral (as were a number of 42's who appeared in the funeral procession) but they were in custody at the time and watched their father laid to rest while they were handcuffed to a Chicago police detective. A number of 42's talked of slugging the dicks and grabbing Frank and Sam, but they finally decided against it.

Which left only Mooney and his associates. In November, 1928, he lost what little hold he had on his freedom. To finance bond and defense money for the delivery-van rap on the 17th, Mooney, Tumpa Russo, and Ralph Orlando attempted to burglarize a clothing store at 3947 West Madison. Again, they went at it in the dead of night, this time at 1 A.M. But the darkness and quiet did not keep them from bungling things once again. To get inside the building they had to go through a brick wall. With hammers and chisels they chipped away at the bricks and mortar but succeeded only in awakening neighbors and bringing on a squad car. Police came at them from all sides. Dust and chips of mortar and brick were everywhere. Mooney, though he had put on a pair of coveralls for the job, was covered with debris. Next to him, lying where he had thrown it seconds before the heat had converged, was his revolver.

Again they were thrown into jail. Bond for attempted burglary and concealed-weapons charges was more than any one of them could come up with immediately. Antonino Giancana this time did not rush to spring his son. So the three of them remained in jail. Word of the pinch got out among the gang and a couple of 42's showed up with food from a nearby restaurant.

Some time later bond money came around and the trio were released. Days later they were indicted on the delivery-van theft. With the burglary rap pending, prosecutors were not zealous about pursuing this charge against Mooney and Russo, though they did convict Orlando on the charge of driving an auto without the consent of the owner. He was sentenced to six months in jail, fined a dollar, and charged no court costs. But on the same day the three were indicted on the attempted-burglary charges. Orlando and Mooney pleaded guilty and were sentenced to one to five years in the state penitentiary at Joliet. Tumpa Russo fought his case, maintaining that he was near the burglary attempt but not a part of it, and his case was stricken. He went back to the Patch and flaunted his freedom. He built a reputation as a burglar, a good one compared to his associates who were headed for Joliet, bought a car, and carried a bankroll.

There were no such times for Mooney. He and Orlando ended

their roaring twenties on March 12, 1929, when they surrendered to marshals and began serving their prison terms. Sam had not yet reached his twenty-first birthday. When the Depression hit months later, he was among more than thirty of the original 42's who were either in jail, maimed, or dead. Police and publicity-prone prosecutors and judges continued to sing swan songs for the gang. They checked off the names, read obituaries, then added to the death knell.

"There aren't 42 members now," one prosecutor was quoted as saying after a rape conviction of two 42's. "Police bullets have accounted for several. Others are receiving their mail at the reformatory at Pontiac or the penitentiary at Joliet."

After the conviction of a small-time 42 Gang burglar, an assistant state's attorney told the press, "Chicago's 42 Gang has virtually passed into oblivion as an organization of young criminals long a moral menace to the city's youth."

Such statements may have made for comforting reading and a publicity boost for the prosecutors' office, but the swan songs had nothing to do with reality. In the Patch, the passing or the absence of every original 42 was met with the appearance of an eager new recruit. Even though the gang ceased to exist as a close-knit organization, it existed as a *culture*. Aspiring punks immediately identified themselves as 42's if arrested. Smart heads along Taylor Street kept an ear out for a reputation and went after the toughest, gutsiest kids in the neighborhood. Despite the deaths of Babe Ruth, the Pargonis, and others, the 42's at the advent of the Depression were as active and plentiful as ever, with new times and new conditions in which to work, and bound even closer by a new and more pervasive era of poverty.

5

SHE WAS A SMALL, slender girl, the youngest daughter of France-scantonio De Tolve and his wife, Maria. The De Tolves had come to Chicago from southern Italy, where they had lived in relative prosperity. But Francescantonio's eyes were on America, and he left his relatives behind for what awaited him there. In Chicago he did well, working as a laborer and saving enough money to buy an apartment building on West Polk in the Patch. His family expanded to seven in all, four boys and three girls, the last one being the fragile yet athletic Angeline.

She was raised in the strictest Italian traditions, seldom emerging from her mother's arm long enough to see what was going on along Taylor Street. When she did get out she went swimming, at the beaches on Lake Michigan or at the public pool at Taylor and Miller. She thrived on the exercise, then was suddenly stricken with rheumatic fever. The sickness was as tough on her as it was on so many other Italian-Americans afflicted with it, causing damage to her heart's valves and leaving her with a permanent heart murmur. She became sickly, and in what was to be a pattern for the rest of her life, she tired quickly with any amount of physical exertion.

Apart from her health, Angeline grew up as her sisters did. They were educated until they were 14 by the nuns at Our Lady of Pompeii. They attended mass and took communion and became devoted to the Roman Catholic Church. Life for Angeline De Tolve was domestic: cooking, laundry, cleaning, taking in tailoring or laundry for extra money. The household was a proper one, as much as Francescantonio and his wife could maintain within the restrictions of their earnings and the temptations of the Patch. For they were not blind, and they knew what went on. Francescantonio knew that only a fine line of discipline lay between an immigrant's family that lost its sons (and occasionally its daughters) to the streets and one that didn't.

With the boys the rules were different, the exceptions broad. Francescantonio De Tolve knew many fathers whose sons hung out with the 42 Gang, and he was well aware of what they did and what happened to them. It wouldn't happen to his boys. His daughters, Rose, Anna, and Angeline, would also be watched. He could lose them only through marriage, and then the courtship, the approach of the suitor, would be a proper one.

By the time Angeline was 18 the gauze had begun to fall from her eyes. She met one boy in particular who took a liking to her, but she did not pursue the relationship because he was one of the "crazy boys." His name was Sam but the boys on the block called him Mooney or, sometimes, Gagiano. The year was 1928, and Sam drove a car and wore flashy clothes, chesterfield coats and wide-brimmed hats like the gangsters in the comics. He was short and skinny, and when he smiled he sort of pulled up one side of his face like a tough guy. Angeline De Tolve met him and talked to him in the stores and soda fountains, she even took a liking to him. But, as she was to learn a few years later, her attraction was nothing like the torch he held for her.

For Mooney, this girl was perfect. She was respectable, came from a good family, too good for that matter, and kindled something within him. He was no longer a teenager. Along with the other 42's, he had gotten on with more girls than he could remember. But they were "bums," girls the guys picked up then banged in hotel rooms or garages, the hideouts, or the back seats of machines. Like Jeanette, who later on became one of the 42's' best gun girls. Mooney and everyone banged her, so much that she was known as the "godmother" of the 42's. Jeanette was loud and a flashy dresser, and she flaunted her looks with more rouge and lipstick than any of the other neighborhood girls dared wear. She smoked and cussed, and like a lot of other gun girls, started acting like the 42's. And, although Mooney took advantage of them, he would never consider getting serious with one. For, as wild as the 42's were, it was still bad form to court a bum.

But, as Mooney got more serious in his courtship of Angeline De Tolve, he met total hostility from her family. He was a hood, a crazy boy of the 42's, and though Angeline was tainted by the very fact that she lived in the Patch (Italian girls who met young men at work or at dance halls found that out all too quickly when they revealed their home addresses and found their suitors quickly repelled), her family, Francescantonio and Maria De Tolve, had far better intentions for her than getting involved with a hoodlum.

The courtship came to an abrupt halt, however, in 1929 when Judge John J. Sullivan sentenced Mooney to prison in Joliet. That was in March, and for the next three years and nine months Francescantonio De Tolve wouldn't see the kid's face around his home. The problem appeared solved.

For Mooney, Joliet was inevitable. He went there instead of to Bridewell or Pontiac because he was considered a hardened criminal, a loser who had come up the ranks from juvenile busts to petty theft and disorderly arrests, finally to a burglary one-to-five. He went there with other thieves, forgers, burglars, gamblers, bootleggers—almost any thug who had gone seriously into crime and gotten caught. He went there to do time, for in 1929 Joliet was a "penitentiary," where the emphasis was on penance. Convicts like Mooney knew it, and though they were put to work in shops where some learned crafts and trades, there was little of what could have been termed rehabilitation. Prisoners counted the days and applied for parole. Social workers and criminologists who visited with them and corresponded with them discovered that the incarceration took little psychological toll, for convicts went in expecting nothing but to do time. Mooney, in fact, referred to prison as nothing but "school."

One thing Joliet did do for convicts like Mooney was to give them a routine. They entered after a disjointed life in the Patch, one that included bizarre diets and odd hours, a lot of booze and even more clap. It was not uncommon for a 42 to go to prison thin and sickly, bleary-eyed, some even suffering from the old ghetto maladies the greaseballs contended with because they didn't have the price of a potato. Forty-twos were so affected because they didn't have the time for one. But in prison that all changed with the uniforms and the regimen. They ate three meals a day and slept eight hours. Some of them even began to get fat. Yet their souls were always back in the Patch, on Taylor Street and in the gang's hideouts and shacks.

The 1930's saw new names on the street. A tough, gravel-voiced punk named Fiore Buccieri started making a name bigger than that of the smart heads of the 1920's. Nicknamed "Fifi," Buccieri began to attract younger kids around him in haunts that had moved west to Ashland and Taylor. The kids could spot him and other 42's because they liked to wear identical wide-brimmed hats, sometimes white ones like those of the gangsters in the movies. Besides Buccieri there were the DeStefano brothers— Sam, and Mario, who was known as "Merle"; little William Daddano, who hung out around Taylor and Loomis and who had been taken in after a shootout and chase with coppers for questioning in the Patsy Tardi murder; Anthony Eldorado, whom the 42's called "Pineapples" because he was shaped like one and also had an affinity for throwing them; Sam English and his brother Chuck, the latter a tall, good-looking kid well liked by the girls; Mike La Goia; and the notorious Battaglias—Frank and Teets.

This edition of the 42's, though they went through the same motions with the police and courts, had grown up in different times from their predecessors. It was the Depression, and though Italian immigrants had come a long way in establishing themselves politically and economically, hard times hit everyone and hit them hard. Goods lost in thefts and robberies weren't as easily replaced. Forty-twos found themselves "junking," going to buildings and stripping iron and copper to sell to junk dealers.

The Depression also meant repeal, however, and a radical reorganization of hoodlums' enterprises. Although the mash cookers still turned out alky from the back rooms of tenements in the Patch, bootlegging and the daily collection of alcohol from house to house sank to a fraction of the business it once was. The gangs kept at it, but also diverted their concessions into gambling and connected rackets. There was also a push at this time to obtain pieces of legitimate businesses: laundries, supply houses, liquor distributing and wholesaling, restaurant supplies, labor unions. In so doing, Capone-level gangsters put many of the older 42's to work as truck drivers and beer runners.

The 1930's also saw a change in the total complexion of organized crime. In New York, the old-time "Mustache Petes"—Joe "The Boss" Masseria and Salvatore Maranzano—were assassinated in the bloody Castellammarese War, and the syndicate there was reorganized by Salvatore "Lucky" Luciano. Luciano in turn set up not only five separate organizations in New York, but also drew up a National Commission composed of 24 bosses from throughout the country. He intended for it to loosely oversee mob interests and mediate differences. But Luciano's Commission was minus one important member, for in May, 1932, Al Capone went to federal prison on an Internal Revenue conviction.

Capone's exodus from Chicago was a loss from which his gang never recovered. Throughout the 1930's, under the leadership of Frank Nitti, moneyman Jake Guzik, Phil D'Andrea, and others, the Capone mob never had the power or earned the revenues that it did under Al. Repeal caused fragmentation and a thinning of the ranks, and even though the hoods got no smarter themselves, the rackets left to them demanded much more finesse than simple booze running.

Mooney got out on parole, but not much of one, shaving only one year three months from the maximum five, a long dose of "school." But on Christmas Eve, 1932, at the age of 24, Mooney walked away from Joliet and took a train back to the Patch. There wasn't a lot to come home to. Hard times had hit his father so badly that he was forced to sell the lemonade store and go back to peddling from a horse and cart. He sold vegetables, watermelons in summer, and ice. Mooney's return meant much to him, as much as the oldest son meant to any Italian father, yet it had been Mooney who had caused so many problems, who spent more time in police stations and jail than out, who was constantly in need of bail money or lawyers' fees or cash for bribes. So, when he got out of the stir at Christmas, in time to welcome 1933 and another year of the Depression, Mooney wasn't looked upon for much. He was not psychologically scarred from prison, but with the stigma of being a convict, with the record he had, he came out an instant loser. Other 42's were in the same straits and got jobs only from relatives, but few held them. Some went into the Conservation Corps camps or other government work projects created by Roosevelt's New Deal. But those groups were as disciplined as prison, and they were the last thing the 42's wanted after a stay in school.

The situation for Mooney was the same as it had been for 42's for years. When one of them returned to Chicago from Joliet, an ex-convict at an early age, he looked to his friends or relatives for chances of getting a legitimate job while he remained on parole. Most of them simply asked him, "Do you really have a yen for being a poor working sap?"

The answer for most 42's was obvious. There was little choice but to get back into the rackets, to hook on with the big-time hoods if possible, to somehow beat the odds of the law and the Depression.

But in 1933 Mooney stayed out of trouble, most likely because he had his eye on getting married. Ordinarily Angeline De Tolve would have been long since out of circulation. She had been engaged to be married while Mooney was in Joliet. But her fiancé had been killed in an automobile accident, and in the emotional period that followed, Angeline grieved deeply. She refused to forget the boy and kept his picture and a silk scarf in a small lacquered Oriental box. Her sorrow made her all the more vulnerable to Mooney, and he was as persistent as ever. The courtship remained rocky. He had nothing to offer but a shady reputation and a criminal record, no money, a Sicilian lineage, a father who was a peddler. Yet Angeline was not a child any longer, and her father was powerless to refuse her her wishes even if he did insist on a proper courtship and marriage.

The wedding took place on September 26, 1933, a traditional Roman Catholic ceremony though not a fancy one. The thin and delicate Angeline De Tolve wore a slim, chic white gown and her mother's wedding ring. As modest as the ceremony was, and as difficult as the relationship with Angeline's family had been, Mooney emerged with a smile on his face, for he had won what he had gone after and waited for for years. The victory would make a difference in his life. At least, for a while.

The Giancanas settled into a small flat at 910 South Hermitage, just a few blocks south and west of where he had grown up on Taylor Street and only a couple of doors down from his father's house. But it was still in the Patch, which meant Mooney was recognized on sight not only by the 42's but by the police. He was arrested occasionally for being on the corner, but through 1933 and 1934 no charges were placed against him. During the fledgling years of his marriage, Mooney stayed clean.

Like so many Italian boys who'd raised unending hell on the streets, Mooney was exactly the opposite as head of his own home. He was a strict disciplinarian and believed Angeline should stay in the house and be a wife and mother. He insisted that the house be cleaned and scrubbed, that meals be prompt. He also yearned for a family, even though Angeline's health made pregnancy no little risk. She was told that childbearing would be difficult for her, that the child could be severely affected. But Mooney was not dissuaded, and Angeline expected their first child in August of 1935.

The doctors' fears were realized in June of that year when Angeline went into labor two months prematurely. In a difficult delivery she gave birth to a three-pound baby girl, a child proportionately as delicate as Angeline. They named her Antoinette, and weighed the hours and days as doctors worked carefully to keep the baby alive. Things went well and the Giancanas celebrated a few months later when the baby was big enough and healthy enough to be taken home.

Yet that joy was also short-lived, for at four months the baby came down with pneumonia. Again doctors worked to save Antoinette's life, this time prescribing mother's milk if she was to live. Angeline was unable to provide enough of it, and the family went daily for the necessary supply to the Chicago Board of Health. Antoinette survived, though the sickness was an omen for years to come. As a toddler she would be as sickly as her mother, having a difficult time well into adolescence.

But she was alive, and Mooney was ecstatic. He prized the baby and showed her off to his friends. He doted on her as soon as she could walk, dressing her up in dark leggings and matching outfits, cooing with the relatives over his firstborn. It had been a victory for Angeline even to have the baby, and the victory was doubly sweet because the child had survived and now was growing into a charmer. And Sam "Mooney" Giancana, the notorious smart head of the 42's, the ex-convict, was a pushover through it all, a beaming, old-fashioned father.

Two years later Angeline was pregnant again. In April, 1938, she gave birth to another girl, this time in a relatively easy birth. The baby was strong and healthy, and they named her Bonita Lucille—Bonnie.

These years for Mooney were his most personal, the most trouble-free time in his life since he'd first hit the streets with the 42's. He worked with his brother-in-law Michael De Tolve in a small envelope and lithographing business and took home a salary of $40 a week. But that kind of money, that kind of life suited Mooney about as much as being "a sap." He still had his contacts, still a street savvy that had been cultivated in the Patch and that counted for a lot among the right people. It was just a matter, in these years, of getting back in with them.

Mooney still had his overwhelming reputation as a wheelman, and it was that ability that impressed those who counted. In the Patch, nobody had a bigger name than "Machine Gun" Jack McGurn, really Vincenzo DeMora, the son of an alky cooker and known in the headlines as one of Capone's top enforcers. Never a 42, McGurn (the name was really a ring name given to him in his early boxing career) grew up around Polk and Morgan, just east of the gang's strongholds. The story circulated around the neighborhood that McGurn's father had been murdered by the booze runners and young Jack had vowed revenge. To sharpen his shooting eye for the day he would stalk his father's killers, he practiced picking pigeons off wires with a rifle. That prowess served to make him a trusted Capone enforcer (it is believed that his biggest hit for Scarface was the St. Valentine's Day massacre). Still, he never severed ties with the boys in the old neighborhood. In September of 1930 a number of 42's attended the wedding of McGurn's sister, and during the reception Jack called them over and set them up in a racket with goods he wanted them to sell.

It was natural for Mooney to gravitate toward a name like McGurn, and occasionally he was seen chauffeuring the machine gunner. But Mooney's stay in Joliet and McGurn's fall from grace within the Capone organization ended that relationship. In February, 1936, McGurn was ambushed as he lingered in the Avenue Recreation Rooms, a bowling alley on North Milwaukee Avenue. Three men formed a semicircle around him and fired away. Then they tossed a valentine onto the body, one that depicted an impoverished couple in front of a sign advertising a household sale.

> You've lost your job,
> You've lost your dough,

Your jewels and your handsome houses.
But things could be worse, you know,
You haven't lost your trousers.

To many the valentine was a direct reference to McGurn's
participation in the massacre seven years before. And, although
it was tossed upon a body wearing a flashy three-piece suit and
spats, McGurn's financial situation was such that informed
sources maintained the card accurately depicted McGurn's
straits. Instead of being rubbed out by avengers from the Moran
Gang, many detectives speculated, he may have been hit by fellow Capone mobsters who considered him broke, ineffectual, and
useless.

Mooney also gained the attention of yet another Capone man,
a square-faced, slow-talking Neapolitan named Felice DeLucia.
He was ten years older than Mooney and had made a name in the
neighborhood when he went to work for Diamond Joe Esposito
in Esposito's Bella Napoli Café at 850 South Halsted. Even then
DeLucia was a man on the run, having come to America with a
falsified passport arranged after he had been found guilty of a
murder in Italy. As a waiter in the Bella Napoli he was known
as Paul DeLucia, and later as Paul "The Waiter" Ricca.

Ricca, because of his exacting sense of responsibility and ability to run things for Esposito, came up quickly in the ranks,
working first for the Genna brothers in their alcohol business
(which was protected politically by Esposito) and then with the
Capone gang itself. Capone's friendship was such that he stood
up at Ricca's wedding in 1927. The Waiter returned the favor—
first with ruthless, precise loyalty, later with disciplined management of the gang's concessions.

It was Ricca, at the time of Capone's fall to the IRS, along with
Jake Guzik, Sam Hunt, the Capone brothers, and Al's bull-faced
bodyguard, Anthony Accardo, who was able to maintain the Capone organization and adapt it to the changing times. In 1932,
Ricca, with his iron jaw and unsmiling expression, his wide-
brimmed white hat, knee-length trench coat, and finely tailored
three-piece suit, met with Sylvester Agoglia, Harry Duckett,
Rocco Fischetti, Meyer Lansky, and Lucky Luciano in Chicago's
Bismarck Hotel. The meeting not only was called to discuss repeal and the problems of reorganizing the mob; it also recognized

Ricca as the man to see in Chicago with Scarface in jail, a man with Luciano's outlook and savvy who could run a modern-day gang.

Mooney then, out of jail and with a life of 42 Gang capers behind him, needed a hook to get him into the big time. He gained Ricca's favor with his ability to drive a car, and by the mid-1930's, the skinny, beak-nosed 42, a family man and a father, was seen in the Waiter's shadows, a well-trained chauffeur with his eyes on the future.

In the meantime, Mooney was a dutiful husband, the loving father of his two little girls, an increasingly strict disciplinarian. Though Angeline oversaw the day-to-day affairs of the children, Mooney made his presence known. He insisted that his girls be perfect ladies, good little dagos. He was authoritative and tough with them in a traditional Italian manner. He also demanded much of Angeline. She had to be the dutiful wife, cooking and scrubbing, immediate in responding to his needs and a housekeeper as well. From the early days Mooney took a special interest in his homes, usually maintaining and furnishing them far in excess of what they were when he moved in. Though Angeline was a tough, resilient woman in her own way, she was very much in the mold of the house-trained matron and acceded to Mooney's insistence on an immaculate house. It became a mania for both of them. As impoverished as they were as newly-weds, as close to the edge of hard times as they and so many families were during the Depression, they insisted on an impeccable house and a full table. What little money there was went into soups in bottomless pots, pasta, breads, and baked goods. The families clung to each other—Antonino Giancana, who struggled to support his remaining family from a peddler's earnings; the De Tolves, who continued in their disapproval of Mooney, however submerged their feelings were through the years of grandchildren with dark faces and shining eyes. And in the midst of the hard times came the good ones. The small Giancana family: Sam, Angeline, the sickly Antoinette, and the infant Bonnie often huddled around the coal stove in their small flat on Hermitage, then on West Lexington. In those times it didn't matter who Mooney was or what he had come from, or about Angeline and her heart or her dead fiancé, or the kids and their sickliness. All that mattered was the warmth from the stove, and how they sliced orange peels and roasted them until they were good and crunchy.

In June, 1937, Guido Gentile wandered far away from his house on South Miller Street in the Patch. Gentile, who used the alias "Joe Greco," took his jalopy onto Highway 20 and headed west, out of Chicago into the rolling cornfields of northern Illinois until he reached Belvidere, just east of Rockford. He was a good 110 miles away from the West Side, from the Chicago police, the G-men. Gentile was what was known at the time as an "honest bootlegger." With repeal came legitimate breweries and wineries and the end of the wide-open Capone-style bootleggers. Moonshining still went on but was looked upon as a relatively honest profession in comparison to the Capone enterprises.

Gentile was scouting for new moonshining territory. With the backing of several partners in the Patch, he was looking for a piece of farm property big enough to hold a full-scale still. That meant a barn for mash cooking and distilling, a fleet of trucks and autos for pickup and delivery, and a network of grain suppliers and local businesses equipped to meet the day-to-day needs of the operation.

Gentile had been given the name of Ed Simons, a Buick dealer and garage owner in Belvidere, and he approached Simons with the proposition of buying a fleet of used Buicks for a business he was about to start. Simons was interested but curious, and Gentile finally said that before he bought any cars he needed a farm for a still. There was no putting off the small intense man who called himself Joe Greco, even though Simons, a rural car dealer of modest means and few pretensions, had a natural wariness of city people, with their three-piece suits and their shiny shoes. But the money Gentile spoke of was hard to deny, and Simons agreed to see what he could do.

A few days later Simons had a visit from Howard Schwebke, a farmer with a spread on Rural Route 1 near Garden Prairie, and Schwebke told him he could no longer meet the payments on a car he'd bought from Simons a year earlier. It was a common occurrence for Simons in the Depression, but this time he offered Schwebke something other than repossession. Schwebke agreed, and suddenly Simons had a remote, expansive barn, just the type the Italian from Chicago had been looking for.

In no time Gentile made good on his commitments. After dropping off $150 for Simons as a commission for finding the Schwebke barn, Gentile began buying used cars and contracting for as many services as Simons could provide. They involved weekly deliveries of gas, oil, and auto parts needed at the barn, goods Simons easily supplied and for which he was paid well. In the process he got a look at the operation the Italians had set up. By the fall of 1937 a huge still in Schwebke's barn was turning out thousands of gallons of alcohol and spirits, and close to 10,000 gallons of mash waited for the cookers.

Gentile was only part of the operation. With him were friends who made the daily trip from the Patch. There was Michael Falco, Jimmy Micelli, Louis Coconate, Sam May, Joe Gizzi, Tony Giacalone, Dick Cramer, Angel Jiannicopulos, and a Sicilian who said his name was Albert Mancuso but who was really Sam "Mooney" Giancana.

For Mooney and the others the still was a natural. It kept them out of the Patch and away from the scrutiny of coppers anxious to send them back to prison, and it was an operation far more lucrative than most rackets in the Depression. There was always a market: in Chicago to wholesalers with strong ties to the old Capone mob, who were always looking for some product to sell without taxes, and in Milwaukee, where Richard Cramer and Elmer Hansen, both associates, were based.

During most of 1938 they kept the still going to capacity. Inventory got so high that Joe Gizzi went out looking for a storage barn somewhere between Garden Prairie and Chicago. In a bar in South Elgin he got to know a 54-year-old chicken farmer named Max Wilcox. Wilcox, who needed a little money to support his 80-year-old mother, suggested the Sorenson barn about four miles south of Elgin. Before he knew it, Joe Gizzi, whom Max Wilcox knew as "Little Joe," had him supervising things at the Sorenson barn. Wilcox didn't know where the alcohol came from or who the swarthy Italian men from Chicago really were, but he did know that they were making a hell of a lot of moonshine somewhere, and that every night it came into the Sorenson barn by the carload.

But the operation didn't stay a secret very long. Internal Revenue agents spread through Belvidere, Marengo, Garden Prairie,

and Hampshire, Illinois, during the fall and winter of 1938, gathering information on the still in the Schwebke barn. On January
17, 1939, a dozen IRS agents surrounded the barn and kicked in
the doors. They found the entire gang hard at work, pouring
alcohol, operating the still. On hand were 8,800 gallons of mash,
1,000 gallons of alcohol, and 1,000 gallons of uncolored spirits.
Only Richard Cramer tried to run, and he was caught before he
got off the farm. In Belvidere, Ed Simons was arrested at his
garage. In Hampshire, Max Wilcox was found tending his chick-
ens and handcuffed.

The group was charged with nine counts of violating federal
statutes against the manufacturing and sale of unregistered alcohol. Before a federal judge in Freeport, Illinois, bond was set
at $5,000 for each man.

This time Antonino Giancana didn't make the trip to get his
son out of jail. Had he wanted to, he didn't have the $500 or the
necessary property to put up. Hence, Mooney prevailed upon his
next best option. Family ties were family ties, however strained,
and with news of his arrest Angeline went to her father for help.
In the cold of January, Francescantonio De Tolve made the trip
to Freeport with the necessary papers. Like Antonino Giancana
and countless parents of 42's on the West Side, he was willing to
put up title to his property to spring his kid. He supplied the deed
to a three-story brick apartment house at 2858 West Polk, a building he'd bought from his brother in 1927 for $15,000 and into
which he'd put $3,000 in improvements. He signified that he was
worth $20,000 above his liabilities and that he had known the
defendant, his son-in-law, "four or five" years. Then, in the uneven scrawl of the immigrant, beneath Mooney's fluid, perfectly
formed signature, Francescantonio added his name. And perhaps owing to the circumstances, or the appearance of nine
criminal violations listed alongside the legal description of his
property, he spelled his name wrong.

Others of the moonshiners depended on friends for bail, and
even then the ties harked back to the 42 Gang. Putting up his
two-story frame house on Elburn Avenue as bond for Jimmy
Micelli was the original smart head, Vito Pelletieri. Co-signing
with him, putting up his Hoyne Street house, was Mike Fillichio,
brother of Mibs and Frank.

The trial began in May, 1939. It was short and quick, with the
government burying the defendants beneath a pile of physical

evidence and a crowd of prosecution witnesses—all small-town farmers and businessmen who'd been well aware of the Schwebke still. Up until the quick-talking Italian from Chicago showed up, moonshining was something done by farmers a few gallons at a time for their own enjoyment. The operation in Schwebke's barn was tantamount to opening a division of General Motors in Garden Prairie, and there were few people in town who didn't know about it.

In exchange for light sentences, all the defendants reversed their not-guilty pleas and were given comparable prison terms by Federal Judge Charles E. Woodward. On nine counts, Mooney received a four-year prison term, fines totaling $2,700, and court costs of $500.

Only the locals pleaded for their freedom. Ed Simons claimed that his was a business relationship with the moonshiners and that he didn't know what was going on inside the barn. He also said he'd quit supplying them in December, 1937. Judge Woodward didn't buy Simons' innocence and gave him a year in jail. Max Wilcox wailed even louder, recounting how he had helped the federal agents in their investigation, claiming that his 80-year-old mother depended on him, then turning out almost the entire town of Hampshire as character witnesses. In handwritten, signed statements, they attested to Max's fine character. "I have known Maxwell Wilcox for many years," wrote Herman Allen of Allen's Corner Garage in Hampshire, "and I have never heard him use any profane language or vulgar talk, and he is a friend to all children in the neighborhood. . . ."

Judge Woodward was touched, even though he noted that Max had once operated a still of his own ("But a small one," Wilcox replied), and he gave the chicken farmer three years' probation.

No such compassion was shown toward the Chicago hoods. As appeals and other routine maneuvers took place Mooney and his associates prepared themselves for the federal penitentiary. Angeline had little choice but to depend on her father for support. She had no money, and with two small children—Antoinette, called Tony, who was almost five, and Bonnie, who now was two—she could do no work apart from laundry or sewing she could take into the house. On October 16, 1939, Mooney surrendered to federal marshals for another stay in "school." This time he was going to Kansas. Leavenworth.

PART TWO

The Rise: 1939–1957

6

IN ITS SIMPLEST FORM, it comes down to three numbers. Any three from 1 to 78. The choice is called a gig, and it's taken from the player along with a nickel, dime, or quarter bet by a runner, who adds it to other gigs he's picked up and takes it to a station. The gigs from all the runners then go from the station to the wheel, where they are matched against the numbers pulled from a can of pellets by the can man. If a gig matches the numbers pulled from the can, it has hit. And a hit, in the right game on the right odds, can bring the holder of the gig $5 on his nickel, tax free and guaranteed. For those are, and have been for centuries, the ways of the game of policy, the numbers.

Like most lottery games, policy dates back to medieval times, to village drawings run by peasants. In America it has been almost exclusively played by blacks, mainly poor classes, who stole from food money to put a nickel down on numbers. The name "policy" is believed derived from the fact that black women pilfered from money meant for insurance policies to play, always inspired by a new number, holding eternal hope for a hit.

The game first surfaced in the 1800's in New Orleans but spread into all big cities with the natural migration of blacks. In Chicago the first numbers man was "Policy Sam" Young, a South Side black who learned the game from an old river-boat gambler named Patsy King. King was a genius of a gambler who not only invented his own games but revised old ones. In Chicago for the World's Fair of 1893, King stayed on and ran the Bucket Shop, a restaurant on Harrison Street that served as a post for his other enterprises. Policy Sam, meanwhile, spread the policy game to the South Side and held drawings under the elevated station at 31st and State, pulling the winning gig out of a derby hat.

With trainloads of blacks coming up from the South every week, the policy games spread quickly. New wheels, the term given to a policy organization (and sometimes referring to the numbers keg itself), sprang up all over. Since the game lent itself to infinite variations, the stakes, the odds, the numbers themselves differed with every wheel, and offered countless opportunities to drop loose change.

A gig can be applied to one of three drawings, called "legs." A single leg is a drawing of 12 numbers, a double leg 24 (the odds decrease as more numbers are drawn), and a short leg a drawing of 6, 5, 4, or 3 numbers. A hit on a 3-number short leg with a $2 gig (the bets most often stay around a nickel or dime but go as high as $2) can mean a quick $2,000—a dollar on a penny—and a temporary farewell to the lower class.

The games are a daily affair, a cheap obsession among the old ladies and the pick-and-shovel workers in the black neighborhoods. A large wheel employs as many as 75 people, runners who hit the houses and the shops, station men, checkers, doormen, guards, cashiers, can men, all working for the 2:30 P.M. or 10:30 P.M. drawing. They pick up hundreds of slips, taking gigs on as many as three and four separate wheels, meticulously record them, then return the numbers drawn—usually printed on both sides of result slips—and pay off the winners. To protect the reputation of a wheel and insure its life, all winners are paid to the penny.

Policy began to flourish on Chicago's South Side at the turn of the century. By the 1920's, it was a major black industry. Wheels became known as the most efficient institutions in the black neighborhoods, and almost everybody played. Runners were incredibly adept, some canvassing blocks and meticulously recording gigs on tiny slips, others generating legends about themselves by memorizing every gig and every player and never messing up. A good memory made it easier if a runner was stopped by the police, even though those who used slips had ingenious ways of stuffing them into the knots of their ties, socks, hats, or, later on, using "flash" paper that burned instantly at the touch of a match.

Games got so big that numbers stations popped up on every block, in barbershops, the back rooms of stores, in markets. Some South Side blocks had as many as five or six stations in them, open from 5 A.M. to 1 A.M., serviced by runners who took bets from an estimated 50 percent of the black population. In the home, numbers pervaded every superstition, every routine. "Dream books" were printed that listed numbers corresponding to objects in one's dreams, or names, addresses, anything with three numbers and a chance. Some numbers became so popular in dream books and so widely played that they were called "fancies," and carried still different odds.

With each number, each game, there was a chance for the player's nickel, but that payoff was nothing compared to the profit margin realized by the wheel. Some games took in as much as $3,500 and paid off only $30 on as few as three winning numbers. With such earnings, policy men easily outstripped legitimate black businessmen in wealth and power, and, in fact, became the barons of the South Side, flashing money and style that rivaled that of the Italian bootleggers and the Irish vice lords. To keep it, policy kings in the 1920's paid as much as $10,000 a week in protection to police and politicians. With few exceptions through the years, they were allowed to operate and flourish unmolested.

Policy Sam Young's domain passed at the turn of the century to "Giver Dam" Jones and his brother Teenan. They were called the "King Bees" of policy, with wheels running at 31st and State, the center of the South Side Black Belt at the time. It held the Old Canadian Club, the Elmwood Club, heavyweight boxing champion Jack Johnson's Café De Champion, the Dreamland Café, the Panama—all quality nightspots that catered to moneyed Chicago blacks who went to them from the theaters—the Pekin, Grand, Vendome, and Mangram—and carried on into the morning hours. If they wanted, they could slip into gambling houses run by the Jones brothers, who were considered experts on poker and other games, but these houses were a side venture, with revenues that couldn't approach policy.

Running it all, with a style that sparkled in the crowds, was

Giver Dam. His character matched his nickname, one garnered from a court appearance. When a judge fined him $100 Jones was said to have replied, "I don't give a damn." The judge then raised the fine to $200 and Jones repeated his sentiments. It went on until the fine was $500. Jones paid it and had a nickname for life.

The Joneses' wheels were eclipsed in the 1920's by those run by Illy Kelly. With his brothers Walter and Ross, Kelly ran the Tia Juana wheel at 29th and State and brought in thousands of dollars a day. He also paid out thousands in protection, but even so had a rocky business history, at times being out of business completely. But when he thrived Illy Kelly ran the Tia Juana, Lucky Strike, Lake Michigan, and Greyhound wheels along with assorted gambling houses. His wealth was incredible, his stature in the Black Belt unparalleled. He and his brothers had a polished, educated manner, and they went out of their way to exploit it and their wealth. They were known for giving handouts to families, for paying rents for scrubwomen and laborers, and for mingling with the people without pretensions. Such public relations entrenched the Kelly brothers' standing, and insured the prosperity of their wheels.

In the mid-1930's, the assassination of Walter Kelly shook the South Side. By that time he had expanded operations into Indiana Harbor and Gary—not only policy, but slot machines and gambling, and the business that associates claimed led to his death, narcotics. He'd been warned against it, his friends said, and he knew the risk and hired a bodyguard. Nevertheless, he was shot to death near his States Hotel on 17th and Washington in Gary.

Competing with Illy Kelly was Jimmy Hilt. He operated the Missouri and Illinois wheels on the South Side so successfully that he was dubbed the "Czar of Policy" in 1923, with a net worth rumored somewhere around a quarter of a million dollars. Hilt showed off every bit of it. He was an extraordinarily good-natured man, who entertained lavishly, drove outlandish cars, and dressed to play.

But even Jimmy Hilt's personality couldn't prevent sieges of police prosecution from time to time. In the reform era of 1927, the wheels came under unmerciful attack by the cops—raids, runners arrested on sight, stations cleaned out—to such a point that drawings had to be relocated daily, often in the private homes of the owners. The problems usually arose when the hue and cry from the clergy was too much for even crooked politicians to ignore. Churches such as Olivet Baptist, Bethel A.M.E., and Quinn Chapel M.E. had thousands of parishioners, and the wrath of their ministers against the evils of gambling never ceased.

The wheels felt the most heat from the politicians they couldn't buy off. But these were few. Instead, the rackets enjoyed the stewardship of Dan Jackson, the power in the black Second Ward. With the blessings of Mayor Big Bill Thompson, Jackson worked hand in glove with the policy kings, even to the point of controlling a gambling house known as the Dunbar Club on South Michigan.

As quickly as the wheels came under attack opposition died down and business returned to usual. More wheels sprang into operation, more kings appeared on the street. Sam Williams owned a pool hall at 35th and State and worked the railroad until he lost his arm in a yard accident. The insurance settlement gave him a stake to start a wheel, which he did with the blessings and backing of Illy Kelly. Pop Lewis was a cultured, college-educated gentleman, who ran the Monte Carlo wheel and soon gave it a reputation for being one of the best-paying wheels in Chicago. With his six-foot-three-inch height, Pop was a handsome, impressive figure, whose style never diminished. He opened the Vincennes Hotel at 36th and Vincennes, with its 200 rooms, ballroom, and banquet halls featuring full orchestras. Black socialites gathered there for lavish banquets and receptions in the 1920's, and later flocked to Lewis' Platinum Lounge which catered to an equally sophisticated black and tan clientele. Buddy Coleman turned the Belmont and Old Reliable wheels into a skein of other businesses, including a tavern, a restaurant, liquor stores, and cleaners. He merged his policy with a bail-bond business, and later became politically powerful. Henry Young came out of World War I a hero and used his reputation to start the Norshore and Black Gold wheels. With Charlie Farrell and Leon Motts, Young soon became worth thousands and invested in homes, office buildings, and a summer resort in Momence, Illinois. And Jimmy Knight, another king with his Iowa and Royal Palm wheels, used his wealth to attract personalities. His Palm Tavern at 446 East 47th Street drew Joe Louis, Henry Armstrong,

Fletcher Henderson, Louis Armstrong, Stepin Fetchit, Bill "Bojangles" Robinson, and hosts of other black athletes and stars.

The wheels weren't totally black. While working in their father's grocery at 29th and State at the turn of the century, the Benvenuti brothers—Julius, Leo, and Caesar—learned the game from Policy Sam Young and began the Blue Racer wheel. By 1929 they were running the Interstate and the Goldfield wheels and doing so well that they were able to hire Policy Sam when he lost control of his wheels. Throughout the Depression, the Benvenuti wheels, like almost all others in the Black Belt, thrived since numbers was the only real hope of the poor man hit hard by hard times. Another white policy king was Petey Tremont, a South Side auto dealer, who ran the Gold and Silver wheel at 29th and LaSalle.

But none of the white-owned wheels, and none of the black-owned ones for that matter, could match the operations of another set of Jones brothers—Eddie, George, and McKissick. Born to Reverend E. W. P. Jones, a Baptist minister in Vicksburg, Mississippi, the boys came north with their father and mother and settled in Evanston, a northern suburb of Chicago. While their father built his congregation, the boys worked as Pullman porters and taxicab drivers, though Eddie was a Howard University graduate. When E. W. P. died in the 1920's, the boys drifted into policy running.

They started with a couple of policy stations on the South Side. They ran them so well, gathering a clientele and establishing themselves as sharp, reliable businessmen, that in 1929 they scraped together $1,500 and began their own wheel. Known as Goldfield, the wheel became immensely popular, and within months they expanded it into three new wheels—the Main, Idaho, and Ohio. In the thirties, when policy was a fact of life in every black block in Chicago, nobody did better business than the Jones Boys. Their headquarters at 4724 South Michigan employed as many as 250 people, including a cluster of attractive women who chatted with customers, and that figure didn't include the hundreds of others working the Joneses' stations, or the scores of runners in the streets. At the height of the wheels, daily grosses were estimated at $25,000, all in bushel baskets full of nickels, dimes, and quarters in such quantities that the brothers bought automatic coin-counting machines to keep up with the flow. Regardless of how large the take and the flurry of activity surrounding drawings and collections, the Joneses' wheels operated like clockwork, as efficient and as well run as many of the marble-lined banks along LaSalle Street, many times more lucrative, and all done behind the closed doors of an inconspicuous building where visitors were admitted by buzzers after receiving the once-over through peepholes.

Like other policy kings, the Jones brothers funneled their profits into legitimate businesses and real estate, so much so that policy became the biggest single source of capital in the Black Belt. They bought the huge Ben Franklin department store on 47th Street, and though most blacks knew it was a front for policy operations, the store did a brisk business and employed 150 people. They bought a food store at 43rd and Prairie and several apartment buildings throughout the South Side. Four hotels—the Vienna Bathhouse, the Grove, the Garfield, and the Alpha—were added to their holdings in the late 1930's. And for themselves and their mother Harriet they bought a villa in Paris, a summer home in Peoria, Illinois, and a villa in Mexico.

It was the Mexican estate, located just outside Mexico City, Lomas Dechapuotepec, that the brothers enjoyed most. At one time it was managed by Ada Smith, known throughout the world as the cabaret singer Bricktop. Though Bricktop performed for the Duke and Duchess of Windsor and was a celebrity in her own right, she kept keen eyes on the Jones house. Any visitor, once he made it past the high iron fences and the elaborate locks, was carefully scrutinized by Madame Bricktop before he got to the family.

Back in Chicago, the light-skinned Jones brothers were immensely powerful and popular figures. They were better educated, better mannered than their policy peers. Eddie, in particular, was an unmistakable figure in his expertly tailored business suits and white shirts, a businessman and a skilled one. He drove expensive Lincolns; his home on South Michigan was custom furnished, with ornate French provincial furniture, wall murals, thick black carpeting, and gold bathroom fixtures. His wife, Lydia, a former beauty queen in the famous Cotton Club chorus, wore satin and mink. His mother, Harriet, was personally chauffeured and waited on as if she were royalty.

But, contrary to popular notions, the Jones brothers, and again most notably Eddie, were not community benefactors. They were miserly and distrustful. Out of the millions they made, none of it went to black charities, black churches, schools, or social agencies. Of the vast real estate they held, none of it was managed by any of the capable black management firms in Chicago. Most of their important financial advisers and money managers were white, and the lavish gifts they did give went to white politicians and bankers and their secretaries in the form of trips to the Joneses' hideaway in France or to the villa in Mexico.

Eddie was even known to rely heavily on his white associates, taking them into his confidence and revealing his family's innermost financial secrets, a practice heavily criticized by his black associates and fellow policy kings. But even his white friends could not keep tax investigators from Eddie's door, and in 1940, with the testimony of Esra Leake, a long-time associate who'd fallen out with Jones, he was convicted on several income tax violations and sentenced to 22 months in the federal penitentiary at Terre Haute, Indiana. There he would get the chance to further his contacts with white financial minds, one of whom was an aging finagler he'd known in the rackets since the Capone days, the other a young man from the West Side with an eye for numbers and a fierce urge to learn more. During his term in Terre Haute, Eddie Jones would get to know Sam "Mooney" Giancana very well.

Giancana was in Leavenworth for only two months, from October to mid-December, but he came to hate the place and would speak badly of it long after. His transfer to Terre Haute brought him closer to Chicago and his family, also within driving distance of associates. There Giancana settled into another session of "school," even taking aptitude tests, which established his reading and writing skills at a sixth-grade level. His IQ scores rated at 71 verbal, 93 non-verbal, with a notation of his poor accuracy but good speed. The totals corresponded with Giancana's general aptitude for mathematics and figures. He seldom wrote down figures, preferring to memorize them, to calculate in his head. As for his other abilities, he didn't much care what the scores showed, because like other compatriots in the pen, he had knowledge as profound and sophisticated as any, but it couldn't be learned in a classroom and wouldn't show up in an intelligence test.

Giancana was 31 when he went into prison, in the prime of his adult life, the budding of his criminal career. All he could do was learn, wise up, await the day when he would hit the street and avoid taking a fall. He was no longer a crazy boy, a 42 Gang screw-up who shot at cops and knocked over cigar stores. And no group of men was better able to counsel him than the inmates of Terre Haute, most of whom were accomplished pros who had erred not as gamblers, thieves, bootleggers, or policy kings, but as taxpayers.

One was William R. "Billy" Skidmore, a hustler who'd sold bail bonds and run gambling joints in the Levee before Giancana was born. He was frequently seen in Johnny Torrio's Four Deuces saloon at 2222 South Wabash before the Capone era. He ran his own saloon at Lake and Robey streets, which served as a head-quarters for pickpockets, petty thieves, and shoplifters, and often provided bail-bond services for them. But his forte was working both sides, firming deals between gangsters and politicians and serving as a go-between and bagman. In 1917 he was indicted with seven others, including then Chief of Police Charles C. Healey, for operating a graft ring among police and gamblers. Healey lost his job, though neither he, Skidmore, nor the others were convicted. In the 1920's Skidmore enhanced his own wealth with casinos that operated safely behind police protection. He also padded his connections with politicians. When Anton Cermak took a seat on the Cook County board, Skidmore suddenly went into the junk business and got a lucrative contract from the county to handle its scrap iron. The junkyard, at 2840 South Kedzie, became Skidmore's headquarters for payoffs and transactions.

But it was the gangsters that Billy Skidmore greased best, first working for Jake Guzik, Capone's paymaster, as Guzik's chief bagman to City Hall and the Kelly-Nash political machine, to the state legislature, and to any other pols who needed attention. In 1929 he aligned himself with Jack Zuta, a gambling head for the Moran Gang, and did similar tasks. The skill of Skidmore was that he could run with both sides, providing services and protecting his own interests without endangering himself.

Few people had as keen an eye for a buck as Skidmore, and although it didn't register with other Chicago gangsters, Skidmore in the 1920's was very aware of the kind of money being made by the policy kings. He wasn't about to break in on it, but with his sense of ombudsmanship, he decided to play upon the numbers kings' need for protection and the Capone-era hoods' love of a percentage. He approached policy men like the Kellys, the Jones brothers, Jimmy Knight, and hosts of others who were running the lucrative wheels, and hit them for a $250-a-week payment to the gangsters in exchange for noninterference in the games. The policy men gladly paid, the hoods gladly took their cut, and Skidmore kept a piece for himself as a reward for being the master bagman.

What Skidmore knew and the policy people didn't was that Capone and his associates weren't really interested in policy as long as their own rackets paid off. In 1925, a South Side nightclub owner by the name of "Bon Bon" Allegretti cornered a policy owner and told him Capone wanted in. The policy owner quickly went to fellow wheel owners, and in typical committee fashion they approached Capone to work out a deal. Capone was surprised, however, and told them he had nothing to do with Allegretti and wanted nothing of policy.

"That's your racket, boys," Capone was reported as saying. "I don't want no part of it." Then he ordered Jack McGurn to bring in Bon Bon and shortly ran him out of town.

That was the extent of the muscle from the organized gangs until Skidmore made his move, an operation he perfected with Jake Guzik, the controller of the gang during Capone's imprisonment, as well as with Zuta, Moran, and their associates. It was that caliber of finesse that a neophyte like Sam Giancana knew nothing of by the time in March, 1942, he met Skidmore in Terre Haute, where the bagman had gone for evading a total of $656,000 in back taxes. Giancana soon sat at the feet of the old master and listened well. School was in.

On the same cellblock was Eddie Jones. The amiable, likable numbers king was not averse to cultivating relationships with whites in prison as he had not been on the outside. He got to know Giancana and Skidmore quite easily and prevailed upon them for favors. Skidmore worked in the kitchens, Giancana on the prison's milk farm, and both were in a position to make Jones's life a little more pleasant. He responded by taking them into his confidence. With Giancana that meant a guided tour through Jones's policy holdings and his personal wealth. He was amazed at how little Giancana knew about the numbers, and how the

West Side gang bangers dismissed the nickels and dimes black cleaning ladies dropped on the games. But, when Jones began talking odds, about single legs, cross-over gigs, hit slips, when he talked about how many people played and how few the wheel paid off, the disinterest of his newest student vanished. No racket Giancana had ever run had such a profit margin, and nothing Giancana had ever gotten into had ever set him up as policy did the Joneses, the Kellys, the Benvenutis. And Eddie Jones went further. Violating a rigid code maintained by numbers men throughout the Black Belt, he offered to set up Skidmore and Giancana once they got out of prison, to put them in their own rackets, not necessarily policy but something with equal potential, to spread the wealth.

Through it all Giancana worked to solidify his friendship with Skidmore and Jones and maintain their faith in him. He was older now, less volatile, less prone to fits of anger and the need for revenge, able to look back at his intemperate days as a 42 and revel in the fact that he'd survived them. But he also felt that he had the ability to control things, to discipline those under him and get things done. Such discipline was the key to anything in the underworld. Skidmore knew it and took a liking to Giancana, promising to work with him on the outside. The two of them hovered over the whims of Eddie Jones, fully aware that the man's resources and his business techniques were diamonds in their futures.

It became a matter of time. Outside the monotonous routines of the penitentiary, the world was changing dramatically, with Hitler, then Pearl Harbor. While Giancana and the others languished behind bars, contemplating schemes and new rackets for the future, the country came out of the Depression and went back to war. Giancana was not due to be released until late 1943, but he applied for early parole. In late 1941 he was notified that his sentence would be shortened by almost a year. If he was lucky, he'd be out of prison before 1943.

Before that, however, he received tragic news from home. His older sister, Lena, his only full sister and a personality who gave Sam his strongest sense of what his mother must have been like, was stricken with an intestinal tumor in March, 1942. Lena had married Anthony Campo years earlier and with him and two

children, a daughter, Catherine, born in 1929, and a son, Leo-
nardo, born in 1933, they lived at 1510 West Harrison. With the
discovery of the tumor, Lena entered Mother Cabrini Hospital
and for a month doctors attempted to keep the malignancy from
spreading. They were unsuccessful. By April the cancer had
metastasized throughout her sigmoid and rectum. On April 9,
1942, she was dead. She died as painfully as her mother, a figure
whom she'd hardly known and whose maiden name she could
not remember (the nun at Mother Cabrini Hospital recorded
Antonia Giancana's maiden name as "Anna Unknown"), and at
the age of her stepmother, Mary Leonardi. That spring, in Mount
Carmel Cemetery in Hillside, Illinois, she was laid beside
them.

Giancana mourned his sister in Terre Haute, then he went
about attending to his own business. Two weeks after the funeral, with his parole nearing, he became concerned about the
settlement of the fines and penalties that had been levied against
him with his sentence and which had not been paid. From prison
he wrote the clerk of the Federal District Court in Freeport and
suggested a solution. On prison stationery, with the impeccable
penmanship of a prison clerk, he wrote:

From: Sam Giancana #104
        U.S. Penitentiary
        Terre Haute, Indiana
        4–20–42

To: Clerk: Federal District Court
        Federal Building
        Freeport, Illinois

Dear Sir,
    I have a communication from Attorney Daniel M. Lyons, U.S.
Pardon Attorney at Washington D.C., relative to my fine and in
which he refers me to you in regard to my proposal.
    You may recall that I was sentenced in Federal District Court
in Freeport, Ill., on October 16, 1939, to a term of four years and
a fine of $3700 of which $2700 was committed, upon conviction
of liquor law violations.
    I am now serving said sentence at the Terre Haute Federal
Penitentiary, having been transferred here, and my sentence
will expire on November 12, 1942.

My purpose in writing to Atty. Lyons as above referred to, was to make an offer to pay this fine of $2700 in monthly installments of $20 or $25. I have no property, as financial assets, but have been promised lucrative employment in an honest, steady business and feel that I can keep up these payments and at the same time adequately support myself and wife in a manner acceptable to our station in life. If such an arrangement can not be perfected, I will be forced to take a "Pauper's Oath," and wait until some future uncertain date to pay this fine. I have no prospects for an inheritance or "windfall," to the extent of the said sum.

You may be informed that in connection with this case there was a tax claim assessed against me also. This claim has been heretofore paid and settlement accepted.

I am aware that similar arrangements to pay fines in monthly installments have been made under like circumstances, and I am confident that you will caucus in the practibility of accepting my offer in this instance.

Please advise me as to your disposition in this matter.

Yours very truly,
Sam Giancana #104

A federal official refused Giancana's offer after telling him that the fines amounted to $2,700, no costs, and a $500 penalty. That left him with no other alternative but the pauper's oath, for his father was hard-pressed to support himself and his third wife, and Francescantonio De Tolve was already supporting Giancana's wife and two children. Neither could afford to spring Sam. Times were better, but not that good. The oath carried a sentence of 30 days, and on December 12, 1942, again as on his release from Joliet ten years earlier, he left prison in time for Christmas.

He returned to a domestic situation even more difficult than before. Angeline continued to struggle with her bad health. Routine housework quickly tired her and she was susceptible to colds and viruses. Her biggest challenge, however, was raising her two girls. Antoinette was as sickly as her mother and found it difficult to match the stamina of her playmates. She was enrolled in a Catholic boarding school in Park Ridge, an unusual arrangement at the time but one her mother insisted on because she couldn't manage the two children, and Tony lived there except for visits home each Sunday. School presented hosts of new problems. Her doctors suggested that she repeat the grade so she could concentrate on staying healthy and growing. Bonnie was a robust, vivacious child, but as a two-year-old she demanded every bit of energy her mother could summon.

The challenge of holding his family together, of relieving some of the strain on Angeline, was important to Giancana. It was one of his utmost concerns upon his release from prison. The draft wasn't a threat, for at his age—34—and with two children and a criminal record, he more than likely wouldn't have been called up. Even so, Giancana took care of his draft status in another manner. He registered at Board #39 at 2312 West Harrison, but not because he was ready to join up. He made every effort to live up to his nickname, to come across as mooney as possible and avoid the military. He ranted and fumed during an interview with a Selective Service official. Asked what he did for a living, he replied sharply, "I steal." Then he ran down a list of events surrounding his criminal record and life on Taylor Street. With every story he cocked his head and stared wildly at the interviewer, shouting how he gave it to this guy and should have given it to that one, recalling every exploit of the the 42's he could come up with, how he traded lead with coppers, flipped cars, and knocked off joints.

The act worked exquisitely. The draft official termed Giancana a true "crazy boy," remarking in official jargon that he was a "constitutional psychopath with an inadequate personality manifested by strong anti-social trends." That was accompanied by a 4-H exemption.

Without having to go off to war, he was free to resume his life and re-establish himself in his home. He did it by exacting the same discipline from the family that he had demanded before. With Tony, though he cherished her and played with her with traditional pride in his firstborn, he was strict and immovable, and reprimanded her for any shenanigans. Angeline, though she had developed a resilience and toughness from her years alone, accepted Sam's presence and acceded to him. She was above all a good, sacrificing Italian wife, and though Sam pushed her to the limit, she resumed that role with endless cleaning and elaborate, punctual meals.

What he had described in his prison letter as "lucrative employment in an honest, steady business" was his job with his brother-in-law Michael De Tolve's envelope company. He took a salary as a salesman and for all outward purposes went about, as he had also written, supporting himself and his family in a "manner acceptable to our station in life." And, as in the years following his stay in Joliet, Giancana stayed out of trouble. Much of his good behavior was due to his total commitment to his family, but also because of Angeline's health. That promised to get worse when she became pregnant in 1944. It was a pregnancy she never should have undertaken, and her doctors warned her about it, but when it came to children in a family as Italian and devoutly Roman Catholic as the Giancanas, warnings from physicians didn't count for much.

As the months passed, Angeline's condition worsened. She was sick daily, her energy sapped by the smallest activities. By early 1945 friends and doctors worried that she might not survive the birth, if, indeed, she was able even to have the baby. Then, three months prematurely, she went into labor and delivered a baby girl weighing one pound, an infant barely alive, whom, as with Angeline's first baby, doctors would struggle to keep breathing.

But this time no complications set in and the baby developed and thrived. Giancana had another daughter, this one named Francine, not the son that he like every Italian father yearned for, but a sparkling baby. Angeline also survived and headed toward recovery.

Away from the house, Giancana dug into other concerns, for at the start of 1943, at a wiser, smoother age of 35, he had to attend to new business. He hit the streets intent on making full use of his prison contacts, on developing the knowledge he'd picked up from Eddie Jones and the savvy he'd seen in Billy Skidmore. Nobody knew what he knew, and he was convinced that nobody had the guts and the shove to fully exploit that knowledge.

7

THE MAN WHO COULD have helped him the most upon his release
from Terre Haute was Paul Ricca. From the day he met with
Lucky Luciano and other syndicate bosses in 1932, Ricca began
working his way to the top of the Chicago outfit. By 1939 he was
on a decision-making level with Frank Nitti, and meeting with
Jake Guzik and Anthony Accardo in the day-to-day workings of
the mob. But in 1943 Ricca and Nitti, with Phil D'Andrea, Louis
Campagna, Frank Maritote, John Roselli, and Charles Gioe, were
indicted in a federal extortion case involving shakedowns of film
makers and theater owners. Known as the Browne-Bioff Case, for
principal witnesses Willie Bioff and George Browne, it was one
of the most effective federal prosecutions ever against Chicago
hoodlums and resulted in ten-year sentences for all. Nitti
avoided his by committing suicide in March, 1943, but Ricca and
the rest were in jail by 1944.

That left Guzik and Accardo in control, and at the time they
were far above Giancana's reach. His only connection was the
recommendation of Ricca and the influence of Billy Skidmore.
More important, however, was Giancana's own initiative, how
much he could show about himself, what he could set up for the
boys.

Back on the West Side he re-established contact with some of
the tougher 42's. Few who'd run with him and Babe Ruth, Pel-

letieri, Fillichio, or Salvi were still around. Most had moved away from the neighborhood and gotten out of the rackets or were dead. But some later smart heads were available, and they were ready with Giancana to get into something big. They were Fiore Buccieri, Sam Battaglia, Lenny Caifano and his brother Marshall, and Willie Daddano. Giancana also looked to business possibilities with James J. Adduci, a well-known West Sider who had been elected to the state legislature in 1934 but made no secret of his dealings with questionable figures back in the old neighborhood.

But none of these could do as much for Giancana as could Skidmore and Eddie Jones. Skidmore greased Giancana's debut before Guzik and Accardo, but to them he was still a 42 Gang crazy boy, and they were willing to sit back and see what he could come up with. In 1944, Billy Skidmore died, but by then Giancana had approached Jones. The policy baron made good on his jail-yard promises, and freely associated with Giancana, several times conferring with him at the Ben Franklin store and even in his home. This was a blatant violation of policy owners' long-standing accord to stay away from the Italians, for the policy men had a deep-seated understanding of what it took to stay in business. They mediated their differences, met frequently with one another and established territories, and almost unanimously kept violence out of the games. The occasional exception came when wheel operators were found tampering with numbers in a technique in which they would rig winning numbers and place their own gigs on them. Called "salting a hit" it was a grievous violation, but offenders were usually drummed out of the organization instead of physically punished. With the Italians, the masters of bombs and machine guns, such gentle tactics were unheard of, and the policy kings wanted nothing to do with them.

But Eddie Jones and his brother George (McKissick Jones was killed in an auto crash in 1944) cultivated Giancana's friendship and explored his business prowess. Eddie bankrolled Giancana with $100,000, ostensibly to branch out into the juke-box and record rackets. His plan was to place jukes in taverns and clubs throughout small suburbs and then go into the city itself.

This money was only part of Giancana's rapidly developing finances, money he made in schemes involving bootlegging with friends from the old neighborhood and, while the war was still on, the counterfeiting of gas and food rationing stamps. The Jones roll was the added push he needed to set himself up in business and buy a house. The business was called the Boogie Woogie Club, a small saloon on Roosevelt near Paulina, and it provided him with a solid base of operations in his old turf. Though the West Side was still the place to do business, it was no longer the place to live. Second-generation Italians like Giancana longed for the day when they could move out, when they could show their friends that they had finally made it out of the hovels where their fathers had settled. Some went to neighborhoods on Chicago's Far West and Northwest Side; some moved north and east a few miles into the Armitage-Sheffield area; others climbed still higher and went into the suburbs. Giancana found a house in the western suburb of Oak Park, a yellow brick house with arched windows and a red-tiled roof. It was a solid, spacious home on the corner of Fillmore and Wenonah streets in a quiet, tree-lined neighborhood. It was the private, unassuming yet elegant house that Giancana had always wanted, a home that fit with his particular tastes and would adapt well to his improving "station in life." Through a boyhood friend, Anthony V. Champagne, who had begun a law practice of his own (Champagne had filed documents for Giancana after his arrest in Garden Prairie in 1939), Giancana bought the house with a $10,000 down payment in April, 1945. He used the name Sam Mooney, one of a number of aliases he would employ in the years to come, completing the transaction with cash for a total price of $22,000.

Back on the West Side he was seen often in the presence of the Jones brothers, and the partnership flourished. But not all of Jones's associates approved of Giancana. One was Ted Roe, a brash, gregarious policy lieutenant who ran his own wheel in conjunction with the Joneses' enterprises. Roe, a mulatto, was known on the South Side as a wild man who never shied away from a fight and ended most of them. He boasted that he never feared white gangsters and that they couldn't muscle in on him if they tried. Giancana did in 1945, attempting to shake him down, it was speculated, more to test Roe's nerve than to get his money. Using a common threat, Giancana said he would expose Roe to the newspapers if he didn't pay him $4,000. Roe laughed at him.

Later, Giancana approached Roe through George Jones. In a

parked car, he outlined to Roe a plan in which he would take on part of Roe's wheel. Roe refused, adding that he wouldn't give Giancana "a quarter." At that Giancana became incensed and began shouting obscenities at Roe. At one time he reached beneath his coat and gave Roe the impression he was going for a gun. Roe grabbed his wrists and began scuffling. Jones shouted for both of them to stop, but for a few more tense seconds the two went at it. Roe said he would stop if Giancana would take his hand off his gun. When both calmed down they agreed to go their separate ways. But Roe never cooled his resentment of the skinny, hollow-eyed Italian. And Giancana felt the same, holding a simmering hatred for the wild-eyed numbers man and vowing revenge.

The next day Roe phoned Giancana just to remind him that he hadn't mellowed. "I know where you are and if you're not gone in five minutes I'll find out how tough you are."

It was a caustic, incredibly bold attack, but at the time Roe had the power and the allies to back it up.

Giancana, with an eye for the future and an awareness of his strengths, said only, "The next time we meet you'll be glad to talk to us."

But he knew that before he could make good on any threats against Teddy Roe he had to make a lot of other things happen. One of those involved his benefactor and associate, Eddie Jones.

These were crucial times for Giancana. He had little going for him and his criminal aspirations but his own nerve and his own ambition. It has long been a fallacy that Chicago's gangsters— mainly the Capone gang and its associates—were a comprehensive, closely knit organization. Nothing was further from the truth. The gang was nothing but the man who ran it and anyone strong enough to make inroads. It was not ethnically exclusive. Though many of its members were Italians, mainly Sicilians (Capone, however, was not), it was also liberally populated with Irish, Jews, Bohemians, Greeks, even a Welshman. It was not, and never came anywhere near to being a "mafia" family or an extension of that underground Sicilian organization. Nor were its founders necessarily members of the Camorra of Naples or graduate Black Handers. Rather, the Capone gang was all of these and none of them. Much like an aggressive corporation, the gang flourished under disciplined leadership and by eliminating or overpowering its competition. Those who became part of it, those who took over after Capone went to prison, were those tough enough to exert their own personalities, to take power and hold it. That meant Paul Ricca, a Sicilian; Jake Guzik, a Polish Jew; Anthony Accardo, a Grand Avenue second-generation Sicilian; or Llewelyn "Murray" Humphreys, a Welshman.

In 1945, as he struggled to get back on his feet after prison, nobody knew better than Mooney Giancana that he was nothing to these men or the rest of the Capone mob. He had been a 42, a wild, unpredictable street punk among other street punks the Capone hoods wanted nothing to do with. He was a two-time loser, a petty criminal who had taken a stupid fall on a botched burglary, then a moonshiner who couldn't pull off a still in the sticks. Those who had operated the Grand Prairie operation were also nobodies, a hodge-podge of neighborhood toughs and chicken farmers, and all of them, with Giancana, had gotten thrown into the can without the protection or the influence of the Capone people. It is likely that the gang knew and cared nothing about the Grand Prairie still or those who ran it. And, once out of prison, Giancana remained nothing to them.

He also had few angles to work. He had a reputation as a superior wheelman with the 42's, but drivers were easy to come by for the outfit and it was a skill that got him no further than had he been an accomplished machine gunner. Giancana also had his own personality to overcome. He was known as a hothead, as a temperamental kid perhaps not in possession of all his wits—"mooney," per his nickname—and if he was to make any headway with the Capone people he would have to bridle his temper and show himself capable of cold, disciplined, cunning achievements.

What he *could* rely on was what he had come from and what he was. The 42's knew no boyhood equals for sheer ruthlessness. If they wanted something they took it. Going on a job took only a comrade with the proposition "Hey, I got something." If they encountered problems they showed their heaters; if they encountered the coppers they threw lead at them or took them on a lam. The 42's were nothing if not the guttiest, most vicious streetcorner gang in the city's history, and its graduates, its survivors, never lost those instincts, least of all Mooney, the whip-nosed, skinny, totally fearless smart head. Now 37 and no longer a kid, he would go to these strengths, those that had survived his boyhood, now tempered with the savvy of prison and the discipline of age. He still had the guts of a 42.

Saturdays were big shopping days in the department store, especially now in early May, 1946, with the neighborhoods again coming alive and the people coming out from the winter. Perhaps no time is more pleasant in Chicago than May, this May, with the war over and people pushing out to start new families, new jobs, veterans home looking for jobs, spending money when they got it. It was that way in Chicago's Black Belt, along 47th street, the bustling thoroughfare of the South Side, and the Ben Franklin department store at 47th near South Parkway thrived on these better times.

The Jones brothers still owned the Ben Franklin, and that meant business was even more lively because of the numbers. Eddie Jones personally oversaw the store's operations, each night checking the receipts and personally escorting his cashier, Mrs. Frances Myles, from the store to her home before retiring for the day himself.

That Saturday night was no different. It was a mild evening, light-jacket weather in the high 50's, and after Jones and Mrs. Myles had counted up—the receipts that day approached nearly $6,000 in cash—he walked with her to his waiting limousine. Inside was his wife, Lydia, who was dressed in evening clothes for a night out, and his driver, Joseph Brock. It was an easy, pleasant ride to Mrs. Myles's home at 4328 South Parkway, just blocks from the store.

As they approached the house, they didn't notice two cars parked along the curb across the street. The Jones limousine pulled up; driver Brock got out and escorted Mrs. Myles to her door, then returned to the car. But, as he was about to drive off, two men ran across South Parkway to Jones's side of the car and jerked open the back door.

They were dressed in long overcoats and hats, and each had a white kerchief over the lower half of his face. Both men held 12-inch sawed-off shotguns.

"Is this Ed Jones?" one of them barked to the startled Jones and his wife.

"I am. Why?" Jones replied.

"Come on, get out. We wantcha," the masked man ordered and waved his shotgun at Jones.

Jones hesitated. The man repeated himself. "Come on, get out. We mean business."

At that Lydia Jones flung her arms around her husband's neck and began screaming. "No! No! You're not gonna take my husband!"

Both men then lunged at Jones and pulled him from the car, then one cold-cocked him across the back of the neck with the barrel of his shotgun. It stunned Jones and he fell to the pavement.

Mrs. Jones screamed hysterically, kicking and struggling with one of the men in an attempt to get to her husband. He pushed her inside, then joined his partner in pushing, even lifting Jones off his feet and dragging him across Parkway and into the back seat of a getaway car. Then a second car pulled up and the two autos sped off, the screams of Mrs. Jones echoing through the streets and bringing neighbors to their doors.

Two police officers, Michael Derrane and William Barber, were cruising in their squad car a block away and immediately heard the screams. They tore around the corner and saw Joseph Brock motioning wildly at a car that had just pulled away. With Brock trailing in the limousine, Derrane and Barber gave chase, not aware of who or what was involved, not realizing that Jones was in the front car and that the car closest to the officers was a backup. The two cops also did not realize that they had gotten into an old-time lam, and that they were tailing a car driven by one of the best wheelmen of the old 42 Gang. All they knew was that, when they got close, one of the men in the rear car broke out its back window and fired off a volley of shots at them. The slugs hit the squad car's windshield and shattered it, then struck Officer Derrane in the shoulder. They pulled up and radioed ahead, but would get no closer to the getaway car than when they last saw it whipping around the corner at 46th Street and heading west.

The abduction made the front pages of the daily newspapers, and three-inch headlines in the black press. There was no bigger snatch than Eddie Jones, and though to many it looked like a common kidnapping and ransom ploy, those who knew Jones and knew the rackets knew better. In the 1930's Jones's brother had been kidnapped and held for a $35,000 ransom, so the threat of abduction wasn't new to the family. But Jones's liaisons with Giancana and other West Side Italians after his release from Terre Haute became a major element in his abduction, and word among fellow policy men was that his gambles had turned on him. Giancana was described by the black press as an ex-convict with "a record as long as your arm," and also as "the worst kind of double crosser." Jones's bankrolling of Giancana was no secret, nor were his dabblings in juke boxes and his general associations with the Italian hoods. These things, coupled with his long-standing and resented penchant for putting his trust in white associates, for baring his business interests to them, painted a clear picture to those in the policy rackets. Reports filtered through the streets that Jones had been seen arguing viciously with Giancana, the latest occasion being only a few days before Saturday night's kidnapping.

But there was also another important aspect that bothered the policy men. Only a few years before, the Harlem rackets had been muscled by Dutch Schultz of the Luciano gang. Schultz and his torpedoes collared every wheel in the city, threatening its owners, kidnapping, beating, and killing any who held out, bombing homes and stations to help persuade the reluctant. It was a ruthless, bloody takeover, with Schultz simply insisting that he was going to put order and organization into the rackets, but meaning that the mob wanted their piece and would have it.

Although there was no indication of such a takeover in Chicago, many considered the move against Jones to be a bad omen. He had been fingered by someone who knew him and knew his routines well. In the hours and days following the abduction, as George Jones and his mother, Harriet, hurriedly flew into Chicago from Mexico, the family remained secluded and uncooperative. Lydia Jones refused detectives entrance to the house and gave them little help in the description of her husband's kidnappers. What first appeared to be an opportunistic snatch now loomed as a complicated crime with layered motives and checkered personalities.

Until they proved otherwise, police kept all avenues open, preferring first to run with the straight kidnapping motive. Yet, when the family heard nothing from Jones's abductors, at least

nothing they would tell police about, detectives brought in Giancana for questioning the following Tuesday. He said nothing and
was released. Meanwhile rumors spread throughout the South
Side that the kidnappers wanted $250,000 in small bills—ones
and fives—for Jones. But police knew nothing of any demands,
and sniffed that that amount in those denominations would fill
three suitcases.

By Thursday, a full five days after the abduction, Mrs. Jones
softened and urged police to intensify their search. Again, word
in the streets was that George Jones and Teddy Roe had been
contacted by the kidnappers and that George had come to town
for the express purpose of getting the large amounts of cash
demanded out of some of the over two dozen banks the brothers
used.

Then it broke. At 1:30 Friday morning, Mrs. Jones got a call
from her husband. In minutes he met police at a delicatessen at
62nd and Loomis. He said he'd been dropped off there a half hour
earlier, with adhesive tape covering his eyes and cotton in his
ears, had been told to wait, and when he thought the men had
left, he removed the tape and cotton and searched for a phone.
He was unharmed and appeared fit and healthy, though tired,
dressed in the same business suit and herringbone overcoat that
he'd been wearing when he was abducted, even freshly shaven.
With wide smiles and tears he said he was the luckiest man in
the world, then hugged his wife, his mother, his lawyer, and a
host of friends.

Jones said he'd been pushed to the floor of the kidnappers' car
and driven around for an hour before tape was put over his eyes
and cotton was stuffed in his ears. It was removed once he was
locked inside a room with a bed, he said, and he stayed there for
the duration, eating sandwiches. He provided no other details,
saying only that he never saw his captors and seldom heard them
speaking. He was so evasive with police that he even denied he
was involved in policy. Details of the ransom were also not revealed, although it was reported that $100,000 was paid.

Little more was forthcoming and shortly after the tearful reunion Jones and his family vanished again, this time boarding the
Golden State Limited for Texas and his estate in Mexico. Police
and prosecutors loudly voiced their disapproval, saying that
Jones was needed for an investigation. Yet most knew, through
various sources, what had happened. The entire abduction had

been planned and executed by the wheelman in the second geta-way car. Giancana set up the kidnapping as a public display of what was going to be the future of policy on the South Side. He took Jones to the basement of his newly purchased home in Oak Park, for he had not yet moved his family in and the house was vacant, and kept him there until he could get word out to George and the family. His ultimatum was clear—the Jones brothers could keep their South Side holdings but they were to relinquish control of the Maine, Idaho, and Iowa wheels to Giancana. It was also suggested that Jones spend most of his time in Mexico; in return he would receive a percentage of the returns from the wheels. Otherwise, he was a dead man.

There were no other arrangements. Although George Jones later released a list of serial numbers for $15,000 of the alleged $100,000 ransom, no ransom money was ever exchanged, or ever recovered. Because Jones wanted to stay alive, he relinquished much more than that to Giancana. At his age, 49, and with his holdings—besides his businesses and real estate, he and his brother owned more than $1 million in blue-chip stocks—he could afford to get out of policy. And apart from occasional visits and appearances in assorted civil court suits, he effectively got out of Chicago. Once he boarded the Golden State Limited, that May morning, 1946, he never lived in the city again.

In the months following, the policy racket was in chaos. Teddy Roe shut down his wheels under an unmerciful attack from vice officers. Other policy men complained that Jones had "brought down the ceiling" on them, that their future was in jeopardy, that the intervention by the West Side Italian hoods threatened their very existence.

They knew only too well. In the following months the owners of the big wheels throughout the Black Belt were hit one by one, intimidated or assaulted into relinquishing control of their wheels. Bombings and beatings followed. Caesar Benvenuti, who had taken over the family wheel upon the death of Julius in 1944, had his home bombed, "Big Jim" Martin, a rapidly rising policy owner, was shot at, then kidnapped. Teddy Roe's home was bombed. Each assault was preceded by a gift sent to the policy king. Neatly wrapped, it consisted of a miniature coffin with a doll inside. Few wheel owners thought it very cute, but they got the message.

What Giancana had done with the takeover of the Joneses'

operation was to convince Tony Accardo, the operating head of the syndicate in Paul Ricca's absence, and Jake Guzik that the policy kings could be taken and that he could manage it. Accardo and Guzik were quickly convinced, and provided Giancana with men and muscle to complete the coup. Within a year after the kidnapping of Eddie Jones, virtually all the wheels were operated by Guzik-Accardo front men, the likes of the Manno brothers—Nick, Sam, Pete, Thomas—Sam Pardy, and many others. The operations remained, but the outfit was now on the fat end of the profits. The entire takeover proceeded remarkably smoothly, and Giancana's favor with Accardo and Guzik, and with Ricca upon his early release from prison in 1947, soared.

He was then given a wider latitude of operations, and also, most importantly, the imprimatur of the mob. He was no longer a small-timer, and to prove it Tony Accardo, the one-time bodyguard and triggerman for Al Capone, the tough but smart kid from the North Side, took on Giancana as his chauffeur. And, although he stood in the background at mob functions and wherever Accardo was seen, he was nevertheless there, his presence finally very evident.

Yet, before he could fully take advantage of his successes in the policy takeover, Giancana had to finish the job. Although the Jones brothers quite readily capitulated, their managing operator and Giancana's early nemesis, Teddy Roe, did not. He and Clifford Davis held on to their wheels and siphoned many customers from the Joneses' operations. Roe, in his typical ebullience, let it be known that no man black or white or Italian could scare him out of the rackets. They could bomb his house, and they had, blowing away the back porch, and they could send him toy coffins, "but they'd have to kill me first," he proclaimed.

But, apart from his public postures, Roe took his precautions. He hired two Chicago police detectives at $20 a night to follow him from his house to policy drawings. He carried a gun, and he kept his home and his wheel quarters heavily armed. But, most of all, Roe never lost his nerve. He was the only policy king who faced off Giancana and any other representative of Guzik and Accardo and did it regularly. Once when Giancana and Gus Alex, a protégé of Guzik, came to talk to Roe, the meeting erupted in a fist fight with Roe charging into Giancana and knocking him down. There was no sign that things between the two of them would ever mellow.

It seemed for years that Roe would be the one man able to get away with it. The threats continued. Roe was once chased throughout Washington Park, speeding at times, he said, up to 80 miles per hour. Though he couldn't be sure, he insisted he never doubted for a second that his assailant was the skinny, vengeful Giancana. But such incidents never interfered with Roe's operations. He lived well, wore monogrammed shirts, alligator shoes, custom-tailored suits, and $50 hand-painted ties with "Theodore Roe" running the full length of them.

Then came the night of June 19, 1951. Driving alone on South Parkway, only a few blocks from where Eddie Jones had been kidnapped five years before, Roe suddenly noticed a car crowding him from the rear and shining a spotlight into his mirror. He claimed later that he curbed his car, thinking the tail was a squad car. Three men approached, he said, and told him they were state's attorney's police.

"Show me. How do I know?" Roe replied.

The three responded by jerking open his door and pulling him from the car. He hit the pavement, he said, knowing right then what was going on, and came up shooting.

Though Roe stuck to that story, investigators found differently. A few weeks earlier, it had become known that Roe was using police detectives for his personal escort service. To keep their jobs they let it be known that they were quitting Roe. In fact, they never did, and were shadowing him that night as he drove on South Parkway near 52nd.

Only a few days before, Giancana and three associates had met to plot their move against Roe. One was Leonard "Fat Lenny" Caifano, an overweight, balding bookie from the Patch who was an old friend of Giancana's and who also had contacts with Tony Accardo. But Caifano was ever a small-timer, eager to do favors, ready to help his friend Giancana complete his move into the rackets. It was Caifano who rented a yacht, the *Lady Lu,* moored in Burnham Harbor on the South Side, and on it conferred with Giancana, Fiore Buccieri, and Vincent Ioli about the prospect of abducting Roe and holding him on the yacht until he agreed to relinquish control of his wheels.

Their plan was about as intricate as any the 42's had ever come up with, and a few nights later the four of them were in the car bearing down on the policy king. As soon as they got out the firing began, most of it coming from the two detectives with Roe.

Caifano was the first to get hit, a slug in the temple that ripped through his skull and exited through his wide-brimmed felt hat. Another hood, believed to be Ioli, was hit in the shoulder before the assailants scrambled back into their car and sped off. The detectives did the same, leaving Caifano a lifeless barrel of flesh in the street, and Roe hiding in nearby bushes.

A few minutes later he called police and claimed full credit for killing Fat Lenny. Then he breathlessly called his wife and told her, "Baby, try not to get excited. I just killed two white men. One for sure and maybe two. But don't get upset. I did it to protect my own skin."

Police charged him with murder though they had no witnesses and no hard evidence. The charges were later dropped, but not before Roe was lionized in the press as being the last holdout against the syndicate.

"They'll have to kill me to take me," he repeated.

By the 1940's they realized that it would be their main source of income in the coming years, with virtually nothing in second place. Let the outfits in other cities push prostitutes, olive oil, narcotics. In Chicago it would be gambling. The main bosses—Paul Ricca, Tony Accardo, Charlie Fischetti, Llewelyn "Murray" Humphreys, and Jake Guzik—preferred it that way, and though they encouraged other concessions, such as juice loans, extortion, union racketeering, and business frauds, none would generate the capital day in and day out that gambling would.

Hence, the mob was not only open to Giancana's schemes with policy, but they were more than willing to delegate responsibility to him if he could create and maintain lucrative gambling setups. He gained the favor of Guzik, a man who, by the 1940's, was in his sixties, a shrewd veteran of Capone and given the nickname "Greasy Thumb" because he could thumb through a stack of bills so well. He handled the gang's cash with the same skill. It was Guzik who oversaw the outfit's gambling endeavors, the slot machines, the casinos, and it became customary to approach him with any plans for something new, secure his word and his backing if necessary, and take advantage of his influence. Although he was considered by many as "retired," he still kept his hand in in Chicago, was seen at his home on South Luella Street or at the Chicagoan Hotel at 67 West Madison, and only seldom joined his wife and children at his opulent home on San Marino Island, just off Miami.

Still, as dominant as Guzik's influence was, and that of Ricca and Accardo, it didn't rule out determined competitors. The war years brought about a boom in gambling activity, casinos hummed, betting on horses and sports events picked up tremendously, and new personalities pushed for a piece of the action. Nineteen forty-three brought about the beginning of a gambling war every bit as vicious as the bootlegging battles of the 1920's. Bosses were challenged, alignments were shaken up, new operations sprang up overnight.

The bombings, kidnappings, and ambushes followed. More than a dozen syndicate figures were killed violently, stuffed in trunks, cut down in busy intersections. Thomas Neglia, a Rush Street operator, was shot to death in December, 1943, as he sat in a barber chair. Two of his associates were shotgunned weeks later. "Dago" Lawrence Mangano, one of the Patch's most ruthless hoods and an early lieutenant of Capone's, was killed in August, 1944.

The violence left no one immune. The ranking bosses took on more bodyguards and watched over their shoulders. That was a break for Giancana. With the imprisonment of Ricca, D'Andrea, Gioe, and Louis "Little New York" Campagna, it was decided by Tony Accardo that the wives of these men would be vulnerable. Upon a recommendation from Leonard Caifano, Accardo approached Giancana and put him to work guarding Louis Campagna's wife. No precaution was too drastic, no one person safe until the gambling wars were quelled.

That was borne out only too well in April, 1944. Guzik was in town attempting to oversee local elections, especially the vote in the Twentieth Ward, where the outfit was switching its support from William Parillo, who had long acknowledged his ties with the Capone gang, to Andrew Flando. On the 14th, after appearing in a small suburban village to pay a court fine, Guzik was reportedly kidnapped from his car at Harlem and Ogden in the western suburb of Berwyn.

Guzik had been riding with his son-in-law Frank Garnett when he was abducted, prompting a frantic call from Garnett to Hymie Levin, one of Guzik's Loop gambling lieutenants. For two days police knew little more than that. Garnett couldn't be found to corroborate his story, and detectives relied on the rumors of informants and random interrogations for leads. They pulled in Harvey Rogers, a freelance thief and bank robber with a reputation for extorting from gangsters—he supposedly robbed Billy Skidmore twice—but learned nothing. They heard from the street that Guzik's associates were getting $50,000 together for his release.

Then, on the morning of the 16th, Guzik was spotted wandering about in a drugstore on West Roosevelt Road. He was noticeably nervous, disheveled, his suitcoat wrinkled, his tie, according to the store's owner, "pulled up under one ear." The normally cool, fastidious Guzik also had a three-day beard. Yet when police arrived he denied that anything was wrong, said that it was all a mistake and he had never been kidnapped. He shrugged off his son-in-law's story. "Frankie's a pretty good kid," he said of Garnett, "but he's new in Chicago and doesn't know our ways." Guzik's ways meant simply that a couple of associates wanted to talk to him and they drove off in a car, he explained. There was no ransom, no shots, no nothing, he insisted. And he never budged from that story.

But it did not sway insiders from speculating that Guzik had been grabbed by someone in the outfit big enough to get away with it and big enough to convince Guzik that a few changes in leadership should be made. But Guzik was nothing if not flexible, a millionaire many times over, and he lived on as elder statesman of what the newspapers were still calling the Capone mob. Paul Ricca, a man twenty years younger than Guzik, a slight, tight-mouthed Italian with a reputation for unwavering discipline, was now the Chicago boss. While in prison from 1944 to 1947, he delegated his responsibilities to Accardo, the thick-faced Sicilian who had once sat in the lobby of Capone's New Michigan Hotel with a machine gun on his lap and who was believed to have played important roles in many of the Capone gang's most vicious and sensational assassinations. Accardo, the son of a Sicilian shoemaker, had the temperament and the brains to do almost anything asked of him, and he, with Ricca, provided organized crime in Chicago with unparalleled intelligence and direction.

Accardo also was arrested in the Loop in February, 1945, for questioning about the Guzik kidnap, among other things. With him were Giancana, by that time his chauffeur, and Daniel Beneduce. It was the first official sighting of Giancana with Accardo, and it signaled his acceptance into the Chicago outfit. His relationship to Accardo, a man only two years his senior but with infinitely more experience, background, and finesse than any 42 gang banger, was that of a younger brother. He was the driver, also a companion, now dressing well and affecting the demeanor of the quiet, unprepossessing Accardo, standing in the background at weddings and wakes, saying nothing but listening well.

On his own, Giancana branched out. He bought two cars, a 1946 Buick convertible and a 1946 Mercury, and had them specially customized. He had a steel plate installed in the rear of the Mercury to make it bullet-proof. Under the hood, where the real action lay for Giancana, he delighted in showing off $950 worth of high-speed heads and special cam shafts. The car was capable of hitting 120 miles per hour, he told friends and relatives, and he had on more than a number of occasions, with reflexes he'd honed as a 42, his head cocked slightly over the wheel, done just that.

At his Boogie Woogie Club he began attracting new faces and new license numbers. Fiore "Fifi" Buccieri became a regular associate, as did Willie Daddano. Others were Thomas Potenza, under whose name Giancana registered one of his cars, Rocco Potenza, James Mirro, and Carlo Urbanati. All were young hoods from the Patch who were still considered small-timers—bookies, gamblers, and runners who were still learning and still earning their spurs. All were looking for something to hook on to, or someone who could cut them in.

Giancana also made the most of contacts from the neighborhood who had gone a little farther or a little faster than he had. One was Jimmy Adduci, the West Side politician with a flair for side enterprises. With Giancana in 1946 he formed Windy City Sports Enterprises, ostensibly to set up softball leagues but actually no more than a bookmaking front. Giancana also opened R & S Liquors, at 1700 West Roosevelt, the 430 Club at 430 South Canal, and the Archer Club. Besides these businesses, he officially listed himself as a salesman for his brother-in-law's Central Envelope Company. The job was more a sponsorship than anything else, for Giancana continued to draw a salary of only

$2,860, little more than $50 a week. In all of 1946 he reported an income of $13,788, with $4,000 of it coming from Windy City Enterprises. It was an impressive figure for an ex-convict with an elementary-school education. This was 1946, good times in a postwar economy, and the year of the abduction of Eddie Jones.

Giancana's income soared in 1947, however, an indication not only of his policy inroads, but also of the fact that the outfit sanctioned his new gambling territories. He kept his hands close to his own neighborhood—in the expanding residential areas on Chicago's Far Northwest Side where subdivisions and shopping centers proliferated. He set up the Montrose Association at 6412 West Montrose, a sophisticated wire room that brought him a declared income of $17,895. It combined with his other enterprises and his nominal salary at Central Envelope for a 1947 income of $28,193.

Times were good and getting better. Giancana opened Club Ozark, 4001 North Ozark, on the Far Northwest Side, in 1948, and it and the Montrose Association accounted for an income that year of $52,526. It was time to give up claim to his envelope selling, and to finagle losses with Windy City and R & S Liquors. The following year Giancana worked out an identical income from the same sources, adding only a token profit from something called the Pascole Club, sustaining debts with R & S Liquors. The pattern was obvious: Giancana was able to set up bookmaking and gambling outlets in virgin areas, in expanding residential neighborhoods where the competition was scarce and the police and politicians vulnerable, and he did it on capital gained from the numbers takeover, where an established, concentrated racket operated as it always had under experienced, adept policy kings.

As for the mob in general, it had its eyes on the nationwide gambling wire services. In the Midwest, the biggest was the Continental Press, a mammoth distributor of track and sporting-events results headquartered in Cleveland. Under the direction of Guzik and Murray Humphreys, one of the Chicago mob's sharpest minds, Chicago gamblers began pirating results from Continental and its distributors, Midwest News Service. Guzik and Humphreys then approached James Ragen, the owner of Continental and demanded he sell Midwest to them. Ragen adamantly refused, and the battle was on. Guzik and Accardo opened the

Trans-American News Service in direct competition. New customers were encouraged by bombing and ambushing Ragen's
clients. Ragen himself was shot in August, 1946, as he drove in
Chicago and died shortly after. His demise ended the war, and
made for a merger between Continental and Trans-American.

The new enterprise was so big and so lucrative that it attracted
Senate subcommittee investigations, and they discovered Continental's "drops," its regular customers, numbering 522 in the
Chicago area. Its wire tickers and telephones provided up-to-the-
minute racing results, the investigators said, and had become the
"life blood" of the outfit. A chief conduit of Continental was R &
H Publishing, owned by and named after Ray Jones and Hymie
Levin, Guzik's veteran lieutenants. R & H featured a clientele
composed of hundreds of ranking and rising names in Chicago's
syndicate, including Joe Guzik, Jake's brother, Louis Campagna,
and Joey Aiuppa, a hood with active concessions in the Capone
suburb of Cicero. Another was listed as "J. Mooney," with an
establishment on Cermak Road in Cicero, and "Sam Cassro,"
with three outlets on South Cicero in Chicago. Both were aliases
for Giancana, and gave evidence of his plans for the fifties.

It was obvious to Giancana that the action in the postwar years,
amidst the baby and housing booms, was not only in the city's
outlying neighborhoods, but in the far suburbs, the villages that
each day were chewing up more cornfields for foundations and
that were run by small-time police chiefs and politicians eager
to talk business. Places like Niles, Skokie, unincorporated areas
of Cook County were gems for Giancana, and he was determined
to hit them with the capital, organization, protection, muscle—
anything necessary to create action and turn over more business
than anyone anywhere in the city. It was not only a way to line
his own pockets, but there was no better way to insure his favor
with his mentors.

The times were also choice for Giancana because he was virtually an unknown. Chicago police intelligence detectives knew
him and knew the progress he was making behind the mob's
scenes. But he was not a personality to the press or the public. By
1951, after the attempt on Teddy Roe's life and the killing of
Lenny Caifano, the newspapers referred to him as Sam "Gian-
canna," and provided little more information about him than his
prison record. Headline writers were still searching for a Capone

Phoenix, the lieutenant or brother who would give them the copy Scarface did. Guzik was a favorite, as were the Fischetti brothers, or Al's younger brother Albert, Sam "Golfbag" Hunt, Claude Maddox, or Louis Campagna. Only Tony Accardo and Ricca, however, were living up to their reputations; their underlings were often new faces that were hard to keep track of. Except in the case of the politicians and law officers who began to see them in their backyards. Fremont "Tiny" Nestor, the rotund police chief of Oak Park, knew very well that the new owner of the house on Fillmore and Wenonah attracted some fast company. By the late 1940's it was no secret to Nestor that Sam Giancana was a comer. He kept surveillance on Giancana's automobiles and the way he drove them, of his clothes, of his spending habits, of the clusters of men in fedoras and long coats who met in his basement at all hours of the night, then left with their chins in their collars.

There was still a job that lingered, still a presence that reminded Giancana and his bosses that not everything and everyone had been delivered. That was Teddy Roe. Through the years of capitulation by the Jones brothers, Roe remained as intractable as ever, a personality every bit as strong as the people who were running his policy associates out of business and freely taking over their wheels. He became known as the "Robin Hood of Policy," a man who not only held out against the mob, but who encouraged competition from anyone who proved himself capable of controlling a wheel, a man who made legends of incidents when he reimbursed players who had been cheated, personally searching out laundry ladies whose nickels had turned them a bundle. All of that was set against his resistance to the mob, a stand that stronger, bigger men hadn't been able to take.

It set well with Roe because such tales insured his wealth. He was still a policy baron, and his wheels paid off with the same odds that put policy men in Lincolns and silk suits while the vast majority of their clients jingled loose change and bought dream books. Six years after the kidnapping of Eddie Jones, Roe thrived, a sign not only of his own toughness and street savvy—there were few men who knew better than Roe when he was vulnerable and how to keep from being set up—but also of the fact that there was really no hurry on the part of Guzik and Accardo to eradicate their competition in policy. The driving force against Roe was the vengefulness of Giancana, his memory for the insults the mulatto had handed him, the sight of Fat Lenny Caifano getting nailed in the street, and, most of all, Roe's stridency, a personality very much like Giancana's. It became very evident through the years that Giancana fought hardest against those who were as strong-willed as he was. He became uncontrollable and unyielding, defying the patience and the wisdom of a Ricca or an Accardo, fulminating revenge until he snapped at close friends and threw newspapers against walls. There was little doubt in his mind from the very day Roe looked him squarely in the eyes and told him he wouldn't give him a quarter, from the times that Roe pinned his arms and kicked his ass, that Giancana would get him.

The scene was perhaps as cold and bloody as any, characteristic of the joyless killing that cluttered so much of what Giancana and his associates undertook in their early careers. There was not even a trace of the reckless adventure that they courted as 42's, of the heat from cops and the wild but thoroughly exciting scrapes and lams that made them feel like big-timers. On the night of August 4, 1952, two white men waited in a Chevrolet across from Roe's house at 5239 South Michigan. They parked there about two hours, shielded by a billboard in a corner lot, noticed at one time by a service station attendant who thought them to be police and asked if they were checking for speeders. At a little after 10 P.M., Roe emerged from his front door and walked toward his new Buick parked on the curb.

The two men jumped from their car and came up on Roe from behind, then leveled shotguns and blasted five times. Three shots hit Roe in the back, one in the forearm, and one tore into his face and jaw as he spun. The force of the shells lifted him off his feet and sent him into a tree; then he slumped into the gutter. Near him lay his wide-brimmed straw hat with pellet holes in the brim; in a holster under his coat lay a fully loaded .38. Roe was dead before he got his hands close to it. Pellets that missed him broke windows in two houses and embedded themselves in three parked cars.

Although the murder was front page, and a sensation among blacks on the South Side, it brought about a curious but prevalent ambivalence on the part of police. Most knew that Roe had been threatened by the mob, particularly Giancana, for years, that he had been offered $250,000 for his wheels, a payment he considered "token." It was even revealed that Roe had met with Giancana six months earlier and agreed upon a settlement that would allow him to stay in business, and on the strength of that agreement he had dropped his bodyguards and his close personal security. (His wife denied it, saying that she and her husband had lived in fear ever since the Caifano killing.) Police, while providing explanations for Roe's murder, chose to clean up and forget it, tacitly espousing the belief that people like Roe courted assassination and the world was better off without them. In any event, detectives in four days following the murder brought in no suspects, briefly questioned the lone witness, and failed to seek out or question any of the mob figures who'd figured in Roe's dealings.

That brought about blistering attacks from black politicians, who'd finally been outraged by the removal of black policy kings by Italian gangsters. With a gallery of supporters behind him, Alderman Archibald J. Carey of the South Side's Third Ward denounced Mayor Martin Kennelly and his police force during a City Council meeting. As the white-haired, aging Mayor sat apparently dazed by the attack, Carey screamed, "The responsibility is on you, Mr. Mayor. We appear before the world as the most godless and callous group of public officials anywhere."

So charged, the Mayor ordered his department to stir things up. At Roe's funeral, a solemn, lavish occasion every bit as grandiose as those of the old-time bootleggers, with 4,000 spectators, a $5,000 bronze casket, flowers costing an estimated $10,000, and 150 white-robed choristers singing and sobbing uncontrollably, Chicago police waded in and arrested Roe's five pallbearers. The arrest and interrogation of 13 West Side hoods, including Giancana and Lenny Caifano's brother Marshall, followed. It did not, however, interrupt a huge reception a week later in Northlake for the son of hoodlum Claude Maddox at which Accardo, Giancana, Sam "Golf Bag" Hunt, Gus Alex, and scores of other mob figures drank and golfed at the Westward Ho Country Club.

Yet, as long and hard as detectives talked to witnesses and hoods, the secret of Roe's demise lay with him. Ironically, in the weeks before his death he had learned that he was suffering from abdominal cancer. It made his resolve that much stronger, his recalcitrance in the face of relatively generous offers by the outfit to absorb his Delta, Indo, and Alcoa wheels all the more grating. He again shoved his fist into the face of Giancana and told him to chew on it. Then he remarked to his wife, "What if they do kill me? I'm going to die of the cancer within a year anyway."

Only days later the stakes that the policy men were killing each other over came to light. The Internal Revenue Service on August 14, 1952, filed tax liens against Thomas Manno and Sam Pardy, two front operators for the Accardo-Guzik syndicate, totaling $2,415,901.14. The total represented taxes, penalties, and interest on income the two men had made on policy since the outfit muscled into it in the middle 1940's. Government agents said it was but a prelude to cases they would pursue against Guzik, Accardo, and others who'd taken over the $30-million-a-year numbers rackets. It wasn't, though Pardy, Manno, and three of Manno's brothers pleaded guilty and were jailed, serving only to showcase the gold mine the outfit had taken. The murder of Roe went unsolved, with no suspects, no solid clues. Only the legacy of the last policy king remained, the event of his death imprinted as indelibly in the memories of black South Siders as anything in their lives. Though they continued to play gigs as fervently as ever, the game was no longer theirs.

9

To the neighbors, the Giancana family was a very normal, if quiet suburban family. The large brick house on Wenonah and Fillmore was on a corner lot, and with a tall fence enclosing the backyard and the garage abutting an alley, the comings and goings of the family went largely unnoticed. By 1950, Antoinette was 15, Bonnie 12, Francine 5, and they were raised oblivious of what their father was doing and whom he did it with. The girls continued to attend private Catholic schools. By the time Antoinette was ready for high school she was enrolled in an exclusive girls' boarding school in Indianapolis.

Although such schooling provided the obvious cover for whatever notoriety Giancana might bring his children, it was also done to ease the burden on Angeline. She continued to struggle with her health, but at the same time she worked feverishly to live up to traditional standards of an Italian housewife. She was devoted to the house, as Sam was, and she repeatedly got on her hands and knees to scrub the floors and keep it uncluttered and spotless. Inside and outside, the house reflected her care. It was a well-built, stately home, if modest, perfectly suited to the family and reflecting Angeline's skill as a homemaker. The grounds were equally well kept, with neat hedges, flowers, grass, all of it fastidiously groomed and tastefully plotted. Without being ostentatious, the home and its grounds reflected the status of the Giancanas: first-generation Italian-Americans who had done better than their immigrant parents, who had moved out of the old neighborhood into the sprawling lots of the suburbs. And, even though it mattered little to Sam and Angeline that they keep up with their neighbors, it was important to them that they reflect what they had and where they had arrived. And it was nobody's business how they had gotten there.

But inside the house the smells and the tastes and the mannerisms remained very Old World. It was important that Angeline preside over an ever-bubbling pot, that her life be her daughters, her home, and the food she put on the table. Sam insisted on such devotion, and also played his part. When he was in town he came home strictly between 5:30 and 6:00 every night and expected the rest of the family to be there. He often took friends with him— two, three, five people at a time—and Angeline simply had to be ready for them.

She remained a stoic, loving wife. She cooked expertly, even if she was exhausted from a day of housework. Pasta, soups, complicated Italian dishes—all of it she made and made well. She continued to be devoutly religious, even though her husband was not. And she deferred to his say in domestic matters. He continued to be unwaveringly strict with his daughters, setting precise times for them to be home, disciplining them severely when they defied him. When they were able to drive, he unflinchingly refused them the use of the family cars when they abused the privilege. He made no secret of his temper, and though it was lined with love and traditional Italian pride in his family and exaltation of his women, Sam Giancana the father was every bit as exacting as Sam Giancana the hood.

The family was also traditionally close-knit, with regular, warm get-togethers with relatives, particularly Angeline's sisters and brothers. The grandparents remained in the center of things, Grandfather Giancana delighting the granddaughters with his grocery and his peddling in the old neighborhood; Grandfather De Tolve scurrying around his home and his property with no regard for his age, always looking for something to keep him busy and once even selling balloons on the corner. The granddaughters would later remember them as the "watermelon grandfather" and the "balloon grandfather."

Though the clan were close and devoted to each other, they

seldom talked about those who had died. The subject of death simply wasn't touched upon or explained. The Giancana girls knew nothing of the death of Sam's only sister, Lena, only that she had died during World War II of some kind of cancer. And they knew less of the death of their grandmother. In a peculiar, yet apparently intentional lie, Giancana told his children not that his mother had died of an infection of the womb but rather that she had been hit by a car. Substituting the death of his stepmother, Mary Leonardi, in place of his mother's, he went even further and told them that she had died saving *him,* that she had been carrying him when she was struck and that the shield of her body kept the auto from killing him. He said no more than that, insisted that the subject not be extended, and left his daughters to carry that vision of their grandmother with them into adulthood.

As manipulative as Giancana could be within his home, he was unable to keep his name and reputation from assaulting his daughters outside of it. By the 1950's he was suddenly discovered by the media, his name and face randomly placed with the lists of Capone-era holdovers that Chicago newspaper writers loved to lionize. In March, 1952, he was listed in a Chicago *Sun-Times* editorial as one of the "Bad 19," a who's who of Chicago organized crime past and present that was contrasted with a list called the "Good 19," made up mostly of civic leaders and law-enforcement officials.

The Bad 19 were household names in Chicago, as well known as the best of the Chicago Cubs or the White Sox. They included Ricca, Guzik, Accardo, Murray Humphreys, Louis Campagna, Sam Hunt, Claude Maddox, Charles Gioe, Eddie Vogel, Ralph Capone, Rocco Fischetti, and Joe Fusco—all names that had been in and out of Chicago headlines since the St. Valentine's Day massacre. But new ones, the younger hoods, weren't as commonly known, Giancana in particular, and Ralph Pierce, Joey Aiuppa, Tough Tony Capezio, and finally the policy heads: Pete Tremont, Pat Manno, and the ill-fated Teddy Roe.

The pictures included were small mug shots, many poorly lit and bad likenesses. Giancana's however, was a direct, frontal mug photo, showing him in his early forties as fuller faced, and more handsome than before. He was still dark-haired and lean, still weighing about 155 pounds over a 5-foot 8-inch frame, but the fleshy face hid the gauntness, the long chin and beak-like nose. In all, his was an unspectacular look, nothing of the jowly, thick-browed Capone of twenty years before, or the bullishness of Tony Accardo.

He was briefly noted, a rising pug among many, while the press kept its eyes on Ricca and Accardo. They were helped considerably by Estes Kefauver, the U.S. Senator whose subcommittee on the effect of organized crime on interstate commerce in 1950 paraded a host of hoods before microphones and photographers. Although uncovering very little, hearings such as the Kefauver Committee's served as a sounding board for law officers and crime commission officials all over the country, and they entertained the public by forcing the grouchy, surly hoods into the open, where they were prodded and poked at by committee members like freshly captured rhinos. Few disappointed; all said nothing.

Accardo was a prime example. A man who shirked all publicity and discouraged exposure, Accardo appeared outside the chambers conservatively dressed, but dour and totally uncommunicative. As Kefauver wrote later, Accardo chose to roam the halls and talk to no one, and came into the hearing room only after his attorney stepped into the hallway and clapped loudly two times. As a witness, Accardo said nothing 140 times and struck Kefauver as "gorilla-like," a term used not derogatorily but descriptively in regard to Accardo's bulk—200 pounds at 5 feet 9—his swarthiness, his thick hands and noticeably hairy knuckles. But Kefauver also observed the tattoo on Accardo's right hand, in the crease of his thumb and finger. It was a dove, and it flew when Accardo clenched and opened his thick fist.

Such was the stuff that carried on the myths and legends of the Capone gang at the beginning of the 1950's, even if it was at the time but a semblance of Al's organization. Giancana fit into it by galvanizing his strengths, tightly managing his enterprises and ever expanding them. He began to build a reputation for being unflinchingly tight, of demanding accounting in his casinos to the penny. His Montrose Association (the outfit became fond of setting up so-called social or athletic clubs complete with memberships, which were simply fronts for casinos and wire rooms) became known as the Wagon Wheel, and in the early years it produced overwhelming revenues. Although it was forced to move to different quarters from time to time—the most expansive and booming being at 4416 North Narragansett in the township of Norwood Park—the Wagon Wheel flourished and lined Giancana's pockets as never before. In keeping with the way he operated, Giancana even charged the outfit a healthy rent for the use of the building.

As his stature grew during this time, Giancana became linked with hosts of new operations. From a trotting club in Melrose Park, a shrimp-exporting business out of Cuba, to rackets in East St. Louis, Illinois, and interests or control of many other casinos and lounges—the Forest Lounge in Niles Township, the Ballard Inn, only a half mile from the sheriff's office in the same area—Giancana was recognized as a master gambling entrepreneur. His successes pushed him faster and further up the mob's hierarchy than any of his peers, and any of the better-known, better-established hoods out of the Capone days.

Little touched him, not even an IRS probe of his income in March of 1951, or a 67-count indictment on gambling and conspiracy charges surrounding the operation of the Wagon Wheel. When the indictment was returned, in fact, sheriff's deputies failed even to serve Giancana with a subpoena; he was never arrested or bonded, and never forced to deal with any of the charges. The officers explained years later that they couldn't find him, even though it wasn't difficult for newspaper writers and columnists to spot him at funerals, boxing matches, restaurants, or simply coming and going from his home.

But such were the times in Chicago and Cook County in the early 1950's. The political and police corruption was blatant and pervasive, noticeable in the strips and haunts in Chicago, obvious in villages and unincorporated areas of the suburbs. The hoods went about their business smugly and openly. Only IRS agents watched them and their books. J. Edgar Hoover's FBI was all but oblivious of organized crime, preferring instead to hunt bank robbers and Communists. Local police were so compromised that they were little but gadflies to the hoods, ineffectual as law-enforcement officers in the strict sense, marginally incisive as intelligence collectors—in fact, doing little but keeping tote boards of meaningless arrests and storing intelligence information, which served as little more than gossip. Homicide detectives in the Chicago Police Department never justified their existence after an outfit murder, and not always because the killings were so carefully and cleanly done; usually they felt the world was better off without the deceased, and that fact alone diminished the necessity to find the killer.

On a lesser scale, few police ever felt obliged to enforce parking laws, speeding laws, or city ordinances against hoods. When Jack Muller, a brash, garrulous Chicago patrolman did do it, as the time he ticketed Accardo's car while it stood outside a Rush Street restaurant, *he* became the object of wrath from his superiors and city fathers, not those violators he nailed. Hence, it was not at all uncommon to see long Cadillacs and Continentals parked outside the front doors of Rush Street saloons, or hoods like Giancana blithely come and go as they pleased while other citizens jockeyed for parking meters or waited impatiently in clogged parking garages.

One exception in the Chicago Police Department was a force known as Scotland Yard. Headed by Lieutenant Joseph Morris and Sergeant William Duffy, the Yard specialized in watching the hoods and amassing dossiers on them. It had its headquarters on Canalport Street, separate from any other station houses or headquarters. Yet Scotland Yard managed to dent the activities of the mob in no substantial ways. After City Hall learned it had tapped the Morrison Hotel, the site of hoodlum meetings but also the place where the Cook County Democratic organization met, the special force was all but stripped of its powers. It became less effective, in fact, than the Chicago Crime Commission, a publicly funded group with a limited number of agents, which did little but attempt to publicly embarrass the mob. Its director in the 1940's and 1950's, Virgil Peterson, became the most eloquent anti-mob spokesman in the city. It was Peterson who filled the pages of the Kefauver Committee's transcripts with meticulous descriptions and intelligence information on Chicago's syndicate. It was the Crime Commission's yearly bulletins that identified mob figures and detailed their activities, and in great publicity bursts urged the public's wrath and contempt for hoods.

But the syndicate felt threatened only by the tax men. It was Accardo's belief that the mob should conduct itself as meekly as possible and avoid attention and scrutiny. His instructions were not unlike those of a gang boss many years before him, one Joseph "Babe Ruth" Colaro of the 42's, who told his gang that driving a hot car and wining the ladies was "inviting the heat." It was Accardo, however, a man who had never spent as much as a night in jail, who felt the tax men the hardest in 1955. The Internal Revenue Service simply was not satisfied with his explanations for his income, and in 1955 the Justice Department appointed a young, politically ambitious Chicago attorney named Richard Ogilvie to head a task force to unravel Accardo's financial intrigues.

It was that kind of federal pressure that made Accardo look for someone to assume day-to-day control of the mob's activities. One of the men he turned to was Giancana, even though speculation ran wild that Giancana was one of a number of troublesome "Young Turks" in the syndicate, a group gaining more power and influence and often killing to get it. The "Young Turk" theory has always been a favorite among police and reporters in Chicago, for the idea of a rising, impatient, and ruthless young faction is a convenient explanation for anything from shakeups to assassinations. It easily lends itself to events in the underworld, particularly in the middle 1950's when the mob was in many ways in transition from the influence and rule of the old Capone lieutenants to the muscle of their young associates. The 1950's saw the deaths of Jake Guzik, Phil D'Andrea, Sam Hunt, Claude Maddox, and Louis Campagna, all of age or ill-health. Three others— Charles "Cherry Nose" Gioe, Frank "Frank Diamond" Maritote, and Alex "Louie" Greenburg, all important mob heavyweights who spanned the years—were assassinated within 18 months of each other in 1954–1955.

After each slaying, the Young Turk stories were trotted out. But closer to the truth was that Gioe, Maritote, and Greenburg had shifted allegiances and had become a threat to the organization. As young as the so-called Young Turks were, they, as in the case of Giancana, held a traditional Sicilian regard for age. Killing a Cherry Nose Gioe for the sake of a power grab or simply to be noticed runs contrary to the very mentality of the outfit. Even a Louis Greenburg, the 65-year-old "Mr. Moneybags" of the mob, who at one time ranked with Guzik as a financier in the Capone organization, a Jew, but one with the closest ties to Capone, Frank Nitti, Accardo, Guzik, and Ricca, was shot in the street because of business complications with the ruling syndicate heads, not a gang of upstarts.

Other rumors about the Young Turks led in 1954 to the creation of perhaps the most preposterous tale concerning them. In April of that year it was reported that Accardo had applied for a passport in order to go to South America because he feared for his life. The story went that he had entered into a serious disagreement with Paul Ricca over control of gambling and vice receipts in South Cook and Kankakee counties. In a meeting with Ricca's representatives, namely Giancana, Sam Battaglia, and Jack Cerone, in an auto parked in front of his suburban River Forest home, Accardo reiterated his position. Then he got out of the car, and as he walked toward his house, Giancana fired a shot over his head. With that, the story went, Accardo relinquished his claims and showed up at the passport office.

The incident, however, probably never happened. No evidence of it or of lingering hard feelings was ever observed by anyone close to the syndicate in the months and years that followed. Exactly the opposite prevailed. Giancana continued to linger in Accardo's shadow, the two of them respectful colleagues of Paul Ricca. It was Accardo who, during those years, taught Giancana everything about the day-to-day mechanics of the mob and its concessions. It was Accardo who demonstrated the restraint, the judgment, the discipline needed to oversee the organization, and whom Giancana looked to as a model of control. It was Accardo, with the total backing of Ricca, who commanded the full force of the 300 or so mob underlings in Chicago and who could have easily retaliated against a bullet over his head with the biggest, most efficient bloodbath seen in Chicago since the Capone move against Bugs Moran in 1929.

Another element that lends serious doubt to the Accardo-Giancana incident is that when it was supposed to have taken place Giancana's wife Angeline lay in a coma in Florida. There were few things that could have moved Giancana from his wife's hospital bed, and probably little but her condition was on his mind.

Still, the story did not easily fade, and Giancana was to become a mainstay of the mob writers' vocabulary as a leader of the Young Turks. Among them were Marshall Caifano; Sam Battaglia, the brother of Duke Battaglia of the original 42 Gang; Jack Cerone; Fiore Buccieri; Gus Alex, the son of a Greek restaurant owner, whose place attracted Capone hoods like Jake Guzik; Albert "Obie" Frabotta; and Felix Alderisio. It was true that all were comers in the outfit, but it was also true that they knew the rules. Business was good, new territories were opening, there was little reason for any of them to move too far too fast.

Giancana's home life suited him perfectly: a wife who was devoted and industrious, close only with relatives, three daughters who, while not being the prides of his life that sons would have been, were still his precious, sacred dago daughters. Following the traditional roles in an Italian family, his daughters were even more easily shut off from the realities of their father's business and his reputation than boys would have been. They were also easier to control, perhaps, except for Antoinette, the oldest and most vociferous, the one reflecting more of her father's character. Bonnie was bright and vivacious, Francine quiet and more introspective.

With things in order at home it was easier to concentrate on business. Ricca and Accardo always believed that, and Giancana sustained the belief. He led a predictable, low-key life, and with associates had an almost priggish disdain for the good times, especially if they involved long-legged women. Part of those feelings may have stemmed from the fact that Giancana didn't have a lot of time to philander, for his expanding concessions made for long hours and demanding supervision. And, if anything, Giancana was proving during these years that he was capable of managing his stores.

With his climb in the outfit came money. His family wanted for little, owned two cars in a time when few families did, took cross-country trips, and vacationed regularly in Florida. In most ways, his relationship with his family during this time was no different from that of any businessman whose family doesn't understand what he does or how he does it, and with his relative obscurity within the mob there were no headlines, few agents, and no bothersome reporters to stir their ignorance. That would come later.

Giancana's biggest concern at home was Angeline's health. Now in her forties, she continued to tire easily from strenuous housework; her heart condition made her vulnerable to common maladies, which afflicted her longer and more severely than usual. Still, hers was a condition more bothersome than worrisome, for there was no way of telling if it would suddenly worsen and threaten her life or remain nothing more than an object of concern.

She was struck suddenly in April, 1954. The family were in Florida when she suffered a blood clot that moved to her brain. Leakage from a heart valve had formed a pocket of blood behind her heart, which ultimately formed the clot. She lapsed into a semi-coma, and with her daughters by her side, she lingered aware, but uncommunicative. She hung on for two weeks until Friday, April 24.

The funeral was a subdued, family affair. The De Tolves appeared *en masse* to bury their youngest sister; the Giancanas were nearly as well represented. Giancana's associates paid their respects, but they didn't bring much attention. The grounds at St. Bernardine's Church in Forest Park, the church Angeline attended faithfully and which benefited nicely from the family's resources, went uncluttered by mob writers or police agents. They, also, would come later.

In the months following Angeline's death, Giancana arranged for a generous, lavish altar in her memory at St. Bernardine's.

At home, he turned over the daily responsibility of his family to his in-laws, Angeline's older sister Anna Tuminello, and Mrs. Tuminello's daughter, Marie Perno, and her husband James. They moved into Giancana's home shortly after Angeline's death and went about raising his three daughters. They became fixtures in the household—Anna Tuminello, with her strong-willed, Old World ways that were similar to Angeline's, and the Pernos, who were younger and closer to the girls, and whose own children later on were often identified as being Giancana's.

The combination of his wife's death and widening mob responsibilities provided an inexorable break from his home life. Giancana began to travel extensively, mostly with Accardo, making the rounds and the contacts necessary. His face appeared constantly in police files, his name added after that of Accardo by intelligence detectives who spotted them around town, and by those in other cities alerted to the presence of Chicago hoods. He was spotted in Miami with Accardo, Murray Humphreys, Jake Guzik, Gus Alex, and Miami gangster Sheriff Kelly. He was among a mob gathering at St. Hubert's Grill in Chicago when Harry Russell, Accardo's representative in Florida's expanding gambling operations, came to town. He went with Accardo and Guzik to Las Vegas on one of many forays surrounding the Chicago outfit's move into the casinos. In 1953 he was arrested with Accardo and held for investigation by Las Vegas police. He met repeatedly with Accardo, Humphreys, Guzik, and various mob gamblers at Fritzel's, a well-known Loop restaurant.

There was little doubt in anyone's mind that Giancana had been fully accepted by Accardo as capable of taking over when he was away, and that Ricca approved of the arrangement. Only one other figure, upon the deaths of Guzik, Campagna, and Charlie Fischetti, remained as well thought of and powerful, and that was Murray Humphreys, the shrewd Welshman whom many considered to be the most innately intelligent hood ever to practice in Chicago. But Humphreys was still Welsh, and no amount of status or reputation could put him above a hard-charging Sicilian like Giancana. As long as Ricca and Accardo ran things—even though they eschewed any "mafia" structure within the outfit and like others before them freely worked with hoods of all races—they put their bottom-line trust in a *paesan,* and that cudgel gradually, singularly fell to Giancana.

Tony Accardo never really relished the demanding day-to-day duties of operating boss. He liked them even less in 1952 when he came under federal scrutiny for selling illegal horsemeat. Again he instinctively chose to get out of sight and try to fight behind the scenes. It was one signal of his increasing reliance on Giancana. The final one, however, came in 1955 when the federal government made an all-out effort to make Accardo account for his income-tax reports. For Tony, the memory of Capone's fall to the tax men was all too clear, and he opted to concentrate on his defense and let the outfit's workings, its minute-by-minute decision-making, fall on different shoulders.

For all practical purposes, the Chicago outfit, the heirs to the Capone gang, the loose confederation of ethnic hoods who had fought each other as punks on the streets, whose fathers had shot at each other over bootleg booze, was turned over to little more than a street-corner tough guy, a 42 Gang smart head who hadn't been able to polish the shoes of Capone-level hoods as a kid but who had proved himself tougher, quicker, more ruthless, more political, more of an opportunist than the lot of them as an adult. Sam "Mooney" Giancana, with the nod of Tony Accardo and the blessing of Paul Ricca, now ran it. To the press he was the new "overlord," the operating head, the enforcer. To police and writers looking for secretive "mafia" intrigues, he was the boss of Chicago bosses, a godfather, a don. But to the folks on Taylor Street, the neighborhood kids who had gotten jobs and gone straight, the relatives of dead 42's, the second- and third-generation Italians who'd moved away at the first chance from the hard times of the Patch, Sam Giancana had simply become a big shot. Nothing more.

But there was one person who never got to see Giancana rise to the pinnacle of his profession, and it can be wondered if he actually would have minded. In 1954, Antonino Giancana, 72 years old, his name now Americanized to Anthony, was stricken with hardening of the arteries and high blood pressure. He was living with his third wife, one Catherine Lombardi, in a new neighborhood. With many of the Italians from the Patch, he'd moved west to the edge of the city to a house at 141 North Long. He still considered himself nothing more than a grocer. He'd never meant to find much in America but better times than he'd known in Castelvetrano. It hadn't been easy, but he'd done it, raised a big family and watched them go out on their own. That a son would do more than that was another story, a bit of fate he no longer could do much about. He'd paid his dues to that son, mortgaged his possessions and borrowed on his grocery stores to get him out of jail, suffered quietly with the embarrassment of having raised a hoodlum. But what Sam did from that time on Antonino wouldn't have to contend with, for on July 25 at four o'clock in the morning, a cerebral hemorrhage convulsed the feisty little immigrant in his sleep, and two hours later he was dead.

PART THREE

Overlord: 1956-1966

10

ONLY A JOHN DILLINGER brought out the best in them, for he was a bank robber and they were masters at tracking bank robbers. Throughout the first half of this century, the FBI did little to crease the routines of syndicate gangsters, James Cagney movies notwithstanding. The Bureau simply had no directive from J. Edgar Hoover to do much about the country's hoods. Not only did the FBI ignore them, but it was relatively ignorant of what they did, how they did it, and the kind of results they enjoyed. The country's knowledge of organized crime stemmed mainly from the activities of Thomas Dewey as a district attorney in New York, then from Estes Kefauver and his Senate subcommittee on interstate commerce in 1950, and finally from the proceedings of John McCellan's Senate subcommittee in 1957 that probed labor racketeering. The Bureau played no role in such hearings, for the simple reason that it had nothing to offer them.

That changed suddenly in late 1957, in the midst of the McClellan hearings, thanks mainly to the curiosity and the guts, not of Edgar Hoover, but of Edgar Croswell. A New York State police sergeant, Croswell knew of the presence of Joseph Barbara and his rambling estate in the hills behind the village of Apalachin. Barbara's background as a bootlegger and beer distributor in New York was no secret to Croswell, and though he could do little about Barbara's decision to live where he wanted, Croswell made a determined effort to keep an eye on him. In the days preceding November 14, 1957, Croswell and his deputies became quite aware of the procession of limousines heading down the winding road to Barbara's home, long black Cadillacs and Lincolns, most with out-of-state licenses, all with two or three heads visible just above the seats.

There was nothing Croswell could legally do about Barbara's visitors, but by Saturday, November 14, with what he figured to be as many as 70 guests assembled, Croswell no longer could stifle his curiosity. He organized what few deputies he had and conducted a raid on Barbara's home, one merely, as he explained later, to see if anything criminal was going on or if Barbara's guests were wanted on outstanding warrants. To do it he blocked the one road leading to the estate, and then waded into the proceedings.

He had no idea of the history he was making. The Apalachin enclave of 1957 was one of the biggest meetings ever of gangsters from all over the country. And, although nobody was sure why they were there, Croswell's raid sent them into panic. Hoods in silk suits and patent-leather shoes bounded out of the windows and patios of the Barbara home, many of them into the dense and muddy woodland surrounding the estate for miles. Those who didn't run were detained by Croswell, identified, forced to produce money and valuables, and state their occupations. Many of those who did attempt to escape were later rounded up by deputies, some of them wandering lost in the woods with mud up to their socks, and burs and thistles clinging to their suits. John Montana, a long-time Buffalo, New York, councilman was spotted trying to untangle his camel-hair coat from a barbed-wire fence. He explained that his car's brakes had failed and he'd gone to Barbara's seeking aid. Other hoods suggested that they were looking at real estate; two said they were trying to catch a train, even though the nearest station was 70 miles away.

The raid made headlines in papers all over the country the next day. Croswell's biggest bag, Vito Genovese of New York, headed the list of some 60 hoods detained and exposed to the public. (Others included New York's Joe Bonanno and Joe Profaci, Cleveland's John Scalise, Joe Zerilli of Detroit, and James Civello of Dallas.) It wasn't Croswell's arrests that made the waves, but the apparent fact that gangsters throughout the country were one with each other, that they met and mediated their differences, and that they formed what appeared to be an insidious brotherhood from coast to coast. No such network had ever been as blatantly exposed before, and the public and politicians clamored not only for action, but for information.

When they turned to the FBI, Hoover shrugged his shoulders and all but said he knew nothing about it. Perhaps because the notion of conspiracy appealed mightily to the director, or because other areas of investigation, such as American Communists, were losing their appeal, Hoover in the days following Apalachin ordered the Bureau and all of its resources to concentrate on dogging hoods.

In Chicago, Hoover's directive meant the dispatch of a special corps of agents, all of them college educated—many with law degrees—free to concentrate 24 hours of each day on any and all of the city's 300 practicing gangsters. Among the Chicago contingent were Ralph Hill, Bill Roemer, Vincent Inserra, and Jack Roberts. They were young, in their late twenties and thirties, and their backgrounds were generally different from those of hoods they were watching. Their professional lives, their goals and ideals, their manners, all contrasted immeasurably. As in other Bureau intelligence operations, the move against the outfit meant the use of a variety of methods, some of them illegal, involving not only day-to-day surveillance but eavesdropping—hidden microphones, phone taps—and the cultivation of a network of informants. By 1958, the Chicago effort was in full swing, and that meant a drive the likes of which hoods such as Tony Accardo, Ricca, Giancana, and their many associates had never run up against. Though Giancana was revealed to have been one of Barbara's guests who got away from Edgar Croswell at Apalachin—sprinting through woods with dash that only an ex-42 could muster—his escape would prove to be only temporary.

His favor steadily rising with Tony Accardo, Giancana at that time began not only to oversee Chicago outfit activities, but to travel extensively throughout the country. That only whetted his taste for more excursions, business and vacation trips to other countries, Mexico, Cuba, South America, even Europe. The outfit had close ties with Miami hoods and set up concessions there and in Cuba, particularly in shrimp importing. Although the outfit's interest in shrimp was only marginal, it provided an excellent business cover for the lucrative Cuban gambling rackets. "Shrimps from Cuba" became a Giancana sideline, or at least a diversion while he concentrated on Havana's casinos.

To do that, however, he had to secure a passport. And for that he dug up his birth certificate. He hardly recognized it. He had no idea who was responsible for "Gilormo Giongona," his name on the document, or for any of the other information. With an uncle from New York, Andrea Giancana, he put together more accurate family information and had it submitted as a delayed record of birth. He officially put his name down as Momo Salvatore Giangano, and changed his birth date from May 24, 1908, to June 15. Then he signed it "Sam M. Giancana." When it was filed by his attorney and boyhood friend Anthony V. Champagne, it became a new source of information for police and reporters, and the nickname "Momo" began to appear regularly in print. But it, like hundreds of other nicknames given to gangsters, was used by newspapermen alone. To his family he was Sam, to his associates he occasionally went as "Mo," but generally, to those who knew him and knew him well, he was "Mooney," the same wheelman and smart-head 42 who occasionally seemed not "to have the right time," Mooney as ever.

With his rise and his travels came visibility, and he appeared to loathe it. Nosey reporters and tenacious agents brought out his moodiness, his surly, irascible temperament, which was easily pricked, easily touched off. His outbursts were so sudden, so savage that observers wondered about his stability.

Yet, with all of his meanness, Giancana possessed one characteristic found in so many Sicilian hoods, a trait exaggerated by observers, perhaps, but that counted for much: a beguiling, lilting charm. Perhaps inherited, perhaps inherent, it was a power able to change the moment. Fellow Sicilians could feel it and knew well enough to watch out for it, knew that these men and their circles somehow removed the specter of what they were, and exuded a feeling of confidence, of ease, of extreme trust. As quickly as Giancana flew into a rage, he was able to envelop those around him into a covin of understanding, and speak with them as one who understood and cared, be it about affairs mundane or treacherous. That charm, as insidious and elusive as it was, was knit with an implied presence of power, that this man, speaking so slowly, calmly, and haltingly, with a voice that went no further than the soft psyches of his listeners, was able to do whatever it was he wished.

Even if that indeed was not always the case (the power of suggestion historically has been more foreboding than that gangsters actually possessed) it worked magic not only with associates, but with women. Few hoods exploited that charisma more than Giancana. After a period of abstinence following the death of Angeline, Giancana went into heat. He hung out at lounges and nightclubs and went after any woman who caught his eye, stringing out a skein of one-night stands in suburban motels that awed his observers. He was rapacious and indiscriminate. He propositioned any woman anywhere, as in the case of a waitress at a West Side café who at first resisted his advances. The woman later told agents that she revealed to Giancana that her husband was a burglar, a fact that opened an avenue for Giancana, for soon after, she said, her husband left the house and never returned. She was convinced that Giancana found out who he was and had him killed, a situation that apparently didn't depress the woman, for she shortly began a lengthy affair with Giancana. Trysting usually in the Thunderbolt Motel in suburban Rosemont (Giancana held part interest), the relationship went on for months until the woman told Giancana she was pregnant. He believed her and provided her with a home and allowance in Lake Worth, Florida. She continued to see him, visiting him in Chicago and in Lake Worth, until the affair faded in favor of newer faces.

One of them was a woman named Bergit Clark, a plain brunette who worked as a secretary at Michael De Tolve's envelope company. As with all of his girlfriends, Giancana overwhelmed her with gifts: jewelry, flowers, clothes, money, trips, the best food, the best clubs. With Miss Clark, it was the gift of a diamond and emerald ring that brought her problems. After she had received the ring from Giancana, one of the stones loosened and she took it to an exclusive Loop jewelry store for repair. Because of its uniqueness, the jewelers were suspicious enough to inquire about the ring and soon discovered that it was part of the take from a robbery of an exclusive West Coast shop. Although pressure was put on Miss Clark—agents attempted to persuade her to cooperate with them in their surveillance of Giancana in exchange for not pursuing the origins of the ring—she refused to turn on her benefactor.

If it wasn't Bergit Clark it was Marilyn "Dusty" Miller, a dancer in the Chez Paree "Adorables," or hat-check girls—almost any woman with a pretty face who was smart enough to ask no questions. Many were young, unsophisticated girls who worked at menial jobs and who were swept off their feet by flowers, limousines, thick steaks, and that charm, that skulking, macho presence, which in some ways terrified them and in other ways was strangely intoxicating.

Giancana even trod forbidden areas, violating not only his own warnings about such things but mob codes in general, when he went after Darlene Caifano, the blowzy blonde wife of Marshall. From Mayfield, Kentucky, Darlene married Marshall in 1945, but the marriage went sour by the mid-1950's. Soon Giancana was seen regularly with her, much to the dismay of Caifano, the small fiery button man frequently sent by the mob to persuade casino owners in Las Vegas to accept new partners or to carry out local contracts. Caifano was strongly suspected of being involved in the Teddy Roe murder, partly because of his executioner status in the outfit at the time, and also because he wanted to avenge the killing of his brother Lenny. It was a mark of how high Giancana had risen in the mob that Caifano was unable to do anything about his wife's choice of boy friends. On the other hand, Marshall took a perverse pride in knowing that his estranged wife was being courted by a boss like Giancana. Darlene was no exception to Giancana's techniques—he lavished gifts on her as he did all the rest—and for a few months, while the Caifanos proceeded with divorce hearings, he was seen with her regularly around his Thunderbolt Motel.

He also developed a relationship with Keely Smith, the stunning jazz and pop singer who made her name with the Louis Prima band. Giancana met her in Las Vegas, where she had built a reputation for her partying and late-night club-hopping. She traveled extensively and saw Giancana in a number of cities where she and the band performed. Though the relationship never flowered past parties and occasional meetings, Giancana proudly displayed an autographed photo Keely had given him, and in a freshly poured piece of concrete around his Oak Park home, he showed friends where she had signed her name.

As his carousing brought attention to him, and the attendant publicity that he so ardently scorned, Giancana pursued seemingly trivial legal problems during these years. And with them too came press reports that held him up to ridicule. They portrayed him at his most quarrelsome, as a petty quibbler who became incensed over minor legal irritations that his peers would have ignored. Through Anthony V. Champagne, he refused to pay his 1956 Oak Park property taxes—a total of $630.60—because he claimed it included a levy on a car, a boat, and a plane that he did not own. He claimed instead that his holdings amounted to $200 in cash, $600 in household effects, and $600 worth of personal effects. Attorney Champagne disavowed federal agents' statements that Giancana's income approached close to $100,000 a month, said simply that "we are personally being discriminated against," then produced an affidavit signed by Giancana that said that he did not own a "boat or a plane." An Oak Park judge threw out assessments on those items, then ordered Giancana to pay $72.52 in delinquent taxes and a $12.32 interest penalty. And the newspapers got another chance to run Giancana's picture and chuckle over the apparent fact that the wages of crime for him were slim. But that did not discourage Giancana from refusing to pay a tax levy of $601.83 the following year, and again going to court.

His dealings within the mob, however, were by no means trivial. His charge to the top was not to be denied, not only because of his lucrative concessions, but also because, like a fortunate politician, he took advantage of the downfall of those around him. By the late 1950's, Accardo was so mired in his income-tax suit, with special attorney Ogilvie turning the prosecution screws ever tighter, that a conviction appeared certain. With Ricca it was. In 1959 he was convicted of income-tax evasion and sentenced to nine years in prison. And, since he was 62, it looked doubtful that he would ever return to his past position in the outfit. Both cases played into Giancana's hands. There was nothing and nobody around strong enough or quick enough to keep him from taking complete charge of the Chicago organization, be it within the outfit, or, like Leon Marcus, outside it.

No politician personified the tradition of Illinois politics like Orville E. Hodge, the gregarious white-haired backslapper who was elected state auditor in 1952. Hodge was a consummate cigar chomper, a back-room finagler who kissed babies and marched in parades, smiled for everyone, then made his deals. What was his was his friends', for Hodge spared no expense in entertaining aboard his yacht, his airplanes, limousines, at his country home or in his suites in the Drake Hotel in Chicago or in Springfield's Abraham Lincoln Hotel. "Come on down," he said to any and all. "It won't cost you a thing. It's all out of my own pocket."

In mid-1956, however, the public learned that Hodge's cash did not come from his own pockets. In three years as auditor, Hodge had managed to skim $1.5 million dollars from his office's budget, and squander an estimated $1 million more, mostly for his personal use. The Hodge scandal rocked the state, for investigators uncovered fraudulent transactions that permeated almost every financial institution with which Hodge came into contact. When he wasn't spending it, Hodge set up intricate schemes involving phony contracts, padded payrolls, fictitious expense accounts, illegal loans, and reams of fraudulent checks. It took investigators and prosecutors months to figure it all out and to arrive at a reasonably accurate total of what Hodge stole. When they did, Hodge went to jail, and the state proceeded, however ineptly, to keep such a scandal from happening again.

Part of the Hodge headlines was a banker and financial schemer in his own right named Leon Marcus. Originally a land developer and real-estate investor, Marcus became a banker when he bought the building housing the Southmoor Bank at 6760 South Stony Island. By 1948, Marcus held a controlling interest in Southmoor and named his brother Hyman president and a son-in-law vice president. Because Marcus had entangled himself in a number of precarious banking deals by the time Hodge took over as state auditor, he was in dire need of any favors Hodge could send his way. Hodge, on the other hand, saw the chance to shield many of his fraudulent transactions through Southmoor. During his three years in office, Hodge used Southmoor as little more than a check-cashing exchange for his phony markers, cashing a total of 89 fraudulent warrants worth $1,024,000. Apart from that, Hodge set up at Southmoor what came to be known as the Brown Envelope Account, a personal savings account made up mostly of embezzled state funds. He deposited $1,300,000 in it alone. Together, Hodge and Marcus used their separate resources to augment each other and prospered nicely until the scandal was uncovered.

Yet, even after Hodge was caught, it appeared Marcus would escape prosecution because he had legally severed his ties with Southmoor. The bank's executive vice president and managing officer, Edward A. Hintz, was not as fortunate, and with Hodge and Hodge's administrative assistant, Hintz was sent to federal prison in late 1956. Marcus, his brother Hyman, and his son-in-law were indicted in 1957 for misapplying bank funds, but by March of that year the case had not yet gone to trial.

Marcus would never get to court. On March 31, after having a Sunday dinner with housing developer Alfred Rado and his wife at their home on Chicago's South Side, he was grabbed by a group of men—believed to have been as many as five or six—as he walked to his car. Rado and his wife rushed to their door when they heard Marcus' screams for help as he struggled with the men, but they saw only the blur of an auto speeding from the scene. His abductors drove only a few blocks from the Rado home, down a dead-end street and into a deserted parking lot for trucks and trailers. There they shot the banker once in the head, and threw his body from the car.

The ensuing investigation dredged up details of the Hodge frauds and added new and equally complex schemes that Marcus had set up with developers, gamblers, politicians, and gangsters. Part of the fascination surrounding the murder was that Marcus' pockets were stuffed as usual at the time. His killers failed to strip him of $1,640.82 in cash, $3,600 in traveler's checks, and bank checks worth $9,440, plus a check from a Cleveland bank, totaling $300,000. But perhaps the most suspicious and perplexing document found on Marcus' body was a receipt for a cash payment of $100,000 to be applied to a mortgage on a Schiller Park motel. The motel was the River Road, formerly known as the Thunderbolt, and the payment was received from one "Mr. Sam Giancana."

A search began immediately for Giancana, and while detectives were looking for him they began to dig into the 61-year-old Marcus' life. What they found was a melodrama of slick business dealings, gambling sprees—he knew no bounds in gin rummy and bridge stakes—secretive dealings with hoods, and a rather blatant affair with an attractive blonde mistress. Police discovered that Marcus spent most of his time with Ruth Weidner, not only socially and as her partner in bridge and gin rummy matches, but at homes he'd purchased for the two of them in Phoenix and Lake Geneva, Wisconsin, and in a well-furnished apartment on the South Side. Miss Weidner identified herself as Mrs. Marcus on many occasions, even though Marcus, the father of two grown children, was still married to his wife, Frances, and sustained a less than estranged relationship with her.

But it was Ruth Weidner who sparked the public's fancy, and who, detectives believed, was around Marcus when he met characters he didn't want to be seen with in his offices at the Southmoor Bank. She was finally found ten days after the murder in Phoenix, Arizona, by Art Petacque, a crime reporter for the Chicago *Sun-Times.* Petacque discovered her to be a charming, agreeable person even though she had dodged police so long, but she said she didn't know a thing about Marcus' business dealings or his killers. She also wasn't anxious to be discovered. "I need publicity like a hermit needs a teeter-totter," she said, and then faded from the headlines as quickly as she had made them.

To a person, each relative, associate, and friend, including Miss Weidner, professed total astonishment at Marcus' murder. "Nobody had any reason to kill Leon Marcus," they repeated, and then attempted, with many homicide detectives, to dismiss the assassination as the work of amateur thieves. The single, fatal wound ran contrary to typical mob hits, they said, because gangsters prefer to ventilate their targets even to the point of finishing them off with a shotgun. These thieves were so bad, the argument went on, that they even bungled the robbery.

With the discovery of Ruth Weidner, the only other figure yet to be found in the murder was Giancana. Intelligence officers reported that he had been seen in Las Vegas, and most recently in Havana, where a clerk at the Hotel Nacional recognized him along with other members of Las Vegas, Miami, and Chicago gambling interests. In Chicago, Giancana had last been seen on the 31st, the day of the killing, in church.

But by the 15th Giancana had decided that he could not remain so coy, and he arranged for his arrest. Two Chicago policemen picked him up at Canal and Cermak Road after, they said, they just happened to spot him. Asked what he was doing there, Giancana answered, "I was just waiting for a streetcar." Where was he going? "East." As coincidental as his arrest was meant to appear, so his attorney Michael Brodkin coincidentally walked into the station house twenty minutes after Giancana's arrest. As Brodkin worked on securing bail for his client, Giancana played his role to perfection for detectives and the cluster of newsmen who had hurried to the station house once they were tipped off to his arrest.

It was that isolated scene that more than any other cemented his image as a gangster in the minds of the reporters who would follow his every move for the rest of his life. Wearing an expensive, narrow-lapeled overcoat, a tailored silk suit and a thin striped tie, a dark, wide-brimmed felt hat, and, not missing a cue, a pair of dark glasses that he never removed, Giancana sat handcuffed to the wooden arm of his chair, alternately smiling, snarling, staring, leering, slyly mugging hoodlike poses, his legs crossed and a thin silk-stockinged ankle dangling a $50 wing tip. Photographers snapped away. Reporters attempted to strike up a conversation, failed, then searched for an adjective to describe what they called Chicago's "Number 3 Hoodlum." Most agreed on "grouchy."

The presiding judge was equally enamored, and though he quickly set bail for the interrogation arrest, Judge Wilbert Crowley was nonplused to discover that the 67-count indictment brought against Giancana in 1951 for his involvement in the Wagon Wheel casino was still outstanding. "Do you mean this man has been wanted for six years?" Judge Crowley exclaimed. He glowered at court officials who explained that sheriff's deputies had been unable to locate Giancana during that time.

Throughout the questioning by police about the Marcus murder, Giancana said he knew nothing. He first explained that he did nothing for a living, that he had been "retired" for twenty years, and then that he did not know Leon Marcus, Ruth Weidner, Orville Hodge, Alfred Rado, or any of the others involved in the Marcus case. Of the receipt found on Marcus' body concerning the $100,000 payment from Giancana for the River Road Motel he said he knew nothing and that he had no connection with the motel or the Southmoor Bank. Where was he the night of the Marcus murder? He had no idea.

It was a predictable, rehearsed performance for Giancana, one that would all but shut out detectives. But it was secondary to his tour de force in his cameo appearance before the press. Although he attempted to snarl perversely, there was a strong fiber within his personality that very much enjoyed the treatment, the display. It had always been said of Capone-era gangsters that they were only as successful as the publicity they got. That same sentiment held with Giancana's generation, even though it outwardly subscribed to secrecy and covertness. The man handcuffed to the station-house chair with the army of photographers fighting for his attention was only a smart head up from the 42's, getting the kind of play that he'd gloated over when he whipped on Taylor Street. Now he feinted, mugged, postured, and gave them his best side. They were very much his reviewing stand, for he had arrived, had attained a pedestal above that of any of those he had grown up with and with whom he'd fought for power, for reputation, for recognition. He had made it, and he damn well knew it. As he left the station, his lawyer having posted bond and attended to the necessary legal details, he told the press to come around later with the photographs and he'd autograph them.

Giancana's connection with the Marcus probe would have gone no further, perhaps, had not his own sense of justice entered in. On Thursday of that week, Harold Dhuse, a fuel-truck driver making deliveries to farms in Will County, southwest of Chicago, noticed a late-model car parked apparently abandoned on Caton Farm Road, six miles south of Plainfield, Illinois. Dhuse spotted keys dangling from the ignition of the 1957 Chevrolet, and decided to contact a state trooper. Unlocking the trunk, the trooper found the body of a young muscular man stuffed inside a drycleaning bag. The corpse had been shot four times, twice in the head. Other marks—two deep gashes in the skull, burn marks on the wrists, abrasions on both knees—gave stark evidence that the man had been tortured.

Within hours the body was identified as that of Salvatore Moretti, 31, one of six sons—including a twin brother Vincent—of the politically heavy Moretti family of Chicago's West Side. Working from their father's poolroom on Roosevelt and Ashland, the Moretti boys ran precincts like nobody before them. Lawrence Moretti was even dubbed the "city's greatest precinct captain," a feat that earned him and his brothers comfortable jobs with the city and county. In 1951 Michael Moretti was charged with killing a teenage boy while on duty as a policeman for the

Cook County state's attorney. He was at first acquitted after a jury believed his story that the shooting was in the line of a narcotics investigation. Later, Michael was reindicted and convicted when it was found the shooting had followed a tavern brawl in which he had been beaten up. During the trial, Lawrence, Pasquale, Thomas, and the twins, Salvatore and Vincent, were caught attempting to bribe witnesses. All of them went to jail, with the exception of Salvatore and Vincent, who were freed because the prosecution could not tell them apart.

Salvatore was then fired from his Park District job and became a used-car "bird dog," a middleman who got buyers and sellers together. But his most active job was as a driver and man Friday for Willie Daddano (and occasionally for Giancana), one of Giancana's rising lieutenants. The way Moretti was found that afternoon in Will County led investigators to believe that it was his dealings with Daddano and Giancana, not as a bird dog, that put him in the trunk. They learned that days after the Marcus killing Moretti had been noticeably upset about something. Then he was given a pair of diamond cufflinks by Giancana and that seemed to settle him. He showed off the cufflinks to friends and appeared pleased with himself. But it was only a ruse on Giancana's part, for Moretti, from what his body looked like, had been punished before he was killed, tied hand and foot and forced to kneel while he was pistol-whipped across the face and skull. Deep rope burns on his neck led a coroner to conclude that he was then strangled to death. Some time later he was believed dumped in the trunk, and for good measure four .38-caliber slugs were pumped into his face and chest. The wounds hardly bled; the shells were found in the car's trunk.

Other evidence told a another story about Moretti's death. All of his pockets had been pulled out and emptied; even the labels on his clothes had been ripped off. But lastly, most obviously, the only thing found on Moretti's person was an aluminum comb.

To those who'd picked up corpses of hoods, the comb was a concise symbol. It fit with all the petty mementos left with victims through the years, from the nickel in the hand of one believed by the 42 Gang to be a stool pigeon, to the valentine left on the body of Machine Gun Jack McGurn, to the tiny coffins sent to Teddy Roe. It was a significant albeit disdainful gesture, rooted in the deep Sicilian regard for signs and symbolism. The comb stood for the act of "combing clean," and was a reference to the body of Leon Marcus, which hadn't been.

Further investigation revealed that the auto Moretti had been found in had been spotted two weeks earlier in Phoenix, Arizona. Police there confirmed its arrival and found that a man identified as Willie Daddano had checked into a motel as "Mr. Tony Daddeno, Cicero, Illinois." Speculation followed that Daddano may have been there to contact Ruth Weidner, Marcus' mistress, or perhaps Marcus himself. Whatever the reason, Salvatore Moretti was last seen alive by his brother Vincent when Sal touched him for $10. Vincent said Salvatore was the only person in the family with any money and a credit rating because the family had gone broke defending Michael in his murder trial. He also said when he'd last seen him Sal had just finished getting a haircut and a shave, a statement believed by detectives, for Salvatore, in as bad a shape as he was when he was found on Caton Farm Road, was clean shaven.

The murder track went no further than that. Chicago police reverted to their old ways of tacitly blessing the work of mob hit men. Police Commissioner Timothy O'Connor pulled his men off the Moretti case, insisting it hadn't happened in Chicago. "I'm glad it didn't happen here," O'Connor said. "He got mixed up with some of those tough Joliet hoods." To which Will County sheriff Roy Doerfler sniffed, "We don't have hoodlums in Joliet. I'm sure it happened in Chicago. I wish they'd stop dumping bodies down here. This happens about twice a year."

As the Moretti investigation bogged down, so did the Marcus probe. But evidence uncovered in the months and years that followed gave reasons for Marcus' killing. It involved Marcus' knack, as demonstrated in the Hodge scandal, for setting up convenient but fraudulent financial schemes. On paper, the $100,000 Marcus received from Giancana was to have applied to a mortgage Marcus' Southmoor Securities, his special holding company, had drawn up on the River Road Motel. Actually, investigators believed, the mortgage existed on paper only, as an income-tax dodge for Giancana. The $100,000 receipt was the visible proof of payment, but actually the money remained Giancana's all the time. Such a scheme would explain why Marcus, after ostensibly receiving the money from Giancana in February, 1955, left it in the bank and never used it or invested it. It was there when he was killed.

Marcus' murder, it is believed, was not tied to the transaction as much as it was to his upcoming trial for mishandling bank funds and making false bank entries. In an attempt to uncover the extent of Marcus' many financial dealings, the prosecution would have questioned the Giancana transaction, and it would have questioned Giancana. With Marcus out of the way, the only things left behind were the mortgage on the motel and the $100,000 in cash. The mortgage was dutifully paid off each month as long as Giancana held interest in the motel. The payments were made by his half-brother Charles, who by that time was going by the name Charles Kane and had only marginal connection with his brother or the outfit. The $100,000 in the years that followed lay untouched, used only by the various owners of the Southmoor Bank as part of their assets, unclaimed by the executors of Marcus' estate because they felt it was Giancana's money, unclaimed by Giancana because it would implicate him in the Marcus murder and because it would bring renewed IRS probes into his income. The money remained for 15 years according to Illinois state law, then it was unceremoniously added to the state treasury. It was a predictable ending to the Marcus and Moretti murders, acts precipitated by questionable financial deals, ended with the silent passage of the money in question. Only Giancana survived unscathed, untouched by the tax men, his public image as a hood sharply enhanced, his private image as an enforcer manifested to his associates as markedly as the comb on Sal Moretti's body.

Soon after, he seemed ubiquitous. FBI agents Hill, Roemer, and Marshall Rutland were watching his every move, and reporters aware of the Bureau's new beat milked agents for any material they could scrape together on him or his associates. Not only could Giancana not avoid personal recognition wherever he went, but he became linked however tenuously with hosts of concessions operated by the syndicate directly and others in which they held only remote interests. If a casino, handbook, or policy operation wasn't controlled by him it was run with his sanction, or with a piece of the action being skimmed and delivered to "the man out west," a reference to him, first of all, then Accardo and Ricca.

An example of such a setup was explained to federal prosecutors in 1961 by Gerald Covelli, a small-time hood who went to prison on auto-theft convictions. Covelli, in exchange for government consideration of his jail term, revealed the detailed setup of the gambling and payoff schemes put into operation on Chicago's hustling Near North Side, an area that attracted the hoods with its Rush Street joints and contained the Gold Coast, one of the city's most opulent areas. With Giancana as overlord, the area was divided by syndicate figures into areas. Concentrating mostly on taverns and nightclubs, the outfit set up bookie operations, police payoff schemes, juke boxes, and loan-shark operations. In some cases, the outfit actually took part interest in businesses when owners got into financial trouble or needed some kind of protection. The combined take during the late 1950's, Covelli said, came to approximately $50,000 a month. Skimmed off the top was an even 10 percent that went to Giancana. "The big boss out west doesn't care who controls the North Side as long as he gets his cut," Covelli said.

Covelli said that the control of the lucrative gambling areas on the North Side became so precise that the outfit sold corners to bookies for a flat $1,500. That payment insured the freedom to operate and total protection from police. About 25 corners were sold in the Rush Street area alone. A percentage of that money became so attractive to police that they also arranged intricate business setups with the hoods. "When a new police captain is assigned to the district, the outfit will explore the possibility of doing business with him," Covelli said. "Until they establish a working relation, they pull out of the district all horse-betting operations, girls, bingo, and B-girls." Covelli's information proved accurate close to a dozen years later when, in 1973, eighteen Chicago policemen, including a district commander, from the Near North Side were convicted of operating shakedown schemes with mob figures that had origins in the late 1950's.

Control of the various saloons and clubs was seldom brought about by terror, Covelli said, but by playing financial angles. No business is as vulnerable to outside problems as a saloon operation, for liquor violations, complications with liquor and bar supplies, police investigations, and general operating difficulties occur constantly. The mob gained its toehold through juke boxes. By placing a box in a club it could see if the place was bustling or struggling, if it had problems with police, if it needed a license to stay open later. Whatever the problem, the mob would somehow work out a way to solve it, and it would have a marker on the club. If outright financial assistance was needed to keep the place afloat, the mob supplied the money and became silent but active partners.

And every nickel that changed hands had some piece of it earmarked for the man "out west." In the course of describing the North Side operations (and Covelli did so with supreme risk, for reliable word was passed that a $20,000 contract had been taken out on him as soon as he began talking), Covelli named names. They became known along with Giancana as the operating outfit, no longer bagmen or errand boys, but, like Giancana, "made" hoods. Top among them was Ross Prio, a short, portly Sicilian who ranked as one of the strongest, richest hoods in the outfit and whose power rivaled that of any in the syndicate outside of Giancana, Accardo, or Ricca. Below Prio was Joe DiVarco, a tough, bespectacled hood who concentrated almost exclusively on his North Side interests but occasionally carried out important murder contracts for the mob. With DiVarco was Jimmie "The Monk" Allegretti, the payoff man and bar politician. Others included the three Doms—Dominick Nuccio, Dominick DiBella, Dominick Brancata; Marshall Caifano, and a name out of Giancana's distant past, Ralph Orlando. Orlando had slugged his way through Taylor Street with the 42's, landed in jail on rape charges and auto-theft raps. Finally, after bungling the midnight warehouse burglary with Giancana and Tumpa Russo in 1928, Orlando went to Joliet for a five-year stay. Thirty years later he was still in the rackets, though nowhere near the status of his old burglary mate, taking care of a slice of the North Side.

Such setups as those Covelli described on the North Side were typical of others operating all over the city, each sanctioned by Giancana. His specialty, however, continued to be his gambling operations in the wide-open suburban territories. In June, 1957, two months after the Marcus-Moretti murders, he was brought to trial for the 1951 Wagon Wheel indictment. He sat bored and silent as the state attempted to prove his connection with the casino from six-year-old evidence, then smiled when the case was thrown out of court. The Wagon Wheel, however, then at its best-known location, on Narragansett in Norwood Township, came under repeated crackdowns from police and prosecutors, usually when it was politically beneficial. The raids generally resulted in the arrests of the casino's managers, but seldom, if ever, interrupted operations for any period of time.

A raid on another Norwood Township joint, this one on Gunnison Street, turned up yet another figure from Giancana's past, the third participant in the ill-fated 1928 burglary: Thomas "Tumpa" Russo. Though Russo was acquitted in 1928, he managed to get himself in enough trouble through the years to make honest employment a problem. He accepted a little help from old friends, kept Giancana's casinos running smoothly, and on a number of occasions took a fall for his boss when the place was raided. Russo was among many needed to run Giancana's ever-expanding, bustling suburban joints. One of the biggest was the Retreat, actually two houses at 6540 North Milwaukee Avenue in Niles Township, just northwest of Chicago. Besides the usual gambling, Giancana also set up a bar—beer at a dollar a bottle —B-girls (women who hustled drinks, primarily), prostitutes, and full-scale horse betting. Running the Retreat was Rocco "The Parrot" Potenza, so named because of his nose and his squawk-like voice, one of Giancana's most trusted gambling managers. To get in, a player had to know somebody; then he passed through steel-plated doors and lost his money totally undisturbed.

Through the years the joints opened and closed, often on the same premises. The Retreat on Milwaukee Avenue later reopened under the name New Riviera Lounge. This time it was run by Thomas Potenza, Rocco's brother, and though it offered the same games, it was much more difficult to get in. One had to pass through the "front" lounge and its two dining rooms, an office, two boiler rooms, a garage, a hallway, then climb 27 stairs before the chips could be heard.

Because gambling operations were fly-by-night businesses— even in the comfortable territories of unincorporated Cook County—they had to be run with speed and flexibility. Few men were able to do it as smoothly as Giancana and his lieutenants. With Rocco Potenza once again, he opened a casino just south of Wheeling, Illinois, far north of Chicago, again in an unincorporated township so sparsely built up that the joint was put into a metal quonset hut. From the outside it looked like an airplane hangar, but inside it was carpeted and air conditioned, and offered any game going, particularly dice tables with $100 bets.

Early 1950's lineup photo. First ever of Giancana to appear in newspapers. Taken during his apprenticeship to Accardo and Ricca in the aging Capone mob of post-World War II. *(Chicago Daily News Photo)*

The family traveling together and staying together. Taken during one of his frequent Hawaiian vacations. Giancana outside of Chicago was not so reluctant to be photographed. Perno family at the time occupied Giancana's Oak Park home and provided parental guidance for Francine, Giancana's youngest daughter. June 14, 1963. L. to r.: Francine, Giancana, Marie Perno, James B. Perno, Annette Perno, and an unidentified man who gave name as James B. Grange. *(Carter Photo Service)*

Taken in a London nightclub in 1962. L. to r.: Christine McGuire,
Dorothy McGuire, Frederick Jones, Giancana, and Phyllis McGuire.
(Chicago Daily News Photo)

At one of his few courtroom successes, Giancana is seen outside
federal court chambers with attorney Anthony Tisci (left), his
son-in-law (husband of daughter Bonnie), and his lawyer for the
case, George N. Leighton (on the right). Occasion was suit against
the FBI for harrassment. Giancana won suit only to have it overturned in higher court. The man over Giancana's left shoulder is
Chuckie English. July 15, 1963. *(Chicago Daily News Photo)*

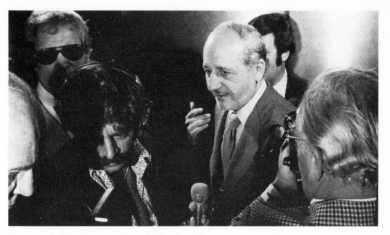

Surrounded by press, the bearded, aging Giancana appears in
Chicago's federal building to testify before grand jury. July 23, 1974.
(Chicago Sun-Times Photo)

The Godfather Room. Remodeled basement room in Giancana's
home, believed site of many mob meetings in his early days. Room
is next to basement kitchen where he was killed. *(Chicago Sun-Times
Photo)*

The murder weapon—.22 automatic, 10-shot pistol with homemade silencer, and clip. Found in nearby Forest Preserve two months after murder. August 27, 1975. *(Chicago Daily News Photo)*

Paul "The Waiter" Ricca, nee Felice DeLucia; until death in 1972, the Godfather of the Chicago mob. Long-time supporter of Giancana.

Tony Accardo, Capone gang graduate and reputed to be the present day Godfather and most powerful mobster in Chicago and the Midwest.

Charles "Chuckie" English, one of Giancana's closest friends and associates, boyhood chum, golfing partner.

Gus Alex, top Giancana underboss of Loop, Near North Side Chicago, still active.

Mad Sam DeStefano, loan shark, the mad hatter of the Chicago mob until shotgunned to death in 1973.

Fiore "Fifi" Buccieri, one-time top enforcer, dead of natural causes.

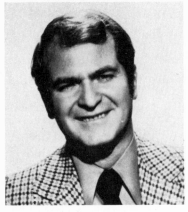

Richard Cain, hood, cop, Giancana's chauffeur, courier, advance man. A brilliant double-dealer, murdered 1973.

Jackie Cerone, top Accardo underboss, still active.

Dominick "Butch" Blasi, long-time chauffeur, confidant to Giancana, questioned by police as one of the suspects in the murder probe.

Marshall Caifano, Giancana lieutenant, convicted extortionist, still active.

Rocco Pranno, fearsome
suburban Chicago enforcer,
lieutenant of Giancana.

John Matassa, sometime
Giancana chauffeur, courier.

Ross Prio, strong underboss, ran
North Side and Rush Street for
Giancana, a don in his own right,
now dead of natural causes.

Rocco "The Parrot" Potenza,
long-time gambling lieutenant
of Giancana.

Charles "Chuckie" Nicoletti and Felix "Milwaukee Phil" Alderisio:
one-time team of executioners. Alderisio (right), now dead but
once considered the most fearsome hood anywhere; Nicoletti still
active, a worthy successor.

Morris Llewelyn "Murray" Humphreys, known as "The Camel"
and "The Hump" to the press,
was "Curly" to the mob. A Capone veteran, Humphreys was
perhaps the most brilliant mob
mind ever in Chicago. A Welshman, professorial, he devised
legal strategies and political fixes
that have yet to be equaled. Died
of heart failure in 1965.

John Formosa, Giancana's Las
Vegas emissary, one-time northern Indiana gambling boss.

Roulette wheels and blackjack tables were nearby, all the games being played with chips, instead of cash as in other joints. A small bar and snack area kept players greased, but the action was for established high-stakes players—only well-known players got in—and it concentrated around the tables, where as much as $25,000 individual losses were not uncommon.

The hut was hidden by abandoned trucks and massive road machinery conveniently parked around it. Even the front portion of the hut was filled with ladders and building materials. Entrance to the tables was located in the rear, and that was watched by two of Potenza's men. Players were even brought in from the Villa Venice, a nearby nightclub Giancana opened in late 1962 with the hopes of someday turning it into an operation as big as clubs in Las Vegas. Until that happened, however, the money was to be made in the quonset hut and other similar establishments.

Another lucrative concession was the juke-box business, and the supply and manufacture of popular phonograph records. The operation was one that had long attracted syndicate gangsters because it gave them access to saloons, and the very nature of the business, like vending machines, lent itself to the use of muscle when encountering pub owners reluctant to take a new machine. A third characteristic, and an attractive one, was that juke boxes served as money laundries—a massive flow of cash that was difficult to monitor and easily mixed with moneys from other sources.

Giancana's move into the industry was through a trusted friend from the Patch, Charles Carmen "Chuckie" English. A good-looking, good-natured hood, English as a youth gained a reputation not so much for being a punk as for being a romancer. He dressed well and got around, courting ladies young and old on both arms. By the 1950's, he was one of Giancana's closest associates and most intimate friends. He opened Lormar Distributing at 5954 West Roosevelt, a complete record-supply house for juke boxes. With the backing of Giancana, the muscle and knowledge of Joseph Glimco, old-time Capone mobster Eddie Vogel, English's older brother Sam, and a veteran in the business, Fred "Juke Box" Smith, English thrived with Lormar. He pushed business into counties outside of Chicago's Cook, and even into Arizona, where he had bought a spacious resort ranch. The McClellan Committee cited English's juke-box enterprise in its rackets probe, naming him a front man for Giancana, and charging him with manufacturing counterfeit 45 rpm records for distribution. In 1959, Special Prosecutor Richard Ogilvie, the same man who had headed the income-tax probe of Tony Accardo, turned his sights on Lormar and vowed to get to the bottom of the juke-box business.

English never slowed his operation, however, and used it as a base to dip into other juke-box-related activities. Lormar prospered well enough not only to cement his relationship with Giancana, but to give him the means in 1960 to buy a ten-room Spanish-style house in exclusive River Forest, a western Chicago suburb that drew increasing numbers of known hoodlums, including Tony Accardo. Giancana, meanwhile, realized sizable earnings from his interest in Lormar, but left it entirely under English's domain.

English was but one of the faces commonly placed with Giancana. As his power and influence grew, he was able to handpick lieutenants and bagmen, bodyguards and chauffeurs. One of them was Dominick "Butch" Blasi, a chunky, bull-necked Italian who served Giancana in more capacities than as a torpedo, and became one of his closest friends. Blasi was not the silent, unfeeling musclehead that many took him for. He had first been brought into the mob by James Belcastro, a top Capone enforcer, who got the nickname "The Bomber" because he was put in charge of bombing competing stills and breweries during Prohibition. Blasi originally was singled out by Paul Ricca to go to Dallas and expand the Chicago mob's interests there, but he was unceremoniously kicked out of that city and returned to be appointments secretary and courier for Tony Accardo. When Giancana made his rise, Blasi was detailed to him in a similar capacity. Blasi soon became much more than a shadow—although he handled most of his boss's mundane chores and some private ones, such as leasing autos and making arrangements for Giancana's girlfriends. He also grew to become a trusted, highly regarded intimate.

There were other couriers, among them Johnny Matassa, a one-time copy boy for Chicago's *American* who joined the Chicago Police Department, then officially drifted to the other side of the law and went to work for the mob. Others were Joe Pignatello, a chauffeur who was later sent to Las Vegas, and William "The Saint" Skally, a dealer on many levels for the syndicate who seemed to turn up wherever there was a dollar to be made. He had arrests for bootlegging, art thefts, gambling, and armed robbery, and in 1953 he was named in a federal indictment as the brains behind a $3 million counterfeiting ring. His counterfeiting abilities also came into play for Giancana and Chuck English in the record business, and he was connected to English's Lormar Distributing by the McClellan Committee.

As talented as Skally was, and as far back as his friendships went—he had close ties not only to Giancana and his contemporaries but to Capone mobsters such as Anthony "Tough Tony" Capezio—his contacts did him no good when he attempted to skim from the outfit. In late 1959, he was entrusted with large sums of mob money that Giancana was directing toward concessions in Mexico, particularly a dog-racing track. Skally acted as courier of the funds, believed to be as much as $1 million in cash, and also as a go-between with Mexican politicians who needed to be taken care of. Throughout 1959, he made as many as eight or nine trips to Mexico City, occasionally stopping off at Las Vegas. Skally, however, was doing poorly in Mexico, and the deal was not getting off the ground. He, nevertheless, was digging deeply into the cash, even though Giancana demanded it back if the dog track did not go through. When it didn't, and Skally could not come up with the money, he was found shot twice in the head in the front seat of a car parked in a church parking lot in River Forest. The car was parked midway between the homes of Accardo and Paul Ricca, two men Skally knew well, but who could not save him from the wrath of Giancana.

Such contracts were carried out swiftly and viciously for Giancana by Felix "Milwaukee Phil" Alderisio. Alderisio and Charles Nicoletti, a veteran of Giancana's West Side, became known as the mob's foremost enforcers as Giancana took over its day-to-day affairs. The two expertly honed the details of their specialty, once even constructing a hit car that contained a false back seat for storing shotguns, a switch to turn off the tail lights, and a fake radio grille used for hiding handguns. The car was discovered one night, with Alderisio and Nicoletti cowering on the floor, near a North Side apartment building. They explained they were only "waiting for someone," and though they were later released, they never claimed the car and it was sold at a police auction. Alderisio made few such mistakes again, and his reputation as an enforcer thrived, entered next to those of other trusted killers, Willie Daddano and Fiore Buccieri. Ne'er-do-wells like William Skally were notches in their guns.

Much of the information about Skally, Chuck English, Alderisio, Joey Glimco, and the dozens of other Chicago hoods who worked the rackets with Giancana's direction and Ricca and Accardo's blessings was brought out by the McClellan Committee, and particularly by its young, aggressive counsel, Robert F. Kennedy. In its attempt to investigate the influx of organized crime into labor and management, the committee, like the Kefauver Committee before it, took testimony from most of the country's prominent hoods. Yet in 1957, the first year of hearings, it was unable to serve a subpoena on Giancana. Although he appeared predictably at business meetings, hangouts, sports events, and at his home, he somehow managed to avoid the servers. The situation got so irksome to the committee that in July, 1958, they suggested serving a subpoena on his oldest daughter Antoinette. Due to Antoinette, coincidentally, that wasn't necessary. On April 4, 1959, she was married to Carmen Manno, a young bartender and aspiring golfer, and in a style not seen among Chicago gangsters since the Capone days, for Father Sam had decided to put on a spread. It took place in the Loop's LaSalle Hotel, no secret to the press, police, federal subpoena servers, or the mob, for by anyone's social standards the wedding of Sam Giancana's first daughter was an *affair.*

Perhaps it was due to the fact that he had never really been much of a father to his daughters, an absentee one at best, or because he realized he had forced them to live in a very closed, secretive society, one that pushed them to schools in other cities, that made them choose their friends wisely, and always, always hesitate to divulge their surname. Or perhaps it was because Antoinette had always had a rough time of it and yet she was most like her father, or because after the death of their mother a wedding was one of the few family times he had to share with them. Perhaps owing to all of those factors Giancana felt it important not only to celebrate the wedding but to fete it.

Or, as more cynical observers were wont to believe, Giancana's bash had little to do with his devotion to his daughter and a lot to do with his standing in the outfit. As the mob's operating boss, he not only could bask in his ability to throw such a shindig, but he was able to demand and get the homage of his associates. The word went out that those who received the engraved, gold-lettered invitations were expected to show up with a handsome cash tribute to the newlyweds. Earlier, the wives of his associates were invited to a "currency only" shower for Antoinette, which raised, much to the resentment of many hoods, a reported $30,000. Keeping one's hold on the outfit meant muscle and politics, and Giancana did well at both.

After the vows had been repeated before thirty or so members of the family, the couple received guests in the hotel's Illinois Room. Antoinette, with her hair dyed platinum blond, stood tall and resplendent in a white satin gown, one very much like that her mother had worn. Next to her stood younger sister Bonnie, her only attendant. Then came Sam, who dressed in tails. More than 400 guests paraded by, friends and neighbors from Taylor Street, many of them Sam's associates and all of them uncomfortable in tight-fitting tuxedoes, their wives in stacked hairdos and sable jackets, but all of them there.

They milled around sipping champagne—Sam had promised Antoinette "a river of champagne"—and then prepared to sit down to a full dinner. But first Sam was told of problems, and again they concerned the press. On the hotel's second floor, a caterer had spread a bevy of guest cards on a table and they were spotted by Sandy Smith, a *Tribune* reporter specializing in keeping tabs on Chicago's hoods. Smith recorded the guest list, which read like one of his year-end mob features. On it were Tony Accardo, Felix Alderisio, Gus Alex, Joey Aiuppa, Joseph Amata, Sam Battaglia, Louis Briatta, Marshall Caifano, Willie Daddano, Joey DiVarco, Frank Ferraro, Albert Frabotta, John Lardino, Chuck English, Chuck Nicoletti, Angelo Perotti—every hood of any consequence in Chicago except Paul Ricca, who was in prison.

Seeing Smith and other reporters gaping at the cards, Giancana moved in and pushed them away, snarling epithets as he went. Reporters tried to explain that it was only proper to report important guests at a prominent social affair, but Giancana wasn't convinced. "Why bother us this way?" he said. "Sure, some of us are ex-convicts, but are we supposed to suffer for a few mistakes we made in our youth?"

Then he went off to join his guests, who were sitting down to a meal of cream of fresh pea soup, boneless half of spring chicken, fresh mushrooms in wine sauce, wild-rice croquettes, fresh asparagus tips in drawn butter, limestone lettuce with sliced avocados, ice cream molded in shapes of wedding bells, slippers, and Cupids, French pastries, and a seven-tiered wedding cake. Whether the guests liked it or not, it was strictly non-Italian fare, from the thin WASP food to the dancing in the prestigious 19th-floor ballroom, where a 15-piece orchestra cooed gently in the background.

It far overshadowed an affair across town in which Joey Glimco, an important mob labor racketeer and featured star of the McClellan hearings, was marrying off his son Joseph, Jr., to the daughter of a Chicago police captain. Glimco also attracted intelligence police, agents, and McClellan Committee investigators, and when he spotted them as he walked into the Edgewater Beach Hotel on Chicago's Far North Side for the wedding reception, he spat at them. Later, he had to hustle downtown to appear at the Giancana fest.

Though Glimco couldn't manage a happy face for the press, Giancana softened later in the reception and chatted amiably with Sandy Smith. He said the McClellan Committee's probe and others like it would "lead to the biggest crime wave ever," for it did nothing but persecute and adversely expose alleged criminals.

"An ex-con can't get a job now," he said. "He has to get a gun and go out and hold people up to get something to eat. There's going to be a lot of crime if this keeps up. It'll be worse than Capone.

"Look at that kid," he went on, pointing to his new son-in-law. "Now everybody is going to hook him up with me. No one will hire him.

"I'll have to give him a .45 and put him to work for me."

At that he laughed out loud. He was completely at ease, a little warmed by the champagne, pleased with the wedding and the reception, and graciously accepting compliments from his friends and relatives.

Asked about the McClellan Committee's attempt to subpoena

him, he again laughed. "They couldn't find me for a year. And I was in Chicago all the time. I like to hide from them. It was fun.

"I'd like to tell them to go to hell, but I guess I'll keep my mouth shut and take the Fifth."

He was going now and enjoying himself. Smith asked him about the fact that his draft board had rejected him as a "psychopath."

"Who wouldn't pretend he was nuts to stay out of the army? When they called me to the board they asked me what kind of work I did. I told them I stole for a living." He chuckled once again.

"They thought I was crazy, but I wasn't. I was telling them the truth."

It was perhaps the most effusive performance Giancana had ever given in public. And he rather enjoyed it, even to the point of wanting to philosophize.

"What's wrong with the syndicate anyhow? Two or three of us get together on some deal and everybody says it's a bad thing. Other businessmen do it all the time and nobody squawks."

Then he went off to oversee the rest of the proceedings. Antoinette and Carmen flew off to a West Coast honeymoon. Giancana stayed behind to pick up the tab: $20,000.

A more troublesome cost, however, was the subpoena it had brought him. On June 8, he finally appeared before Senator McClellan and his committee, its counsel Robert F. Kennedy, and a sarcastic committee investigator named Pierre Salinger. Giancana, in his customary dark glasses but wearing a conspicuous hairpiece, had only a three-by-five card in front of him, on which was printed the Fifth Amendment. He read from it when Kennedy asked him about the $520,846 in income he had reported in the years 1950–1957. Then Salinger quoted for the committee the interview Giancana had granted Sandy Smith. During it Giancana smiled and laughed. Kennedy then asked, "Are you going to tell us anything or just giggle? I thought only little girls giggled." Giancana took the Fifth. Senator McClellan asked if he was happy being a thief. Giancana took the Fifth.

He repeated himself when Salinger asked about Leon Marcus and his murder. Then Salinger pieced together a scenario of the mob's move into rackets in Lake County, just north of Chicago's Cook County. He said that Giancana and Accardo had gone to Los

Angeles in 1953 to persuade Anthony Pinelli, a one-time Chicago hood, to return to the Midwest and take over the Lake County concessions, including juke boxes, gambling, pinball machines, and prostitution. Pinelli accepted the offer, according to Salinger, and in the next few years turned the county into a lucrative part of the Chicago outfit's holdings.

Giancana listened impassively, then took the Fifth. In all, he read from his notecard 34 times.

Yet outside the hearing room he reverted to the style he'd started with Sandy Smith. To another reporter he mumbled, "Those birds got me all wrong. What a rap. You'd think I control every racket in the country."

"Don't you?" the reporter replied.

"Cut it out," he said. "Cops all over the country think I have it my way. I can't understand why they dragged me into this Lake County business."

The reporter suggested he tell his side of the story to the committee. Giancana guffawed, laughing so hard that his glasses almost fell from his face. But the reporter persisted: "When was the last time you were in Lake County?"

"C'mon," complained Giancana. "I have difficulty remembering the states. Don't throw counties at me."

But that was enough chatter for him. When the reporter asked another question, Giancana mumbled, "It's getting stuffy in here." Then he went for the elevator.

From Washington and the hearings, he flew off to Mexico for a two-week vacation. As talkative as he had been outside the committee's chambers, he had managed to keep quiet inside them. But he was taking his chances, bumping against a public eye more penetrating than he had been used to. And it plagued him most at home, where he was unable to keep from getting embroiled in petty legal problems. As his steps were dogged ever more closely by federal agents, police, and the press, Giancana began to rue the very fact of his visibility. The exposure they brought his way soon began to bog him down, to the point where the more he appeared in public, the more he lost face, enough so that he developed an unsettling paranoia about it.

A typical incident occurred when he arrived back in Chicago from Mexico in late June. Alerted by FBI agents, customs officials at Midway Airport searched every inch of his belongings. Giancana complied affably, even when he was asked to take off the pants to his silk suit. It was a check of his wallet that changed his mood. An agent found his driver's license in the name of Frank DeSanto, 50, 3436 West Adams. When asked about it Giancana growled, "It's a guy I know. So the license is in his name. So what?" So it was enough for customs agents to notify the Illinois Secretary of State's office.

If the incident at customs didn't convince him, the word came down from Tony Accardo. As powerful as Giancana was, he had broken some important outfit rules by his display at Antoinette's wedding. Accardo abhorred that kind of exposure. He felt it inexcusable for any mob figure to associate with reporters or get chummy with them, and he was even more wary of the possibility that someone in his cups would babble on about things. As a general rule, Accardo advised against any such public contact, that it was better to put one's hat on, keep a stiff jaw, and walk away. When Giancana hadn't done that, when he had acted so cavalier as to talk about the McClellan hearings, and even given credence to the existence of a syndicate as he had with Sandy Smith, it was within Accardo's power to take him aside and give him the word.

He may not have had to do that, given the embarrassment Giancana had suffered at customs. In any case, Giancana went about preparing for yet another wedding in total secrecy. His daughter Bonnie, only 19 and perhaps more sensitive than Antoinette to the publicity her father brought on, prepared to marry Anthony Tisci, a young, good-looking law student who worked as secretary to U.S. Representative Roland Libonati. Although Libonati had a notorious reputation as a friend of gangsters and a foe of anti-crime bills—he considered Al Capone a personal friend—Tisci was a low-key, serious person who disliked personal publicity. In deference to him and the wishes of Bonnie, Giancana arranged for the wedding and reception to be held in Miami Beach at the Fontainebleau Hotel.

He managed it very well. On the Fourth of July, the day of the wedding and also the day Tony Accardo traditionally threw a grand lawn party for the entire outfit at his home, Giancana was nowhere to be found. The *Trib*'s Sandy Smith hustled to Accardo's party to take up his vigil. (Smith had this down to an art. In

1956, he rented a room in the house adjoining Accardo's yard and spent the entire Fourth watching Accardo's party from a window.) But this year, with Accardo in trouble with the federal prosecutor, the party was held at the house of Jackie Cerone, an Accardo lieutenant. Only twenty or so guests showed up, Smith noted, and no Giancana. Accardo came, looking subdued in slacks and a sport shirt—in past years he'd decked himself out in Bermuda shorts—and drove his wife's Volkswagen. It left Smith with the impression that times were down for the mob, or at least Accardo, and that the lawn bash wasn't what it used to be. He had no idea that the bulk of the outfit were in Miami Beach at the Giancana wedding.

It was no secret in Miami, however. After a ceremony at St. Patrick's Catholic Church, the wedding party and 200 guests waded into a private reception at the Fontainebleau. Things were lavish—this one cost Giancana $10,000—but by no means as open as Antoinette's wedding. The guests, many of them conspicuous with their dark glasses, passed by suspicious guards, who stopped and checked everybody. A Miami society columnist managed to slip by and grab a glass of champagne, but before she could lose herself in the crowd, which she described as subdued and self-conscious, she was spotted and escorted out. Though Giancana himself once again presided in grand fashion over the affair, though he once again had been touched by the loss of another daughter and had been observed dabbing at his eyes as he gave her away at the altar, he granted no interviews and allowed nobody not a part of the proceedings to get close to him.

The strategy was a success on the Chicago front too, but for a different reason. On July 6, 1959, Queen Elizabeth and her entourage were due to visit the city. The town and its newspapers were agog over the event. On one of the few occasions in its history, Chicago preferred to ignore the doings of its gangsters in favor of royalty. Only the *Tribune* made a small mention of Bonnie Giancana's wedding to Representative Roland Libonati's secretary, and that was tucked deep inside the paper. The papers instead were pawns before the Queen, filling pages with parade routes, features, and news stories about the hubbub surrounding her visit. The *Sun-Times* ran a long "open letter" to the Queen, headlined "This Is Our Chicago." In it, the paper gushed over the city's beauty, its history, its parks, its newly completed $183 million Congress Expressway, its museums, its Montgomery Ward and Sears corporations, its schools, its river, which flows backward to keep its pollution to itself and not contaminate Lake Michigan, its slum-clearance projects, and even its orchestra. The letter made no mention of its biggest tourist attractions, however, the site of the St. Valentine's Day massacre, Dion O'Banion's flowershop, or Al Capone's old New Michigan Hotel, and it failed to note that its gangsters still thrived and maintained the city's Capone-era reputation. The Queen didn't seem to notice, though, and after a State Street parade with Mayor Richard J. Daley at her side, she said that she found Chicago "wonderful." In souvenir issues of the day's newspapers she wouldn't find a story on the Giancana event (it was reported more fully in New York City's papers) and she wouldn't know how well it went.

As smoothly as Giancana had pulled off his daughter's wedding this time around, it would be only months before he would again flop in public. Officials in the Illinois Secretary of State's office investigated his driver's license and found that it had not only expired in November of 1958, but that it too was probably fraudulent. They had reason to believe that someone else had taken the driver's license test and signed Giancana's name, spelling it "Gianciana" in the process. Hence, the office not only sought to revoke his license but to serve an arrest warrant for the phony license discovered at customs. It wasn't until October that they found a chance to do it.

It came when Giancana was forced to appear before Richard Ogilvie and his special federal grand jury probe into the mob's juke-box and Rush Street affairs. On October 6, Giancana appeared for 25 minutes before the grand jury, at the U.S. Courthouse in Chicago's Loop. Waiting for him, along with two dozen reporters, photographers, and cameramen, all back in form after the Queen's visit, were officials from the Secretary of State's office ready to serve him with notice of his license revocation. With them were Illinois State Police, who hoped to be armed with a warrant for his arrest. But the troopers' timing was just off.

Knowing what he was in for as soon as he stepped out of the grand jury room, and totally piqued by the whole affair, Giancana literally ran out of the room and into an elevator, then ran from the elevator toward the street. "Persecution! This is persecution!" he yelled at reporters, and then added a choice string of obscenities. On his heels, as he went for Dearborn Street and a taxi, were Richard Gorman, his lawyer, a horde of reporters and photographers, and secretary of state investigators with their license revocation. The state troopers were left flatfooted at the door because the warrant they needed to make their arrest hadn't arrived yet.

But they were hardly missed, for Giancana and the corps behind him barged through midday crowds, knocking some people off their feet. Giancana himself sprinted right into traffic, causing tires to squeal and autos to swerve to avoid hitting him. He jerked open the door of a cab and pulled Gorman inside with him, then shielded his head with a newspaper. The cab was held up in traffic long enough for the license-revocation notice to be thrown through the window onto his lap. The arrest warrant showed up five minutes after he had made his escape.

But again he had made his appearance, and bungled it badly. Newspapers filled front pages with shots of his jog into traffic. Journalists reveled in his disdain for them, and they faithfully described him as the most ill-mannered hood in town. A month later he was quietly found guilty of the violation—a judge noted that the physical description of "Frank DeSanto" on Giancana's license matched that of Giancana himself—and paid a fine of $100.

No year to date had been as rough on him publicly as had 1959. But his power went undiminished. He was 51, the aggressive, shrewd operating director of a large metropolitan business organization, and he could roll with the punches of his social gaffes. Also, mob patriarch Paul Ricca was in prison, and without his direct hand there would be no serious threat to Giancana's position, even if things went sour. The following year things were to get worse for Tony Accardo. A jury would find him guilty on all counts of income-tax fraud and sentence him to a six-year term in the federal penitentiary.

11

BY 1959 the FBI effort against the outfit in Chicago was in full swing. Agents were becoming more sure of their adversary and of themselves; their techniques were better defined, more effective. The assignment was more exciting for them, more diverse than anything they had ever done before, and they began to relish the beat. The better they got, the more committed they became, and the better they were able to get inside the lives of the men they tracked. To other police agencies, and to the hoods themselves, the "G" as FBI agents were dubbed, were "Boy Scouts," straight shooters who couldn't be bought, who conveyed a righteous indignation for the crimes hoods committed. And the agents played on that reputation, developing an *esprit de corps* that was remarkably competitive yet complementary. Individual agents were responsible for particular hoods—Roemer watched the stylish, professorial Murray Humphreys and Jake Guzik's protégé Gus Alex; Hill had Giancana; Rutland had Frank "Strongy" Ferraro, Giancana's underboss; and so on through the outfit—yet they all covered for each other, passing along information, knowing full well that they had to intermingle as well as the outfit did.

Though the Bureau wasn't the only agency watching the hoods —in Chicago and suburbs as many as six other forces, police and non-police, federal, state, and local, kept some kind of tabs on the mob—it was clearly the most far reaching. Its network of agents was international, its communications, resources, and manpower far more sophisticated. Local agencies, those that weren't in some way corrupted or co-opted, were no match for the syndicate and had no idea how to gather effective information on it or how to conduct worthwhile surveillance. Many didn't try. It was no secret that various village police forces were "taken care of" by the mob to the point where their officers often patrolled mob hangouts and residences to guard them from problems, and from federal agents. Scores of Chicago policemen on all levels did the mob's bidding, and scores were on its payroll. Those who weren't, particularly Joe Morris, William Duffy, and their Scotland Yard group, were scarcely able to function as much more than information gatherers, and little of what they got was hard evidence of crimes committed.

Other efforts came from county or state officials, too often an official looking to make a political reputation. In most cases they dispatched untrained, unsophisticated deputies to trail hoods, and their efforts amounted to little more than publicity-oriented harassment. Dogging the syndicate meant little as long as it did business indoors, away from and out of sight of its tails. What information such surveillance uncovered was little more than names, faces, license numbers, and itineraries. Nothing, again, for all the man hours spent, that provided hard evidence of lawbreaking.

FBI agents soon learned to work around other agencies. And they learned even sooner of the folly of gadfly surveillance. In the early days of their efforts against Giancana, Hill, Roemer, and the others decided to attempt a clamp on him from the moment he left his house. They assembled agents in a fleet of nine autos, all spaced around Oak Park, all with radio communication, and primed to shadow Giancana everywhere. It took fifteen minutes for Giancana, with his best 42 Gang instincts, to spot the tails and lose them. Agents drove in circles trying to pick him up, chattering over their radios, nearly colliding with each other. Later in the morning Giancana helped out by driving up alongside them and saying, "Here I am."

The agents tried to adapt to the habits of their prey, and that meant thinking like hoods. It was another task they took on eagerly. Though Hill, Roemer, and Rutland were G-men through and through: the suits, ties, white shirts, the black surveillance autos, they were smart enough to see past the stereotypes of cops-versus-robbers. They never apologized for the standards of the Bureau, and they took pride in being labeled Boy Scouts, but they still developed a keen appreciation for the personalities, the intelligence, the relative strengths and weaknesses of the men they tried to put in jail. Likewise, their own personalities permeated what they did: some were witty, profane, eager to bait hoods; others were close-mouthed and businesslike; some were titillated by the hoods' sexual exploits; others politely looked away; some were secretive about what they saw and heard; others were uncontrollable gossips. Each was in many ways susceptible to the television Efrem Zimbalist, Jr., image, and at the same time each was an exception to it. To a man, they had an almost fanatic commitment to their incorruptibility, and they believed that they achieved far better results against the mob because the hoods knew they would not nail them on tainted evidence or a phony rap, concocted evidence, hearsay, or perjury. With that, the agents went about their business and the hoods went about theirs.

At first the agents tried selective surveillance, which meant they watched a hood closely until they could establish his routine and his hangouts. In the early days of FBI surveillance, Ralph Hill once dogged Marshall Caifano wherever he went. Caifano soon became aware of his tail, but had no idea who Hill was or what he was doing. Finally, Caifano stopped and confronted him.

"Mr. Hoover wanted me to take time out and see if you guys were doing anything around here that we might be interested in," Hill replied.

"No, no," Caifano assured him. "You can tell him we don't do nothing that you guys could work on."

"Well, what do you guys do?" Hill asked.

"Gambling most of the time," Caifano said. "We got joints, some books. We do a little juice loan, some juke boxes. Nothing you guys would want."

Hill milked him, "All right, it's just that I got to do my job and make a report. It won't be anything more than that."

He explained he had to fill in the gaps. He asked Caifano who did what, and Caifano never hesitated. He proceeded to run down some of the bosses, which territories they controlled, and generally capsulize the basic Chicago organization. Hill nodded and gave the impression he was satisfied.

"Listen, we've got to sit down for a talk. Let me get it down so I can make my report. Then that'll be that," he said.

Caifano agreed. He saw no reason why he shouldn't take care of the Feds and get them off any outfit case. He okayed an afternoon meeting with Hill at a nearby restaurant and parted company. Hill was overjoyed, not only with the information he'd already gotten from Caifano, but at the prospect of what was to come.

Things were interrupted, however, by an ill-timed newspaper story. The day before they were to meet, a Chicago paper reported that the Justice Department was probing organized crime. Shortly after the headline appeared, Hill received a call from Caifano. "Tell Mr. Hill that Mr. Caifano don't want to meet with him any more."

With or without Caifano, Chicago agents were on the verge of making substantial intelligence gains on the mob. Roemer's surveillance of Murray Humphreys and Gus Alex produced the fact that they were frequent visitors to a second-floor tailor shop on North Michigan Avenue. Roemer at the time didn't know the shop was really the headquarters of Frank "Strongy" Ferraro, a mob underboss with a strong standing in the outfit. Until more was known about the shop, agents were not aware how strong.

To get a watch on the shop, agents stationed themselves in an apartment of a friend living across the street. What they found amazed them. It was not only a favorite spot of Humphreys and Alex, but it was a regular morning meeting place for the syndicate's top people. Also appearing were Giancana, Joey Glimco, Accardo, Ferraro, and others, all of them promptly there at nine o'clock. And they assembled, from what the agents could see with binoculars, in order to sit down to hard business.

Hill and Roemer dearly wanted to get an ear into the shop. They filed for permission to install a hidden microphone, but frankly were not optimistic that Washington would okay it. The Justice Department at that time had never authorized such surveillance anywhere in the country. But permission came through. For months they tried to figure a way to tap the tailor shop, which, owing to its location, was seldom unoccupied or unwatched. Finally, after a series of Sunday-morning attempts, they got inside and even then encountered problems. The equipment was unsophisticated—the mike was of World War II vintage and was as big as a soft-drink bottle—and implanting it meant stringing wires throughout the building. They were also blessed with a technician who was competent but clumsy. Once, while stringing wires in a crawl space between floors, he lost his balance and fell onto the ceiling of O'Connell's, the restaurant below, causing the ceiling to buckle. Still, the equipment was finally installed, the microphone placed behind a radiator. It picked up every sound in the room and was never discovered. Nor was the bulge in the ceiling.

The microphone provided a mine of information. Almost on cue, Humphreys, Giancana, and company showed up at the shop, which, agents then learned, they referred to as "Schneider's," and talked into the bug. Only the noise of the radiator in winter obscured the pickup, and agents remedied that by going in with their technician and installing other mikes so that reception was stereophonic. They heard from the hoods' own lips who had the power and how it was distributed, who put the fix in and where it was put, what decisions were made and who was affected, who had the solutions. They heard stories, anecdotes, family problems, even a history of mob decisions as told with relish by Murray Humphreys. And nobody but Humphreys became suspicious, for the agents closely guarded the secret tap and told not even fellow law-enforcement agents or close press contacts. They also took pains to stay away from Schneider's and insure its relative anonymity, wanting the hoods to think that there was no reason to interrupt business as usual. They escaped electronic sweeps ordered by Humphreys by intercepting the order and shutting off the mikes. In all, the ears in Schneider's remained intact for five years, and were to be the biggest, most reliable source of information on the Chicago syndicate anywhere at anytime. Humphreys occasionally had second thoughts. Often he opened the morning meetings by announcing, "Good morning, gentlemen, and anyone listening. This is the nine o'clock meeting of the Chicago underworld."

The mikes in Schneider's also supplied agents with an unusual insight into the relationships of the top hoods with one another. Again, Humphreys, the veteran conjurer, whose specialty, challenged by no one, was political fixing, was most notable. Though he was Welsh, Humphreys played the role of an Old World Sicilian Mustache Pete. He was eloquent and anecdotal, always reasoning slowly and logically, supplying a bit of history or the context of a decision made by Capone, Guzik, or some other past lion that was applicable to a present problem.

He went into elaborate detail one day describing how Paul Ricca was sprung from prison. Convicted of conspiring to extort money from film makers and distributors in the famous Browne-Bioff case, Ricca was sentenced to ten years in prison in 1944, and after that faced prosecution on mail-fraud indictments. Humphreys told his compatriots in Schneider's that his aim was to get the additional indictment dropped, then lobby for early parole. To do it, he said, meant a lot of cash and high-powered influential lawyers.

The indictments were dismissed as a result of the efforts of a Dallas lawyer who was a friend of then Attorney General Tom Clark. The parole situation was pursued by a St. Louis lawyer who had been associated with Truman campaigns in Missouri. Money changed hands, according to Humphreys, in Chicago's Stevens Hotel, now the Conrad Hilton. Humphreys never said how much it was and the details of the transaction were not divulged. But Ricca and three other Capone hoods were paroled after having served three and one-half years in jail, the minimum sentence.

The early release prompted a Congressional investigation. Results were inconclusive because the Congressmen could not obtain the parole board records. They later publicly said that Attorney General Clark had not told them all he knew about the situation.

Clark, who was later appointed to the Supreme Court, saw his reputation sullied by the incident. A 1952 Chicago *Tribune* editorial called him "unfit" for a Supreme Court position for his "considerable role" in the release of Ricca. But Humphreys, as he explained in Schneider's, found the episode memorable. Of many maneuvers, he reminisced, certainly one of his best.

Humphreys was listened to, and generally heeded, but because he was not Italian his was never the last word. Ricca always sat by, the embodiment of the godfather, the wise, ruminating patriarch whose word was steel. Accardo's presence was always felt, his voice and mannerisms as foreboding as his appearance.

Once, when Gus Alex appeared on the verge of a nervous break-down (owing in great part to the heavy surveillance from Roe-mer), he was given some practical advice by Accardo. With his husky, raspy voice, Accardo said, "Take it easy, Slim. Go away to the mountains like I do and chop wood. When I chop wood, I chop and chop and chop and I don't think a nothin' till it's all been chopped. Then I come back all cleaned out and I can go back to work again."

Giancana, given the force of his opinion and the place he had taken in the mob hierarchy, was a voice to be reckoned with. Though he lacked the grace, the wit, the style and eloquence of Humphreys, the control of Ricca and Accardo, he made up for it with a sharp edge for in-fighting, a volatile presence that had to be dealt with. His power was undeniable. One session at Schneider's involved a request for money from Sonny Capone, Al's only son. It became apparent that the Chicago outfit provided a monthly sum for Capone's widow, Mae, and Sonny, both of whom lived in Florida. Sonny, at the time, was operating a res-taurant and doing poorly, and requested an advance of $25,000. A discussion and vote followed and only one person vetoed the request. That was Giancana. But that was enough, and Hum-phreys dictated a short note to be sent to Sonny Capone, com-municating the mob's refusal.

The microphones in Schneider's gave rise to the need for oth-ers. Agents again requested and received permission to plant them in offices, apartments, lounges—anywhere the hoods did business. With each one the agents took pains to keep it a secret, and then attempted to keep far away from the site. Once in place, it became more productive than the legwork of scores of agents. Washington knew it—permission for electronic eavesdropping had to come from Hoover himself but not necessarily with knowledge or consent of the Justice Department—and soon Chi-cago set an example for electronic surveillance for other cities. To agents it wasn't a matter of violating constitutional rights as much as it was a situation of fighting fire with fire. With the encouragement of Hoover, and along the way that of Justice Department officials, especially Attorney General Robert Kennedy after 1961, the Bureau took the position that micro-phones, as well as other surveillance tactics, were weapons to be used to defeat an enemy.

Working against Giancana, Hill and Roemer dearly wanted to get a microphone into the place he did most of his business. That meant the Armory Lounge, at 7427 West Roosevelt Road, in the western suburb of Forest Park. It had become the site of a constant procession of hoods wanting to talk shop. Little if anything was done on the phone, for most phones were tapped, or at least the hoods thought they were. Decisions were made in conferences in the Armory, in a back-room office just to the left of the kitchen. Hoods entered the Armory through a side door and approached Dominick Blasi, and he went back to tell Giancana who wanted to talk.

For months Hill, Roemer, and Rutland watched the Armory, trying to devise a method of tapping it. One of their chief obstacles was the Forest Park police. Its members had a cozy relationship with Giancana and patrolled the Armory around the clock. A break surfaced through a busboy. Agents noticed that he stayed on long after the place closed up, apparently scrubbing it down. One night they pulled his car over, posed as narcotics officers, and searched him. They found a set of keys. The man explained that he worked for "Mr. Sam" and that those were keys to the Armory. To follow through with the ruse, they took the man downtown and appeared to book him. He was terrified that they would tell Giancana they had stopped him and he would lose his job. The agents assured him that they would do no such thing, and after they had made duplicates of the man's keys, they freed him and again vowed their silence.

Swift late-night visits to the Lounge were then conducted, again with the help of the electronics technician. Again there were complications. While installing the microphones behind the shelves and soup cans in the back-room office, the technician accidently flipped on the switch to the neon sign out front, and at 4:30 in the morning it began blipping wildly. Another time he tripped the switch to the juke box, and it blared for long seconds. But once again the microphones went in undetected and stayed that way even though agents had to visit the place again and again to adapt the mikes to the changes in the Lounge. Once, for no apparent reason, the back office was remodeled and Giancana decided to take his business out to a table in the lounge area. That meant a microphone in a baseboard near the table, and results were mixed because of background noise.

The Armory mikes were immensely productive, however, and provided a look at the working structure of the mob as well as the specific details of Giancana's operations. Agents learned that the mob did everything by relay, that is, Giancana was indeed the boss and everything had to be cleared through him. Most of his time was spent handling problems, conflicts, and operating decisions. At all times his word was binding. Various lieutenants and associates would come to him with requests or problems, and he would attempt to do what he could. Then he would call in whoever could take care of the problem—Joey Glimco if it dealt with labor, Murray Humphreys if politics, etc.—and he would lay it on them. It was done this way not only because Giancana ran things and wanted to know what was going on, but also because he didn't want individual hoods going directly to one another with problems. The relay system was rigidly observed and painstakingly attended to. Giancana demanded it be followed with the same discipline that he demanded in all mob operations. Defy the system and a man was asking for problems of his own.

There was one other haunt of Giancana's that interested Hill and Roemer as much as Schneider's and the Armory, and that was the office of Chicago's First Ward Democratic organization, generally believed to be the political base for the West Side Italian district and others like it in the city. It was believed to be not only sympathetic to hoodlums but their functioning associates. The boss of the First Ward was John D'Arco, a member in good standing of Mayor Daley's Democratic organization, who had grown up on South Bishop Street in the Patch. But the brains of the First Ward was Pat Marcy, another graduate of the Patch. It was Marcy and D'Arco, and their dealings with the many West Side Bloc politicians, city officials, and city police, and their pipeline to Giancana and company, that agents most wanted to listen to. Soon that office too was wired.

The bugs made for a tightly knit sound screen, which Giancana could not avoid no matter how hard he sprinted for his car in the morning or how much rubber he laid getting out of his garage. It not only served to fill in agents on what he was going to do, but it gave them a background on what had happened years before. As in the conversation Giancana had with Stephen Magaddino, the outfit boss of Buffalo, New York, following the Apalachin fiasco of 1957. It had been Magaddino who argued that the conclave should be held at the estate of Joseph Barbara, despite Giancana's objections and his insistence that the meeting be held in Chicago or one of the surrounding suburbs because Giancana was so confident of his control over the areas that he guaranteed no intervention. He repeated that claim in his later talk with Magaddino, and took the opportunity to scold the Buffalo chief.

"I hope you're satisfied," he said. "Sixty-three of our top guys made by the cops."

"I gotta admit you were right, Sam. It never would have happened in your place," Magaddino said.

"You're fuckin' right it wouldn't. This is the safest territory in the world for a big meet.

"We could have scattered you guys in my motels. We could've given you guys different cars from my auto agencies, and then we could have had the meet in one of my big restaurants. The cops don't bother us here.

"We got three towns just outside of Chicago with the police chiefs in our pockets. We got what none of you guys got. We got this territory locked up tight," Giancana added in a boast that he himself hardly realized was mostly wishful thinking.

Apart from the microphones, the Bureau's thrust against the mob included an intense effort to recruit informants. Bill Roemer was generally responsible for cultivating them, and Roemer, a hulking yet soft-spoken ex-boxer, was unusually adept at it. Given that being a stool pigeon within the mob is the quickest method of exterminating oneself, it was a measure of Roemer's finesse (and the leverage of the Bureau in court) as well as the federal pocketbook, that he was able to create and sustain his roster of informants. They were so plentiful, and so well placed, that they ultimately matched and corroborated the best information the Bureau was getting from its microphones.

Agents learned, for example, the inside story of Apalachin, and that Giancana got away by running out a back door and hiding in the adjoining woods for hours. The meet was called by New York's Vito Genovese, who, with Lucky Luciano exiled to Italy and Albert Anastasia recently killed in a Manhattan barber chair, wanted to tighten his control over the New York mobs and also purge the outfit of untrustworthy chiefs. Essentially, it was one of the Genovese's moves to gain sanction for his designs in

New York, and galvanize support from leading hoods across the country. He later blamed the disruption of the Apalachin meet for his 14-year prison term on charges of conspiring to peddle narcotics.

It was from the tap on Schneider's, however, that agents received their first information about the "Commission," the national board of syndicate chiefs that assembled from time to time to discuss major mob issues and settle disputes between organizations. The information surfaced because of the relationship between Giancana and Accardo. Having taken his place as operating boss in 1957, Giancana also replaced Accardo as representative to the Commission. Because he felt Accardo still to be his mentor, and on an equal footing with him as far the Chicago hierarchy went, Giancana relayed the proceedings of the Commission to Accardo each time it met. That was a violation of the Commission's rule of total secrecy, but Giancana did not hesitate to tell all.

He told Accardo, and agents, in September, 1959, of the changes in Commission membership, a total that ranged from 6 to 15 representatives through the years. Then Giancana ran down the ranking members in 1959, and they included, besides himself: Raymond Patriarcha of New England; Stephen Magaddino, Upstate New York; Joseph Zerilli, Detroit; Joseph Profaci, Vito Genovese, Thomas Lucchese, and Joseph Bonanno of New York; Joseph Ida, Philadelphia; and Joseph La Rocca of Pittsburgh. Through the years that membership changed, and Giancana kept agents informed via his pipeline to Accardo. For the Bureau, it was a mob history lesson in capsule form, up-to-date information on what was happening and who was calling the shots, an invaluable aid to their nationwide deployment of agents and other microphones.

From the Armory, agents picked up information that made for new surveillance, and even intervention in potential outfit assassinations. In early February, 1962, Jackie Cerone, one of Accardo's top men, talked at length with Giancana at the Armory Lounge about killing Frank Esposito, head of a construction union in Chicago. Though the reason Esposito had to go was not revealed, the mechanics of how Cerone was going to get him were. With Giancana's sanction, Cerone planned to kidnap the union boss somewhere around his home in Hollywood, Florida.

Upon learning that Cerone was going to a house in Florida as a base of operations, agents went down there before him and fully bugged the premises. On schedule, Cerone rented the house and, with his brother Frank "Skippy" Cerone, Fiore Buccieri, David Yaras, James "Turk" Torello, and Vincent Inserra, went down to Florida and proceeded to stalk their prey. Their plans included grabbing Esposito around his house on North Surf Street in Hollywood so it would appear that he had been kidnapped, then never found again. If that didn't work they talked of bringing Phil Alderisio to Florida and having him contact Esposito on the pretext that Tony Accardo wanted to meet with him. Esposito would then be grabbed as he showed for that meeting. Regardless of how they made the snatch, the plan called for Esposito to be taken out in a power boat rented by Skippy Cerone, killed, then his body cut up with an ax and thrown into the Atlantic.

Once down in Florida, Cerone, Buccieri, and their friends lounged inside the rented house and soon got to trading stories about some of the memorable murders they'd undertaken. As agents listened to every word, grisly details of executions were light-heartedly recounted in perhaps the most candid, spontaneous conversations ever heard from the mouths of organized gangsters.

The most spectacular, and gruesome, was that concerning William "Action" Jackson, a 300-pound juice-loan collector suspected of being a federal informant. The story was repeated of how they took the massive hood to a mob-owned rendering plant, tied him hand and foot, then decided "to have a little bit of fun," as Buccieri told it, and hang him on one of the plant's meathooks. Jackson howled in pain, and to increase it his torturers stripped him then shot him once in the knee. Then they proceeded to work him over with an arsenal of baseball bats, ice picks, and a blowtorch. Buccieri even found an electric cattle prod, which he pushed up Jackson's rectum, then at intervals poured water on it. Jackson, who was barely conscious but whose bulky body squirmed and shook on the hook, lost all control of his bowels. "Boy, did he stink," Buccieri added.

The enforcer hung there for two days before he died, prompting Buccieri to remark that he was "sorry the big slob died so soon." Photographs were taken of his mutilated corpse and saved as reminders for other mobsters inclined to talk to police. Then he was put into the trunk of his auto and driven to lower Wacker Drive in the Loop. The car sat for four days in the heat of August until a passing patrolman smelled the stench.

As the group in Florida laughed over the memory, James Torello paused to wonder. "I still don't understand why he didn't admit he was a pigeon."

The conversation went on. Jackie Cerone told of how he ambushed Big Jim Martin during the mob's policy takeover. He leveled him with a shotgun blast, but didn't kill him because the ammunition was "old stuff." He wasn't aware of it at the time, however, and reported to Accardo that Martin had been taken care of. Another hood interrupted Cerone to say that whenever he used a shotgun to kill someone he made sure the ammunition was fresh.

Luckily for Frank Esposito, the agents stepped in to prevent another killing. They did so by staying one step ahead of Esposito's stalkers. When Cerone and his men crouched in bushes near Esposito's home waiting for the labor boss, the agents parked in front of the house until the hoods took off. When Esposito was shadowed by a carload of hoods as he walked from his home to the beach, agents again appeared. The hoods even tried to grab Esposito by using a woman to draw him near. But again agents intervened and interrupted the attempt. They continued for about a month, until Esposito prepared to return to Chicago, then they prevailed upon local sheriff's deputies to guard Esposito. The sheriff stationed uniformed officers around his home, and that finally was enough to lead Cerone and friends to abandon the hit.

Throughout the operation, the hoods never knew why the agents appeared at such opportune moments. Esposito did, however, for back in Chicago agents approached him and told him of the situation, hoping that he would cooperate with them and not only tell what he had done to earn a contract, but also testify against his stalkers. He refused, and instead denied that such a thing had gone on. "It's a lot of bunk," he said later. "I don't believe it. Why, I don't even know those guys [Cerone, Buccieri, et al.]. I'm not scared of anybody. I don't need any bodyguards."

As it turned out, he didn't, for the contract was inexplicably called off. That didn't particularly upset the Bureau, nor did Esposito's lack of cooperation. "The important thing," said Roswell Spencer, a chief investigator for the Cook County state's attorney's office, to whom the protection of Esposito was entrusted once he returned to Chicago, "is that he's still alive to keep his mouth shut."

The very nature of the Bureau's infiltration of the outfit created potentially deadly situations. Informants ran the constant risk of discovery and instant execution. Even the suggestion of being a stool was enough to get a man killed, for the mob, especially with people they didn't like very much anyway, seldom demanded unquestionable evidence of a man's treachery before they ordered him killed. Such was the case of Action Jackson. The juice collector was never an informant (which answers James Torello's question) but a friend of his was. The Bureau did approach Jackson but he refused to cooperate, a fact lost on the mob in the face of reported sightings of Jackson meeting with agents. His fatal mistake was not to report agents' advances to Giancana. That he discussed much with his friend, and that that information sooner or later was used against the mob, convinced the outfit of Jackson's leanings.

Agents sometimes couldn't even save their informants from being killed. A microphone once alerted Hill and Roemer to a contract granted on one of their own contacts. They alerted him to it but he wasn't convinced and wouldn't take precautions. They also attempted to get county officials to watch their man, or, if possible, to move him out of the area. Those officials were also skeptical, and with the reluctance of the informant himself, agents were unable to do anything. It was only a matter of time, however, before the informant got it. Walking up to his house in the middle of the afternoon, he was leveled by a shotgun blast.

As much as such events frustrated and angered agents, they fought temptations to intercede and use their information to set up hoods they despised. They approached that with Giancana on many occasions, for with his volatile temper, his vile, acid anger, he never charmed agents, or made them forget what he stood for. The very nature of law enforcement involves a unique relationship between the cop and the criminal. Each works a world of the streets, making arrangements, deals, promises—all with an unstructured, pragmatic set of rules and a feeling for the other guy and what he is made of. Officially, that which separated Sam Giancana from Bill Roemer and Ralph Hill was the edge of the law. Yet the three of them were linked more closely than they could have known by the appeal of what they did for a living—more specifically, by the factor of risk involved in it. There was little fear to be found, and a definite, telepathic communication, even an understanding.

Except that in the case of Giancana there was absolutely no affection involved. With Accardo, agents developed a feeling of respect, a sense that within the framework of what he did for a living he had a degree of class and intelligence. The same applied to Paul Ricca. Murray Humphreys engendered appreciation for his immense intellect, his finesse, and again within the perspective of his vocation, his civility. But Giancana did nothing but stoke the fires, little but antagonize and hiss obscenities, even at the height of his power. They admired his strengths and his ability to keep his power and to organize his people, but they loathed the man. Ralph Hill discovered that Giancana read the *New York Times* and the *Wall Street Journal* each morning, and that surprised him. But he also listened to a conversation Giancana had with Milwaukee Phil Alderisio after the two had returned from separate European vacations. Alderisio waxed as eloquent as he could about the beauties of the Greek and Roman ruins and wondered if Giancana wasn't equally touched. Giancana sneered at him and said, "Ruins ain't shit."

It was that charm that pushed Hill, Roemer, Rutland, and the others to keep up their close to round-the-clock surveillance on the man, to keep the microphones planted, to go out of their way to try to score against him.

12

OF THE THREE SISTERS she was the tallest, the youngest, and the prettiest. With a glossy smile and wide, glittering eyes, Phyllis McGuire bubbled the all-American charm that made the McGuire Sisters one of the most popular trios in the 1950's. The daughters of Asa and Lillie McGuire, they first harmonized in the choir of the First Church of God in Middletown, Ohio. Asa McGuire accompanied on the guitar while Lillie, the pastor of First Church, raised her arms to heaven and smiled in gratitude for three of the most beautiful, talented little girls any mother could wish for: Christine, Dorothy, and Phyllis—Phyllis just a bit taller and placed in the middle, but blending with her two sisters so well that most believed Middletown, Ohio, would not be able to keep them long.

They soon performed outside the church, first at the Paramount Theater in Middletown, and then in their first professional break, a 1952 national television appearance on Arthur Godfrey's "Talent Scouts." Singing "Pretty Eyed Baby," they broke Godfrey's applause meter, so impressing Godfrey that he immediately signed them as regulars on his weekly variety program. With other Godfrey stars, Frank Parker and Marion Marlowe, Haleoke, and Julius La Rosa, the sisters became household figures. First dubbed "the Three Little Godfreys," the McGuires had little trouble outstripping Godfrey's popularity with a list of perky, bouncy popular hits such as "Something's Gotta Give," in 1955; "The Naughty Lady of Shady Lane," "Picnic," "Melody of Love," and finally, in 1958, "Sugartime," a number-one hit that put them on the cover of *Life* magazine.

Through their early successes they remained the sweetness and purity that their fans wanted, sugar in the morning, evening, and at suppertime. They began earning upward of $100,000 a year each, yet said they still tithed and contributed to the church. They dressed alike, giving people the notion they were triplets, and they steadfastly insisted they didn't smoke or drink. And at concerts and nightclub appearances they never failed to smile and brim with enthusiasm, often bringing their parents along and introducing them to tumultuous applause.

But off-stage, the McGuires couldn't kick up their heels fast enough. Dorothy McGuire started it when, it was reported, she was carrying on a torrid affair with Julius La Rosa behind the curtains of the Godfrey show. It was a double scandal because Dorothy was married to Kenneth Brown, an Air Force sergeant in Korea. For months the on-again, off-again romance of Dorothy and Julius screamed from headlines in fan magazines, so much so that Arthur Godfrey publicly castigated the two stars. Finally Asa McGuire, the girls' father, held a press conference to disavow the rumors, saying that Sergeant Brown and Dorothy were loving partners, and that Brown even wrote his in-laws from his post in Korea.

But that was wishful thinking, for in 1958 Dorothy divorced Brown. That same year, Phyllis divorced her husband, a radio-television announcer named Neal Van Ells, who worked in Dayton, Ohio. Although the divorces somewhat shocked their fans, they didn't lessen the popularity of the McGuire Sisters as much as did their age—the girls were in their late twenties at the height of their popularity—and the unpredictability of popular music. Still, they drew and drew well wherever they appeared.

In the late 1950's, they made one of their many stops in Chicago, this time appearing at the Chez Paree Lounge. Among the patrons in the crowded club were Bill Roemer, Ralph Hill, and Marshall Rutland. They had come at the urging of their wives, who had always wanted to go to the nightclub and were anxious to see as popular a group as the McGuire Sisters. As they had expected, the show was a smash, the sisters performing with the same zest that had made them famous. Midway through the show, they stopped and exchanged informal chatter with the crowd. Helping was club comedian Billy Falbo, a popular Chicago figure, and Falbo took the opportunity to salute prominent persons in the crowd. One of the first he noted was "Jimmy A," the Rush Street mob lieutenant, Jimmy Allegretti. At that, Roemer, Hill, and Rutland exchanged troubled glances, for they had been on the organized-crime beat for many months and knew the likes of Jimmy Allegretti. But they had no suspicions of the McGuire Sisters, and gladly applauded when they got back to the microphone. When the sisters pointed out their parents, Lillie and Asa, who were sitting at a front table, the agents and their wives increased their applause, nicely satisfied that the spotlight had shifted from Jimmy A to the best of the First Church of God in Middletown, Ohio.

But it wasn't long before all lost their illusions about the innocence of the McGuires, at least, about Phyllis. In the 1960's, the trio began lucrative engagements in Las Vegas, and there Phyllis became fond of the gambling tables. She played the casinos with abandon, covering her losses with her considerable earnings. She also partied a lot, getting a reputation for liking a good time, a woman who used her talent and her ravishing good looks to make the most of what Las Vegas had to offer.

It was at a gambling table at one of Las Vegas' biggest casinos that she captured Giancana's attention. She was gambling heavily, having run up a debt of more than $100,000, when Giancana sauntered over and began chatting with her. But what he said had nary the impact of what he did. By this time the Chicago outfit had made deep inroads into Las Vegas, having taken over sizable percentages of key casinos while leaving ownership in the name of representatives. One of these was Morris Dalitz, a one-time Cleveland hood who had bought into Las Vegas in the late 1940's, beginning with the Desert Inn. It was in one of Dalitz's casinos that Phyllis was ringing up her marker. Giancana went over to the house manager and told him he would take care of the debt, which he did, not by paying it but by telling Dalitz to eat it. He then sent his best wishes and a suiteful of flowers to Phyllis, signed affectionately, "Mo."

It was the usual advance by Giancana, gifts and favors for women that knew no restraint, furs, jewelry, autos, money, vacations, high times, cold cash. While a boss like Tony Accardo was niggardly with his money, even to the point of mowing his own grass at his River Forest mansion because he didn't think it was worth it to have it done, Giancana gave money away with both hands. Few women who trod his circles could resist, not at first and not for long, and Giancana had no dearth of soft fingers on his arms. Phyllis was no exception, except that she fell for Giancana. She was totally taken by his charm, his power, his generosity, and she began a close, devoted relationship with him.

From Las Vegas she traveled to clubs all over the country, and Giancana followed her. He sat at front tables when she sang in New York, Miami, Hot Springs, Arkansas, and at small summerstock theaters, where she labored in plays like *Annie Get Your Gun.* He did it at severe professional expense, for Chicago hoods complained loudly that he was letting the rackets slide, putting matters in the hands of Dominick Blasi and not being around long enough to give direction or to preside over important meets. But it didn't faze Giancana. He was certain of his power, so certain of his control that he kept right by Phyllis' side. In October, 1961, he flew off to Europe to be present for the sisters' appearances there.

In London he began the many nights of partying after the sisters' performances. By this time he was a fixture with Phyllis and at least nominally accepted by the sisters, a situation he no doubt helped along by his generosity. For all of his surliness in business affairs and in public appearances, Giancana was capable of being a lamb in private, a sociable, charming guest, a good-natured father figure with just a touch of the Old Country. He loved good food and plenty of it, thick steaks, shrimp, his anchovies and tomatoes, carafes of red wine. And inestimably, he carried his strength as he knew it from the mob, the intrinsic power that went along with who he was, again that Sicilian blend of macho charm and implicit danger that lingered beneath the surface, the sense that he could do what he wanted to do and one dare not cross him. All of that held a repugnance for most, but allure to others; for Phyllis, once the unblemished, frivolous little Godfrey girl, it carried an infatuation.

He openly toasted the sisters in a London nightclub where they had gone with Frederic Jones, their hairdresser. The five of them were spotted by a British photographer, and in a rare, almost unheard-of instance of candor, Giancana posed with his glass of wine high, a half smile on his lips, his left arm wrapped around Phyllis. The photographer snapped away, the sisters holding polished professional smiles, thinking nothing amiss, Giancana searching for his expression, not sure what to think.

The photo session, as innocent as it seemed, had enormous repercussions. Though Phyllis' affair with Giancana had become known among friends and relatives (agents and intelligence police were oblivious of it for months before being tipped off by a newspaperman sometime in 1961), the public had yet to get the word before wire services spread the London snapshot. The reaction was nothing short of outrage. America had seemingly lost another of its cherubs, and this time in the worst way. Chicago newspaper columnist John Justin Smith headlined his objections: "Wake Up, Phyllis! Your Pal, Sam, Is a Hoodlum." He went on to chart the romance in most distressed tones, then reiterated Giancana's criminal past, and ended with "Next time you are with this man, look at his hands. You may not see any blood but you will see hands that have created human disasters."

But the outrage did nothing to dampen the relationship, though it would permanently change Phyllis' relationship with the press, not to mention her fans. Giancana continued to follow her and the group through Europe, to Rome and Madrid, and always he feted them with lavish dinners and receptions. His presence became accepted by the sisters, Christine and Dorothy at first not sure how intense the relationship was getting, but adapting easily to Giancana's style, an undeniable energy that had served him well in his climb through the Chicago mob and now won him favor with them. Phyllis, for her part, was not publicly divulging her feelings, but privately she admitted she was falling in love with Giancana. Rumors quickly sprang up that she had married him in a private European ceremony, and though the story was never confirmed, she did little to deny it.

Back in the States, the sisters continued to receive Giancana's attentions. In Miami he entertained them lavishly at the Fontainebleau Hotel among others, and particularly at a restaurant operated by Rocco and Joe Fischetti, ex–Chicago hoods whose brother Charley had been a powerful Capone lieutenant. In Las Vegas, Giancana invited them into his casino hotel suites, when, that is, he wasn't lounging with them in their own elegant chalet apartments. In New York City he stayed at the sisters' Park Avenue apartment. In all, it was a cross-country, international affair, with vacations to Mexico, particularly Acapulco, and San Juan, Puerto Rico, a setup that suited Giancana because he saw himself by then as a roving world boss, touching base with the country's top hoods while exploring new territories for expanding mob concessions. Phyllis fit in nicely not only because he was smitten by her as he had not been by any woman since the De Tolve girl took his eye on Taylor Street thirty years earlier, but also because her life style conformed nicely with his and it could be used to his good advantage.

Las Vegas became the center of things, appropriately because its enormous gambling concessions were created by organized mobsters and continued to reward them, and also because the strip attracted entertainers and personalities. It was a natural matchup: hoods who considered gambling and gamblers as a chief source of laundered revenue, and entertainers who catered to the high times and the big money and the power of the silk-suited men who handled things under the tables.

Benjamin "Bugsy" Siegel had started it all in 1946, certain that he could lure highrollers into the desert because of Nevada's quick divorce laws and legalized gambling. He arranged loans and contracts to get things moving, a difficult task in the harried postwar years made easier by his underworld associates, and soon began pouring millions of dollars into his Flamingo hotel and casino, a name taken from the bird that haunted the Hialeah Race Track, which he had once owned. Siegel never quite pulled it off. The Flamingo mired him in debt, as high as $5 million, mostly to the mob, a debt that the organization, headed by Lucky Luciano, Meyer Lansky, would have to absorb if Siegel couldn't pull Flamingo and Las Vegas off. After a disastrous opening and months of floundering, the operation began to show a profit, but Siegel had already sealed his fate. To hedge against financial ruin, he had skimmed money off the top of mob loans and the Flamingo's building budget and placed them in his own bank accounts. Lansky and Luciano found out, and in June, 1947, just as the Flamingo operation had begun to pay off, Siegel was shot through the head as he sat in his living room in Beverly Hills. Days later, representatives of Lansky showed up at the Flamingo and took over its operation. Other casino hotels followed, many with mob financing (some with union, especially Teamsters, pension-fund moneys), and Las Vegas began to mushroom.

It remained "open" territory as far as the mob was concerned, free for any and all syndicates to enter and operate and invest. They came in sprinting, aggressively setting up front organizations and representatives to shield mob investment and ownership by syndicate bosses. No group came in more quickly than the Chicago outfit. In the early 1950's Ricca, Accardo, Humphreys, and Guzik saw the future of Las Vegas, the enormous potential of its tables and the vulnerability of casino operations. By that time also, Chicago's outfit had made its reputation as a rogue organization, unpredictable, ruthless, almost impossible to control. Stemming from Capone and his power, the reputation was carried on by Ricca, and later pushed to extremes by Giancana. Nobody in New York or the rest of the country had the power or the persuasion to stand up to the Chicago outfit, or would try in Las Vegas.

Chicago's first inroads into Las Vegas came in 1953 when Marshall Caifano was sent there by Accardo to bird-dog, to set up business with casino owners and even to strike out after smaller, one-time extortion attempts. The latter often involved bailing out a highroller, lending him money for the tables, or arranging to take care of his debts at excruciatingly high interest rates. Caifano quickly cornered Louis "Russian Louie" Strauss and for months stayed with him while Strauss gambled his way deeper and deeper into debt. When Strauss was unable to satisfy Caifano and his sponsors, he was taken out for a ride in the desert and never seen again. The incident proclaimed that Caifano and Chicago meant business when they made contact, and it also provided Strip gamblers and hoods with an inside joke, answering when they were not about to pay for something, "I'll pay when Russian Louie hits town."

Caifano's activities were but a prelude to wider interests Chicago was pressing. In its developing years, the Flamingo operation was taken over by Gus Greenbaum, a hustler with ties to the Capone organization that went back to Prohibition and continued with its maneuverings into the Trans-American gambling wire services. Greenbaum went to the gang for large chunks of capital to infuse into the Flamingo and keep it solvent, loans that totaled up to $1 million. In return, Accardo, Ricca, and

Guzik wanted a piece not only of the Flamingo but of the Riviera, a newly built hotel that had hit difficult times and whose management had approached Greenbaum for help. The plans never fully developed, however, mostly because of Greenbaum's failing health, his own addiction to gambling, a drug problem, and finally his inability to run things as well as he once had. In December, 1958, Greenbaum and his wife were found brutally murdered in their Phoenix apartment, and though Greenbaum was a problem out of the way, the outfit swallowed the debts he owed them.

They were to be made up and then some by new forays into the Strip. When Giancana took control of the Chicago outfit he coveted Las Vegas like no territory he had ever seen. He would have preferred to go there himself and set up shop, but because Nevada state gambling authorities attempted to keep close checks on the presence of known syndicate figures in casino operations, he instead delegated a handful of envoys to break the ground. They could either muscle their way in, usually demanding "points," or hidden shares, in casinos (points varied in worth from hotel to hotel and from year to year, but generally ran between $50,000 and $125,000), or threaten violence, or they finagled holdings by supplying capital, paying off bad debts, and generally being ready with a buck whenever casino owners needed it. Ideally, their money would come from the "skim," the taking of money from the daily "first counts," when the money is taken from the rooms and first tabulated by casino owners. An effective skim means money going right into the hands of mobsters, be they hidden owners or extortionists, before it is reported as earnings, before owners, stockholders, or anybody else connected with the casino is paid off. It is steady, unseen, incalculable cash as clean and unfettered as any money hoods can take.

Giancana sent off as many as seven men to do his Las Vegas bidding. One was Joe Pignatello, his first chauffeur and bodyguard, who went out to the Strip and set up a lounge–pizza parlor as a base for his other activities. Others included John Drew, a Chicago bookie; John Formosa, who ran the outfit's concessions in Lake County, Indiana; two union racketeers, Gus Zapas and Eugene C. (Jimmy) James; and Marshall Caifano. But perhaps the most important and effective Chicago emissary was John Roselli, a long-time Chicago hood who made inroads into the movie industry and went to jail in 1944 with Paul Ricca and others in the Browne-Bioff extortion case. It was Roselli who maneuvered Chicago's interests toward two casinos, the Desert Inn and the Stardust. A chief stockholder in both casinos was Mo Dalitz, the one-time Cleveland hood with whom Giancana and the Chicago outfit had close ties.

The negotiations with Dalitz were lengthy and complex, overseen not only by Giancana but by the shrewd business mind of Murray Humphreys, and they at one time or other included at least six other mob representatives, all making quick trips between Chicago and the Strip. The outfit was still interested in getting their piece of the Riviera Hotel, taking up where Accardo and Ricca had left off with Gus Greenbaum. They wanted six points of the hotel, valued then at $125,000 apiece. By late 1960, the deal with Dalitz had reached its final stages. Dalitz flew to Chicago and in two days the transaction was made, giving his silent Chicago partners working shares of Dalitz' Stardust and Desert Inn arranged for in previous deals and a hidden piece of the Riviera. It was a remarkable success, albeit characteristic of the Giancana-Humphreys blend of muscle and business acumen. It resulted in an estimated $1 million initially skimmed from the three operations, and a continuing $65,000 a month coming in directly to Giancana.

Giancana celebrated by spending more and more time around the Strip. Again, he did it in the company of Phyllis McGuire. In 1961 she leased the Green Gables Ranch, a large spread four miles outside Las Vegas in a place called Paradise Valley. Giancana spent weeks there, often wearing loud cowboy shirts and a ten-gallon hat. His new interest in the casinos brought visits from various hotel employees—managers, croupiers, dealers—each ushered to the ranch at the request of Giancana and receiving suitable instructions as to how best to serve their employer. From his vast experience with numbers runners and bookies and casino managers in Chicago, Giancana knew that he had to get the word through that if employees chose to steal or even cheat they should know full well who they were stealing from. Once that was taken care of, he basked in the company of Phyllis for weeks at a time, enjoying the sun, the games, the privacy, and the satisfaction of yet another concession under control.

Though he'd become *the* man behind the scenes, his pockets and the coffers of the Chicago outfit swelling from Las Vegas wagers, Giancana was persona non grata on the Strip itself. The Nevada Gaming Control Board made a concerted effort not only to bar known hoodlums from owning or investing in casinos, but also to keep them out of them. It was a sincere if superficial attempt at keeping outward propriety attached to the business of Las Vegas. To do it the board issued its "black book," a list of eleven underworld figures who were to be barred from all gambling halls. Prominent on the list was Giancana; others included the heads of organized crime families with interests in Las Vegas.

As specious as the "black book" attempt seemed, it generally kept people like Giancana out of the halls. It even stood up in court, for in 1963 Marshall Caifano, also listed in the book as a result of his activities in the 1950's, sued the state and the Desert Inn on grounds that he was being deprived of his civil rights. In October, 1960, Caifano was ejected from the Inn after a stormy confrontation with gaming board officials and casino owners. The state officials trailed Caifano as he visited several casinos, and when casino owners failed to eject him, the officials stopped all gambling and proceeded to inspect cards, dice tables, and other paraphernalia. At the Desert Inn (oddly enough, the casino with the biggest share of mob ownership) house managers opted to eject Caifano instead. A federal judge ruled not only that the Inn could eject people like Caifano, but that the state could bar those like him on grounds that they were threats to the health, morals, safety, and general welfare of its citizens. The judge also ruled that the state has the right to protect its gambling licenses, and that a person like Caifano, with records of felony convictions, including extortion, gambling, and bank robbery, was a threat to gambling establishments and could be kept out of them.

That ruling and other actions by the state gaming board made it tougher for Giancana to move freely in and out of the area. To do it, and to travel unhindered wherever he went, he constantly used aliases, from random names like Michael Mancuso and R. J. Landholdt, to his favorites, derivations of family names. He often used the name Flood, the last name of a brother-in-law, or T. Ischi, from son-in-law Anthony Tisci, or the name DePalma, the last name of his third son-in-law, Jerome DePalma. When less inspired, he simply doctored his own name: Giancanel, Giancaco, Gincani.

For practical purposes, perhaps, but also in affinity for the ruse, Phyllis McGuire also took on a variety of aliases whenever she traveled with Giancana, her favorite being "Pat McGovern." But accompanying him and sharing his life style was not without problems. Phyllis was later questioned about the use of her telephones and her various residences as points of contact for Giancana and his many associates. He used the sisters' ranch in Las Vegas and apartments in Beverly Hills and New York City as bases from which to take and forward calls. Her credit card was used hundreds of times, sometimes as often as a dozen times a day, for long-distance calls from Giancana to Dominick Blasi, Anthony Tisci, and other associates and relatives wherever they were. Countless calls were made on the card from Phyllis to Giancana's home in Oak Park, or the Armory Lounge, many of them personal, others, no doubt, clustered around important Giancana movements or business transactions. As the relationship continued, her telephones became a switchboard through which Giancana passed his word, sometimes in his name, other times from "Jones," or his favorite "Mr. Flood."

In the midst of it all, Phyllis would take time out to try to prop up her badly tarnished image. In a tearful private interview with New York columnist Dorothy Kilgallen, in 1963, she vowed she was giving Giancana up. "It's terribly unfair, but I promise you it's true," she said as she paced the floor of her Manhattan apartment while Kilgallen listened intently. "Look at me and see if you can't tell by my eyes that I'm not lying. I'm not going to see Sam again." She went on to say that she had to clear the air of rumors about her secret marriage in Sweden to Giancana, that because of it she had been receiving hate letters and had been the object of angry gossip columns, including some from Kilgallen. "Sure, I've been seeing Sam," she said. "I've been with him in Las Vegas and in Florida and Europe. I'm a grown woman. It seems to me I have a right to see a man if I like him. But I swear I'm not married to Sam, and I never will be."

Her motives were transparent, however, geared mainly at protecting the trio's professional standing. She said that producers of variety shows and television specials were becoming reluctant to book the sisters because of the scandal surrounding her and Giancana. She told Kilgallen that she couldn't understand it, couldn't see what connection her love life had to do with the medley of McGuire Sisters' hits beamed cheerfully into the television rooms of middle America. But then she said she could and did know quite well what "image" was all about, and that she was giving up Sam because of it.

It was nonsense, for she remained "Pat McGovern" and her telephone credit card number remained in Giancana's use. Nobody knew it better than the federal agents following them. They began to know Phyllis as well as they knew Sam, their relationship, their spats, their secrets, even their intimate moments. And they were unable to convince her (for they tried as they tried with every person, every girlfriend who came into contact with Giancana) to break down her ties to him and secure intelligence data. They directed their efforts as much against her as against him.

In mid-1961, as the two of them flew from Phoenix to New York, they were met at Chicago's O'Hare Airport when the plane made an intermediary stop. It again was the same crew of FBI agents who lived with Giancana whenever he came to town: Bill Roemer, Ralph Hill, Marshall Rutland, John Bassett, and Vincent Inserra. When the plane pulled in and Phyllis and Giancana stepped off, Bassett and Inserra approached her with a subpoena, one supplied by a grand jury in session but aimed only at harassing her into talking to agents. At the sight of the agent Phyllis became livid, the veins in her neck tightening, her smile vanishing.

She slapped at the subpoena. "And who are you?!" she snarled.

Bassett and Inserra identified themselves and their occupations. Then they said that the subpoena gave them the power to take her downtown with them, or require her to appear there the next day. But if she cooperated, they said, they could talk in a private room in the airport and the subpoena would be withdrawn. Taking quick note of the alternatives, and possibly knowing the reaction of Giancana, who was following at some distance behind her, she composed herself, replaced the gleaming smile, and said she would be glad to cooperate.

As she was accompanying Bassett and Inserra down the airport corridor, Giancana appeared and flew into a rage at the sight of the agents and Phyllis' exit.

"Where the fuck is she going?" he bellowed.

"She's going to have a nice little talk, Mo," said Roemer. "About you and what you do."

He fumed and tried to collect himself, frustrated at the presence of Hill, Roemer, and Rutland, who, by that time, relished every meeting and every opportunity to bother him.

"Whataya wanna know?" he said. "*I'll* tellya, I'll tell ya anything ya wanna know."

"Okay," said Hill. "Tell us what you do for a living."

Giancana folded his arms in front of him. "Easy. I own Chicago. I own Miami. I own Las Vegas."

But his cooperation went only that far. "Where in hell is she?" he barked, growing edgy and impatient.

"She's singing," said Roemer. "The whole story is coming out."

Giancana snarled, by this time drawing attention to himself from the various people sitting in the waiting areas. "Fuck you," he said to the agents. "Fuck your boss, too. Fuck your boss's boss."

Then he turned and walked angrily back on board the plane. It was some minutes later that the plane pulled away from the terminal and started for the runway. Phyllis was still talking with Bassett and Inserra, telling them nothing and reneging on her promise to cooperate. Plans had been made to get her on a later flight to New York to rejoin Giancana. Then Giancana's plane suddenly pulled back into the terminal, the walkway was connected, and Giancana himself came storming off. In his hand he carried Phyllis' hat and purse.

The agents went wild. They began whistling and catcalling and telling him that the handbag suited him well, kind of matched his personality. At that Giancana lost his temper. "You cocksucker!" he shouted at Roemer. "You motherfucker!" He made no attempt to control himself or keep his voice down. "I ought to get Butch here with his machine guns and take care of you pricks."

Roemer responded quickly, his adrenalin flowing, his 200-pound, 6-foot-2-inch frame leaping toward the runty, balding Giancana with all of the rancor he had for the man. "Is that a threat?" he said, towering over Giancana. "Are you threatening a federal officer, Mo?"

"Take it any way you want," Giancana said, then he sat in a chair and stared straight ahead.

But Roemer was hot, and untrue to his casual, low-key style, he went for Giancana, egging him on and hoping on hopes that the hood would take a punch at him. Roemer waved his arms and announced broadly to anyone in earshot: "Ladies and gentlemen, here he is! Chicago's number one hoodlum, the city's biggest form of low life. Right here. Responsible for more scum, more crime, more misery than anyone alive. And you people are lucky, you don't have to put up with slime like Sam Giancana. You can pass through this city and go on to wherever you live and not have to put up with what this animal does to this city. But here he is, folks, get a good look at him!"

Roemer had surprised even himself. The waiting area and terminal corridor were jammed with people listening and trying to figure out what was going on, many of them craning to see who it was sitting in the chair. Hill and Rutland could not contain their pleasure.

Giancana, sitting, stewing, clenching his teeth in a straight-ahead stare, finally got up and headed for the plane. Then he turned and faced off with Roemer, "I'll get you for this. You lit a fire tonight that will never go out. You'll rue the day. I'll get you."

Then he disappeared on board. Shortly after, shielded from the crowd by an agent, Phyllis followed after him. Then, just before she boarded the plane, she paused and turned back to the agents and offered her hand. "Sam was not a gentleman tonight. I want to apologize for him." She smiled sweetly. "But I hope you'll always remember me as a lady."

Giancana angrily stormed back and jerked her into the plane.

13

Since his days in Hoboken, New Jersey, the skinny, good-looking Italian kid with big ears had never apologized for the origins of his last name or the people he'd come from. Many of them were hoods, *gumbas* from the neighborhood who helped here and there, who watched over him and promised they'd do what they could for his career. There was never any doubt that Frank Sinatra could sing. People like Willie Moretti, the patriarchal New Jersey mob boss, only wanted to make sure he made it to the top, and Sinatra, a "good boy," never forgot him.

In 1946, when the nation's top hoods gathered with Lucky Luciano in Havana, Cuba, to figure out what to do with Bugsy Siegel and the Las Vegas fiasco, Sinatra was there and had a warm reunion with the exiled Luciano. As he went on in show business, small men in silk suits often bought tables for his performances, giving rise to speculation that it was help from these friends that got him through the early years with the Tommy Dorsey band and his early acting attempts.

Before long, he met Giancana, an inevitable meeting not only because of the company Sinatra sometimes kept, but also because he was close to Chicago's Fischetti brothers, Rocco and Joey. Joey Fischetti was an entrepreneur of sorts, opening restaurants and attempting to get into show business and entertainment, keeping his ties with Sinatra strong. Sinatra also loved

Chicago, loved to perform there and then crash into a downtown restaurant with a dozen friends and eat and drink until dawn. He quickly took to Giancana, not only because of his power, but because Giancana's energy was infectious, his nature aggressive, and his ability to command the attention of powerful men around him something that Sinatra felt within himself. The two of them partied together, ate and drank together. Sinatra entertained for Giancana, introduced him to his circle of friends, especially women, in Hollywood and whenever he entertained in his home in Palm Springs, California, and always, most importantly, he respected him, never apologizing for him or his association with him. He was very much unlike fellow Italian-American Joe DiMaggio, a man who would have nothing to do with hoods of any sort. As much as Giancana reveled in his closeness to Sinatra, he fumed at the mention of DiMaggio, often openly challenging DiMaggio's right to act as if he were better than his *paesani.*

Sinatra, on the other hand, with a personality as vibrant yet volatile as Giancana's, knew no bounds to his hospitality toward the people he liked. His parties were lavish, often raucous affairs, with food, booze, and women in constant supply. With the high times came pranks, practical jokes, and juvenile hijinks. Peter Lawford was present in the Fontainebleau Hotel in 1960 when Giancana and Sinatra tried to outdo each other at tossing cherry bombs. Lawford lost his temper when one was tossed under his chair, and he went after Giancana, only to be menaced by one of Giancana's ubiquitous bodyguards. Sinatra and Giancana, meanwhile, continued to run through the hotel lighting firecrackers even to the point of boarding nearby yachts and tossing them below deck.

Sinatra, at the time, was very close to what became known as the Clan, or the Rat Pack, a group of actors and entertainers who got together for club openings or Las Vegas appearances, television, even movies. It was a loosely knit group with many members, most notably Sinatra, Lawford, Dean Martin, and Sammy Davis, Jr., but it also included from time to time Joey Bishop, Tony Curtis, Janet Leigh, Robert Wagner, Natalie Wood, Shirley MacLaine, and Jimmy Van Heusen. They became identified with one another, supportive, and almost as if to live up to the image they began to party with each other in raucous affairs that equaled anything Sinatra or the rest had thrown before.

Running to bases in Las Vegas, Hollywood, New York, Palm Springs, the Rat Pack attracted untold hangers-on, including show-business personalities, Las Vegas types, hoods like Johnny Roselli, Giancana's Las Vegas–Hollywood connection, starlets and long-lashed women who thrived at such goings-on, and politicians. Lawford was then married to Pat Kennedy, sister of then Senator John F. Kennedy, and Kennedy had a reputation for enjoying the high times and his brother-in-law's crowd. In early 1960, when Kennedy was just getting his presidential campaign together, he visited Lawford while he and the Rat Pack were filming *Oceans Eleven,* a movie about a group of ex-servicemen who band together to rob Las Vegas casinos. By this time Kennedy had become a close friend of Sinatra and often stayed at his home in Palm Springs. That night in March he kicked up his feet with the Pack as they partied and slapped each other's backs at the Sands Hotel. Flashbulbs popped and nobody hid the fact that they enjoyed the evening immensely, particularly Kennedy, who no doubt found his entertainer friends a faster crowd than that in Washington. Part of the appeal was the women, stunning, aggressive girls who were always around, always available, many of them dancers or starlets or simply pretty faces. And it was no secret to Sinatra and the rest of the Rat Pack that Kennedy never ran the other way when they came out of the woodwork, and the Pack went out of its way to make sure they were there.

When Kennedy's bid for the presidency gained intensity, members of the Rat Pack did what they could. Their support meant money and visibility, and Kennedy did not hesitate to take advantage of it. But Sinatra went further than that, pushing in his own way and with his own methods in order to make things move behind the political scenes. He wanted nothing better than to see Kennedy get elected. He talked with friends about the possibility of his Palm Springs home becoming the summer White House.

Knowing full well Giancana's political influence on the city of Chicago and its politicians, Sinatra discussed the issue of the Kennedy election. It was no idle discussion. From the days of Johnny Powers to the present, the mob has had close control over certain aldermen, committeemen, ward heelers, even state and congressional representatives. Giancana was a business partner of State Senator James J. Adduci. His daughter had married the legislative aide of Congressman Roland Libonati. From the days when he was a slugger in city elections, votes could be influenced, stolen, even created if necessary, for such was the legacy of Chicago politics. Sinatra didn't necessarily ask for any of this, he only asked that Giancana do what he could do.

It wasn't a matter of pulling anybody's teeth, for the appeal of John F. Kennedy to politicians in the city of Chicago was enormous. He was an Irish Democrat, a creature as close to the very soul of Chicago's Mayor Richard J. Daley as anything on earth, and he was a Roman Catholic, a fact Daley appreciated each morning as he stepped into mass. Daley's blessings alone insured Kennedy a massive Chicago push, one that Giancana and the outfit hardly had to supplement. But the fact remained that the notorious West Side Bloc, the handful of legislators and ward politicians who ran the river wards, the working-class Italian, Black, Latin, and Polish wards that skirted the Chicago River, had enormous control of voters and voting returns. They also had an intimate relationship with the outfit, one that meant financial support and influence, one that cut across city politics, judges, even state and federal representatives, to the degree that they not only conferred with people like Giancana, Tony Accardo, and Murray Humphreys but they took orders from them, drew up election slates with them, even resigned when the word came down. Hence, an order from the mob to work for Kennedy only insured a total Chicago effort of the kind that historically had been known to work miracles in the early-morning hours of vote counting.

Giancana, however, made no commitment without expecting something in exchange. What he expected from Sinatra, Giancana told his associates, was a hotline to the White House that would get the federal government and its tenacious agents off Giancana's back. Giancana, in a gush of wishful thinking, had confidence that Sinatra could come through, that his influence with the Kennedy boys might be strong enough.

The 1960 Kennedy-Nixon election played into Giancana's hands, for with the race so close the winning margins came down to the outcome of a few states. Illinois was one, and it hung in the balance all night as Daley's forces, and the master vote counters of the city's river wards, worked feverishly to deliver their man. The state swung to Kennedy by a few thousand votes and in many minds was the deciding factor in Kennedy's win (actually, Kennedy would have won anyway when Texas returns came in for him). Illinois, the Daley machine, would be ever in John F. Kennedy's favor. And Giancana privately celebrated, exulting every time he spotted Sinatra at arm's length from the new President.

The months that followed, however, could not have been more bitter for Giancana. Sinatra's influence on the Kennedy boys proved nonexistent in matters of government policy. As it turned out, Sinatra was closer to Joseph Kennedy than anyone else, and his influence on his sons was minimal, if not also nonexistent. When Robert Kennedy was appointed Attorney General not only did he not lessen the government's thrust at syndicate crime, but personally directed its increase. J. Edgar Hoover was kept on as FBI chief and his policies in the Bureau remained intact. But it was Bobby Kennedy's zeal in taking on the mob that dramatically changed things. He publicized the mob, railed against its cancerous effect on the country, then he drew up a list of hoods he personally wanted to go after. And heading the list was none other than Sam Giancana—Peter Lawford and the Rat Pack notwithstanding.

The Kennedy push made life harder for agents like Bill Roemer. Scores of new agents were assigned the organized-crime detail and Roemer found himself with five assistant agents to direct and oversee. Also, in the most demanding duty, Roemer had to supply daily information on mob doings to Washington so that Kennedy himself could review it. Kennedy wanted fresh material on the teletype every day, not just about hood comings and goings, but intelligence material. And Roemer, Hill, Rutland, and the others were pushed to the limit to supply it. The crackdown on Sam Giancana was just beginning.

Giancana was furious, feeling not only threatened and harassed by the government, but that he had misjudged Sinatra. Those close to him were equally angry, for nobody went untouched by the new government heat, and nobody was unaware that it came from the people they had worked to elect. The federal effort against organized crime was outwardly the biggest effort ever, meaning not only increased surveillance and prosecution, but the passage of new, tougher racketeering laws, and laws to make prosecutors' legal weapons more effective against heretofore sacrosanct outfit enterprises. And at the top of it was Bobby, the baby-faced Kennedy, assailing the cavalier life styles of hoods, their vicious form of justice, the collusion between mobsters and politicians, and through it all naming names, especially those of the Chicago bosses. Giancana cursed at the sight of the Attorney General, and fumed at the very mention of the Kennedy name.

It got to the level that he and his lieutenants seriously considered doing something about it. It had always been a tradition with the Chicago mob to confront problems outright, be it a fix with the feds, a persuasive suggestion tinged with threats, or an outright execution. Talk came to that one day as Giancana talked about the Kennedy problem in the Armory Lounge with his Las Vegas emissary, Johnny Formosa. Formosa thought the Rat Pack could deliver and they hadn't.

"Let's show 'em. Let's show those fuckin' Hollywood fruitcakes that they can't get away with it as if nothing's happened," he said.

Then he mentioned Sinatra and his solution was simple. "Let's hit him."

It was a contract he gladly would have carried out for Giancana, and he would go it one better. "I could whack out a couple a those guys. Lawford, that Martin prick, and I could take the nigger and put his other eye out."

Giancana didn't discourage him; but he didn't issue the contract.

"No," he said, knowing full well that he only had to say the word to see it done. "I've got other plans for them."

For years the Villa Venice was known as a clip joint, a roadhouse type of restaurant where a lot of things went on and a lot of money changed hands. It was located on Milwaukee Avenue near Wheeling, Illinois, far northwest of Chicago, a rural, unmolested site free from curious cops or unwanted visitors. In 1956 Alfred Meo, owner of a restaurant in the Chicago suburb of Norridge, bought the Villa Venice. It was a transaction that interested authorities because Meo's Norwood House in Norridge was a well-known hangout for hoods, most notably Tony Accardo and Paul Ricca. Though Meo put down $80,000 for the Villa Venice, and registered his wife and relatives as officers, it was common knowledge on the premises that Giancana was the owner. Whenever he showed up, there was little doubt about it, for he charged through the place issuing orders to even the lowliest busboys.

In 1961 Meo sold the restaurant to a group headed by a man named Leo Olsen, but investigation of the sale revealed that the new owners were still only a front for Giancana. After the sale, extensive remodeling began for the purpose, according to Olsen, of putting the club in shape to feature name entertainers and attract Las Vegas–style crowds. His intentions, he maintained, were to get the likes of Eddie Fisher, Dean Martin, Sammy Davis, Jr., and Frank Sinatra to kick off the new policy and do it with style. Other changes included the letting of contracts to various restaurant-supply firms either owned or operated by syndicate figures, a fact Olsen didn't mention, but which became quickly apparent to investigators.

In late 1962, Olsen's plan for the gala opening of the Villa Venice materialized when Fisher, Martin, Davis, and Sinatra all arrived in Chicago for their respective appearances. The opening was a smash, with ticket demands too numerous to fill, even with the stiff conditions set up. To get in, one had to pay $10 per person, but minimun reservations were for an entire table of ten, $100 right off the top before anyone got through the door. A sizable portion of the tables were taken by Giancana and his friends, as well as other associates, who knew it was good practice to be seen and who also didn't mind taking the wives out for a night of Rat Pack entertainment.

As an added feature, a shuttle bus setup was arranged to transfer nightclub patrons to Giancana's impromptu casino located in a quonset hut only two blocks away. There was no dearth of takers, and as the drinks flowed at the Villa Venice, as Fisher, Sinatra, and the rest sang at their best, the dice rolled, the wheels hummed, and the money flew in the plush surroundings of the quonset hut.

Hill, Roemer, and Rutland were fascinated by the operation and made it a point to interview the Rat Pack members. What they found was that each one was appearing gratis, as a personal favor to Sinatra. They would say little more than that. Eddie Fisher, for example, talked to agents in his downtown Chicago hotel suite. His answers rambled; he referred to his good friend

Frank Sinatra. In the middle of the interview he was interrupted by a phone call from comedian Louie Nye, and after a few words, Fisher hung up and told the agents he would no longer say anything. "That was my attorney Louie Nye," he said, "and he advised me not to talk."

Sinatra, on the other hand, said he was doing this as a personal favor to Leo Olsen. He said he was a lifelong friend of Olsen's, that he had grown up with him in New Jersey and it was a pleasure for him to help him get started. Nobody else, including someone like Giancana, had a thing to do with it, Sinatra insisted.

But Sammy Davis, Jr., was a little more candid. Sammy freely invited agents into his penthouse suite in the posh Ambassador East Hotel even though it was morning and he was wearing nothing but a tight pair of black slacks. He offered the agents the run of the place, including an elaborately stocked bar. They were more interested in why somebody like himself would cut short lucrative Las Vegas engagements to work at the Villa Venice, and for nothing.

"Baby, that's a very good question," he said, then smiled, feinted, as if going through a piece of his act. "But I have to say it's for my man Francis."

Or friends of his?

"By all means."

Like Sam Giancana?

"By all means."

They asked him to elaborate.

Davis cocked his head and shot them his characteristic sideways glance. He paused, took a deep drink, then exhaled.

"Baby, let me say this. I got one eye, and that one eye sees a lot of things that my brain tells me I shouldn't talk about. Because my brain says that, if I do, my one eye might not be seeing *anything* after a while."

He left it at that. The agents left it at that. The Villa Venice attracted full houses for the duration of the Rat Pack's run—almost an entire month. Each night Giancana showed up and hosted lavish receptions in his upstairs suite in the restaurant, parties that the performers rarely missed. And the quonset-hut casino ran at full tilt, taking some of its customers for upward of $25,000. Then, as quickly as it had opened and became one of the top Chicago clubs, the Villa Venice closed, its entertainment policy was suspended, and the restaurant was used only sporadically for receptions and parties for hoods and their families.

To the agents who listened to Giancana from the other end of their microphones, the reason for the sudden closing was obvious. A month-long reparation from Sinatra and company was all that Giancana needed. They listened as he counted up the returns for the Villa Venice and the quonset-hut casino. The total topped $3 million. All of it was free of overhead, free from strings of IOU's, for Giancana had cashed in on one of his biggest. His "other plans" for Sinatra and company had come to pass; he was satisfied. The Kennedy problem was something he would deal with in other ways, at other times. To his credit, in one of the few instances of such importance in his life, he had turned a problem to his favor without killing somebody.

Sinatra was to suffer further financial problems as a result of his close friendship with Giancana. By 1963 Sinatra had bought into the Sands Hotel in Las Vegas, and had become owner of 50 percent of the stock of the Cal-Neva Lodge in nearby Lake Tahoe. That put him under the scrutiny of the Nevada Gaming Control Board, the same commission responsible for the "black book" of undesirable hoods. Under state law, catering to any of the hoodlums listed in the black book was grounds for license revocation. The board meant it, and when Giancana continually appeared at the Cal-Neva, staying there with Phyllis McGuire as honored guests of Sinatra, it moved to challenge Sinatra's right to hold a gambling license.

The board's evidence was strong, for not only had Sinatra freely associated with Giancana throughout 1963, but the relationship went back to the late 1950's. When customs men had frisked Giancana in 1958, and the infamous bogus-driver's-license incident ensued, they found Sinatra's private telephone number. When Joe Pignatello, Giancana's one-time chauffeur and bodyguard, was set up in Las Vegas and attempted to gain gambling licenses, his case was pushed by Sinatra, who said he would vouch for Pignatello's character. Pignatello was still turned down. Finally, the board maintained, when Giancana was not with Sinatra in Las Vegas or Cal-Neva, he stayed at the singer's home in Palm Springs.

When approached by the chairman of the Nevada State Gaming Commission, Sinatra lost his temper. His association with hoodlum elements had become an increasingly sore spot. He maintained that he could see whom he wished on a social basis, and he resented questioning of his business ventures. He replied to the board official with an outburst of obscenities, then followed with what was interpreted as a threat the board official said in an attempt to scare the board out of pressing the case. He ended the conversation by saying that he would continue to do what he pleased, and see anyone he wished, regardless of what the board thought about it. With such a response, and when a Sinatra employee at Cal-Neva refused to answer a board subpoena on the issue, the commission formally moved to revoke his state gambling licenses.

The issue simmered for a while as Sinatra took a beating in the press and answered reporters' queries with "I don't know what the hell they're talking about." But in October he formally announced that he was divesting himself of all his Nevada holdings, the Sands stock, which was valued at $380,000, and the half ownership of the Cal-Neva, put at $3 million. It was a stiff price to pay for his friendship with the little Chicago hood, though Sinatra stated that Giancana had nothing to do with his decision. He had decided that he would not waste his time trying to convince Nevada officials of his good intentions and that his investments had become too diversified anyway. He had been named a vice president of the Warner Brothers movie studio in Hollywood and was going to devote all of his energies and income to the entertainment world.

It was an important bit of strategy for Sinatra. His professional reputation would have been badly damaged if he fought the gaming board in court. It would only serve to sharpen the public's focus on his friendship with Giancana and other mob figures. It would peel back the layers of friendships that went years back in Sinatra's life. It would expose the personal, psychological bond he had with his *paesani,* one that he didn't choose to reject and that he didn't think he had to reject. An assault on them was an assault on him, no matter where he went in show business or what kind of crowd he ran with, presidents and senators included.

The stories leaked out anyway, and they were difficult to gloss over. Earlier that year, Giancana had been at the Cal-Neva with

Phyllis and the sisters as they completed an appearance there. Also present was a small, wiry Canadian named Victor LaCroix Collins, who served as the trio's road manager. Collins had originally been a rancher on the Calgary ranch of Lowell Williamson, Christine McGuire's husband, but he signed on with the group and oversaw most of their tour arrangements. While lounging with Phyllis in her chalet at the Cal-Neva, Giancana invited Christine, Dorothy, and Collins in for a drink, a nightcap after the trio's performance and the dinner Collins had had with the two sisters. As the time passed, the discussion drifted over to Phyllis, and Collins began to criticize her. Voices soon began to rise; Collins became upset as did Phyllis, and she stood up and began shouting at him. He stood up and pushed her back into her chair.

At that, Giancana jumped Collins and the two of them began scuffling and rolling on the floor. Collins was stronger, younger, and tougher than Giancana, even if he wasn't as experienced, and soon took the advantage. He was pummeling Giancana handily when Sinatra burst in. He pulled Collins off and pinned his arms behind him. The McGuire sisters shrieked and scrambled to get out of the way. According to the state and federal investigators, Sinatra held tightly to the Canadian while Giancana regained his balance and his strength. Then, while Sinatra exposed him like a human punching bag, Collins helplessly absorbed the combination of punches Giancana could muster.

14

When FBI agents prowled through the back room of the Armory Lounge, the room where Giancana held court amidst the linens and soup cans and tomato paste, they came upon a carton of the most unlikely gadgets. They were electronics devices, eavesdropping equipment mostly, as costly and sophisticated as any the agents themselves were planting. Upon closer scrutiny, it became obvious that the equipment was government material—specifically, material purchased by and perhaps still belonging to the Central Intelligence Agency. The agents were dumbfounded, and in days following they made contact with the CIA to find out what business they might have been doing with the likes of Sam Giancana.

The electronics gear was physical evidence of a perverse CIA operation aimed at Fidel Castro, Cuba's fledgling Premier, most definitely involving Giancana, his associates, and his resources. Initially, the FBI was told that the CIA was only making use of underworld figures on an intelligence-gathering basis, and when the story broke in the press in the middle of 1963, the Agency's rather murky explanation of the plan went no further than that. It was many years later that the real CIA goal was exposed: Castro's assassination.

Soon after the fall of Fulgencio Batista in 1959, the CIA began its campaign to discredit the unfriendly Castro and lay the groundwork for his demise. Their attempts, and more serious efforts to follow, smacked of the worst spy-counterspy plots, and contained some of the choicest comedy. Their activities, running roughly from 1959 through 1965, included at least eight assassination plots against Castro, and the potential use of high-powered rifles, poison pills, lethal cigars, even exploding underwater seashells.

The Agency began in early 1960, intending only to mar Castro's public image in the eyes of Cubans and to puncture his seeming charisma. They first considered sabotaging his speeches, proposing to spray his broadcasting studio with a chemical that would produce results similar to an LSD trip. That was shelved when the chemical was found to be unreliable. Another chemical was tested for use in coating a box of cigars that would be smoked by Castro prior to a speech and would cause him to lapse into a confused stupor. Another plan involved an effort against Castro's beard, his apparent badge among the people. Because Castro had planned trips outside Cuba (in the early days of his regime he did not completely break off relations with the United States), particularly to New York, it was thought that the beard could be eradicated by use of a strong depilatory. The plan was to dust his shoes with thallium salts when he left them outside his New York hotel room to be shined. The plan, and the beard, never came off because Castro canceled his visit.

The CIA's efforts grew more deadly with time, however, and centered on what the Agency called "neutralizing" Castro's influence. That meant assassinating him, and perhaps his brother Raúl as well. An early plan again included Castro's beloved cigars, this time dipping them into a botulinus toxin, a poison so potent that he would die after putting one in his mouth. It is unknown if the plan was ever attempted, but preliminary contact with Cuban nationals who would carry out the cigar switch proved fruitless. It was then, in mid-1960, that the Agency came up with the idea of contacting members of the underworld to commit mayhem on the Premier.

It is unclear exactly who in the CIA decided to go to the hoods, but first contact was made between Colonel Sheffield Edwards, director of the CIA's Office of Security, and Deputy Director for Plans, Richard M. Bissell, Jr. It was Edwards who approached Robert Maheu, an ex-FBI agent who had been on the CIA payroll since 1954 on a limited basis. Maheu, who was operating a Miami-based detective agency at the time, was asked to contact John Roselli, the Las Vegas mob representative of Giancana. The premise was simple but sound: that the underworld would perhaps have strong contacts in Cuba left over from its pre-Castro gambling concessions. Actually, the mob did not have effective Cuban contacts (or, at least, they never surfaced) but it had plenty of interest in the project. In Batista's regime, the outfit, specifically Meyer Lansky and the New York families, had designs on turning Cuba into a second Las Vegas. It pumped millions of dollars into hotel-casinos and related businesses. When the revolution erupted, the mob, in traditional bipartisan spirit, financially backed both sides, only to have Batista run off to exile with many of the outfit's millions, and Castro shut down the casinos. (Castro stopped all gambling activity when he first took power, then reopened the casinos to foreign tourists in February, 1959, only to close them permanently in September of 1961.)

Maheu had known Roselli in Las Vegas, and though he claimed not to have been aware of Roselli's mob connections, it was evident to him, in his words, that Roselli "was able to accomplish things in Las Vegas when nobody else seemed to get the same kind of attention." Roselli was to be told that efforts against Castro could be the first step to the outfit's recovery of their Cuban investments. He was also to be offered a figure of $150,000 for Castro's head.

Maheu, Roselli, and a CIA agent met for the first time in early September, 1960, at the Brown Derby restaurant in Beverly Hills. Roselli was suspicious and reluctant to get involved, and insisted on contact with a higher government official. He suspected the CIA was involved but wasn't sure. The second meeting was successful, and Roselli agreed to go to Miami to recruit Cubans for the operation. He also went there to lay out the scheme to Giancana.

Although the idea of being a government agent in the strictest sense was repugnant to Giancana and any hood, there is little doubt that a Castro hit contract, even if done in the service of the CIA, probably intrigued him. It has been said that, even in their almost daily disregard for the law of the land, mobsters remain intensely patriotic, grateful for the U.S.A. and the opportunity it provided them and their fathers. Roselli repeated that sentiment, stating that the mission "was for the Government of the United States, this is the least I can do, because I owe it a lot," and even refusing payment. He may have believed what he said, but a candid interpretation would reveal that Roselli, real name Filippo Saco, was working an angle against deportation proceedings against him. Born in Italy and, it was believed, brought illegally into this country, he amassed an extensive criminal and prison record from his days with Paul Ricca and the Capone gang. Government action against his citizenship was in motion when he was approached by the CIA. A mission on behalf of the CIA and national interest might wash away his problems, he figured. With Giancana, it may have been a matter of money—the $150,000 would have tempted him—but more precisely it was the outside chance that he could pave the way for the mob's retaking of Cuba, a feat that would put him in overwhelming favor with the national syndicate, even to the point of placing him at its head.

First, however, he had to convince himself that the CIA was really serious about the venture, enough, anyway, to commit money and services, and not just interested in letting the mob take the chances. He was introduced to Maheu by Roselli in Miami Beach. Roselli referred to him as "Sam Gold," and said he would serve as a backup man. Also present was Santo Trafficante, a long-time friend of Lucky Luciano, who had run Cuban enterprises. Roselli referred to Trafficante as Joe, and said he would be the chief courier to Cuba. In meetings that followed, Giancana met often with Maheu to hammer out particulars of the Castro attempt, but initially to avail himself of what Maheu and the CIA could do for him.

Giancana was very suspicious of what Phyllis McGuire was doing when he was away. He was also extremely jealous. When rumors reached him of her accompanying nightclub comedian Dan Rowan, he decided to see how serious it was. He could have easily arranged for any one of his underlings to dog Rowan and McGuire, but he chose instead to let Maheu do it. In October of 1960, Maheu arranged for another Miami detective agency to send a man to Las Vegas and place a microphone in the wall of Rowan's apartment. Instead, the detective proceeded to tap Rowan's room telephone. In the process, the detective left equipment unattended in the room, where it was discovered by a maid.

Local police then arrested the man and he ultimately passed the blame to Miami and Maheu. Roselli finally paid the detective's bail.

Maheu insisted that the tap was necessary (from the CIA's point of view) to keep Giancana in Miami and his attention focused on the Castro operation. He claimed that Giancana was so aggravated when he learned of Phyllis' seeing others that he threatened to go to Las Vegas himself. But the circumstances of the tap may have been different, including the possibility that the CIA was worried that Giancana was leaking information to friends and associates about the Cuba effort. Sources told them that Giancana had openly boasted of the caper to friends and assured them that Castro's death was imminent. The Agency then attempted to eavesdrop on Phyllis to determine if she knew of the plan and was spreading the story. Roselli himself was worried about Giancana, and said they attempted the wire tap to "have him keep his mouth shut." Overwhelming evidence indicates Giancana's skepticism of the whole affair, including the CIA's sincerity and its competence. When told of the detective's arrest in Las Vegas, he was convulsed with laughter, according to Roselli: "I remember his expression, smoking a cigar, he almost swallowed it laughing about it."

Still, the planning went on. The CIA suggested a simple, direct execution, but Giancana, though he would have enjoyed such a hit, opposed the idea because he said it would be difficult and dangerous. He, instead, suggested poison. A quantity of pills containing the deadly botulinus toxin (which, in CIA laboratory tests, thoroughly did the job on monkeys) were produced and delivered to Roselli. Though the exact events are unclear, it appeared that Castro, because of either superior intelligence forces or dumb luck, was one step ahead of his stalkers. Once a high-level aide working for the CIA was to have slipped the pills into Castro's drink, but failed when he was demoted and lost access to the Premier. In another instance, Santo Trafficante claimed to have a contact (termed by the CIA an "asset") who owned a restaurant frequented by Castro and who wished to eliminate the Premier and further his own activities in Cuban rackets. The Cuban wanted money for expenses and communications devices to pull the operation off. All of this was arranged, and Maheu, Roselli, Trafficante, and the Cuban met at the Fontainebleau

Hotel in early 1961, before the disastrous Bay of Pigs invasion. At the hotel, Maheu, according to Roselli, "opened his briefcase and dumped a whole lot of money on his lap," along with the capsules that "couldn't be used in boiling soups," but would work nicely in water.

An associate of Roselli and Giancana, Joseph Shimon, also claimed to have been present at the delivery of the pills. Shimon said he went to the Floyd Patterson–Ingemar Johansson heavyweight boxing match in Miami with Maheu and later was told that Maheu had a contract to assassinate Castro. With Roselli, Giancana, and Maheu, Shimon shared a suite in the Fontainebleau and saw the capsules, believed to be five or six gelatin pills, to be used to kill Castro. They would be slipped into his drink, Shimon was told, and he would become ill in two or three days and then die. Maheu told him, "Johnny's going to handle everything; this is Johnny's contract." A few days later he said he got a phone call from an excited Maheu, "Did you see the paper? Castro's ill. He's going to be sick two or three days. Wow, we got him."

But Shimon also said that Giancana confided his continuing skepticism about the entire campaign. "I'm not in it. They are asking me for the names of some guys who used to work in casinos. Maheu's conning the hell out of the CIA."

Whatever happened, the poison capsules apparently never got to Castro. He stopped frequenting the restaurant owned by Trafficante's friend, and even if he had, CIA officials said the "go" signal had never gone through. At some time, it is believed, the CIA-backed Cuban had an opportunity to give the pills to Castro and either Raúl Castro or Che Guevara. But again the "go" signal never came. The money and pills were returned to the States. The Bay of Pigs invasion followed shortly after.

Though the Bay of Pigs led to the exit of Deputy Director Bissell, one of the early supervisors of the Castro effort, the attempts against the Premier went on. Under William Harvey, the CIA remained in contact with Roselli, but told him to cut off his dealings with Maheu and Giancana, both termed surplus and "untrustworthy" by the Agency. More pills were secured and transferred to unnamed Cubans, only this time they demanded weapons and electronic equipment to aid in their mission. Explosives, detonators, rifles, even a bazooka, handguns, radios, and boat radar—all costing an estimated $5,000—were purchased with CIA money, then loaded into a rented truck. The key was given to Roselli and he was to deliver the goods to his Cuban contacts. While the CIA agent and Roselli watched, the truck was driven away by the contacts. In the days and weeks that followed they waited for progress reports. None came. Four months later, this time late 1962, Roselli and his CIA agents decided that nothing was going to happen. Indeed, they had no assurance that the pills, the guns, explosives, and electronic equipment ever made it to Cuba, or were used in an assassination attempt. They also decided to break off contact with their Cuban agents.

Still more efforts at fantasy were considered. In 1963, the CIA considered rigging an exploding seashell and positioning it where Castro commonly went skindiving. The skindiving suit itself was mentioned, and plans were explored to contaminate the breathing apparatus with a tubercule bacillus. A diving suit was even purchased and dusted with a fungus that would produce a chronic skin disease. But, even as the CIA couldn't get close to the Premier's cigars, or his shoes, his beard, or his drinks, they also couldn't molest his wetsuit.

But word of their attempts made other government agencies furious. The FBI was particularly upset because it compromised their efforts against Giancana. When the Bureau investigated the Las Vegas–Maheu wiretap connection, it felt itself compromised because of the danger of exposing covert CIA operations abroad. In early 1962, another development arose that put the FBI in a delicate position. An investigation of Roselli uncovered the existence of a mutual friend of Roselli and Giancana, and also, most importantly, of President John Kennedy.

She was Judy Campbell (Exner), a dark-eyed, dark-haired divorcee, whose marriage to actor William Campbell had ended in 1960. She first met Roselli in Hollywood during the 1950's and dated him when her marriage broke up. She was then one of many women present on the fringes of Hollywood crowds, women who gravitated toward the action, be it with hoods, movie stars, entertainers, or politicians. When Kennedy made the Las Vegas Scene in March, 1960, he met her through an introduction from Frank Sinatra and began an intense, if surreptitious relationship. From his election and through mid-1962, White House phone logs recorded 70 calls between the two.

Campbell's relationship with Giancana also came via Sinatra, this time in Miami only weeks after her meeting with Kennedy. Whatever she had going with the then Senator—she claims to have had a four-day tryst with Kennedy at the Plaza Hotel in New York City in March, 1960—little of it rubbed off on Giancana. He was seeing Phyllis McGuire regularly at the time, and even though he often accommodated willing new friends, his fling with Judy Campbell was momentary at best. Chicago agents, who were listening to several microphones on Giancana and monitoring his telephone calls from a variety of hangouts, only briefly encountered her. She came to Chicago for a week and wandered around the Ambassador West Hotel, making it plain that she was trying to get closer to Giancana and his Oak Park home. Finally taking a room in the Oak Park Arms Hotel, she was seen coming and going from the hotel to the Giancana house for a few days after, then she left town. She made no phone calls from the house, and none to the White House. In fact, little of Giancana's business, either professional or social, ever generated from his home telephone. Phone logs of his business spots revealed one phone call, this one from the Amberlite Lounge, where Giancana occasionally hung out, to a Miss Campbell.

Her fling with Giancana may have been significant in light of the fact that she was also seeing the President, but it is doubtful that she was a conduit between the two. Giancana regarded most women, perhaps only with the exception of Rose Flood, his sister-in-law, as untrustworthy and unreliable. He told them nothing of his activities, little about his friends, and nothing of his plans. Phyllis McGuire in her years by his side was all but ignorant of the intricacies of his business dealings. Her telephones may have been used as his switchboard but she was never a confidante. Giancana's daughters, while coming to know many of his associates and mob friends, also were told nothing of what he did. In fact, when new faces appeared at meetings or at the home, the daughters often dug up books on Chicago's mobsters to learn what they were supposed to do for a living. (The daughters, as the years passed, also became somewhat resentful of Phyllis McGuire and other women their age who saw their father. As far as Judy Campbell was concerned, her face was unknown and unremembered in the household.)

Judy Campbell fit nicely into Giancana's routine because she barely dented it. He carefully adhered to the mob's general code of silence, his alleged gabbings about the Castro plot notwithstanding. If he did spread word of it to friends, or girlfriends, it was probably because he considered the whole venture a lark, and one only remotely concerned with him. Had it been hard and cold mob business, he would have said nothing. He once illustrated this when sitting in a bar shortly after a government raid on a mob meeting resulted in the arrest and exposure of a number of top leaders. A mob lieutenant approached him and asked if he had heard of the raid, and Giancana, sitting and staring straight ahead, with a rigid expression, didn't answer him, as if to say that he knew damn well of the fiasco. The associate didn't read his irritation and kept pumping him for a reaction. Giancana remained unmoved, finally staring up at a long sailfish mounted on the wall above the bar. "You see that fuckin' fish?" he said. "If he'd kept his mouth shut he wouldn't a got caught." Then he went back to his drink and said nothing more.

The very idea of one woman bedding a Kennedy and a Giancana, however, fired the worst fears in others. When Campbell's name mixed with that of the two, plus John Roselli, on FBI reports (reports that didn't originate from Chicago, for agents there had no record of sounding any alarm about the Campbell situation, or even keeping a close watch on her), J. Edgar Hoover moved to do something about it. On February 27, 1962, he sent a memorandum concerning Judy Campbell to Attorney General Robert Kennedy and Kenneth O'Donnell, Special Assistant to the President. Though it was a delicate situation for Hoover, it was no doubt one that he relished, for with his sense of position playing and his feel for keeping a tight hold on his job, nothing better suited him than a potentially serious indiscretion by a President.

Almost a month later he had lunch with Kennedy and O'Donnell, and while alone with Kennedy for a short time, he revealed the information he had on the President, Campbell, and Giancana. The word must have been devastating to Kennedy, for White House phone logs show one more call to Campbell, only hours after the Hoover luncheon, and then no further contact. Even the Rat Pack—Sinatra *et al.*—became unwelcome guests, and hosts, for in the months that followed Kennedy contacted Peter Lawford prior to trips to California and requested that

Lawford find him suitable accommodations, meaning somewhere other than Sinatra's Palm Springs home.

The FBI still had the problem of the CIA's involvement with Giancana, especially the issue of prosecuting the illegal Las Vegas tap of Dan Rowan's phone. In a series of meetings between FBI and CIA people, a decision was reached not to prosecute in order not to endanger sensitive CIA sources and activities. The Bureau swallowed hard, and its Justice Department boss, Robert Kennedy, when told of the operation and the use of Roselli and Giancana, registered his anger. CIA General Counsel Lawrence Houston was present.

"If you have seen Mr. Kennedy's eyes get steely and his jaw set and his voice get low and precise, you get a definite feeling of unhappiness," Houston said later. Kennedy agreed with J. Edgar Hoover when Hoover said that the CIA used horrible judgment in contacting Maheu and then Roselli and Giancana. To Houston, Kennedy said simply, "There is not to be any contact with the mafia without prior consultation with me . . . if you ever try to do business with organized crime again—with gangsters—you *will* let me know."

That officially ended the Castro neutralization attempt as far as the Justice Department was concerned, and CIA memoranda indicated that Roselli was told that the operation was off and the $150,000 reward offer withdrawn. As far as Giancana was concerned, it had never been something he took very seriously. He never received any payment, even for expenses or hotel bills. Likewise, Roselli received no CIA money except for brief hotel stays in Miami, a fact that suited his sense of patriotic duty. But Giancana always held on to the outside chance that the CIA contact might do him some good in the face of the unremitting FBI effort against him. At one time, Chuck English, Giancana's long-time friend, associate, and golfing partner, whom the agents considered somewhat of a clown prince among mobsters, seriously remarked that they should lay off, that "we're on the same team."

Though the remark was later disavowed, the message was clear to agents. Once they got over their aggravation at the CIA use of Giancana, they used it to needle him. They laughed and said it was good to see him joining the force, hoping the idea of

Giancana's role as a government agent would filter back to his top-level associates. "C'mon, Mo," they taunted as he walked through airport corridors and putted on golf courses. "We'll show you our badges if you'll show us yours."

15

IT WAS A LARGE, aggressive construction company, doing millions of dollars of jobs each year, but until this one, never in the city of Chicago. When it won the bidding on the motel, a large Loop structure with an underground garage, the firm went to the proper offices in City Hall and took out the necessary permits. Construction began on schedule and proceeded without any significant problems. Building anything in the city, especially in the Loop area, meant dickering with unions, inspectors, suppliers, subcontractors, the usual persons involved in the trade, but it was nothing this firm hadn't dealt with before and couldn't handle now.

One morning, however, the firm's construction foreman showed up at the job and found work at a standstill. Not one hammer was being raised. It wasn't long before a man showed up and identified himself as a Democratic precinct captain, specifically of the very precinct in which the motel was being built. The captain had discovered that the construction firm had not taken out any insurance on the building, or if it had, not with brokers familiar with the ward Democratic office. He suggested that the firm contact an outfit called Anco Insurance, on North LaSalle Street in the Loop. When the firm did, it quickly learned that Anco was owned and operated by the Democratic ward alderman, and the Democratic ward executive secretary, all, specifically, of the Democratic First Ward.

The Anco people were most receptive to the construction firm, almost as if they had been expecting them. Policies were drawn up and premiums paid. Scarcely had the ink dried, when work started up again back at the site. It went on without problems, with city inspectors increasingly amiable, and even Chicago police squad cars lingering around the area during off hours just to make sure things were not molested. By the time the last concrete was poured and the finishing touches completed, the construction firm was most pleased, having all but forgotten the time missed by the work stoppage, and recommending to other firms doing work in the First Ward that proper insurance coverage was a great idea.

Whether it knew it or not, the out-of-town construction firm was simply taking part in an honored political tradition in Chicago and most definitely in its First Ward. Consisting of Chicago's Loop and sections of the Near West Side, the First Ward has long been the domain of versatile politicians like Hinky Dink Kenna and Bathhouse John Coughlin, men who were as much at home in the Levee's saloons and brothels as they were in the back rooms of the ward headquarters, often because the two were one and the same. They freely aligned themselves with Big Jim Colosimo, Johnny Torrio, Al Capone—working the politics of the ward around the needs of its businessmen, regardless of what business they were in. They controlled political jobs, city services, permits, licenses, even the jobs of city workers, including policemen, prosecutors, and judges. They controlled political slates and, in the best forms of buying, slugging, and bribing, they controlled the votes, in some years down to each individual vote.

As the years passed and the power of individual hoods rose and fell, so the politicians followed suit. The First Ward, which in 1947 was merged with the old "Bloody Twentieth," which included the Patch, saw its politicians fade quickly if they fell out of favor with the reigning hoods, or if a new boss wanted a particular protégé in power. But most pols were most flexible, sustaining the lucrative insurance operations for the hundreds of businesses in the Loop that needed coverage, or keeping a close watch on the many wire rooms and books that operated and making sure they didn't operate without the blessing of the mob. Out in the ward's residential areas, precinct captains were building their IOU's with the people, helping them with permits, licenses, smoothing over problems with the police, attending wakes, weddings, sending a basket of food for an anniversary. Everyone needed help from the ward office at one time or other, especially immigrants who didn't know the language and had little clout, or their sons who needed jobs or sometimes got in trouble. What the precinct captains wanted in return was a vote, and if they didn't get it, a chicken, a bottle, or a couple of dollars could be found on election day to help things along. It was a routine, day-to-day contact with people of the neighborhoods that began years ago with Johnny Powers and continued through the years with new faces, new favors.

For these same politicians, the backing of the outfit meant survival. At one time mob help included dozens of vote floaters or sluggers who went out and coerced the voters, but later it meant sheer money and influence. Mob heavies could convince potentially strong rivals that they should not run, that their health meant more to them than an election victory. Mob money could launch a campaign and keep it visible. What the outfit wanted was position—in the police department, where key men could either thwart efforts against mob businesses and hoods themselves or could quickly alert hoods to such moves. (It has long been a fact of life that syndicate inroads into the police department are so deep that confidential information concerning them is known within hours after it hits department files.) The mob also wanted position in the legislature, where key members could attempt to thwart laws aimed at curbing syndicate ventures or new laws providing wider police powers in fighting organized crime. On a lower level, the mob wanted police and judges it could control. When it got them, no matter how strong or tenuous the relationship, it cultivated its favors carefully.

No one was better at working such strategy than Murray Humphreys, a veteran of the fix from the days of Capone. It was Humphreys who insisted that playing the angles was more effective than resorting to out-and-out muscle, although he knew that mob leverage worked because of the fear it engendered. With police, especially high-ranking officers who were in a position to do great favors when the situation arose, the mob worked at improving their positions in the department. That even meant tipping them to heists and robberies, most involving fringe mob associates or freelancers, and having the coppers show up and make outstanding arrests. With one notorious Chicago police officer, mob setups resulted in wild shootouts in which thieves were left riddled with service revolver bullets. The officer soon got a reputation for being the toughest of the tough, even retired with it (and, when so doing, decried the present-day attitudes that supposedly weaken police powers) and few knew that he was the outfit's man in a pinch.

With judges, the same deception was exploited. Humphreys and associates encouraged their judges to be tough at all times, particularly on minor offenses involving hoods. The judge was to get a reputation as a hanging judge and amass a record against hoods that showed no mercy and gave no hint of collusion or favoritism. There would always be a time when a big favor would be needed, and an outfit judge with a tough, anti-crime syndicate record could better deliver.

But mostly the mob influenced ward politics on a day-to-day level: the unending business of collecting and granting favors. When Jake Guzik took control of the Capone gang fortunes, he installed his trusted aide Benjamin "Buddy" Jacobson as ward secretary or "fixer." And Jacobson often publicly boasted that he was the man to see. "I am the fixer in the First Ward," he'd tell anyone in earshot. "I've been the fixer for over forty years. I take care of everybody, including policemen, politicians, and judges. Everybody who needs anything comes to me for favors in my ward. This is my function."

Through the years those who came and went included Morris Eller, Peter Fusco, Peter Granata, Sam Romano, Andrew Euzzino —all local and state politicians. But none shone more brightly or made more noise than Congressman Roland Libonati. "Libby" was a round-faced, wattled veteran of the Capone era when being seen in the presence of gangsters wasn't a shame. He boasted of his friendship with Scarface and Jack McGurn, even proudly posing with them at a Cub baseball game in 1931, only a short time before he began his first term as a state legislator. Later he went to the U.S. House of Representatives. At both places he worked openly, and with a talent for malapropisms that left his colleagues in tears, for measures that would benefit his underworld friends, especially anti-crime bills. With a seat on the powerful House Judiciary Committee, Libonati's leanings were not harmless, since federal agents watched him openly consort with Murray Humphreys, Paul Ricca, and several other hoods. He also was in a position to accommodate friends and relatives of the hoods. When he hired a legislative aide, it happened to be a young lawyer named Anthony Tisci, later to be the husband of Bonnie Giancana.

With the passing of Jake Guzik and the rise of Giancana in the late 1950's, the power structure of the First Ward changed to meet Giancana's wishes. Buddy Jacobson was replaced as executive secretary by Pasqualino Marchone, a sharp, keenly intelligent graduate of the Patch who had Americanized his name to Pat Marcy. It was Marcy whom Giancana looked to as the brains behind the ward, a man capable of running its politics with skill and power, rivaling the best of the behind-the-scenes men in Cook County politics. It was Marcy who became the pipeline, the fixer, the man in the First Ward who could get the job done no matter what it took. In its grand scheme of things, the mob often designated key personalities to ostensibly stay out of the rackets and work only in infiltrating influential areas such as politics, the courts, the police department. However unrealistic their thinking may have been, Marcy was their choice to penetrate City Hall, starting from his base in the First Ward.

Up front, Giancana's man was another old neighborhood chum, John D'Arco. Though D'Arco possessed a remarkable likeness to Capone himself, he managed to stay out of trouble as a kid growing up in the Patch on South Bishop Street. His parents attempted to keep him off the streets and out of reach of the 42 Gang. His godfather was Corrado DeSylvester, a sharp college student who, while at the University of Chicago (one of the few kids from the Patch who went to college at all), studied with John Landesco and researched important sociological studies of the Italian-American communities in Chicago, one of which concentrated on the 42 Gang.

Even with such influences, D'Arco narrowly evaded early jail sentences. In 1931, while still a teenager, his parents died and he went to live with an uncle in Yonkers, New York. But his friends from Chicago contacted him and persuaded him to return to the West Side. He did, and shortly after was implicated by a woman who said that D'Arco and another boy robbed her on the Oak Street Beach. DeSylvester made the trip to court on his godson's behalf, but could not persuade the judge to drop charges on his word that D'Arco was out of the city when the crime was said to have taken place. A trial some months later vindicated D'Arco, partly on DeSylvester's testimony, and he went free. Through the years, perhaps innocently, perhaps owing to D'Arco's influence within the police department, records of the arrest and charges were lost.

But incriminating information against D'Arco came later from another source. When Giancana was detained by customs officials in 1959 upon his return from a vacation in Mexico, they found among his possessions a notebook that contained the name and phone number of D'Arco. When FBI agents learned of it, they confronted D'Arco, asking him how an upstanding citizen and public servant could afford to be listed in a hood's address book. D'Arco recoiled at the accusation, but instead of denying any connection with Giancana, he turned on the agents. "You can't touch me in this town," he said to them. "As long as my constituents don't squawk and the man in City Hall backs me, I can do anything I wish." He paused, then repeated himself, "You guys can't touch me."

D'Arco, with Giancana's blessing, succeeded at his political moves, first as state senator, then as First Ward committeeman and alderman. By the late 1950's, evidence of the Giancana-D'Arco-Marcy combine was so strong that federal agents chose the First Ward office as another home for a microphone. In no time they listened as the political word came in, as the favors were done, as the clout was dispensed.

What Giancana attempted to accomplish with the help of the First Ward and West Side Bloc politicians (the name given to a handful of state and federal politicians from areas controlled by the syndicate) was to somehow get the federal monkey off his back. With Humphreys, he worked overtime to try to get a jump on pending legislation, especially that which involved wire-tap and surveillance powers, and then block it. They were also keen on trying to work out another early parole for Paul Ricca, the victim of income-tax convictions. (Ricca entered prison in July, 1959, to begin a three-year sentence, and was released in October, 1961.) Humphreys made frequent trips to Washington to pursue that and related business, as well as pursuing it at home with Pat Marcy and others.

But things got worse instead of better. With increased federal surveillance, the possibility of exposing its politicians in compromising situations loomed ever larger for the mob. Its dealings with the West Side Bloc involved favors and cash, usually kickbacks and percentages. Such moneys were taxable, and grist for a government case. Giancana decided in 1962 that politicians were no longer to be seen with the outfit, no matter what the reason or how innocent the dealings. If the mob were to lose any of its loyal pols, a major source of power and revenue would be endangered, and everybody would suffer.

Such thinking was part of the reason Giancana decided Libby Libonati was no longer the man for Congress. As loyal as he was, Libonati was a clown and his antics would do nothing but bring more heat on the mob. During Giancana's problems with FBI surveillance, Libonati proposed a bill in Congress that would have made it a federal crime for agents to keep criminals, especially so-called hoodlums, under surveillance. Penalties would be stiff: a $5,000 fine and ten years in prison or both. The bill got nowhere, and though Giancana may have sympathized with it, he preferred to fight his enemies in other ways. He told Libonati he was through. Libby demurred but in early 1963 announced that because his wife was so sick he would not run for re-election. He was replaced by Frank Annunzio, a younger, sharper politician, a one-time First Ward committeeman with a clean record even though it was revealed that he was a partner with D'Arco and Buddy Jacobson in Anco Insurance. (Annunzio later sold his interest in Anco.) Annunzio retained legislative aide Anthony Tisci, and even raised his salary from $13,000 to $19,000 a year.

It wasn't Annunzio or Tisci who brought problems, but John D'Arco. Though D'Arco, as committeeman and alderman, generally kept things going, he was never as important to Giancana as was Pat Marcy, and never as well thought of. When Giancana sent word down that no politicians were to be seen with hoods, he went out of his way to get through to D'Arco. Nobody knew that better than FBI agents, and from it they saw a golden opportunity to try to embarrass D'Arco or somehow lessen his image before Giancana.

Their chance came in late 1962 when they intercepted a luncheon meeting between Giancana and D'Arco at the Czech Lodge in North Riverside. Agents Roemer, Hill, and Rutland headed out to the restaurant, intending to plop themselves in the laps of Giancana and D'Arco and make them fully aware that the government knew of their relationship. At the Lodge, Roemer spotted Buddy Jacobson sitting at the door acting as a lookout for D'Arco, whom he'd accompanied to the meet. Roemer, however, pushed his way past Jacobson, nodded at the bartender, and flashed his badge, then walked into the rear dining room, where D'Arco was huddling with Giancana.

"Ho, ho, ho, it's Mo!" Roemer announced, then he shot out his hand to the flustered D'Arco. With a politician's reflex, D'Arco shook it. "Why, how are you, John? It's good to see you again," Roemer added, bubbling with good cheer and trying to give the impression that he saw D'Arco often and knew him well. Giancana glowered, then steeled a rigid expression on his face, but not before he visibly kicked D'Arco in the shins as the alderman was shaking Roemer's hand. D'Arco quickly pulled his hand away and attempted to sit down. But the impact had been made. Roemer lingered a few seconds, then walked out as casually as he had come in. Shortly after, Giancana left, with the same scowl glued to his face.

From the moment Giancana saw D'Arco stick his hand out to Roemer, he'd made up his mind, but he still went through normal channels to get rid of D'Arco. Meetings with Humphreys, Accardo (who had managed to beat his 1960 income-tax conviction in federal appeals court but had not retaken control of the outfit from Giancana), and trusted underbosses Gus Alex and Frank "Strongy" Ferraro were convened, and Giancana presented his case against D'Arco. He wanted him out, and the more he thought about him, the more upset he got. D'Arco was a buffoon, Giancana wailed, a bumbling idiot who didn't deserve what the outfit gave him; in fact, he had become a liability. To state it simply, D'Arco didn't deserve to live. It took Humphrey and even Paul Ricca to calm Giancana down, to convince him that hitting D'Arco would bring on more problems than it would solve.

The lapse with Roemer in the Lodge would have been enough to lose D'Arco his job, but an added point against him was the lessening revenues produced by First Ward gambling due to increased heat from the Cook County sheriff's office and the FBI. The feeling was that D'Arco should have had the clout to prevent such a crackdown, or at least lessen it. It was finally decided that he was out as First Ward alderman, but that he could retain his committeeman position, and also his piece of Anco Insurance.

It was a reprieve for the shaken D'Arco, but hardly a comforting one. The day after the Czech Lodge incident he appeared pale and haggard in City Hall. He complained that he didn't feel well, and that night he entered the hospital. It was reported that he had suffered a heart attack, and though that was never confirmed, the announcement went out shortly after that he would not be a candidate for re-election. He said it more candidly to a hospital visitor: "They told me if I didn't quit, I'd wind up in a box."

Giancana's choice was his nephew-in-law Anthony De Tolve, who during his law school days at DePaul University was known more for his piccolo playing than his acumen. De Tolve was a state senator at the time, having been elected for a third term to the seat he took over from D'Arco in 1951. In the statehouse he became known for antics equal to those of his federal counterpart, Roland Libonati, often entertaining the gallery with wild speeches that he interspersed with jigs danced in the aisles, even wailing away on his piccolo at Springfield parties. But, on strict orders from his uncle-in-law, De Tolve ran his aldermanic campaign very low key; in fact, it was almost nonexistent.

Because Mayor Daley was assailed in City Council by his few critics for the sham of First Ward politics, the press took up the bleatings and went after De Tolve. That wasn't easy, for even though he was supposedly running a campaign De Tolve made no appearances, no speeches, granted no interviews, printed no campaign posters, and even refused to answer the telephone. His office on West Van Buren reminded reporters of an old speakeasy, with its iron bars on the doors, padlocks, and peepholes. But that did not mean that an opponent was picking up the slack, for in the First Ward even those who want to reform things think better of it. De Tolve's Republican opponent, though as difficult to find as De Tolve, was a token quail who was humiliated in the press for his nonexistent campaign. (Partisan politics do not interest the mob. Peter Granata was the First Ward's Republican committeeman and state legislator and a loyal syndicate man.)

It was De Tolve himself who was his own worst enemy. It became obvious to Giancana and others that the merciless press ridicule of De Tolve was potentially a worse problem than anything D'Arco had ever brought on. De Tolve was also the last person expected to fit in with the mob's new attempt to keep a low profile. That was clearly illustrated when De Tolve finally talked to a reporter who had been dogging him for weeks. "Let's get one thing straight: I haven't been hiding," De Tolve told him. "I'm just busy, all the time busy." But he wasn't specific, adding only, "I go for all that cultural stuff. I'm busy, all the time busy." With that, the papers went to their talent for nicknames and dubbed the candidate, Anthony "Busy-Busy" De Tolve.

It was enough for Giancana. Only days before the election he decided that Busy-Busy had to go. The announcement was made to First Ward precinct captains that they were to instruct the voters to write in Michael FioRito. The choice was engineered by Pat Marcy, for Giancana had been unable to make up his mind. More than anything, FioRito was an unknown quantity, which bothered no one, not even the voters who wrote him in by an overwhelming margin.

But even FioRito was to have problems, for the irate segment of Daley critics in City Hall investigated his background and found that he wasn't even a resident of the First Ward. In the previous year he had listed three residences, one on the North Side of Chicago, one in the exclusive suburb of Wilmette, and one in the First Ward's Conrad Hilton Hotel. Sheriff's investigators found numerous other irregularities, most in affidavits filed on behalf of FioRito just prior to the election. It was enough heat to raise even Mayor Daley's ire, and he demanded FioRito resign. The outfit threw in the towel, and after only 19 days in office, FioRito quit. He left the office vacant, something which didn't really bother too many people, for only weeks after the furor passed John D'Arco was found to be back at work doing most of the things he had done before he shook Bill Roemer's hand in the Czech Lodge. Although a lot of things had changed in the months that had followed, most ultimately had stayed the same.

Even Mayor Daley withstood the nonsense and the scorn heaped upon him by opponents in City Hall. With his usual aplomb, Daley simply took no responsibility for the actions of aldermen or aldermanic candidates. When D'Arco resigned and newspapers printed damning charges that his demise was engineered by Giancana, Daley replied, "This is a matter for the people of the ward. I do not interfere with any campaign for alderman in any ward. I have been told by Mrs. D'Arco that he has refused to run because of his health. He has been a fine alderman."

Daley, for his part, has always preferred to take such a position, casting no stones at First Ward politicians or those in three others of the city's 50 wards with strong syndicate ties. There was little question in anyone's mind that he could purge the organization of such influences, but he didn't wish to. His power thrived on diversity, allowing individual power brokers to do their favors and make their deals as long as they did his will in City Council and delivered the vote. The First Ward had always delivered, raising nary a whimper in City Hall (even when the Mayor bulldozed much of the Patch in the 1960's in favor of Chicago's Circle Campus of the University of Illinois, John D'Arco and his organization were hard-pressed to object), and beginning the council's voting—usually by snapping to attention when a roll was called and looking to the Mayor's council leader for the thumb up or the thumb down.

Even when the Mayor and the the city of Chicago were held up to contempt from out-of-town critics of the mob, Daley blustered indignation. When New York hood Joe Valachi cited the Chicago outfit as having the country's strongest political, police, and judicial contacts, Daley feigned outrage. "This man is not doing Chicago's reputation any good. Real people recognize Chicago as a great city despite what has been said by his kind. Chicago is a fine city of churches and schools. We have a great police department. His statements are without truth. While we have our faults, let's not start to agree with someone like him. I don't like to hear these figments of imagination and hallucinations."

After the tremors passed, the memories of the Libonatis and Busy-Busy De Tolves prized more by newspaper reporters than anyone else, politics went on as usual. The First Ward aldermanic spot was finally bestowed on Donald Parillo, a young banker who was the son of William Parillo, a West Side politician with long-time allegiances to Capone and Jake Guzik. Son Donald took immediate criticism not only for his family ties, but also because he was involved in businesses with notorious mob ties: the Meadowmoor Dairy and the Parr Loan and Parr Finance companies. Meadowmoor was a textbook study of hidden mob interests; the Parr companies were known not for their clients but for their victims, for police found that its officers and employees were well-known juice-loan operators. When William "Action" Jackson was put on the meathook by James Torello and Fifi Buccieri, he was working as a collector for Parr Finance.

Parillo talked his way through such allegations, clearly showing himself to be an alderman meeting Giancana's requirements. He ascribed his inordinate wealth to good business and inheritances. His mob friends were leftovers from his father's days in the old neighborhood, and furthermore he resented the innuendo that accompanied his name simply because it was Italian. He did nothing as alderman but serve the people of the ward, he said, doing favors and attending to needs. He even donated his meager aldermanic salary to charity.

Meanwhile, the business of the ward also went on. It was simply done more discreetly. D'Arco met Giancana and Humphreys, or the rising First Ward power Gus Alex, in autos in shopping-center parking lots, while Butch Blasi kept lookout for unwanted intruders. Jacobson and Marcy made frequent trips to deliver the ward's payoffs, deliveries occasionally witnessed by FBI agents. They watched, for example, one December morning as Giancana left his house at 8:00 A.M. and drove to a nearby Oak Park restaurant. At 8:30 Jacobson came and sat across from him. They talked idly, then Jacobson produced a manila envelope and Giancana opened it. He displayed a packet of currency two inches thick, a total, agents later discovered, of $10,000 in cash, the percentage of the Anco Insurance profits due Giancana.

With business like that, there was no need to disrupt things in the ward, no need to dislodge D'Arco. Yet anyone close to Giancana knew that the D'Arco episode had disastrous effects on him. The pressure of the FBI, the face of the smiling Bobby Kennedy in the Justice Department, Sinatra be damned, the constant need to look over his shoulder were more aggravating than anything he'd encountered. Also, the increased government pressure was taking its toll not only on the First Ward revenues, but on all the mob's concessions. It was simply much easier to operate when the G were not around. And, though top-echelon hoods realized that, it was difficult for them not to attach some of the blame to Giancana personally, to his flamboyance, his club hopping, his newspaper photos with Phyllis McGuire, his constant traveling, his uncontrollable temper, a temper never so obvious as after the Czech Lodge incident.

Nobody said it better than Buddy Jacobson, the one witness,

besides D'Arco and Roemer, to Giancana's explosion.

"... and all of a sudden there they were. These guys walked in and Mo, why he kicked John in the shins! And John says I don't know him! And *I* don't. How he knew me I don't know. The same guy as always. Roemer. With those two guys they say are always with him, Hill and Rutland. I didn't know what to do or how to do it! The thing is they are so fucking smug! ... world by the ass. And how do you fight them, you can't stop them ... like fucking gangbusters.

"Smart cocksuckers. Why, John is sick, dead. Said we know you, Buddy. Used to be with Guzik. They been givin' Mo fits. He hates them. Hill. And they say Rutland is the guy that Frank Strongy ... you know, he's the one caused Frank all that trouble.

"They can't do nothin' with those guys. They never seen such guys. Nobody can sit with them.

"You know it wouldn't be so bad, but how do you fight that kind of thing? In the 41 years I been here I ain't seen nobody like them three. They walked into that place like the goddamned Marines!

"I never saw them before but right away I said to myself, we're in trouble. See, I can spot a wrong guy after all this time.

"Three big, cocky, arrogant, like get the fuck out of the way, you fucking bastards. I knew they had to be heat, and when I heard Roemer say to the bartender, FBI! I knew we was dead right then. Fucking cocksuckers!

"If only there was some way somebody could sit down with them. And what do they get out of this? Like a bunch of boy scouts. Hump says he can't do nothing with them.

"And sweet talkers? You'd think they was the three nicest guys in Chicago. But dirty? They would burn their mothers if she crossed the street on a red light, what with their honor. I think they would. Dirty pricks. I *never* seen Mo so mad!"

It was as accurate a picture of Giancana's feelings as any, for in mid-1963 he chose to do what no other syndicate hoodlum had ever done, what the mob traditionally had avoided at all costs: he decided to sue the bastards.

16

APART FROM WHAT he had become, apart from the power, the wealth, the entourage, the lights, and the law, he was still a tradition-bound Sicilian. He cleaved to what few private moments he found. They came most often on Saturday mornings when he would drive back to the old neighborhood to buy fresh-baked Sicilian bread, so warm he could hardly slice it, or wine, a bottle of anisette, or some thin-sliced prosciutto. With the food came the talk in Italian with the old-timers, the tailors, the shopkeepers like his father.

Other moments came when he drove in for lunch, usually to the Vernon Park Inn. No matter what happened to the neighborhood, what places and faces came and went, the Inn stayed on Vernon Park and Aberdeen. Sicilians and Italians through the years, immigrants and their children, came and went to the Inn daily. On Thursday they came for *al trippa,* the steaming tripe dinners. On Friday it was *pasta e fagioli,* beans with pasta, or the fish salad with its garlic, olive oil, squid, shrimp, and whitefish. Or they ate *baccalà,* or codfish, with red sauce, with potatoes boiled in the sauce, and ripe olives.

Giancana was no different. He went to the Inn often and ate the food of his youth, talking with grease running down his chin to Sam Tufano. "Pop O'Zeke" they called him, in Sicilian the "thin one," because Tufano was robust and fat. He ran the place for his *paesani,* with nothing fancy, just the food and the conversation. He had once cooked for Al Capone, everyone in the neighborhood knew that, the same dishes that he served in the Inn. And he asked no questions, knowing full well who was who and what they came from. When Giancana came in, he sat alone at a formica-topped table in the rear dining room and felt perfectly at home, talking in low tones to Pop O'Zeke, phrases laced with Italian, nods, unspoken understanding. The bill seldom came to more than $3. The Inn stayed through the years without so much as a sign out front, the old-timers coming and going even if some of them had to drive in from barren suburbs. When Pop O'Zeke died, his son Sam, Jr., with his stoop shoulders and bug eyes, carried on, changing nothing, serving beer and wine, the tripe, the codfish.

No matter how much he got around, Giancana never outstripped his origins. He was still family oriented, acquiescing to the warmth and the common ground of his brothers and sisters, his aunts and uncles, and especially his own daughters. For his entire life he had fraternized mostly with family, on weekends, holidays, birthdays, anniversaries, often sitting out in backyards or in basements after eating too much and talking old times. The death of Angeline had fragmented those relationships, and the fact of his long absences made him that much more detached, but there was still nothing as important to Giancana as family, and nothing that disturbed him more than for it to be threatened.

Likewise, he held an affinity for his Italian *paesani* that went deeper than formalities. As quick as Italian gangsters are to kill those who've wronged them or betrayed the organization, they are as quick to mourn them. Giancana again was no exception to such double standards, feeling perhaps genuine remorse for the demise of a hood he had ordered killed. The flowers that dripped from the caskets of the Genna brothers of Prohibition days flowed from caskets in Giancana's era, as in the funeral of Joseph Mendino in 1961. A hood whose heart gave out, "Crackers" Mendino was born on the West Side and worked his way through the ranks to where he was a trusted juke-box, pinball, and gambling lieutenant. Tony Accardo and Jack Cerone were his pallbearers. Giancana, Gus Alex, Chuck and Sam English, Ross Prio, and a score of others attended. Murray Humphreys flew in from Tucson, Arizona. Again, though a relatively minor, unsensational wake, it was another private, important moment for Giancana and his friends, a time they felt too private and personal to be tampered with.

But such traditions meant nothing to the watchers. Although FBI agents were usually more than willing to stay away from Giancana as long as they had their microphones wired, he had no such luck with other agencies. Sheriff's deputies (particularly those under Richard Ogilvie, the politically ambitious prosecutor who had convicted Accardo on tax fraud in 1960 and who'd turned his sights on the likes of Giancana after his election as sheriff in 1962) were most bothersome, waiting for him outside his house when he got up in the morning and staying with him until he turned out the lights at night. Along with scattered details of Chicago police, the deputies became fixtures around the Giancana home, and the quiet corner with its immaculate lawn and clipped shrubs was stripped of its anonymity. Neighbors, who generally knew that Giancana lived there, had never before paid much attention. They had little reason to worry about the gardeners who worked on the place or the relatives who came and went, or to wonder about the few times they spotted someone from the house, occasionally Giancana himself, lazily walking the family's poodle. But that changed with the constant presence of the unmarked cars, the staring men in brush cuts, the relative unease felt at the prospect of having someone silently watching.

They watched his friends, daughters, relatives, associates, anyone who came anywhere near him. And they watched him, which irked him because he considered them rank amateurs. Still, it got so that he poked a pair of binoculars through the curtains of his windows each morning and checked the streets for cars. Then he phoned Frank Eulo, a Cicero gambling lieutenant who lived just two blocks away, to see if any heat was parked down there. If they saw nothing, he ran out the back door into his garage, revved up his two-year-old Chevrolet hardtop—he still preferred older cars with souped-up, proven engines—and roared off. He drove himself and drove as he always had, giving his tails as difficult a time keeping up with him as he had the coppers chasing him as a 42. When he returned at night he usually drove around the block a few times before squealing into his garage and sprinting into the house.

Usually he fumed over the tails; sometimes he played with

them. Once, after coming out of a nightclub in Oak Park with a blonde girlfriend and a clusters of others, he decided to give his trackers a run for it. This time it was a crew of Chicago police intelligence officers using a Cadillac as an unmarked car. At first, he let the woman drive and the officers stayed close behind them. Then he took the wheel and sped off at speeds of 80 miles per hour through the streets of Berwyn and Cicero. When the officers speeded to keep up, they attracted the attention of an Oak Park squad car, which pulled them over. While they were curbed, Giancana pulled up with a wry grin and said that he may have been the cause for the high speeds. When he noticed the car following him, he said innocently to the village police officers, he speeded because he feared for his life. Then he burst out laughing.

Yet he became increasingly upset about the surveillance, and grew paranoid about it. Virtually no part of his affairs was immune from them. Wakes and weddings were carnivals for reporters tipped by the deputies; even family gatherings were dogged. In the past the family had often invited school friends of the Giancana girls in for parties and birthdays, sometimes even opening the house to neighborhood kids. But the constant presence of police curtailed even those activities.

Once, when one of Ogilvie's deputies had parked in the alley behind the house, he was approached by Francine Giancana, then still in high school.

"I'd appreciate it if you would move your car back a little," she asked, forcing herself to confront the cop. "I have girlfriends coming over and I don't think they know anything about all this."

The deputy nodded and pulled his car around the block. A while later Giancana appeared and approached the car.

"I just want to thank you for the nice way you treated my daughter," he said.

The deputy was surprised, having expected a tongue lashing.

"That's all right. I don't have anything personal against her," he answered. "In fact, I don't have anything personal against you."

At that, Giancana became livid. "Then what in the hell are you doing here!?" he shouted.

With the deputies, and the attendant publicity, came the crazies. A North Side Chicago evangelist who preached out of a panel truck decided to make gangsters his personal missionary project. With a Bible in one hand and a sheaf of religious tracts in the other, he made the rounds of the suburban homes of the better-known hoods, knocking on front doors. He caught Giancana on a hot Saturday afternoon, and Giancana was somewhat nonplused when the evangelist, who was tall and gaunt and looked very much like the farmer in Grant Wood's "American Gothic," asked him if he was a Christian. "Yeah, sure," Giancana answered, then closing the door, he added, "Now beat it."

With their microphones telling them more than they could have ever found out on their own, FBI agents were more than willing to stay away from Giancana and give him the impression that he was out of their watch. They generally believed tail surveillance to be folly, that sitting outside a hood's house at night and following him during the day usually benefited them little, and they discounted the efforts of local police. Occasionally sheriff's deputies would approach them and boast about how they had stayed with Giancana throughout the previous night, and the agents would commend them, encouraging them to stay at it yet telling them nothing of their own intelligence work.

Still, they saw the effect of tight physical surveillance on Giancana, that it bothered him and made it difficult for him to meet freely with associates, particularly bookmakers and gambling bosses who counted on close business ties. They saw how it aggravated him, at times kindling his uncontrollable rage. In late 1962, because Giancana was operating more and more out of the city and in foreign countries, agents decided to increase their efforts against him. With his temper and his volatile moodiness, they saw a chance to disrupt the man's routine, his private affairs, his very equilibrium to such an extent that they were certain it would cause him to make mistakes. He had little of the control of Accardo or Ricca, none of the *savoir faire* of Murray Humphreys, and the lack of such, more than anything, is usually what gets criminals caught. So Roemer, Rutland, Bassett, and four other agents decided they would try to push him to the limit.

They decided in late spring, 1963, on "lockstep," a 24-hour tail on Giancana that would know no bounds, watching him day and night, no matter where he was, what he was doing, who he was with. Lockstep was entirely a personal thing (and not unanimously agreed upon, for Hill, who moved to another detail in 1963, disagreed with the tactic, feeling it would not only be as unproductive as tactics used by other agencies, but that it would jeopardize the existence of their microphones) and while not ordered by the Bureau (though sanctioned by it) it was eagerly taken on by the agents. With it, Roemer, Rutland and the others hoped Giancana would crack, even take a punch at them and risk a charge of assaulting a federal officer, but most of all that he would make a mistake. For they knew that Giancana had to oversee the day-to-day operations of the mob and he depended on getting around to scores of secret, private liaisons. Lockstep was meant to interfere as much as possible, to make him a leper among his own, and to those outside the mob with whom he often met.

After a while, he became almost desperate to elude them. He drove even more furiously, once squealing around the corner and pulling into his garage so fast that he lost control and ripped into the side of it. Once he tried to lose agents by going through a nearby car wash. Attendants who knew him and saw him coming stepped aside and cheered, "Go, Mo, go!" only to watch agents meet him as he emerged from the tunnel.

Even on the golf course Giancana had no peace. As he became a man of means, Giancana developed a passion for the game. He played regularly, usually with Chuck English, Johnny "Haircuts" Campanelli, Sam Pardy, and often with his second daughter, Bonnie. It was a chance not only to get some fresh air, but with the wide, open surroundings of a course he found it the perfect place for privacy. That meant he could carry on business, even if it meant that couriers had to run back and forth between the clubhouse and the greens, or that associates had to play a round. The course became his office, one that he dressed for—and Giancana was always stylishly decked out in brilliant crimson slacks, yellow shirts, beanies, golf gloves, and matching shoes. Once business was taken care of, he played for blood, even though he was generally an average hitter with a nagging hook. He couldn't approach the game of other hoods like Marshall Caifano or Jack Cerone, Accardo's underboss, who played well enough to win pro-am tournaments.

He played even worse with "lockstep." Roemer and Rutland readily stocked their own clubs in order to stay close to him.

Usually that meant that they teed off right behind him and played on his heels. Roemer, a superb athlete and strong, long hitter, often drove into Giancana's foursome, not wanting to hit anybody but not minding if a drive bounced between their legs. Often the agents would crowd Giancana's foursome right up to the greens, then stand yards away as the hoods putted out. And Giancana, whose putting was the strongest part of his game, three and four putted with regularity as the agents watched and snickered. And he became more and more incensed about it. He was a man who took his game so seriously that he had his gardener cut practice greens in his backyard. He bet on each hole and took his opponents' money with glee when he won. And often, with agents as his witness, he played liberal "winter golf" rules, frequently coming upon his ball buried in the rough, then waiting until his opponent wasn't looking and kicking the ball onto the fairway. Even then, he played a mediocre game.

The constant assault on his affairs, both business and private, drove him to a measure never before undertaken by an outfit boss. In early 1963, after long consultation with his son-in-law and attorney, Anthony Tisci, he decided to seek an injunction against the FBI on the grounds of harassment. Tisci went after a civil-liberties lawyer, and after being turned down by many because of Giancana's reputation, he approached George N. Leighton. A graduate of Howard University and Harvard Law School, and a black man, Leighton had gained a reputation for being a specialist in civil rights cases, having handled legal affairs for such as the Black Muslims' founder, Elijah Muhammad. He had never represented a hoodlum of Giancana's stature; in fact, Leighton hardly knew anything about him.

Tisci took Leighton to Giancana's home, where the three of them discussed the merits of the case. What Tisci had in mind, essentially, was a suit to be filed by his father-in-law against the Bureau, its local agents, and its local director. Leighton agreed to take the case on its merits, but only after convincing himself that the Bureau was indeed depriving Giancana of his constitutional rights to privacy. He then took an extensive survey of Giancana's neighbors to see what they thought of him as a resident of the community. The results astounded Leighton. For a man with so grisly a reputation, Giancana's neighbors spoke glowingly of him, for whatever motives, casting him as a model citizen of a quiet village.

The neighbors' portrait of Giancana matched that which Leighton perceived in his preliminary chats. With Tisci always present, Giancana was courteous and soft-spoken, agreeable, even docile. Leighton at one time got the impression that he was as much a curiosity to the hood as Giancana was to him. As they talked in Giancana's refinished basement recreation room, Giancana came on as a modest, retiring gentleman.

The crux of Leighton's representation of Giancana, however, and Leighton was intent on spelling this out from the moment he began discussions with him, rested on Giancana's willingness to swear that he was a law-abiding citizen. He had to swear to as much in court, which would mean, in perhaps the most precedent-setting aspect of the suit, opening himself up to cross-examination by government attorneys. For an outfit boss to do this in federal court was unheard of. Historically, hoods suffered quietly, believing publicity was poison and attention something to be scorned. Leighton, however, said that to prove harassment one had to maintain that he wasn't a lawbreaker. There could be no choice on this point. He would pursue the injunction on those grounds only. Giancana agreed.

To bolster his case, Leighton not only hired a camera crew to take pictures of police around the house, on the golf course, even in traffic, but he hired the services of a private detective to act as an objective witness to FBI surveillance tactics. Don Ricker was a quiet, unassuming private eye for the John T. Lynch Detective Agency and it was his assignment to spend a week going wherever Giancana went, doing what he did. Ricker had read about Giancana and knew who he was supposed to be, but he took on the job with relative ease, being assured by Leighton that his job would be simple and involved only keeping his eyes open.

Ricker began one week in early June, a week allegedly of business as usual for Giancana. At the Giancana house Ricker met Tony Tisci, then Giancana, who came on as polite and modest as he had with George Leighton. Much of the time was spent lounging around the house, sitting in lawn chairs, drinking beer. Giancana drank little; Ricker occasionally drank glasses of Pryor's beer Giancana drew for him from a barrel in the basement. Leighton showed up occasionally and held private, intense conferences with Tisci and Giancana. Giancana's wife's niece, Marie Perno, and her husband James were there, as were Francine and various other relatives who came and went. For Ricker, it was a placid, somewhat dull scene of suburban living. Except that parked along the curbs of Wenonah and Fillmore streets were the agents: Roemer, Rutland, Bassett, still in lockstep.

It was Leighton's wish that Giancana do with Ricker what he normally did, and Giancana even did a little more. That Sunday, for the first time in as long as the agents could remember, he found his way to mass at St. Bernardine's Church in Forest Park. They followed him in, sitting a few pews back. The scene soon became a parody, for Giancana was as comfortable in church as he would have been at a ballet. He attempted to be devoutly submerged in the proceedings, except that he was just a little rusty. When he wasn't snarling back at the agents, who were smiling at him, he looked at the people around him for cues for when to sit, stand, and kneel. As mass went along, he got worse. The agents could hardly keep a straight face, watching and whispering under their breath, "Kneel, asshole. Sit down, asshole."

From church they proceeded to Mount Carmel Cemetery in Hillside to visit the grave of Giancana's father and that of Angeline. Then they were joined by family and a few relatives, usually Rose Flood, and went out to eat. At all times Giancana was on his best behavior, speaking quietly but seldom, blending into the family gathering as a retiring, gracious grandfather.

Only when he was alone with Ricker did his personality begin to emerge. Once, while passing a Catholic church near his home and spotting agents' autos lined up in the parking lot, he hissed, "Those cocksuckers." He was referring to the church fathers, not the agents. "I give them more fuckin' money and then they go and let the G use their lot."

At the Armory Lounge Ricker watched Giancana devour plates of tomatoes and anchovies smothered in salad oil, until Ricker began craving the dish. They followed that with steaks, almost always, even though Giancana welcomed Ricker to anything he wanted. They also spent a couple of afternoons on the golf course, where they were joined by Chuck English. They apologized to Ricker for not having clubs for him, so he rode along in the golf cart. Again he had no difficulty spotting the agents, their cars lined up along the fence, their drives and approach irons plop-

ping just behind. Giancana and English remained polite, perfect
gentlemen in Ricker's presence, serious about their wrath at the
agents and pointing them out with a curt "There's another one
of the bastards." But mostly they went about their games, acting
like buddies, joking about shots and lies, dressing well and enjoying themselves.

Ricker himself soon became a believer. Giancana told him to
walk over to a drugstore on Roosevelt Road just to see what the
agents would do. Ricker started off and drew an instant escort.
They never stopped him or asked him who he was, but the agents
watched his every move, went into the store with him, then followed him back to Giancana's. When he returned to his home
that night, Ricker told his wife about it and of Giancana's atti-
tude. "Oh, he's pissed off about it," he said. "But hell, I would be
too. They're going way too far."

In the evenings, Giancana and Ricker went out driving, and
the parade was on. With an audience, Giancana was eager to
show off his old skills as a wheelman. With agents crisscrossing
his tail, he'd look at Ricker, smile, then say, "Let's lose the cocksuckers." To Ricker's amazement, he turned the rather drab gray
Chevrolet (Tisci's car) into a blur of speed. He took corners without braking, cut down side streets, through alleys, across parking
lots, never letting up, always certain of where he was going no
matter what suburb they hit. "I got my start this way," Giancana
said as he leaned into the accelerator and twisted the steering
wheel with one hand. It struck Ricker that he was truly enjoying
himself, that here was Sam Giancana, a man who could not only
afford to own any car but have people drive it for him, instead
wheeling his own machine, whipping corners, dousing lights
and driving blind through intersections, chortling over the fact
that he hadn't lost it. For indeed he had not. Though he was thirty
years and untold psychic miles away from Taylor Street, he was
still a 42, still on a lam with Babe Ruth, Vito, Salvi, and Patsy
Pargoni, still grabbing butter and eggs, packing a heater, and
running from Sergeant Leyendecker. He took delight in doubling
through an alley and waiting silently in a parking lot for the
agents to catch up. "Watch 'em. Watch those dumb bastards," he
said, and minutes later the agents and deputies would squeal
down the streets, windows open and radios crackling obscenities
about their lost mark. And he took delight in moving darkly out

of the lot and easing up to the agents, then tripping his brights, "Here we are, fellas," before howling off again. And on the way back, while sliding the car through traffic, he talked about how they used to do it, how they grabbed a machine and made it scream, "back," and he said it in passing, "in the good old days."

In court, Giancana was very much under the thumb of the proper, articulate George Leighton. The attorney, son of Portuguese immigrants, was methodical and unflamboyant, a black lawyer who had spent most of his career defending poor people against criminal charges, black people suing for their constitutional rights. He looked upon the Giancana case the same way. He was anything but a high-priced mobster lawyer in patent-leather shoes who performed like a toady for his clients and banked the professional drubbing he took off thick fees. Leighton was also very conscious of his future as a lawyer, and hence pursued the Giancana suit on the broadest grounds possible, believing that if he won rights for a person with as bad a reputation as Giancana, and did so using the Constitution and not court technicalities as his premise, he would win a victory for the people who were not gangsters but who nevertheless saw their rights casually abused. In late June, he filed a petition on behalf of his client demanding that FBI Director J. Edgar Hoover and Chicago head Marlin Johnson be enjoined from harassing his client. "Regardless of what Mr. Giancana's reputation may be, his civil rights are being violated," Leighton claimed. "No citizen should be subjected to such harassment. It is a violation of the Constitution."

The petition claimed that in his home in Oak Park Giancana was violating no laws and that continued FBI surveillance destroyed the "tranquility of the general neighborhood." It recounted the surveillance at the golf course, church, restaurants, and complained that friends and family were told by agents that Giancana was a "man of bad reputation with whom they should not associate." It charged agents with using field glasses to look into his home, with taking movies of his comings and goings, interrogating those seen in his company, and frequently using high-powered cameras to photograph anyone appearing in the windows of his home.

Leighton filed affidavits signed by various employees of the

Giancana household attesting to the presence of the FBI. A maid
said she was approached by agents and told she was working for
"the biggest hoodlum in Chicago," and that agents even visited
her home and asked her for her Social Security number. But the
real action began when Leighton and his client appeared before
Judge Richard B. Austin in U.S. District Court. It was a page-one
event, for never before had one of Chicago's hoods voluntarily
gone to court to testify about anything, and reporters were there
to take his every word. Leighton methodically produced his evidence: the survey of neighbors, affidavits, and then a roster of
witnesses. Among them was Ricker, then the photographer
Leighton had hired. He said that when he began to shoot movies
of the FBI agents they gladly cooperated. "Take this side," one
said to him. "It's my best side. Then I'll take a picture of you and
put a nice number under it." Besides his footage, Leighton requested that news footage shot by a local television station be
shown. "Why not?" replied Judge Austin. "Since this is the season
of reruns, I'll feel right at home watching those, too."

Next came Mrs. Rose Flood, Giancana's sister-in-law, a ma-
tronly engaging woman who said her sister (Anna Tuminello)
lived in the Giancana home and that since the surveillance began Mrs. Tuminello's heart condition had grown worse. "This
makes her very nervous," said Mrs. Flood, and added that she
visited the Giancana house daily for as long as three or four
hours. "It makes me very nervous. The whole household is in
turmoil. They follow Mr. Giancana down alleys . . . even when he
goes to mail a letter. We're terrified." She complained that the
agents watched the family as they had an outdoor barbecue, then
followed them to a restaurant. Judge Austin asked if they went
to the restaurant because the barbecue was bad, and Mrs. Flood
replied that she went there with Giancana because they liked the
place. When they emerged agents followed her home.

Giancana's golfing buddy and juke-box czar, Chuck English,
also testified. He began by telling of his regard for the FBI for
being against "commies, bank robbers, and spies." He was surprised, however, at their efforts against Giancana. English talked
mostly about surveillance at the Fresh Meadows Country Club,
where he said he often talked to agents as they golfed behind
Giancana and him. English said he took a ribbing one day from
Marshall Rutland and Fred Cook about a pair of red Bermuda
shorts he was wearing.

But it was Giancana who was the star witness. He took the stand in a perfectly cut gray sharkskin suit and a matching silk tie. He told how agents watched him everywhere. At the Armory Lounge they "park across the street and see that I don't sneak out the back door." At his home they shadowed him when he went out for walks. "Once I went walking in the park and two fellas popped out of a car to follow me. One of them says, 'We'll give you protection, Sam.' I says, 'I don't need protection.' Then one of 'em says, 'Why don't you make it easy on yourself and get out of town? Or maybe out of the country.' "

Then the lights were dimmed and Giancana moderated movies he said he had taken himself. The scenes were taken from a visit to the family's mausoleum at Mount Carmel Cemetery, then at the Fresh Meadows Country Club. "I took over the camera now. There's the north end of Roosevelt Road."

"There's no north end of Roosevelt Road," Judge Austin corrected.

"There are the guys on Roosevelt Road," Giancana went on. "They're parked. I tried to get in front of them but they got away."

The rest of the footage was taken on the golf course. Much of it was out of focus. "That's on the second green," Giancana said. The camera showed a group of four men. "That's Roemer. Playing right behind us."

Then Leighton summarized by identifying Bill Roemer and other agents. He also made a serious plea about the golf-course surveillance. "Maybe you'll appreciate the position of a golfer," he said to Judge Austin, "who is about to take his eighteenth putt and looks up to see six FBI agents watching him."

Austin shook his head and answered, "The most I've ever had was four putts."

But at the conclusion of Giancana's appearance, after the films and the at times almost facetious recounting of the agents' tactics and Giancana's efforts to elude them, Leighton asked his client the trial's most important question. It was the one Leighton had primed him for from the beginning. Was he, Sam Giancana, guilty of breaking any local, state, or federal laws that would warrant such FBI surveillance? Never hesitating, Giancana answered, "No." Then Leighton turned to government attorneys and said his client was open for cross-examination.

An opportunity like that one had seldom dropped so effortlessly into the laps of the U.S. Attorney's office. With it, they could grill

Giancana on everything he had ever done or that they suspected him of doing. They could ask him about any personality in the Chicago syndicate. They could ask him about any of the details FBI agents had picked up in four years of listening to the proceedings at Schneider's or the Armory Lounge or the First Ward Democratic headquarters. They could ask him about crimes committed: rackets, scams, extortions, bribes, hijackings, narcotics, prostitution, any and all mob enterprises. Even hits and hit contracts. And Giancana would have to answer the questions, or face binding contempt charges.

But, as Giancana sat wide-faced and vulnerable in the witness chair, aides of U.S. Attorney James P. O'Brien quietly waived their right to cross-examine, saying they had no questions.

It was a remarkable decision, which surprised George Leighton, and it infuriated FBI agents. For they had seen the opportunity and prepared a fusillade of questions that could have kept the court intrigued for days. But the word had come down from Washington, from the Justice Department and then Attorney General Robert F. Kennedy. They claimed that the Giancana petition was improper and that the U.S. District Court lacked jurisdiction in the matter. To have taken advantage of cross-examination rights, they maintained, would only have lent sanction to the petition. But the agents privately fumed over the decision, believing it to have been a colossal bungle, a case in which the government attorneys were caught unprepared.

Yet the government's strategy continued. When Leighton subpoenaed Marlin Johnson, head of the Chicago FBI office, he took the stand and refused to testify. In a scene reminiscent of the Senate McClellan or Kefauver hearings, Johnson answered Leighton's questions by reading from a notecard. "I respectfully decline to answer the questions based on instructions from the U.S. Attorney General, order No. 260–62." Leighton asked him about agents, Bureau autos, surveillance techniques, but each time Johnson replied by reading from his notecard. Before he was excused, he'd done it 13 times.

Judge Austin, however, had heard enough. His order came down shortly, a ruling against the FBI. He ordered a reduction of surveillance, including a limit of one car parked within one block of Giancana's home, and only one car to follow him (instead of the usual three tails), and, sympathizing with Giancana's golf game, ordering agents to play one foursome behind the Giancana group. Austin lashed out at the FBI for its tactics, suggesting that they were "an admission of ineptness and a confession of failure to obtain the information sought by methods normally used." He said he doubted foreign spies in the U.S. were subjected to such tactics. Then he added injury to the insults by citing Marlin Johnson for contempt of court and fining him $500. It was a move that infuriated Department of Justice officials in Washington and one that they said would be appealed. Locally, Roemer, Rutland, and the other agents considered it a slap at their efforts, but they said nothing, and went about their modified surveillance routines. Yet privately they seethed, feeling ire not for Judge Austin but for Washington. Perhaps the biggest fish in the country had been set up, and the government, their bosses, had blown it.

For Giancana the decision came as a remarkable surprise. He was sitting slouched in a chair next to Leighton when Austin began, looking bored and rather peeved that he had started this thing in the first place. When he realized the judge was ruling in his favor, he sat up, then eased a wide, smug smile over his face. Outside the courtroom, he was handed a long cigar by Dominick Blasi, and with Tisci and Leighton he lit up and filled the corridor with smoke. Although Tisci coughed repeatedly on his, Giancana puffed away, the cigar being a trademark of his to the degree that his code name among associates was "Cigars," even though the press had not picked up on it enough to make it his middle name. They continued inside Judge Austin's chambers while the judge signed necessary papers. And just behind them, standing impassive and tolerating the smoke, was Marlin Johnson. Though Johnson said nothing, the scene was one of the few public indignities he had to face in his FBI career, for he was there to sign a bond statement in lieu of his contempt fine. Judge Austin could have put him in jail.

Austin's ruling, however, was little more than a moral and limited constitutional victory for Giancana. Austin had not enjoined the FBI from watching him altogether—Austin pointedly noted that the Bureau had the power to keep surveillance on anyone it saw fit—but only from lockstepping him. Furthermore, hours after Austin's ruling, three unmarked cars drove up to Giancana's home and parked. They were deputies of Sheriff

Richard Ogilvie. "We watch hoodlums from time to time," said Ogilvie, and then added that he welcomed a suit from Giancana, and looked forward to the chance to cross-examine him. He made no secret of the fact that he would take on where the FBI agents left off.

Giancana was furious, once charging out and confronting the deputies personally. "Don't you know that you're illegal here?" he shouted. His daughter Francine and Joseph DiPersio, a 69-year-old gardener and caretaker who had a criminal record that included mob-related offenses, walked down the street and copied license numbers of the deputies' autos. The cameraman used in the FBI suit was called in to photograph the deputies, and did so with a camera propped in the kitchen window of Giancana's home. It was done on the advice of Leighton, who prepared to file an amendment to the original petition that would include other police agencies.

But the damage was already getting out of hand, for the new surveillance by Ogilvie's men was a *cause célèbre* after the well-publicized FBI suit. Giancana's house became a tourist attraction, with hundreds of cars circling the streets to get a look at the hood or his family or the grim-faced deputies. The deputies themselves made no attempt to be covert, and neighbors complained not only about the carnival atmosphere but the noise the deputies made at all hours of the night.

Giancana's nerves were assaulted. He carried a camera with him and frequently stopped what he was doing to take footage of Ogilvie's deputies. One of the most tenacious was Lieutenant James Donnelly. Once when Donnelly was bumper to bumper with Giancana at the busy intersection of Roosevelt Road and Harlem Avenue a few blocks from his home, Giancana suddenly got out of his car, and while motorists around him honked and cursed, he slowly photographed the deputy. He switched roles on the golf course, standing on the edge of the green shooting film while Donnelly tried to line up a putt. Donnelly said later that Giancana ruined his golf game that day, but as bad as it was it still was better than Giancana's. "He plays a terrible game. Constantly to the left and in the rough." And later it became personal, Donnelly said, as in one instance where Giancana came over to his car upon departing from a restaurant and simply began shouting obscenities at the deputies.

Meanwhile, government attorneys appealed the ruling, arguing before the U.S. Court of Appeals that Austin's decree was legally ineffective, that the judge had no right to interfere with the authority of the FBI, which, importantly, is an arm of the executive branch of the federal government. In late July the appellate court agreed, reversing Judge Austin's order. It ruled not only that the judge had no authority over the Bureau, but that civil-liberties statutes (at that time) were not applicable to federal officers. The appeals judges also said that Austin could not rule because financial damage to the plaintiff had not exceeded $10,000. That was an aspect of the suit Leighton had not pursued, and later he admitted he had erred in not realizing that in filing a civil-liberties suit substantial financial loss had to be demonstrated. Giancana's freedom, he guessed, was worth millions, and nobody came forward to contradict him.

Then, as quickly as it had taken the headlines, the case dropped out of sight. Leighton's appeal to the Supreme Court was ultimately denied a hearing. The newspapers played with the phenomenon of a gangster going to court, and finally editorialized that it was difficult to generate sympathy for Giancana. Chicago's *American,* the remnant of the Hearst newspaper in the city, sneered, "As the chief bum in an organization of bums who find murder more congenial than work, he deserves as much consideration as a chigger."

The only real winner in the case, even though he had to abide personal smears in the years that followed for his handling of the case, was George Leighton. He felt immense pride in making the point for civil rights in yet another important case. He considered it a high point in his career, and generally felt it responsible for various honors and commendations he received thereafter from civil-rights and legal-rights groups, even for further professional awards. He went on to judgeships, even being named candidate for a Federal Appeals Court position, one that necessitated investigation of his background by the FBI. That probe was highly positive.

Giancana, on the other hand, after the smoke of early victories had cleared, found himself no better off. In an attempt to rid himself of surveillance and exposure, he had engendered more publicity, to the point where he and his family were public spectacles. Through it all, the outfit seethed. Tony Accardo and Paul

Ricca were severely critical, yet their criticisms were cushioned by the overwhelming power Giancana had at the time. He did what he wanted to do. But the rumblings were heard, surfacing as they did frequently throughout Giancana's rise, that he was unfit to rule the mob, that he brought it more harm than good, that his problems made more for everybody else. Meetings were held without him in which strong underbosses railed about Giancana's lack of cool, his affinity for the bottle, for the high times, for anything but the cold, monotonous business of mob affairs. Names like Sam Battaglia, Jack Cerone, even Giancana's own enforcer Willie Daddano were brought up as possible replacements.

Though it came to nothing, the furor of the FBI suit passed and was an item of mob and legal history, the incident took a toll on the stature of Giancana, which would not be immediately visible but which would linger then surface in the years to come. When he pursued his suit against the FBI, when he appeared in court and did so without shielding his face from anybody, he was a strong man doing his own will. There would be a time, perhaps, when he would not be so strong.

And, as always, the agents, Roemer, Rutland, Bassett, and many others, would continue to watch him, to listen to him, to dog him.

17

Sometimes life in the mob is fun. Take me, a guy
with an eighth grade education. I've beat big businessmen, bankers, legitimate millionaires, guys with all
kinds of education. It's a nice thrill. . . .

Sometimes in the mob you have to do things you
don't like. Sometimes people that were real close to you
have to be put to sleep. It has to be done, because the
orders come down, and it's either you or them . . .

—Vincent Teresa, *My Life in the Mafia*

THE DEALS CAME and went, the opportunities endless, the days
flush with money to be made.

In 1965, Giancana was 58 and a millionaire many times over.
But money per se wasn't the object, not the obsession, for the
realities of his profession prohibited outrageous wealth. Whatever he needed, whatever he wanted, he got. The money was
always made available. It was, however, but a cushion beneath
the power he held. His word was law in Chicago, Cook County,
Gary, most of the upper Midwest. His interests reached into
Miami Beach, St. Louis, Arizona, California, Las Vegas, Mexico,
Central and South America. The revenues, the percentages,
counted into the millions, estimated by some at $2 billion a year.

But his ferocious will was what counted, what went un-
checked. As a Commission member, a hood among hoods, he
knew no equal, not in any one man, only, at best, from the combine of New York families. To a man they were afraid of him, of
his power, of what he could do, or would do, if crossed. It was fear
identical to that felt by the lowest-level hoods in Chicago, the

thugs who collected juice, the thieves, the lackeys, that if Sam Giancana gave the word you were a dead man.

His concerns were endless and compounded by the fact that everything had to be cleared through him. It was no exaggeration to say that he personified organized crime in Chicago, and anywhere else for that matter, because as operating boss he had his finger in every pie, cutting a percentage of deals, deciding on new concessions, okaying hit contracts, exacting discipline, smoothing out disagreements, interacting between the older dons and the young hustlers.

By watching Sam Giancana in the 1960's, one saw the mob in all its capacities.

He oversaw the diminutive, tough Marshall Caifano in 1963 when Caifano made contact with Ray Ryan, a multi-millionaire who frequently lost big money at the dice tables in Las Vegas. Caifano huddled with Giancana, got the okay, and approached Ryan with a typical mob business offer: pay $60,000 a year or be killed.

In April, 1963, Caifano and Charles Del Monico, known as Charles Turine, made the move on Ryan. Ryan laughed and said he wasn't intimidated, then said he was going to the FBI. The response distressed Giancana, and he quickly dispatched five lieutenants to Las Vegas to discuss the matter with Ryan. They did, but Ryan wasn't impressed and talked freely with federal agents. A year later, Caifano and Turine were convicted on extortion and racketeering charges and given jail terms of ten and five years, respectively.

But in case anyone got the idea that the mob and Giancana could be beaten with impunity, that notion was changed during another of Caifano's trials. This one involved Lewis Barbe, a fringe associate of the Chicago outfit who went to the FBI and turned state's evidence in an insurance swindle he'd worked with Caifano. His decision to stool meant a contract on his life. He received telephone threats, then noticed shadowy characters tailing him. One night in a Chicago restaurant a man walked up to him, bent down in front of his face and blew several shrill blasts with a doorman's whistle. Barbe began to shake, knowing that it was a symbol for the whistle he was blowing on the mob.

When the trial began, Barbe showed up with a revolver in his coat pocket. A bailiff spotted it and he was charged with carrying a concealed weapon. But even the revolver wouldn't have helped him on the afternoon of January 27, 1964. Leaving the Criminal Courts building after a day's proceedings, Barbe entered his car parked nearby, turned the ignition, and heard the explosion. The blast blew him completely out of the car, and though it did not kill him, it very nearly tore his legs off.

Such contracts were part of the discipline of the mob, something Giancana exacted mercilessly. Only occasionally was his will overturned. It happened in the case of Bernie Glickman, a balding promoter who was a close friend of Tony Accardo. A Jew and a Sicilian, the two of them ate breakfast with each other on Sunday mornings so often that Accardo developed a fondness for lox and bagels. Glickman owned the Cool Vent Awning Company and mob aficionados used to laugh at how easy it was to spot the houses of Chicago hoods by their Cool Vent awnings.

But boxing was Glickman's real game. He promoted and managed fighters, starting with Sonny Liston and proceeding in the early 1960's with Ernie Terrell. In 1965, Terrell challenged Muhammad Ali, and Glickman and the mob were anxious to set up a championship fight. With his Chicago interests, and the backing of Accardo, Glickman set up the bout for Chicago's Soldier Field, only to have New York mobsters insist that the fight be held there.

To settle things, Accardo sent Glickman to New York with Milwaukee Phil Alderisio, one of the mob's top enforcers. Once there, however, Alderisio, a vicious hood who had never liked Glickman in the first place, decided that Bernie was trying to cheat the East Coast mob and turned against him. Glickman, furious, afraid, and caught in the middle, for the first time in his life saw no way out but to go to the FBI. He agreed to testify against New York and Alderisio, but only on the condition that he not be forced to implicate Accardo. The government agreed.

Again, such a breach of mob code moved Giancana to issue a contract on Glickman. In protective custody of federal agents, however, Glickman talked for hours about the mob-infiltrated boxing world. But a lapse in security allowed Alderisio to get to him. In Glickman's suburban Chicago apartment, Alderisio attacked him, choking him and clawing at his face. The commotion brought landscape workers around and they pulled Alderisio off, then agents showed up and enforced the peace. Glickman, however, sat shaking, his face bleeding and his clothes disheveled, afraid for his life.

Grand jury proceedings began and Glickman, under the questions of U.S. Attorney Edward Hanrahan, a young, politically aggressive Cook County Democrat, told his story. Yet, at the close of Glickman's testimony, the pressure on Hanrahan became too great and he went after the big man involved, Tony Accardo. Glickman froze and refused to answer.

His silence damaged his credibility severely. Hanrahan was furious, and even though he himself had blown the hearing, he blamed Glickman. He returned him to the FBI, wrote out a small check for witness fees, and told Glickman to go home. Agents, realizing what had happened, were enraged. Glickman was caught in the middle, no longer a government witness or ward, no longer an ally of the outfit. In fact, knowing the lethal hand of Giancana, he realized he was a dead man.

There was little the agents could do but attempt to keep Glickman alive. They decided, and did so against all Bureau precedent and without authorization, to approach Accardo himself and explain the situation. A meeting was set up. The agent was to come alone at midnight to the Sears parking lot at Grand and Harlem in the western suburbs. He was met by Accardo's bodyguard and taken to Accardo two blocks away. Then, in one of the most unlikely meetings ever, a strait-laced federal agent, one of Robert Kennedy's best, strolled shoulder to shoulder with a top mob boss and talked things out.

The Glickman matter was fully explained, and Accardo, perhaps in consideration of his old Sunday-morning breakfast mate but against mob order, agreed to call off Glickman's hit. He also volunteered to put Glickman into the psychiatric ward of a Chicago hospital so he could rest and solidify his jangled nerves. But Accardo vowed that he wouldn't be harmed, a promise that only a hood with the power and stature of a man like himself could make. He still possessed the necessary influence on Giancana. Then he talked to the agent about other matters, in all talking and strolling in the darkness of early morning and the gaze of his torpedoes, until 2 A.M.

Glickman remained alive if shaken, regaining his health and his equilibrium, assured that the killer Alderisio would stay away from him. He later retired to the sun of a western state.

But other contracts on mob stool pigeons were not swayed. Forgiveness was not one of the mob's habits. When low-level hood Louis Bombacino turned some years later, testifying against Jack Cerone, Accardo's top lieutenant, Bombacino became a marked man. The government provided Bombacino with a new identity and a new home in Tempe, Arizona, but in 1974, years after the Cerone trial, he filed a civil suit using his real name. A few months later, he turned the ignition on his car and heard the explosion, the last thing he ever heard.

Besides the hit contracts, the unending discipline, Giancana kept a watch on even minor doings of his minions. With support from Ricca and Accardo, he enforced the narcotics ban in Chicago, from ordering hits on a handful of low-level hoods who got into drug dealings in the 1950's, to warning freelancer Americo DiPietto against getting involved. DiPietto, however, was liable to get into anything, as in 1963, when he was indicted for possessing $10,000 worth of stolen toasters. Police found them in 300 cartons stacked in his garage.

Or the Rush Street doings. When bosses there bickered over how much to tip cabbies for dropping off suckers to mob-controlled nightclubs, Giancana ordered Gus Alex, the Loop boss, to set the standards. It seemed like nickels and dimes until one looked closely at the "nut," the total amount club owners had to share with the outfit. From every watered-down $2.50 drink, 15 cents went to the girl who pushed it, 35 cents went to the club for overhead, 75 cents went to the club owner, and the rest, about $1.25, went "out west," to Giancana. Out of every drink. There were no exceptions.

When he wasn't consumed with day-to-day operating decisions, Giancana maintained rapport with Paul Ricca, his long-standing sponsor, a man venerated by functioning hoods in Chicago and across the country. Ricca gave every appearance of being little more than a white-haired pensioner. He spent his days lunching with old friends or watching the planes come and go at O'Hare Airport. He feared only the Immigration and Naturalization people, who pressed deportation against him. He'd aged much since the days when he casually ordered executions by saying, "Make-a him go away," but he'd lost none of his stature. Giancana listened to Ricca and heeded his advice, knowing

full well that he dare not jeopardize the backing of the diminutive patriarch.

Relations with other hoods weren't as important, but they were
every bit as sensitive. The mob was full of psychopaths and mo-
rons, and keeping order among them was a challenge to the
mettle of any boss, be he an elderly don like Paul Ricca, or a
power broker like Giancana. Nobody tested the patience and discipline of both men more than Sam DeStefano, a freelance juice-
loan operator and terrorist who was the pre-eminent clown
prince of the Chicago outfit, a buffoon with no equal. A graduate
of the Patch and the 42 Gang, where he was known as Jack
Napoleon, DeStefano through the years had somehow gained the
favor of Ricca and Giancana, a standing that kept him alive. For
nobody made more enemies, or talked more, or louder, than De-
Stefano, the mad hatter.

Despite a criminal record as sordid as any, DeStefano stayed
in the extortion and juice-loan business and meted out his justice
for recalcitrant debtors with a knife or an ice pick. In 1955, he was
accused of killing his younger brother Michael because he had
become a drug addict, and afterward stripping his body and
washing it clean of the stain of narcotics. But his most savage
acts were saved for tardy juice-loan clients or fellow hoods guilty
of double-crossing him. He regretted not having participated in
the "Action" Jackson mutilation, when the fat collector was
killed on the meat hook, but he did keep snapshots of Jackson's
mutilated body. In another instance, DeStefano abducted and
chained a would-be juice competitor to a radiator and, in full
view of the man's wife, tortured, beat, then urinated on him.

There was no limit to his perversity. Clients, fellow hoods, and
police did not hesitate to categorize him as mentally deranged.
Prosecutors and law-enforcement officials used that angle to cul-
tivate him as an informant, but never succeeded. They also delighted in watching him make a public spectacle of himself, an
event that happened regularly when DeStefano was indicted or
subpoenaed. Once he showed up in court in a wheelchair with a
bullhorn he used to bark orders. In court he occasionally defended himself, usually presenting a defense that said he was too
sick to have done what was charged. During proceedings he wore
house slippers, took out vials of pills and poured them down his
throat, even got friends to testify that he was saddled with a

colostomy bag at the time the crime in question took place.

There was no end to his antics, his raucous courtroom appearances, his outrageous quotes, even his endless calls to newspaper reporters that rambled on so long that the reporters handed the phone to each other to pass the time. But he never lost his capacity for violence, or threats of it. In a Federal Building elevator he singled out the government's witness against him and asked if he hadn't heard rumors that his eyes were dimming, his memory permanently fading in the near future, and that he was scheduled to do some fishing, a reference in mob jargon for the probability of lying on the bottom of a river.

The icy streak of killer ran through his veins and shone in his eyes. He killed with no reluctance, with much joy, with manic uncontrol. It was never better illustrated than in November, 1963, when he went after Leo Foreman, a sometime associate who had fallen far behind in juice-loan payments and had even threatened DeStefano with a gun. DeStefano, ever the proper hood, went to Giancana first to get a contract on Foreman and two others. He came away with Foreman's and proceeded to lure him to his home on the pretext of giving him some stolen diamonds.

With DeStefano's brother Mario, another part-time hoodlum; Anthony Spilotro, one of the young rising figures in the outfit; and Charles Crimaldi, an outfit contract operator, the deed was done against Foreman. They invited him to Mario DeStefano's home in suburban Westchester and in a basement sauna bath–bomb shelter they shot him, but did not kill him.

Crimaldi, who turned state's witness, described what followed:

Foreman rolled on the floor, moaning from his gunshot wound, when Mario stabbed him a couple of times with a butcher knife. "Leo kept moaning and I asked Mario, 'Why can't we kill him?' I said, 'Why can't we put a bullet behind his ear and get him out of his misery?' Mario said, 'Don't worry about it.'"

About then Sam DeStefano walked in, dressed in pajamas. "He started swearing at Leo. He told him, 'You thought you'd get away from me. I told you I'd get you. Greed got you killed.'"

Foreman then started begging Sam, whom he called "unk" from when they were on better terms, for mercy. "Please, unk, oh my God," Foreman said, according to Crimaldi. Then Sam took a gun and shot him in the buttocks. Then Mario stabbed Foreman a few more times and he stopped moving. Then Mario picked up one of Foreman's arms and cut a piece of flesh out of it. Then Spilotro and Sam DeStefano took the knife and did the same, taking turns cutting into Foreman's corpse.

But it wasn't the memory of the grisly torture and butchery that bothered Sam. It was the look on Foreman's face after he was dead. It held a glazed, unmoving smile. "Look at him," Sam said. "He's laughing at us. Like he's glad he died."

It haunted him, and later DeStefano, while gleefully recounting the details of the Foreman killing to associates, would cower and shake at the memory of Foreman's expression. He even had nightmares about it, saying that he was startled and awakened by the sight of Leo Foreman laughing and smiling at him in death.

Foreman's body was found five days later in the trunk of a car.

The deals came and went, the opportunities endless, the days flush with money to be made.

As with the sections of the city of Chicago, various outlying suburbs were distributed to mob lieutenants. Depending on the makeup of the community, the character of police and politicians, and the ingenuity or muscle of the hoodlum, various suburban communities did business under the rigid thumb of the outfit. Construction contracts, licenses, gambling concessions, anything the mob was interested in came under its representative's jurisdiction.

Nowhere was mob influence more prevalent than in the blue-collar western suburbs of Northlake and Stone Park. There one went to Rocco Pranno, a tall, thin hood who was quick to threaten and quick to go to his boss for permission to enforce. True to many mob clichés, Pranno often threatened to break legs with a baseball bat or dump people into the river with cement shoes.

In the fall of 1960, the International Paper Company of Framingham, Massachusetts, decided to build a plant in Northlake. They hired a superintendent to go there and oversee the preliminary plans and contracts. Four days after he arrived, he got the word from Pranno: no payoff, no plant.

The price was set at $20,000 cash. The superintendent went back to his bosses and was told to negotiate. A series of calls, meetings, and huddles followed, many involving direct calls to Giancana in Miami, San Francisco, Reno, and New York City.

Finally, Giancana returned to Chicago and met with Pranno in Northlake, then again at the Armory Lounge. A $16,000 price was set.

More negotiations were held with International Paper, some via long-distance telephone. The deal was debated by Giancana, underboss Ralph Pierce, Murray Humphreys, Frank Ferraro, and Gus Alex. On November 14, 1960, a certified check for $16,000 was turned over to Pranno.

Pranno's muscle had been backed up and remained intact, a fact he emphasized to an associate a short time later.

"The Man told me that I had Northlake and Stone Park," Pranno said.

"Who? Accardo?" his associate said.

"Hell, no. My guy is Mooney. He told me I had Northlake and Stone Park for good."

Then Pranno mentioned that a good chunk of the International Paper payoff was going directly "out west." Operating fees, he said, needed to stay in with "the Man." (Pranno was later found guilty of extortion and imprisoned.)

Such was business as usual for the outfit, in the early 1960's, even though developments in those years had not gone as smoothly for the mob as they would have liked. The occasional setbacks, the bothersome federal surveillance were phenomena to be weathered. There were still deals to be made, services to be rendered. The crime syndicate existed because people wanted it to, or so the newspapers said. It also existed because Giancana, and others working for him, held to the centuries-old truth that fear is the most awesome form of leverage. Giancana would not have lasted 58 years had he ever lost his nerve, or his capacity to kill or to order killings.

He remained untouched, at the top of the heap, snarling obscenities at federal agents when they subpoenaed him or his girlfriends, when they trained binoculars on his home. Through lapses, leaks, informants, mistakes, the usual number of subordinates fell and were imprisoned, the number increasing with the passage of tougher interstate racketeering laws. But the Giancanas seldom were implicated. Layers of associates stood between them and the commission of a felony. And though the syndicate showed signs of weakening internally—many of the second- and third-generation hoods simply felt little of the Old

World reverence for silence or unconditional loyalty to the group
—it was all but impossible to find a reliable witness to go on the
stand against those at the top. Only foolish mistakes or clever
prosecutors would dent their standing, and there were few of
either around.

In 1965, with what he had and what he had become, Giancana
was as vicious and menacing as ever, a personality easily kindled
to anger, tempered with the restraint of age, perhaps, but showing not a trace of cracking, mellowing, or weakening.

Outside one of countless grand jury proceedings he stood in the
company of his lawyer and his bodyguards. He was there only
because of a subpoena. As usual, he was dressed in his silk suit,
his pressed shirt, gold cufflinks, the polished, spotless alligator
shoes. Momentarily, an associate approached, whispered in his
ear, and Giancana responded by reaching into his pocket and
withdrawing a sheaf of bills folded in a gold, initialed money
clip. He pulled a couple of bills away and handed them to his
companion. A government lawyer, seeing the transaction and
feeling particularly brash in the captive presence of the hoods,
nodded at the money roll.

"Hey, Sam, how about a loan?" the lawyer said.

Giancana eyed him. "Whattaya need?" he said.

"Oh, about $500," the lawyer said, pleased with himself and the
smirks he generated within his group.

"Whattaya got for collateral?" Giancana continued, his voice
even but unamused.

"Whattaya need?" the lawyer shot back.

Giancana paused, then looked the young prosecutor straight
on. "How about an eye?" he said.

The lawyer dropped his smile, didn't respond.

PART FOUR

The Fall:
June 1, 1965–
June 19, 1975

18

WHEN JOSEPH BONANNO was abducted in front of his Park Avenue apartment building on October 21, 1964, an event that shook the New York underworld as only the kidnapping (and presumed slaying) of a mafia boss could, repercussions were sharply felt in Chicago. The outfit there was well aware of Bonanno's run-ins with Giancana, and of the fact that they had feuded and competed with each other in areas outside of their respective home regions, most notably in Arizona, where Bonanno and his family had made their second home, and where Giancana's close associates Sam and Chuck English had purchased a huge ranch; also in Las Vegas, California, and Wisconsin. But the feud had been contained mostly inside mob circles, and generally debated and handled in meetings of the National Commission, to which Giancana and Bonanno both belonged. Yet, when Bonanno was snatched, the worst was imagined, that the abduction of a Bonanno was pure Giancana, and it introduced the possibility of a gang war more vicious and far-reaching than any in history.

The missing Bonanno was the least of Giancana's problems. Word was quickly spread that he had nothing to do with it even though the feud still lingered. Attention was turned, instead, to Giancana's internal command, and in late October it became evident that his control over the Chicago outfit was suffering badly. Discontent consisted of more than mere complaints from underlings not getting what they thought was theirs. The mob was being prosecuted and penetrated by a host of outside forces. Revenues were down, surveillance was tighter than ever, high-level rackets bosses were being supoenaed and indicted by federal grand juries. And, through it all, Giancana continued to come and go as he pleased, often spending less than one week out of every month in town, partying and celebrity stumping wherever he went.

Accardo and Ricca had warned him about it all along, but it got to a point where they could no longer keep from doing something about their runaway operating boss. Rising mob lieutenants were hungry for Giancana's head, and eager to divide up his power. Finally, a meeting was held in the Armory Lounge at which all the top-level outfit bosses, including Giancana, were present to talk about Giancana's leadership. It was an agitated, fiercely contested affair, breaking soon into a group close to Accardo and Ricca that challenged Giancana's right and ability to run things, and a faction supporting Giancana. The Accardo-Ricca people were bitter about what Giancana had done through the years, most particularly his penchant for bringing publicity and heat: the FBI suit, the traffic violations, the constant anti-press and anti-government surliness, which seemed only to bring more publicity and more heat. They then railed about his repeated absences, which made the gossip columns, at the expense of pressing mob matters. His absentee bossism, they contended, left the outfit at a loss for discipline and direction. Things, in short, were falling apart under him.

Throughout the meeting, Giancana sat by hard-pressed to keep back his anger. But he sensed that it was no longer possible for him simply to announce that he was listening to no one, that he was boss and he would do what he wished. For, as much as he called the shots with this group, they were also his base of power, and if they turned against him it might ultimately get to the point where he would no longer have the sluggers to preserve his dominance. The Chicago outfit had always run more like a corporation than like a family. Giancana knew that, knew the power of Accardo and the patriarch Ricca, and though he fought for his command, he also lobbied for position. A compromise was agreed upon that meant the naming of an operating director to run things in Giancana's absence. The Accardo-Ricca group wanted Jack Cerone, a scheming, gambling lieutenant who was close to Accardo. Giancana wanted his gravel-throated executioner, Fifi Buccieri. Neither would budge, and another compromise was struck, this time in the person of Sam "Teets" Battaglia, a west suburban underboss who had risen through the mob's ranks after wild beginnings with members of the 42 Gang in the Patch.

The meeting ended with things ostensibly unchanged, but those close to the mob and its working realized that Giancana had emerged with his power sharply eroded. Some felt that he was boss in name only, that it would be only a matter of time before Battaglia ran things completely. Criticism like that Giancana had taken was theretofore unheard-of as far as his rule was concerned; there was little question of the fact that Chicago bosses were very nervous about the Bonanno affair. Clipping Giancana's wings was one way of meeting the crisis. But perhaps most significant was the fact that the meeting ran contrary to the will of Giancana and his control over the outfit. He didn't want realignment. He didn't want Battaglia to step in on a part-time basis. He didn't want any changes, yet they went through, and he left having to accept them.

The Bonanno question also remained more of a problem than most realized. Murray Humphreys, for example, a veteran of the worst mob uprisings, was so wary of it that he took elaborate security precautions in the days following. He answered his phone only if callers used a prearranged code—three rings, hang up, one ring, hang up, one ring, and Murray would answer. He also installed a burglar alarm on his apartment in the well-guarded Marina City complex. Even though he lived on the 51st floor, he had bars and railings built onto his balcony so that it looked like a cage.

Bonanno's troubles were ample cause for alarm. He had been called to testify before a New York federal grand jury, but it was his run-ins with other bosses, particularly Giancana, that upset the bosses of syndicated crime and necessitated a meeting of the National Commission in late October. It came only three days after the Chicago meet concerning Giancana's rule, and as a measure of his fall from power, he did not represent Chicago in the Commission. For the first time since 1956, Tony Accardo made the trip.

Privately, Giancana seethed over the challenge, and he fought against making any more concessions. He had supreme confidence in his power, in those close to him, even to the point where it was rumored that he ignored a request from the Commission that he talk over his problems with Bonanno in front of them. He would show no weakness, no signs of conciliation. His acute paranoia thrived—he was certain those within and those outside were trying to get him.

At no time was that more evident than when federal agents attempted to subpoena him to testify in front of the New York grand jury probing the Bonanno disappearance. At the time Giancana was traveling cross-country, using new and varied aliases, moving at odd hours and taking quick flights to avoid surveillance and escape trackers. He was spotted, however, just after midnight as he boarded a plane in New York. Using the alias Sam Volpe, he had almost managed to take his seat unnoticed when agents confronted him and stuffed the subpoena into his hand.

He was furious. He cursed them at the top of his voice with obscenities that echoed through the boarding ramp. He took the subpoena and threw it on the floor, then continued with his tantrum until he drew a crowd. He pushed through them, never once lowering his voice or tempering his choice of words, and paced through the terminal. When baggage attendants stopped and stared at him, he charged at them and swore at them, accusing them of being FBI agents. Finally, he turned and went for his plane once again, determined to board anyway. FBI agents stood in his way and told him that if he ignored the subpoena they would put him in jail. He answered with more profanity, then stalked off. The next day he appeared in front of the grand jury and said nothing.

It was a foreshadowing of what was to come. In the spring of 1965, federal prosecutors, along with the contingent of FBI personnel in Chicago that had been dogging Giancana for close to seven years, moved to make an all-out attempt to prosecute the outfit. That meant, essentially, that the government, after its long intelligence thrust against organized crime, an effort that knew no parallel in Bureau history for its intensity and also for the amount of information acquired, owing largely to the massive electronic surveillance, the telephone logs, and the army of mob informants, was going to put up or shut up. First of all, however, local attorneys had to convince their bosses in the Justice Department that a grand jury investigation was warranted, and that it would result in indictments instead of just impressive headlines.

The effort was again headed by Edward Hanrahan, the politically heavy U.S. Attorney. Hanrahan was fully ready to make his mark at the expense of hoods, an area more inviting for a man with his close political ties to the Daley Democratic Organization than a probe into political corruption. He was assisted largely by two young aides, David Schippers, a blond, crew-cut Chicagoan who had grown up in the city's neighborhoods, and Sam Betar. It was Hanrahan's job to go to Washington and plead their case before Attorney General Nicholas Katzenbach and his aides, including Henry Peterson and Archibald Cox. It was an uphill fight, for even with the mountains of information the FBI had gathered against the outfit, Washington was not convinced that hard evidence, enough for indictments and convictions, existed. Hanrahan and Schippers argued that even if it was not available in all cases, they had enough to make significant inroads and put mobsters in jail. Only Katzenbach was convinced, but his word was enough to launch the probe.

Right from the very beginning, Giancana was the prosecutors' target. Yet they long hid that fact. Ricca was not considered because of his continuing problems with deportation; an offer of immunity might endanger deportation efforts against him. Accardo was rejected not only because he had beaten his 1960 tax conviction, but because since then he had kept a low profile, supplying federal agents with little hard evidence of mob activity apart from his meetings with other hoods. Giancana, on the other hand, was the active operating boss, the man who figured in all decisions, who traveled, who made and carried out connections, who left a trail of circumstantial evidence everywhere he went. The government was convinced that it had enough hooks to sink into him, and it asked the FBI to give them everything it had.

What resulted was a dossier of intelligence information on Sam Giancana that covered almost every activity he'd undertaken in the last seven years. It detailed extortion attempts against individuals and corporations, his hidden interests in

gambling dens and Las Vegas casinos, his involvement with professional boxers, his hidden real-estate holdings, the murder
contracts he authorized, his participation in national crime syndicate dealings, his contacts with politicians, his South American and Central American gambling concessions, and hosts of
other mob dealings that ultimately led to him. For the record, the
probe was looking for federal offenses consisting of bribery of
federal officials, interference with interstate commerce by
threats or violence, interstate travel in aid of racketeering, intimidation of voters, vote buying, importation of narcotics, income-
tax evasion, income-tax fraud, or violations of the Federal Communications Act.

But privately Hanrahan and his aides were looking for a hood
who would crack, Giancana preferably, because he thought the
government had him cornered. Their strategy involved presenting specific evidence, mostly eyewitness reports of meetings,
with informants who would back up that information, and then
endless logs of telephone calls between specific parties that
would form a web of circumstantial evidence of the purported
act. Information gained by electronic surveillance—the many
microphones—was inadmissible before the grand jury, but it did
provide the groundwork for the cases, and it gave the prosecutors
the goods around which to build. Lastly, and often most importantly, the prosecutors used wild speculation about crimes or
motivations, and then hoped that it would serve to confuse, and
frustrate, the witnesses. In all, the government tried to show, if
not the commission of crimes, then a course of conspiracy, and
if that did not work, they would go to other charges, including
perjury and obstruction of justice. It was an effort to use all tactics, all weapons and legal maneuvers, including the granting of
immunity, to put hoods in jail. Or, at least, one hood.

What followed in the month of May, 1965, was a parade of
scores of witnesses, all answering federal subpoenas. It was a
daily show-up of mob figures, friends, associates, business partners, girlfriends, even relatives. For the record, prosecutors were
saying nothing, but behind the scenes they were feeding information to trusted newspaper reporters in a calculated scheme to
keep the outfit off guard. If it could not predict the path of prosecution, the mob wouldn't be able to form its defenses and cement

its alibis. Hence, Schippers and his fellow lawyers would tip reporter Sandy Smith (who had moved from the *Tribune* to the *Sun-Times*) to what the government was going to do the next day, and Smith would break the story, or he would even plant a story with shadings of truth, or calculated inaccuracies, most of those specifying which areas the government was probing.

The government, for example, subpoenaed Americo DiPietto from his cell in Leavenworth, where he was serving a 20-year sentence for narcotics trafficking. The story went out that the probe was interested in narcotics, when actually the government had nothing on DiPietto outside of what it had convicted him on originally, and the subpoena served as a government tactic. It also served as a bluff, as a way to make Giancana, or any other hood who'd had dealings with DiPietto, nervous about the possibility that a man under a 20-year sentence would talk. DiPietto, for his part, fought the subpoena with a vengeance, claiming that if he did appear before the grand jury in a closed hearing room, he'd be set up to look like he had talked. He was then a dead man, he contended. When he was forced to appear, he was terrified, and refused even to give his name. To compound things, Schippers kept DiPietto in town for two days, and he sat in front of the jury each day for an hour and said absolutely nothing, but this gave the impression that he needed both days to tell everything he knew.

Others followed, mobsters big and small. English, Buccieri, and Alex came. Rocco Pranno appeared and refused to talk about the situation in Northlake and Stone Park; then the mayor and city officials, even businessmen in the two suburbs, followed him. John D'Arco, Pat Marcy, and Buddy Jacobson were questioned about the First Ward and Anco Insurance. Then came Anthony Tisci, Giancana's son-in-law and formerly aide to U.S. Congressman Libonati, and Tisci's present boss, Congressman Frank Annunzio. Lewis Barbe showed up to talk about how and why his auto was blown up. Teets Battaglia, the newly acclaimed surrogate operating boss, was subpoenaed. He came wearing a beanie-type fedora of the same style as many of his associates. When asked why, Battaglia tipped it and said, "We got 'em at a discount." Butch Blasi, Giancana's trusted bodyguard, appeared, then Richard Cain, Leo Manfredi, and Jackie Cerone.

On the other side of the probe, still within earshot of the FBI's well-placed microphones, Murray Humphreys was working harder than anyone else to attempt to outwit the government. It was then that he again showed how shrewd he was, that his years as the fixer had given him a head for legal maneuvers rivaling that of a sharp lawyer. Had he been able to work without tipping his hand inadvertently to the government, had he been able to brief witnesses privately and instruct them on how to evade and avoid the traps set for them in the jury room, the probe might have ground to a halt. Instead, FBI agents listened as he instructed and counseled his associates at Schneider's, then they briefed Schippers on Humphreys' moves. Schippers in turn would feed to the newspapers information that was intended for the grand jury to read and that would as much as possible thwart Humphreys' strategy, usually by implicating the witness in other mob activities and crimes even if unrelated to the current probe.

Humphreys himself, in the smooth, wise manner that he carried so well, even tried to grease his own way through the hearing. Before a witness got to the grand jury chambers, he went from a waiting room through a door, then into a short corridor before opening another door into the hearing. Within that corridor, in almost a last breath before he went on record, a witness often attempted to get a look at the prosecutor, sometimes one to intimidate him, or to bluff him, or to feign disinterest. Humphreys used the corridor to make his pitch. He took Schippers aside, and with all the paternal charm of a man forty years older than the young prosecutor Humphreys said, "Look, kid, I know you're just in this to make a name for yourself. You're looking for the type of business you can get once you leave here. . . ." He trailed off. Schippers faced him and refused to play the game. To him it was a thinly veiled offer of a bribe: take it easy and we'll handle it when we're through. Humphreys had done his homework on Schippers, as he had on Hanrahan and all the prosecutors, and he knew that Schippers came from a Chicago family with long-standing political ties. Normally, those were Humphreys' kind of people, even their sons who became lawyers. But, with Schippers, the fact of his background made an offer from Humphreys all the more contemptible, and he responded only by offering the hood the open door to the grand jury.

All the proceedings weren't as stark; in fact, the prosecutors at times toyed with their witnesses. Such conduct stemmed from the fact that after a few days the government lawyers felt little fear of the hoods. They considered them to be meatballs: bumbling, insecure, illiterate thugs who were incapable of functioning without the security of the group or the direction of the bosses.

The Buccieris, Frank and Fifi, though riding on reputations for being bloodless killers, were buffoons for the prosecutors. Frank Buccieri was known to have had a girlfriend who had been a Playboy Bunny and a nude centerfold in *Playboy* magazine. All were subpoenaed, and as evidence the prosecutors came up with a picture of Frank and his girlfriend and the horse he had given her as a present, a token that provided Buccieri with the nickname "The Horse." Along with that photo, the prosecutors brought out the nude centerfold of the girlfriend and showed it to the jury and relevant witnesses for identification, even to the point of stamping "Grand Jury Exhibit #..." on her bare buttocks. When Buccieri's brother Fifi appeared, both photos were shown to him. Schippers asked, "Did you know that this young lady got a horse from your brother Frank?" Fifi took the Fifth Amendment. Then Schippers paused and said, "Did you know that your brother is nicknamed 'The Horse'?" Fifi again took the Fifth. Schippers then added, "Is the horse named for your brother or your brother named for the horse?" The grand jury members could hardly keep from laughing. Fifi appeared frustrated and a little angry at the apparent good cheer around him, and with a voice rubbed hoarse from a throat operation, he rasped, "I take the Fifth on the horse and the broad."

Ultimately, the prosecutors had to show their hand and zero in on Giancana. Until the last moment, they were determined to keep the fact that they had wanted him from the very beginning a secret, and even then they refused to reveal publicly the tactics they would use to squeeze him. Because the probe was so widespread, the grand jury, knowing of Giancana's many contacts in show business and politics, anxiously anticipated the appearance of movie stars and entertainers. Occasionally they inquired about Frank Sinatra and others of the Rat Pack, but prosecutors decided that none of the Hollywood clan, or the Kennedys, would be of any real use and decided not to issue them subpoenas. But with Phyllis McGuire there was no choice.

It was finally disclosed that the network of telephone calls between McGuire and Giancana and hosts of his associates was one of the strongest aspects of the government's case. A total of more than 3,000 telephone calls, most of them long-distance, had been logged by federal agents since the romance began, some spanning the Atlantic, many cross-country, countless others—as many as 50 a month—placed from a phone in the Armory Lounge. Complicated schedules had been assembled by FBI agents showing a path of calls between Giancana and pertinent associates around the time of a specific transaction. And most of these somehow included McGuire, either as a conduit of information, or simply as a base of communications. Use of the telephone in such cases, the government was attempting to show, was a violation of the Federal Communications Act. In late May, prosecutors decided to subpoena McGuire and make her account for her participation.

She showed up at the Federal Building as radiant as ever, the famous Hit Parade smile, her bouffant hairdo and heavy make-up, with bright red lipstick, carefully in place. She was treated like the star she was, now 35 years old and by no means a disappointment to the crowd of photographers who pushed to get close to her. At no time did she take her wide, photogenic smile from her face. She was an entertainer, and though she stayed close to her attorney, Thomas Wadden, of Washington, D.C., she was determined to get through her appearance with style.

Inside the Federal Building, the smile faded and she told David Schippers of her fear of testifying. In many ways, it was a ploy on her part to give the impression that she was an innocent party. But through it Schippers detected machinations, a street-wise presence that to him revealed McGuire to be capable of holding her own with the likes of Giancana. Before she testified, however, Schippers attempted to push home a lever. Away from her attorney, he told her that, if she was frightened of Giancana, she shouldn't be, for everything said in the grand jury chambers was absolutely secret. Schippers' advance was quickly rebuked by Wadden, who went on to scold him for talking with his client in his absence. Schippers took the reprimand, certain that his chat with McGuire would filter back to Giancana, hoping it would plant more seeds of distrust.

In front of the grand jury, McGuire pleasantly refused to say anything. Again, Schippers kept her there for the full hour. Outside the hearing room, she approached him and said that she would be more cooperative if he would assist her in avoiding publicity, mainly, she said, the legion of photographers waiting in the lobby. Schippers agreed, and then went about setting up an elaborate escape route down freight elevators and out the back way. He went with her, and finally they made it to the rear of the building unnoticed. She thanked him profusely, reiterating the fact that the publicity was hurting her family and her career. They parted, and McGuire got into a taxi. Then she instructed the driver to take her around to the front of the building. She got out of the cab and proceeded to tell reporters that she had cooperated with the prosecutors and answered all of their questions. As cameras and television crews closed in, she smiled and repeated her good intentions, then she was interrupted by her attorney, who had finally caught up with her. He told her quite frankly to shut up.

The incident could not have better played into the strategy of the government, for it totally unnerved Giancana. He had yet to be called before the grand jury, and he privately fumed over the entire affair. McGuire's appearance and her ensuing press conference pushed him to the brink. He spent long hours in suburban lounges drinking and stewing over the proceedings, usually with Butch Blasi, and within sight of a government agent.

The night after McGuire's appearance he sat in the Go-Go Lounge, on Roosevelt Road in Forest Park, with Blasi and a blonde woman in her forties. He was noticeably upset, occasionally raising his voice at the woman and berating her for looking at other men. At times he put his head down on his arms and appeared to be sick. Then he perked up and bought drinks for everyone in the house, also for the band, a low-budget rock 'n' roll group called "The Missing Links."

The agent attempted to be inconspicuous, but because there were few people in the lounge, he was spotted when Giancana's woman friend casually looked over at him. Giancana loudly barked at her and she snapped back at him. Then he shouted, "Don't give me that shit. I saw you eyeing that guy all night." The agent, who was not known to Giancana, finally went over and offered to smooth things over by buying them all a drink. Blasi motioned at him to stay away. He went over to the bar to buy drinks, but the bartender told him not to bother. It was a smart move on his part, and he proceeded to drink undisturbed while Giancana continued to rave. Towards 1 A.M., he finally announced the source of his displeasure. "I can't move!" he shouted. "Every time I turn around someone's taking a picture of me." But he saved his choicest rancor for Phyllis McGuire, finally standing and shouting a string of obscenities in which he claimed that although he had lavishly romanced her throughout the years, she was now turning on him. He bellowed, "I'm getting fucked!"

The outburst was duly reported to the prosecutors the next morning. It was good news. Schippers believed the probe was getting to Giancana, goading him, pushing him to the limit. McGuire was scheduled to testify again that day and Schippers decided to throw everything he could at her. Inside the grand jury room he unloaded an arsenal of incriminating evidence against her, accusing her of complicity, reciting records of dozens of phone calls between her homes in Las Vegas, California, New York, and Canada and wherever Giancana was staying. He let up only long enough for her to take the Fifth, then launched into another tirade, raising his voice and shooting accusations at her as if she were on trial. She emerged from the room a half hour later red-faced and embarrassed, rushing quickly past the press, her smile for the first time gone from her face.

The same day it was Giancana's turn. He appeared dapper and trim, tanned from his daily rounds of golf, wearing a smartly tailored suit, complemented with a sleek silk tie, gold cufflinks with inlaid rubies, sunglasses, and always the narrow-brimmed hat cocked just above his forehead. He was accompanied by Thomas Wadden, who was also representing him, and the two of them cooperated to the extent that they had to. Giancana at first came off as soft-spoken, even self-effacing, occasionally exchanging remarks with prosecutors by talking out of the side of his mouth as if he were mimicking a movie version of a gangster.

Slowly his irritation with the proceedings began to show. He was easily unnerved, especially by the small shows of arrogance on the part of Edward Hanrahan. Prosecutor Schippers always met Giancana and shook his hand. Hanrahan refused. That nettled Giancana, and after repeated attempts, he pursed his lips and shot angry looks at the U.S. Attorney. But it was another ploy by the government that riled Giancana more. In past weeks the prosecutors had used an identification picture of Giancana that had been taken after he had worked in the yard or around the house. He was shabbily dressed, his thinning hair mussed, and he looked totally unkempt. The photo bothered Giancana, and as soon as he appeared before the grand jury he asked to see it. His reaction was extreme, for few things could upset him quicker than ridicule, especially that aimed at his appearance. The picture went so far as to change his conduct and steel his resistance to any of the proceedings. It became obvious to the prosecutors that almost anything in Giancana's character could be attacked except his vanity.

Once past the preliminaries, the maneuvers, the insulting stares, the posturing, the government got into its attack on the man they really wanted. A task force of FBI agents had prepared a series of 250 questions covering his numerous mob activities through the years, questions carefully placed and interwoven so that they would leave no room for Giancana to wriggle free. Initially, they centered around extortion from businesses and manufacturers in Northlake and Stone Park, the case involving Rocco Pranno among others, and activities in the Democratic First Ward office, on both of which the FBI thought it had evidence and witnesses sufficient to convict. But the questions to be thrown at Giancana would hit everything, according to William Hundley, chief of the Government's Organized Crime and Racketeering Section, under whom they had been assembled, so the greatest number of events would be covered and follow-up questions could pick at specifics.

"You will note several of the questions appear to bear little or no relation to the two specific areas of inquiry," Hundley wrote in a memo to Schippers. "This is a deliberate effort on our part not to disclose at the time of the witness' first appearance the scope of the grand jury investigation." He said that the questions also had little chronological or logical sequence, something deliberately done to divert Giancana and prevent him from lying his way through them. The government knew all too well that their attempts to nail Giancana would fail if he could anticipate the probe and simply lie about his doings. They then would have no alternative to admitting they had no case and ending everything.

After months of preparation, the prosecution was ready. Giancana had appeared as subpoenaed. The roster of questions representing the government's effort against him in the past seven years lay in David Schippers' hands. At few times in the history of the government's effort against organized crime had one prosecutor had so much information against one man. The initial questions filled 13 pages. Follow-up questions would fill dozens more.

"Are your home telephone numbers listed in the telephone directory? If so, what is the listing? Are they listed under your name? By whom are the bills paid? . . . What is your relationship to Phyllis McGuire, if any? Does she have a telephone toll credit card? What is her credit card number? Have you ever used Phyllis McGuire's credit card in placing toll calls? . . . Are you acquainted with Dominick Blasi? Has Phyllis McGuire ever called Dominick Blasi at your request? Have you ever called Dominick Blasi using Phyllis McGuire's credit card? . . . Are you acquainted with Rocco Pranno? Did you go to the Key Club in Stone Park on November 5, 1960? Did you meet Rocco Pranno there? Did you discuss the International Paper Company? Was the figure $20,000 ever mentioned? . . . Are you acquainted with Roland Libonati? Have you ever actively participated in his elections? Have you ever exercised any efforts to control his voting in Congress? Are you acquainted with Frank Annunzio? Have you ever exercised any efforts to control his voting in Congress? . . . Who is Benjamin Jacobson? Has Jacobson ever given you any money? . . . Have you ever met John D'Arco at the Czech Lodge? . . . Who is Anthony Tisci? What is his relationship to you? to Dominick Blasi? to Roland Libonati? to Frank Annunzio? to Phyllis McGuire? to Peter Granata? to Anthony De Tolve? to John D'Arco? to Benjamin Jacobson? . . ."

The pattern was well laid out, even to the point of calculating evasive tactics, occasionally even throwing in irrelevant questions to confuse Giancana, or to make him wonder about things that had gone on behind his back. A question about John Matassa, one of Giancana's chauffeurs, was followed by a random query about Matassa's relationship with Keely Smith. Actually, there was no relationship between the two as far as the government knew, but asking Giancana about it would make him think twice about what had been going on and thoroughly aggravate him.

But nothing disturbed him like the possibility that someone would talk. The appearance of Phyllis McGuire, the manner in which she emerged shaken and distraught after her second hearing, had noticeable effects on Giancana. Prosecutors were certain that he suspected her and that it totally unnerved him. There was also the possibility that the government would use the granting of immunity as another weapon against him, a tactic that would pit him against the rest of the outfit. The mob, Murray Humphreys specifically, knew immunity would be granted, but they didn't know to whom. At Giancana's initial appearances, in which he answered all government questions with the Fifth Amendment, no indication was given that immunity might be forthcoming.

Then it came. Once McGuire rushed out of the Federal Building for the second time, the offer was made to Giancana. It was one he could not refuse, that no grand jury witness by law could refuse. Judge William J. Campbell, armed with every immunity statute available, quickly read Giancana his privileges, a grant so far reaching, the judge said, that he could thereafter ignore parking tickets. Then he asked Giancana if he was willing to answer questions in accordance with the order.

Giancana turned to his lawyer and conferred briefly, then he looked back at Judge Campbell and said, "Yes, sir."

He was then ordered to appear immediately before the grand jury. Wadden, his lawyer, then turned to Schippers and asked, "Now what are you going to do?" The question was more of a challenge than anything else, for the general consensus of the mob and its attorneys was that the prosecution was bluffing, that it had banked on total refusal by Giancana to talk. Schippers replied by handing Wadden an additional roster of questions, then said, "I'm going to keep your man in the grand jury for six months."

A series of legal maneuvers followed, mostly concerning attempts by Wadden to narrow the scope of the prosecution. He attempted to get a ruling from Judge Campbell that would make the immunity grant apply only to questions already asked by the government. He desperately wanted to head off a *carte blanche* foray by the government into Giancana's dealings. Judge Campbell refused and said the witness had to answer to everything.

Suddenly confronted with the odds, the book of questions

Schippers had handed his attorney, the possibility that others would be immunized and testify against him, Giancana reneged on his offer. He refused to talk. His choice was really no choice at all. If he talked under immunity, there was little chance he could keep from perjuring himself. If he talked without lying, the mob would blow him away. If he refused, he would be cited for contempt of court and held liable. He decided to clam. He answered two questions: What is your name? What is your address? Then he took his Fifth Amendment rights.

The prosecution returned to Judge Campbell. The judge ascertained Giancana's unwillingness to cooperate (a decision he stuck to even though Wadden made last-ditch attempts to get him to talk), and then held him in contempt of court. The judge's action was swift and definite. He instructed that Giancana be taken into custody by a federal marshal and put into the Cook County jail until he decided to talk. It was the first time ever the talk-or-jail tactic had been used against a hoodlum, this time against the biggest Chicago had to offer. Judge Campbell said the offense was not "appealable or bondable," and added, "You have the key to your own cell. Whenever you decide to obey the lawful order of the court, notify the U.S. marshal and he will bring you before the grand jury."

With that, more than twenty years since he had last been there, Giancana went back to prison.

19

His FIRST MEAL was pork sausages and baked beans. He picked at it from within an eight-by-ten maximum-security cell in the basement of the Cook County jail, still wearing his blue-gray pinstriped suit and a thin silk tie, observed silently by two men in adjoining cells, both of them awaiting murder trials. He had been fingerprinted, given a blood test and a chest x-ray, and $22.31, his only personal possession on him, was inventoried. He was told he wouldn't have to wear prison denims because he wasn't under sentence. He replied by refusing to talk to any reporters. The three basement cells would be guarded round the clock.

Outside, his lawyers furiously filed motions of appeal. Wadden worked along with Chicago attorney Richard Gorman, but the two of them found no success. Briefs were filed, hearings were called, but nothing presented before Judge Campbell, the U.S. Court of Appeals, or U.S. District Court Judge Michael L. Igoe could remove the order. Meanwhile, Giancana languished in jail. He was prohibited from using laundry facilities and told he had to wash his silk shorts in the cell's basin. Days passed, and with no progress on his appeals, he reluctantly settled into the routine. It wasn't easy. His daughters and Attorney Anthony Champagne ministered to his needs, once bringing him a stack of fresh underwear and socks, but he chafed under his confinement. He

273

alternately shouted at guards, stared at the wall, then erupted in unprovoked outbursts. He often shouted only, "I won't talk!" Other moments he was quiet and seemingly absorbed, once asking for a small dictionary to pass the time.

It had been some time since he had been forced to awaken at 5 A.M., as was jail procedure. But he did it every day, then ate a breakfast of oatmeal, coffee, and a sweet roll in his cell. In the morning he occasionally washed his clothes in the lavatory, swept up the floor, mopped it, then made up his bunk. For lunch he ate meals like macaroni and cheese, white bread, and cocoa. Most of the afternoon he was confined to his cell, and he slept or read magazines, occasionally listened to popular music on a radio. His daughters and lawyers visited, and all noticed the most conspicuous piece of furniture in the basement complex. Only 20 feet away from the cell next to Giancana's was the county's unused electric chair.

Scarcely more than a week after he was incarcerated, he came down with violent stomach cramps. He had a history of stomach problems, some years earlier had had abdominal surgery, and the heavy, starchy foods in the prison diet apparently took their toll. He was then put on a diet of milk and raw whipped eggs. Perhaps at no time of his life was he more uncomfortable, and he was nearly powerless to do anything about it.

He wasn't cheered by what was going on outside his cell. The mob was being run by committee. In the Loop Gus Alex, Jackie Cerone, Ralph Pierce, Murray Humphreys, and Hy Godfreyd met not only to talk over the problem of the continuing grand jury probe, but also to make decisions previously left to Giancana. Sam Battaglia, the intermediate operating boss, was assuming more and more responsibility, and he became recognized in the press, newspapers that Giancana read well, as the new boss.

Giancana's lawyers, meanwhile, were getting nowhere. In late June, Giancana put the word out from his cell that he was ready to give $100,000 in cash to anyone who could think up a way to spring him. The offer was serious, and though federal prosecutors laughed about it, they were amazed at the fuss it raised in legal circles, even to the extent of moving certain lawyers to make random inquiries of government attorneys about how to shake the talk-or-jail order. Known mob attorneys dug for any tactic, any order that would free Giancana. But none were found, and no help came from a U.S. Supreme Court refusal to free Giancana pending a ruling. For the first time, observers began to talk realistically about the possibility that the Chicago boss would be in jail for the life of the grand jury, which meant until June, 1966, one full year after he'd entered.

Schippers and Hanrahan, meanwhile, gloated over their catch only long enough to continue their probe. It was guessed that they would offer immunity to others, especially to figures involved in the First Ward Democratic organization. But no immunity was issued, even though hoods under subpoena fully expected it. Members of the outfit during that time became incredibly edgy, on occasion calling prosecutors and asking if they had plans to subpoena them in the next few weeks, explaining that they wished to go on vacations with their families. The fear of immunity and prison was constant. When Chuck English, Giancana's close friend and juke-box lieutenant, was subpoenaed, he appeared in old clothes and carrying only $5. He was certain he would be in jail that night.

Things were not going well with Giancana's son-in-law Tony Tisci, either. Long the object of controversy because he was congressional aide first to Roland Libonati then Frank Annunzio, Tisci finally announced he was quitting his job. He gave ill-health as a reason. It was not a phony excuse, for months earlier, at the age of 36, he had been stricken with a heart attack and had undergone heart surgery at the Mayo Clinic. Doctors told him to limit his activities, and engage only in the private practice of law.

Other setbacks in Tisci's legal career gave him problems. Only a year earlier he had brought suit against the Chicago *American* for libel. Asking $16 million in damages, he accused the paper of linking him to underworld activities because he was associated with his father-in-law during Giancana's 1963 suit against the FBI. Tisci's suit seemed to most observers to do little but hold him up to more ridicule because of his family ties. In August of 1964, a Cook County Circuit Court judge ruled against him.

When he was subpoenaed to appear before the federal grand jury in May of the following year, Tisci took the Fifth Amendment to all questions. That prompted a local government watchdog agency in Chicago to call for Tisci's disbarment. He reacted to the pressure by resigning his government post. That prompted his boss, Congressman Frank Annunzio, to lament, "I'm hoping for the day when the American people will mature to the point that the sins of the father are not heaped upon the children."

Giancana was in the maximum-security cell until mid-July, when he was ordered moved to the federal tier of the jail. The change was more comfortable for him—it permitted him a chance to mingle with other prisoners and the new area was cooler than his old cell—but it caused nothing but problems for his jailers. A prisoner of his rank kindled unrest among the rest of the inmates, according to prison officials. Some convicts attempted to cater to him, others attempted to pick fights with him. Guards had little control over the situation, since in the new cell Giancana was allowed as much as 16 hours' time daily in a bullpen with 55 other prisoners.

By late August, more rumblings were heard, and a full-scale jailhouse scandal loomed over the treatment Giancana was receiving. It was discovered that, through a system of couriers, he was being smuggled many of the luxuries he enjoyed on the outside. They included his $1 Cuban cigars, then only after they had been properly refrigerated, whiskey, and elaborately prepared steaks. He also benefited from the use of a stove, refrigerator, dishes, and cooking utensils in his cell. He often roamed the tier well after curfew, and messages were carried to and from him.

The reports prompted an investigation by Sheriff Richard Ogilvie, preceded by new restrictions clamped on Giancana. He was again given round-the-clock surveillance, and a log was to be kept recording all movements, visitors, and even the names of anyone who talked to him. Ogilvie also asked for permission to put Giancana back in the maximum-security section of the jail. The prison warden defended his guards, saying none of them babied Giancana or gave him any preferential treatment.

For his part, Giancana laughed at the reports. His weeks in jail had made him no more friendly to outside interviews, but he did ask reporters why they were making such a fuss about him. In a sport shirt, slacks, and slippers, he sat on his prison cot and read a book while a reporter tried to get him to say something. "I have no comment about anything," he said. But, when a guard arrived with lunch of creamed chipped beef, applesauce, and bread without butter, he looked up at a reporter and said, "Special treatment, huh?" Later he added, "I get along okay."

Days later, however, two guards admitted they had done Giancana's laundry for him on several occasions. They were summarily fired. Another guard, who admitted that he was a close friend of hood Sam DeStefano, failed lie-detector tests and was also fired. It was this guard, investigators found, who had taken care of most of the favors done Giancana, and he had received up to $75 a week to do them. Most involved cigars, liquor, and specially prepared foods brought to Giancana when he was in the maximum-security cell. They were done at the behest of DeStefano, the mob crazy man who needed all the favors he could get from a boss like Giancana.

When the furor died down, Giancana continued to languish, causing little trouble. He was visited frequently by his daughters, by the ever-faithful Champagne, and by his attorneys, who were pressing his appeals. Thomas Wadden's Washington partner, Edward Bennett Williams, asked the U.S. Supreme Court once again to consider Giancana's appeal, and though Giancana spent Thanksgiving of 1965 in jail, he hoped that the Supreme Court would get him out by Christmas.

Even with Giancana in jail, the grand jury probe was going at full speed. The outfit was sharply on the defensive. The press kept printing stories stating that Sam Battaglia and Murray Humphreys were soon to be jailed as Giancana was. Only Humphreys didn't buy the government's game, and told associates that if he was questioned he would supply answers and beat them. The old fixer gave it his best. He was aging, in his late sixties, blind in one eye, and suffering from painful shingles, which prevented him from comfortably wearing a hat. Nevertheless, just to confuse the jury, he showed up to testify wearing a hat and an eyepatch.

Once the questions came, Humphreys dodged and hedged and bluffed as best he could. But the evidence in the hands of the prosecutors was too much even for him, and they soon tripped him up with evidence conflicting with his on places he'd been and people he'd met. Following his appearance, the grand jury voted an indictment against Humphreys for perjury.

Knowing through FBI intelligence that Humphreys intended to leave town to beat the arrest warrant, the government moved quickly to serve it. They also set another trap for him. They leaked the story to the press in order to make it fully known that Humphreys was wanted. The warrant was then given to Bill Roemer, the agent who had tracked Humphreys for years, and Roemer headed for Humphreys' Marina City apartment.

It was a place Roemer had been often, a task he didn't mind doing. His work against Humphreys had engendered a respect for him, a feeling that, regardless of the crimes of his past, as a senior hoodlum he was cunning, cool, and very much a worthy adversary. There were few other hoods like him. When Roemer approached the door of the apartment, he heard voices inside and knew Humphreys was there. Humphreys' brother answered the door, however, and said Murray was gone. While he stood in the hallway, Roemer spotted a blue blazer he knew belonged to Murray draped over a chair. He made a mental note of it, and left. Humphreys, meanwhile, collected his goods and hustled off to a train, headed for his wife and children in Norman, Oklahoma, where they lived on a ranch. He went there, Roemer knew, to say goodbye to them before going to prison.

He was finally served in Oklahoma, and he explained that he had left Chicago not knowing that he was wanted. That statement set government prosecutors in motion, for with a little luck they hoped to show that Humphreys indeed knew he was wanted, as Humphreys was well aware of everything that went on around him, and that he left Chicago in an unlawful flight to avoid prosecution. Roemer set out to prove it. What he found led to a solid case against Humphreys, one of the few ever put against him in his career. Roemer not only found reliable witnesses who identified Humphreys on the train to Oklahoma and wearing the same blue blazer hanging in his apartment, but he also found eyewitnesses who swore that Humphreys sat down in a train seat and proceeded to read a Chicago newspaper story with the headline that he was wanted on perjury indictment.

Again Roemer went to Marina City with an arrest warrant, this time accompanied by other agents and certain he would get his man. After announcing who they were, they were confronted at the door by Humphreys, who held a gun in his hand. They could have shot him right there, but instead disarmed him and proceeded to search the apartment in conjunction with the arrest. Humphreys attempted to stop them, saying they had no warrant.

He jostled with them, something he rarely had done in the past few years; and this served only to illustrate how frail and sickly he had become. He had suffered heart attacks, and was taking nitroglycerin tablets. But the agents' presence totally unsettled him, and he continued to struggle.

That night, as Roemer was home taking a shower, he was called by a newspaper reporter and told that Humphreys had collapsed from a heart attack. The veteran fixer, who had lived through 66 years of wars from the Capone days on, had schemed his last.

The appeals failed one by one, first the U.S. Appellate Court, then in December the U.S. Supreme Court refused to consider the case. Although the offer of $100,000 still stood to any lawyer who could spring Giancana (rumors persisted that the sum had been pushed to $1 million), no breakthroughs appeared imminent. The death of Murray Humphreys stripped the mob of yet another legal mind, and it chipped away from the status quo within the mob that gave Giancana his power base. In meetings monitored by the FBI, it became apparent that Sam Battaglia remained titular boss, and that Giancana's power had been distributed among the top-level associates.

In jail Giancana sometimes wore colorful Bermuda shorts on hot days, days he would have probably spent on the fairways in his baby-blue golf cart, or practicing putts on his backyard practice green with fellow hoods. Other days he dressed in suits without a tie, appearing as if he expected to go somewhere that afternoon.

By 1966, the strain had begun to show. He complained occasionally of stomach problems, but mostly he grew more and more silent. What was considered a coolness, a subdued resilience, in the first months of imprisonment became moroseness as the weeks passed. Results of the prison diet began to show; he became gaunt, his eyes sunken. A guard once remarked, "He's so quiet, it's pitiful."

His daughters kept up their frequent visits, especially Bonnie, who was planning a move to Arizona because of her husband's health. And Tony Champagne, the long-time chum who dutifully administered to Giancana even though Giancana occasionally ridiculed him behind his back, and regarded him capable only of handling minor legal chores, appeared regularly with specially prepared food. Usually it was prohibited by jail officials, now closely watching such favors, but after some months even Giancana refused it.

The grand jury continued to work. In March, 1966, Rocco Pranno and two associates were convicted for their Northlake extortion schemes. Speculation continued to center on who, if anyone, next would be granted immunity, and when the First Ward politicians and their alleged mob associates would feel the pinch. Finally, eyes began to turn to the June 1 expiration date of the grand jury and exactly what new move the government would take against Giancana.

Surprisingly, very little was happening behind the scenes. Contrary to the belief of the media, the government's strategy never was to run down the list of top hoods and grant them immunity. That, it was felt, was an abuse of the statute. It was done against Giancana not only because prosecutors felt they had the best case against him, but because they honestly believed he would crack. There was a pervasive feeling among prosecutors that Giancana was not, as mob associates would say, a "stand-up guy," that if he thought he could talk and get away with it, weathering the consequences on the outside with his well-developed mob standing, then he would talk.

As far as the Justice Department in Washington was concerned, it was adamant about the need to develop hard evidence against Giancana and anyone else, and win convictions. As one Justice Department official said to Schippers, "Indict them, try them, convict them. Don't bullshit them."

But, along the way, the man responsible for directing the investigation failed. Edward Hanrahan, as U.S. Attorney and a strong Daley Democrat, began to fade during the months of the grand jury. He became less and less communicative with his aides, finally to the point of losing trust in Schippers. Throughout Giancana's prison stay, he never approached Schippers, Sam Betar, or the others on the prosecution team with followup strategies against the hood. He became paranoid about the press, even at times going to great lengths to avoid interviews with inquiring reporters who addressed him by his first name. As the months of spring, 1966, approached, Schippers finally confronted Hanrahan. "Ed, what are we going to do about Giancana?" Hanrahan replied, "Don't worry about it."

But those in Washington were worried about it. Attorney General Katzenbach and his aides were under criticism for Giancana's jailing, because it had been done on a technicality, not on solid criminal evidence, and was a shaky premise for further government moves against organized crime. Hence, with June 1 and the life of the grand jury nearing its end, Washington gave indications that it was opposed to reimmunizing Giancana before a new grand jury with the same talk-or-jail ultimatum.

What would have been needed to change their minds was strong new evidence of continuing crimes. One area where that evidence was available, as far as the FBI was concerned, was in the First Ward. Hanrahan did not pursue that route of prosecution. Speculation held that strong pressures were put on Hanrahan, not from his bosses in Washington but from his benefactors in City Hall. Schippers, for his part, was not convinced they had enough First Ward material to run with. Schippers still believed they could press on with their immunity strategy and break Giancana. It was his idea to again put Giancana before the grand jury in its final days and declare that the government had an ongoing investigation and that the jury was going to end its tenure with unfinished business. That, he argued, would be cause to indict Giancana for obstruction of justice. The plan, however, never came off.

In the final days of May, amidst the routine of the jury's hearings, Schippers got a tip from a Washington friend that Katzenbach and his aides had made a final decision against reimmunization of Giancana. He got the call as he briefly stopped at his office while awaiting a quorum in the jury room. Suddenly, the reality of losing the prize fish hit him. He dropped his papers and sprinted down the hall to Hanrahan's office to attempt to get to him before the Washington call came through.

At the door, he spotted Hanrahan on the phone. A secretary said that he was talking to Fred Vinson, one of Katzenbach's top aides. Moments later Hanrahan faced him and said, "We can't do it."

"Let's do it anyway," Schippers said.

Hanrahan shook his head. "I don't think I can."

"Look," Schippers pleaded. "You want to be Governor of Illinois? There's no one way to be elected faster than for getting fired for going after hoods."

Hanrahan stopped and looked at his aide. The mention of public office had always made him hungry. But he again shook his head. "I can't," he said.

The word came down to Giancana just before the weekend. His lawyers did not want him to get too optimistic; there was always a chance the government would present another twist. A standing subpoena was believed the next move, and it would require Giancana to stand by to testify at all times. But generally the belief held that they were not going to nail him for a second time. He read every line of the newspaper reports and thoroughly enjoyed the quandary Washington and Chicago prosecutors were in. He occasionally hummed out loud, talked back to guards, made wisecracks. Then he went about preparing for his exit.

His last day in jail was to be Memorial Day, 1966, and he awoke early and ate for the last time the prison breakfast of oatmeal and coffee. Then he shaved and put on a suit of the cut he had been wearing when he came in a year before. Outside the jailhouse the usual army of reporters, photographers, and television crews were waiting, something they did poorly. The prison's warden told them he would bring Giancana out "when we are ready. Nobody is going to get near him." In early afternoon Anthony Champagne came for a short visit then left without talking to anyone.

For reasons they would not divulge, prison officials catered to Giancana's wishes to be released secretly, even to the point of rigging an elaborate escape. At five in the afternoon, after newsmen had been waiting for hours and were angry, a huge prison van drove into the jailyard's driveway. Its drivers told reporters they were delivering prisoners and had no papers mentioning a pickup of Giancana. Ten minutes later, the van drove out, this time with only one man in the front seat. Most reporters ignored it, but on a hunch one photographer got in his car and followed it into traffic as it headed for downtown Chicago. At a stoplight, the photographer jumped out of his car and onto the van's fender so he could look into a rear window. Inside he spotted a guard sitting in a corner, and Giancana stretched out on the floor. By the time he could report to his colleagues, the van had reached the Federal Building and Giancana was released from the office where he had originally been taken into custody. In minutes he was in a car with Butch Blasi and headed for his home in Oak Park.

His freedom touched off days of charges against all sides of the grand jury probe. Headlines charged incompetence, bungling, even the suggestion of a fix. Judge William Campbell, the same judge who upheld the government's right to jail a recalcitrant witness, released the grand jury and excoriated the Justice Department in Washington, but not its local prosecutors. ". . . After his [Giancana's] imprisonment, many Department of Justice statements—at least one by the Attorney General personally— were made to the effect that the government had scored a major victory in the battle against organized crime by the imprisonment of this witness," Campbell said in dismissing the grand jury. "The fact is that they have never prosecuted him for any crime nor asked you to indict him for any substantive offense."

Yet Campbell did not hold Hanrahan responsible, and added that he was an "able, conscientious and knowledgeable prosecutor" under orders from Washington not to indict Giancana. Hanrahan added that he agreed to release Giancana "reluctantly but obediently, on the instructions of my superiors."

Such cheek outraged Washington, and while at first they were willing to take the heat for Hanrahan, they moved quickly to discredit him. "His statement was unconscionable," an unnamed Justice Department official fumed. "A complete act of disloyalty." Other sources added that Hanrahan had presented them no hard evidence meriting further prosecution of Giancana but simply wanted to press more contempt charges or an obstruction-of-justice charge. "This route was neither proper nor desirable," an official said, "No matter whether his name was Jones or Smith or Giancana, he had been in jail for a year. It would have been questionable, to say the least, to then bring a criminal contempt charge against him for basically the same proposition, failure to answer questions after being granted immunity." Then, to make himself look guiltless, the Washington source said, Hanrahan misled Judge Campbell into believing that Washington had tied his hands. "I've been around here [the Justice Department] a long time and I've never seen such an act of connivancy and chicanery in my life."

For the record, Washington stated that Hanrahan's tactics with the use of immunity would ultimately be appealed before the

Supreme Court and the entire immunity statute would be challenged on grounds that it was being used just for selective persecution. They suggested Hanrahan pursue evidence supplied in other areas, specifically in the First Ward, and give the grand jury some solid evidence to ponder.

For its part, the FBI and agents close to the case seethed over Hanrahan's handling of it and his attempt to blame it all on Washington. They fully believed that Hanrahan had bungled the prosecution. To prove it they released incriminating evidence concerning the First Ward. With names, dates, and details on vote buying, influence peddling, and even payoffs by the likes of John D'Arco, Pat Marcy, and Buddy Jacobson, not to mention the many West Side Bloc politicians, the Bureau attempted to illustrate the kind of evidence Hanrahan had and refused to act upon. It was hard evidence, the Bureau argued, enough to grant immunity to others and force a witness showdown over alleged acts in violation of Federal Communications laws, interstate racketeering laws, and the influence of federal officers. Documented was $30,000 in payoffs to Giancana from individuals in the First Ward office.

The information made instant headlines. It backed reports that Washington had urged the use of immunity in the investigation, but that Hanrahan had not moved. It backed allegations that Hanrahan either knew little about the law and effective uses of federal statutes against the mob or that he was reluctant to use them. It made Hanrahan's statement that he never had anything on the First Ward people "that we could go on" seem ridiculous. When asked about the payoffs, he shrugged and argued, "I would like any lawyer to tell me what federal violation exists when $10,000 is paid by one person to another."

Such statements were enough for Washington. They continued to mince no words in describing Hanrahan's bungle. They criticized Hanrahan's incompetence and his sloth during the year of Giancana's imprisonment.

Rumors persisted in Chicago, on the other hand (and were not discouraged by Hanrahan), that a deal had been made in Washington between Giancana and agencies there. If they let him out of jail, the story went, Giancana would cooperate behind the scenes to nail other top hoodlums. Schippers and other Chicago-based prosecutors who had seen the rug pulled from under them preferred to believe the story. Why else, they argued, would Washington be at a loss for a clear explanation of why they wouldn't let Hanrahan reimmunize Giancana?

For FBI agents, however, those intimately familiar with the evidence available for use against Giancana, there was little question in their minds of where to lay the blame. The same kind of evidence was used to convict Rocco Pranno for his shake-downs in Northlake, and in November, 1965, to convict Phil Alderisio for his extortion attempts against a Denver millionaire. But those were Northlake and Denver, not Chicago. Thereafter, few federal agents were again able to hear the name of Ed Hanrahan mentioned in regard to Sam Giancana without much resentment.

Throughout the months that followed, reports surfaced that Hanrahan was preparing new thrusts against Giancana and that he was prepared to ask for an indictment. Nothing ever materialized. Sympathetic politicians who saw Hanrahan a victim of his Washington superiors scored Attorney General Katzenbach for his decision, then vowed congressional investigations. Nothing ever materialized.

That night, his first night home in a year, he was feted by his family and friends. The house was lit up until the early-morning hours. Reporters hung around outside waiting for the glimpse of Giancana they had missed at the jailhouse that afternoon. He never showed. During the night, one of his daughters came out of the house and paused to chuckle at the press corps. "Too bad, boys," she said. "You blew it."

20

IF THERE WAS any doubt in his mind about what he was going to do, there was none in the minds of the outfit. Giancana had become too hot. His year-long legal battle had again made the mob visible and controversial, not only a target for aggressive young prosecutors, but a guinea pig for jurists and legislators. There was little mystery in how Paul Ricca and Tony Accardo felt about it, for in their minds the mob worked best when people never heard about it or saw it, when politicians and columnists branded the notion of a crime syndicate as myth.

As for his position as operating boss, there was no way the mob was going to let him take it back. Federal agents were aching for a new chance to nab him on something and put him back in prison, and their efforts, if Giancana was again at the center of mob business, would jeopardize the entire outfit. Giancana himself knew the situation and knew he needed a change of scenery. His only concern was hanging on to what he had. Even that was difficult, for Ricca and Accardo were under pressure to strip him of his holdings in favor of Sam Battaglia or Jackie Cerone.

In the end, Giancana would have to pay attention to the judgment of Ricca, for the old man had been through similar blowups before. But, in a meeting with Ricca late in June, Giancana heard things he didn't want to hear. The general thrust was that Giancana had to lie low, most desirably get out of Chicago and the country altogether until things lapsed back to normal. If he did, he argued, what would keep him from losing what he had? Ricca's answers did not convince him, and he left the meeting noticeably angry.

Although he had traveled extensively, choosing a country to live in wasn't an easy task. A big factor in his choice was Richard Cain, a square-faced, good-looking master of all trades, a man equipped to complement Giancana and his hold on Chicago. A sometime cop, sometime detective, con man, linguist, hoodlum, Cain was charming, stylish, proud, yet a consummate liar, and always an enigma to anyone who knew him.

Cain was one of the Patch's brightest products. Born in 1924 and raised around Taylor and Marshfield during the Depression, he picked up the street savvy of the old 42's, dropped out of high school but was so gifted that he read and assimilated anything, even built an impressive vocabulary and a knowledge of literature and history.

Unknown to most, it was Cain's parentage that laid the groundwork. When Cain was only four years old, Billy Ranieri was kidnapped and held for ransom. Though Cain was too young to realize what was going on, his entire family was involved, for Billy Ranieri's father went to Ole Scully, the courageous sewer contractor who had mobilized fellow contractors into a White Hand Society against the scourge of Black Hand extortionists. Scully was the same man little Dickie Cain knew to be his grandfather. And though Cain hardly remembered holding the hand of his mother, Lydia, Ole Scully's youngest daughter, during the funeral after Scully was murdered just prior to the Ranieri trial, he was brought up with constant reference to his grandfather and what he stood for, and more importantly, whom he stood against.

Cain's career was not as inspired. In 1952, he went to work for a Miami detective agency, was fired for misconduct including theft of company checks, then joined the Chicago Police Department. He rose quickly through the force, but soon was involved in a scandal surrounding the murder of a petty extortionist who preyed on homosexuals, then another controversy involving a raid and theft of cash from a notorious South Side madam.

But the ax fell in 1960, when Cain, while on furlough from the Richard J. Daley–dominated police force, moonlighted for Republican State's Attorney Benjamin Adamowski, a one-time Daley mayoral opponent and long-time political foe. Cain was investigating police officers, mainly the upper ranks, Daley officials, and especially Daley's own commissioner of investigations, Irwin Cohen. Cain was caught and suspended from the police department, and ultimately he resigned.

Still, Cain wasn't finished with Chicago. After he spent time in Miami training Cuban nationals for the Bay of Pigs invasion, he returned north to go to work as chief investigator for Cook County Sheriff, Republican Richard Ogilvie. Ogilvie was the same prosecutor who had convicted Tony Accardo in 1960 on tax evasion and who had built a reputation for aggressive, honest law enforcement. Against everyone else's better judgment, he hired Cain as his top investigator. Ogilvie told friends who warned him of Cain's complicity, of his shabby record, of his uncanny ability to play both sides of the law, that he thought he could control Cain. He was in for a rude surprise.

Once Cain got on the job, he was a cyclone of activity. With his knowledge and penchant for investigating vice crimes, he made sensational raids and arrests of gamblers, dope pushers, handbooks, pornographers, abortionists, and prostitutes. He went into offices of his targets and read the contents of their desks upside down, then memorized most of it. His raids were quick and devastating, often semi-legitimate. Those who worked closely with Cain had a pervasive suspicion of many of his operations. Many seemed almost too easy, as if they had been set up for Cain. Others, especially those that threatened operations of well-known syndicate members, had a way of falling through.

Cain soon pushed his luck once too often. In October, 1963, a semi-trailer truck with $250,000 worth of drugs was stolen from a warehouse in suburban Melrose Park and found empty in Chicago a few days later. The case went unsolved until almost four months later, when Cain, with three of his deputies, armed with machine guns, and followed by a cluster of reporters and television cameras, kicked open a door of a room in a Rosemont motel and discovered cartons of the stolen drugs valued at $43,000. The raid made headlines. Cain attributed his success to good police work and well-placed informants.

But nine months later the entire case and so-called raid blew up. It had been a phony, and a badly bungled one. Cain, with the

help of the mob, had set it up. He and two others were indicted
for perjury, obstruction of justice, and conspiracy. In 1964, all
were found guilty. Cain was fired by Ogilvie, though the Illinois
Supreme Court later reversed his conviction.

Figuring he had about run out his luck with police work, Cain
went back to the outfit and the people with whom he had more
in common than anyone else. A man of Cain's capabilities was
a natural for Giancana, not only because he was intelligent and
able, but because he was fluent in many languages and could
readily interpret for Giancana as he traveled throughout the
world. Cain was especially close to the people of Mexico and
South and Central America, regions Giancana saw as prime
gambling territories.

Giancana's acceptance of Cain, however, was a revealing, perhaps a dangerous proposition. Not only was Cain keenly intelligent, by no means a goon or a lackey willing to jump at his boss's
commands, but he was also contentious and supremely self-
confident. His strongest characteristics were the strengths of
Giancana, including, not insignificantly, his ambition. And,
though Giancana's power lay in his ability to discipline and organize, Cain was not the average, old-neighborhood-style thug. The
two men would either supremely complement each other, or
chip away at each other. Those who knew them both in 1966
waited to see the results, knowing that with Giancana and Cain
the wait would not be long.

Eager to jump into any situation, Cain seized the opportunity
to introduce Giancana to a friendly foreign country. He convinced him that he could operate in Mexico as easily as he had
in Chicago. In fact, Cain said, he would use his contacts to lay the
groundwork.

The arrangements were made, the necessary leave-taking
from the family, from the grandchildren who were growing up
and beginning to pay attention to their grandfather, the agree-
ments made with associates and long-time friends. But none of
it was done ostentatiously. Agents still watching Giancana knew
nothing of his plans though they detected changes. Their information was no longer firsthand, for Justice Department officials
in Washington put severe restrictions on electronic eavesdropping to the point in July, 1965, where all microphones were ordered shut off. The decision effectively ended the daily glut of

data intelligence agents collected from their targets. Now they were forced to rely almost entirely on informants and physical surveillance, and information was slower in coming. By the fall of 1966, they discovered that Giancana was no longer in Chicago.

He settled first in a penthouse suite of a Mexico City apartment building on Amsterdam Avenue. His plan, one sanctioned by the Chicago mob, was to function as a roving ambassador for the outfit. With money made in its American concessions, he would seek out foreign investments, preferably lucrative gambling casinos in South and Central America, including "junket" boats, floating casinos catering to highrollers from the States. Such enterprises were not new to the mob, for ever since Cuba was discovered in the days of Lucky Luciano, the gangs had known that gambling in south-of-the-border countries was lucrative, and often easier to set up and control once local government officials were taken care of. If nothing else, overseas investments also served as depositories for mob funds.

Before long, however, Giancana had to get his personal finances in order. By Mexican law, aliens are not permitted to own property or business enterprises, hence all of Giancana's business had to be set up in Mexican corporations. To do this, Richard Cain again came into the picture. He introduced Giancana to a Mexico City attorney named Jorge Castillio, a shrewd legal mind with powerful political connections owing to his close and long-standing friendship with Mexican President Luis Echeverría. It was Castillio who provided Giancana with his base in the country, even to the point of directing him to real-estate agents and setting up provisions for Giancana to establish his residence in the style he had always enjoyed.

His first home was a modest walled estate in the suburb of Cuernavaca, at Las Nubes #2. It was a comfortable house, not altogether private, however, because the rolling terrain around it allowed those who wished to look onto the grounds. But Giancana quickly settled into his new routine, one that included his beloved golf game. He played almost daily, introducing himself to his golf partners, many of whom were tourists or winter residents, as Sam DePalma, and explaining, if anyone asked, that he was a banker from Chicago.

He also resumed his relationship with Phyllis McGuire. She frequently visited Mexico in late 1966 and into the new year, often arriving at the Mexico City airport and being met there by Richard Cain. From time to time intelligence agents kept surveillance on Giancana, a move that challenged Cain with the task of losing the tails. This he did with delight, often in the company of McGuire. Agents easily verified, however, the constant flow of couriers from Chicago to Giancana. Dominick Blasi was one; Johnny Matassa, his occasional chauffeur, another; and both brought large sums of cash across the border. There was little question that Giancana was operating on a large scale, and that the outfit had vested interest in his dealings.

Shortly, he began to move around, leaving Mexico for long periods of time to pursue concessions in Central and South America. He spent a lot of time in Rio de Janeiro attempting to set up casinos there. He traveled to Haiti, where East Coast hoods had set up casinos under that country's ruler, François "Papa Doc" Duvalier, but it was reported that he was unable to do the same. He also had sights set on Panama City, an enterprise he pursued with Hy Larner, the long-time Chicago envoy to Central and South America; and on Caracas, Venezuela, and on the Dominican Republic. It was in Santo Domingo that Giancana had pursued Chicago interests as early as 1963, when it was learned that he was going to travel to Europe to meet with the notorious Porfirio Rubirosa, the Dominican ambassador to France. (In fact, it was the possibility of a meeting with Rubirosa in 1963 that had been one factor in the Chicago FBI's decision to put 24-hour lockstep surveillance on Giancana. That meeting never came off, and Giancana later proceeded with his civil suit against the Bureau.) In the Dominican Republic in 1966 Giancana was aided by Leslie Kruse, a veteran Chicago gambling boss.

His ventures were similar to those of another veteran hoodlum on the lam, Meyer Lansky. Although Giancana possessed little of Lansky's business genius (even the toughest New York hoods through the years bowed to Lansky's prowess, realizing that his schemes doubled and tripled their money), he nevertheless had the ability and the contacts to make significant foreign inroads. His transactions were part of an overall change in the mob's financial thinking. Because of increased problems with U.S. government agencies, and tougher federal racketeering laws, coupled with IRS statutes, the mob looked for new ways to launder their money, to invest it in legitimate businesses or get it out of the country altogether. Tony Accardo was a strong proponent of this, and with Giancana's exit from Chicago, his decisions were law.

Giancana's foreign advances matched others already made in the Caribbean, most notably in Jamaica and the Bahamas, two places where they had encountered resistance a few years earlier. The islands were choice areas for gambling junkets. The Chicago mob in 1963 bought a 65-foot yacht expressly for that purpose, and went about setting up offshore gambling vacations for well-heeled American tourists.

Back in Cuernavaca, he continued to maintain his low profile. Those he came into contact with on a social basis did not know who he was or what he did. He began to hang out in nightclubs less and less, preferring instead occasional afternoon stops at sidewalk cafés, where he idled away the time sipping drinks and smoking his ever-present cigars. To make up for the luxuries not readily available in Mexico, he ordered things such as suits and shoes tailor-made. He often called in a local tailor, pointed out a suit in a copy of *Playboy* or *Esquire,* then ordered one exactly like it.

He also lost close contact with his family. Although his daughters and their families occasionally visited him there, he was not one to write postcards or long letters. When they did come down he was warm and gracious as he always had been. Often he took them for drives to small Mexican towns, where they would stroll through the streets and visit the local Catholic church. At all times he had pockets full of pesos, and as the small Mexican children gathered around him, he tossed handfuls of coins to them. He loved the attention, the way the kids laughed with him and tugged at his sleeves. Some tried to give him Chiclets gum in return but he refused and laughed and threw more pesos in the street. And, though he seldom brought it up, the scene was not a strange one for him, for 50 years before, when he was but a kid of seven running the streets of the Patch, the finely dressed bootleggers like the Genna brothers or Diamond Joe Esposito used to walk the neighborhood, or ride slowly through in their plush jalopies, and the small dago kids would run under their hands or jump up on running boards and scream with delight as the bootleggers threw pennies at them. But that had been 50 years before, a long time ago, or maybe not so long.

But life for Giancana was still business and staying in business. He applied for but was unable to get resident alien status in Mexico, even with Castillio's help. His status in Mexico, in fact, was anything but stable. Friendly government officials there had to be taken care of, and there was always the threat of a scandal that would put Giancana out of grace. There also existed the interest of the American government; even though they could hardly bring about Giancana's ouster from Mexico, they stood by ready to take him if the occasion arose. The situation was precarious enough for Giancana to apply for citizenship in other countries, something he did without success in Guatemala because of his criminal record.

Back in Mexico City he continued to enjoy visits from Phyllis McGuire, and occasionally he traveled with her to engagements in places like San Juan, Puerto Rico. Richard Cain accompanied him more and more, moving often between Chicago and Mexico, and even representing Giancana in places like Peru. The movements of each man were not closely followed, for once outside Chicago Giancana did not merit full-time FBI surveillance as he had before. Only occasionally did agents check on his doings apart from the general correspondence they received from international police agencies whenever Giancana traveled to a different country. Once, on a spring weekend in Mexico, agents followed him as he rented a fishing boat and proceeded to rendezvous with another boat two miles off shore. Through long-range camera lenses, they watched Giancana pad about the deck of the boat in a white hat, a white long-sleeved cardigan, his white sneakers, dark glasses, and the trademark long cigar.

Giancana never lost the paranoia that he had developed owing to the tight FBI surveillance in Chicago. While spending time in Acapulco, he happened to notice an American tourist staring at him on the beach. The tourist, a Chicago lawyer who recognized Giancana, had alerted his wife and told her that there was a chance Phyllis McGuire might be around. The two of them eyed Giancana once too often, causing him to get up from where he was sitting on the beach and, with a bodyguard, walk around the area craning their necks in an apparent attempt to discover federal agents. Later that day, the American tourist was interrupted by a bellboy, who asked for his room number. He gave it to him without thinking that it was probably Giancana's method of finding out who he was. And, though nothing more happened, Giancana shortly checked out of his hotel and left the resort area.

His wish for privacy increased the longer he stayed in Mexico. When golfing with new partners, he never revealed his real name. Occasionally, however, he came close to destroying his cover, for on the course he was prone to temper tantrums whenever his shot would desert him. His string of obscenities belied his true profession, and after startling his partners, even caused them to inquire about the short, dapper man who said he was a banker by the name of DePalma.

Even those tourists and Americans living in Mexico whom he invited into his home for the most part were unaware of who he was. Most of them were casual friends who spent nights playing cards, an activity Giancana increasingly enjoyed in Mexico. Castillio, who occasionally fraternized with Giancana, knew, as did Max Gluck, an American designer who worked at length on Giancana's various residences. But other card-playing cronies did not, or at least they didn't until September, 1967, when a sensational *Life* magazine series written by ex–Chicago reporter Sandy Smith appeared. In them, Giancana's exploits were fully documented by the reporter who best knew them, and the accompanying photographs captured Giancana in many of his best poses. It was a severe setback to his attempts at anonymity, and he was enraged.

Shortly after the *Life* articles, an Illinois scandal broke concerning Giancana and the license plates spotted on a car he and Richard Cain were driving around Mexico. No record of the plates was listed in Secretary of State files in Illinois. When reporters began digging, they finally found a receipt for them signed by Nicholas Ciaccio, one of Secretary of State Paul Powell's top aides. Ciaccio could not explain how it happened, or how Giancana got the plates, or even who owned the white Oldsmobile Cain and Giancana were driving. When an application for the plates was finally uncovered, it was signed by Harriet Blake Cain, the fourth wife of Giancana's talented associate.

Problems substantially more severe surfaced only a short time later in nearby Tucson, Arizona. Giancana's daughter Bonnie Tisci, her husband Tony, and their child had settled there after Tony's heart attack, and lived virtually undisturbed until the night before their ninth wedding anniversary in July, 1968. That night, the picture window of their home on Camino Escuela Drive was shattered by a shotgun blast. Pellets were embedded in the wall of the living room. A second shot damaged an auto parked in the driveway. Nobody in the family was hurt; in fact, it was not known whether Bonnie and her child were in the house (the damage was reported to police by a caretaker). Tony was in Chicago at the time.

To mob watchers, the shotgun attack on the Tisci home had dangerous ramifications, for living in the same area was Giancana's one-time nemesis, Joe Bonanno. In May, 1966, while Giancana was in prison, Bonanno had suddenly reappeared in New York City, ending a year-and-a-half absence which began with his "kidnapping" in October, 1964. Although the story was never fully disclosed, it was believed Bonanno had engineered his own abduction because of escalating disagreements with fellow bosses. Prior to it he had spent time avoiding fellow New York bosses by going to Canada and California, and he had almost totally fallen out with members of the National Commission. His recalcitrance so upset Giancana that he once shouted out in a Commission meeting, "Kill 'im! Why don't you just kill the guy!?" But Bonanno beat them to such a solution by vanishing. His reappearance precipitated what became known as the "Bonanno War," a power struggle between remnants of the Bonanno crime family and those wishing to replace it. By 1968, close to a dozen men had been killed before Bonanno more or less gave up and retired to Tucson.

Only two weeks after the Tisci home was shot at, two dynamite blasts rocked the Grace Ranch nearby, a spread owned by Peter Licavoli, a transplanted Detroit mobster. The next night a small bomb exploded in the barbecue pit of the Bonanno house on Elm Street. More explosions followed through the summer, some at the houses of Bonanno associates, others near the homes or businesses of persons in some way connected with the underworld. Arizona authorities feared they were in the midst of a full-scale gang war.

A year later, the true story came out. Three Arizona men were arrested and later testified to their roles in the bombings of the Licavoli and Bonanno residences. The men divulged, however, that they were working not for hoodlums but for David Hale, the special agent for the FBI in Tucson. It had been Hale, the suspects said, who devised and planned the attacks against the hoods in an attempt to foment a gang war. He also had drawn up a list of several other potential targets. And it had been Hale, on the night of July 3, 1968, one trial witness said, who had shot out the front window of the Tisci house.

David Hale soon resigned from the Bureau and refused to testify in subsequent hearings on the bombings. He was not prosecuted. A key government witness—one who allegedly witnessed the shooting at the Tisci home—was found murdered. The men who admitted their involvement in the bombings pleaded guilty to a misdemeanor charge and were fined.

In Mexico, meanwhile, Giancana settled into what looked to be a permanent stay. He again applied for resident alien status, and even though it was refused, he believed he had sufficient influence with the government to insure his residence there. True to his long-established love of fine houses and furnishings, he went out looking for a new home. Again Jorge Castillio steered him to real estate agents who would do his bidding. They showed him an estate in the La Quintas section of Cuernavaca, a place called San Cristóbal. Described by some as a castle, San Cristóbal was an expansive, walled home bigger and more sumptuous than anything Giancana had ever lived in. It had always run against his tastes to live in rambling, ostentatious mansions; his home in Oak Park suited him perfectly. But San Cristóbal was too good to pass up, and he purchased it in mid-1969 through Castillio from an American couple for $150,000.

He lived there with more privacy than he had ever known. Only intimate friends came in for evenings of card playing. No federal agents kept tabs on his phone calls or his visitors, and no microphones overheard his business transactions. Only one thing changed drastically in his life, and that was the fading of his affair with Phyllis McGuire. Because they had been so close for almost a decade, it became noticeable when the romance faded. She only occasionally visited him in Mexico; he seldom traveled with her or attended her shows. She was reported living in Las Vegas, seeing other men, and attempting to rekindle a career that had all but completely dropped out of sight.

Giancana continued to travel extensively. He was spotted several times not only in South America but in the Mideast, in Beirut, and Teheran. He became a member of a country club in Beirut under the name "Sam Ginco." He also traveled through Europe, to Spain, and especially to Athens. He was met by hosts of couriers and associates. Many, it was believed, were delivering cash intended for deposit in secret trust accounts Giancana was setting up for the mob. Occasionally, he re-entered the United States, usually to meet his daughters and their families in Las Vegas for a holiday. Sometimes, family members visited him in Mexico, including the close and trusted sister-in-law Rose Flood, a woman agents believed served as courier and confidante to Giancana in mob matters.

Then a new face appeared with Giancana. Around 1970, he was seen in Europe, especially Athens, with a woman named Carolyn Crumbley Morris, a 48-year-old divorcee and mother of two children. A blonde, attractive woman, Morris had divorced her husband, a wealthy New York music publisher, in 1970, and lived with her children in Santa Monica, California, when she wasn't traveling with Giancana. She was a sophisticated, refined woman, and when FBI agents questioned her about her relationship with Giancana she refused to tell them anything. Later, however, she admitted that she was fond of Giancana, in fact, she said, in love with him. The feeling was mutual, apparently, for Giancana shortly began making quick trips over the border to visit her in California.

As quickly as he entered the country, Giancana left, either for Mexico or other points. He was not about to take the chance of being served another subpoena and being forced to play legal games with another federal grand jury. Back in Chicago the FBI and IRS, aided by special federal strike force teams, continued their efforts against mobsters. They continued to gather evidence and win cases against upper-level hoods. In 1967, Giancana's successor Sam "Teets" Battaglia was convicted with two associates on federal charges of extorting money from the owner of a construction firm. Despite appeals and maneuvers by Battaglia's lawyers, the conviction held and Teets, the unofficial 42 who often outdid all others in the Patch at getting in trouble, was sent to Leavenworth with a 15-year sentence.

Battaglia's duties were handed to Joey Aiuppa, the aging Cicero rackets boss who up until then was highly regarded, but not looked upon to oversee anything more than his own territories.

But with Giancana's absence, and the prison terms of Felix Alderisio, Marshall Caifano, and Battaglia, Tony Accardo, who still wished to escape the day-to-day pressures of operating boss, found himself scouring the mob hierarchy for someone who could take over. Aiuppa, a sharp, well-qualified hood, had endeared himself to mob writers some years before when he was arrested in Kansas for illegally hunting mourning doves. According to state game officials there, Aiuppa and friends killed the birds as they perched on telephone wires. All told, the slaughter amounted to more than 1,400 birds. Aiuppa, from then on, was dubbed, "Joey Doves."

It was Aiuppa who also filled in for Giancana at his beloved Armory Lounge. Just before Giancana was released from jail in 1966, the Lounge became known as Gianotti's restaurant. Mrs. Mary Gianotti said she only operated the place and paid rent to Aiuppa. Although Aiuppa and friends were occasionally seen there, the restaurant no longer was the center of activity it had been with Giancana. The microphones remained in place, left there to be discovered by any remodeler who might puncture a wall, but long since turned off by federal agents. If agents had been able to place a bug anywhere close to Aiuppa, they would most likely have chosen the Luxor Baths on North Avenue in Chicago, where the new underboss often went to sit with associates in the steam and the towels.

Giancana also left his house to sit quietly in the care of relatives. The Pernos remained there, coming and going without the escort of federal surveillance. Caretaker Joseph DiPersio, already in his seventies, moved into an upstairs room with his wife, Ann, and kept the premises in the shape Giancana demanded. The furniture remained intact, polished, well preserved if seldom used; the paintings and cabinets full of figurines were undisturbed except for periodic dusting. The grounds outside were kept in excellent condition, the shrubs clipped and pruned, the putting green expertly mowed, the flowers and grass watered and fresh. In all, the place was in readiness for Giancana's return at any minute.

21

THOUGH RICHARD CAIN spent much of his time with Giancana in Mexico and other countries, he was unable to avoid yet another federal indictment in late December, 1967. In one of the most sweeping federal efforts against crime syndicate hoods and their professional accomplices, the government indicted 24 men, including Cain and top-level Giancana lieutenant Willie "Potatoes" Daddano, on a variety of charges involving bank robbery, hijacking, and interstate theft. According to government witnesses, those indicted were professional thieves working under the auspices of the mob and Daddano. In the years since the federal clamp-down on organized gambling, the mob sanctioned forays into theft and armed robberies simply because it needed the revenue. Daddano, a wizened, ruthless hood who had grown up in the Patch and later carried out orders for Giancana, oversaw the loose cadre of thieves from a suburban bowling alley, where he lounged for hours munching shoestring potatoes, per his nickname, and answering to the name Dr. Miller.

Though most of the others indicted were named for various robberies or hijackings, Cain's problems stemmed from a 1963 bank robbery. In an amazing story pieced together by three state's witnesses already in jail for the robbery, Cain was charged with having administered lie-detector tests to members of the robbery team under orders from Willie Daddano to determine which of them was a federal informant. Cain, at the time sheriff's investigator, was to have used county equipment in the tests, and for so doing was indicted for violating federal bank robbery statutes, being an accessory before and after the fact, and for conspiring to hide information about a felony.

As the story came out, on the morning of September 23, 1963, six men, all convicted professional thieves, robbed a Franklin Park Savings and Loan Association of $43,000. A few days after, however, federal agents rounded up the entire robbery team, prompting Willie Daddano to suspect that one of them was an informant. Once the men were released on bail, he ordered them all to take a lie-detector test administered by Cain. One of those forced to take the test was Guy Mendola, a thief with a long record of participation in professional robbery rings. Mendola was shot to death outside his home in August, 1964, in a killing which it was thought at first was related to the bogus motel raid after the warehouse drug burglary. But in 1968 Mendola's murder was believed connected with his problem in passing the lie-detector test after the bank job.

Apart from the complications of the bank robbery and the hosts of other thefts pulled off by those involved, the 1968 indictment of Cain again gave the media a chance to fascinate themselves with the lapsed copper. He announced that he was going to defend himself in court, an act not as cavalier as believed but linked to his lack of money. Nevertheless, it was again a chance to showcase his intellect and his style, something Cain dearly loved to do.

During the proceedings he sat apart from Daddano and the others, doing so because he actually believed he wasn't one of them, not a greaseball hood, instead, a civilized, intelligent ex-lawman indicted on a flimsy technicality. He played the angles. He amassed a portfolio of newspaper clippings about himself as evidence of prejudicial publicity, each one filed and underlined by Cain in his neat, orderly penmanship. He called two convicted murderers, who supplied a different version of the cause for Mendola's murder. He called character witnesses, jousted with the prosecution, and continued his relentless deprecation of the government's witnesses.

But the evidence against him was overwhelming, particularly that of a former deputy, who took part in the lie tests on orders from Cain but who testified he had no idea of the reasons behind them. In October, Cain, Daddano, and the three other defendants were convicted. Daddano received a 15-year sentence. Cain was sentenced to four years in prison and fined $13,000. He filed appeals but was imprisoned later that year in a federal penitentiary in Texarkana, Texas.

He remained there into 1969, reading, writing sentimental poetry, philosophizing in letters to friends and newspaper contacts back in Chicago, referring to himself as a political prisoner. At one time he helped addicted inmates into withdrawal through hypnosis, another science that fascinated him. He was enraged when he was prohibited from working in the prison library and from teaching English to the Mexicans in and around the prison. But he remained cocky and cynical.

Yet seldom did he charge himself with being the cause of his problems. He maintained a maddening aloofness, a casual cynicism even though he was discussing his own failings. And he continued to deceive his friends. During his heyday in Chicago he often bragged to friends how he could manipulate the press. He occasionally called columnists over to his table and fed them an intentionally false story, then chortled when it appeared the following day. In prison, writing to Chicago *Today* columnist Jack Mabley, the one Chicago writer who constantly gave him the benefit of the doubt, Cain enclosed a well-crafted poem he said he had composed. Mabley was so impressed he printed it at the end of a column on Cain, only to be embarrassed when he discovered that the poem was not Cain's, but one composed one hundred years earlier by Christina Georgina Rossetti.

In late 1971, Cain was released, and he lost no time getting back to Giancana. He had always aspired to become a big operator and Giancana was his hook. He worried only about his twin daughters, Karla and Kimberly, who were in their late teens and dangerously involved with drugs. His mob duties were more pressing, however, and he went about scouting new territories for Giancana, writing once from Colombia, again from Peru.

His proximity to Giancana also engendered a fondness for the aging boss, and Cain often spoke well of him. He not only considered Giancana a close friend, but one that he felt duty-bound to watch out for, an uncharacteristic stance for anyone close to Giancana. Cain nevertheless felt Giancana was vulnerable to those who wanted to use him, particularly Phyllis McGuire, and as the years passed, Cain developed suspicion of the sincerity of her affection for Giancana.

He bought Giancana gifts, once at Christmas buying him a gag golfball implanted with an electrical device that would allow a player by remote control to cause the ball to pop out of the hole. It was a costly, albeit affectionate gift, and Cain and Giancana laughed long over it. But Giancana, the purist he was about his golf game, said he would never think of using it. That was the end of it, and the gadget was stacked among his countless other golf novelties.

Without Giancana, the Chicago outfit took less of the headlines, prompting journalists in the early 1970's to write long stories about how aged and graying the mob was becoming. In reality, only the familiar faces were departing, most of them dying of bad hearts or livers or lung cancer, and they left their concessions to lesser-known lieutenants. Milwaukee Phil Alderisio died in prison; Fifi Buccieri succumbed to cancer. Sam English, Chuck's brother and an important juke-box boss, died of a heart attack. Ross Prio, the North Side underboss, died in 1973, then his top lieutenant Jimmy Allegretti died while serving a federal prison sentence.

But no loss sapped the outfit like the death of the Patriarch. In October, 1972, Paul Ricca, the old waiter whose word was listened to always, died in bed. His fight with the immigration officials finally ended in his favor, for he evaded deportation a full 15 years after a federal judge revoked his citizenship. At one time he might have accepted deportation back to Italy, as he showed by spending many hours around the Al Italia terminal at O'Hare Airport. He listened well to the Italian tourists who talked his native tongue as they hustled down the corridors. But the government of Italy would not permit Ricca to enter that country, and his case remained in limbo until he died.

His death left the reins of the mob totally in the hands of his old friend Tony Accardo. As Accardo stood near Ricca's bier at a West Side funeral home, he silently greeted fellow hoods who came to pay their respects. He would now delegate day-to-day authority through Joey Aiuppa, Jack Cerone, and Gus Alex, and they would attempt to control rising lieutenants eager to step in.

Accardo would also have to contend with Giancana, a task made easier not only because many of Giancana's most ruthless executioners had died or gone to prison, but because Ricca had always stood strongly behind the upstart operating boss. Ricca had had immense respect for Giancana's abilities, and had generally overlooked his flaws. He had been a godfather in all respects to Sam, and his death would tell.

Ricca meant much to others, too. His word was enough to keep a man alive, to cover lapses that would have ordinarily been cause for a murder contract. One of those who thrived under Ricca's graces was Mad Sam DeStefano, a man who had made enough enemies and committed enough mob excesses to have warranted extinction on many occasions. But DeStefano survived, partly because he also managed to earn the favor of Giancana. The 1970's, however, brought him added criminal indictments and ensuing courtroom appearances that sustained his reputation for being the mob's premier loon. In March, 1972, he was sentenced to three and a half years in prison for threatening a government witness. While appealing that, he faced a murder indictment for the 1963 torture murder of Leo Foreman.

As the months passed, however, it looked as though his health, not his enemies, would finally kill him. He had a history of stomach and abdominal problems, and in early 1973 was diagnosed to have cancer. Still, with DeStefano's antics, nobody took his demise seriously unless it was accompanied by a coroner's report. That was to come in April of that year.

On the morning of the 14th, a brisk, sunny Saturday, the 64-year-old DeStefano dressed in casual work clothes and prepared to work in the yard of his home in a neat residential section of Chicago's Far West Side. He was alone in the garage at just after 10 A.M., a new broom in his hands, when he looked up into the barrel of a shotgun. The blasts knocked him off his feet, one catching him in the heart, the other severing his left arm just above the elbow. He landed on his back, spread-eagled on the concrete, his feet facing the street. Two spent shells and his eyeglasses lay nearby. It was a half hour before a friend came to the house and found him.

The usual speculations followed the slaying, only more so in the case of DeStefano. Homicide detectives named dozens of people who may have wanted DeStefano out of the way, including his brother Mario and Anthony Spilotro, both of whom were scheduled to be tried with DeStefano for the Foreman murder and who feared his courtroom antics. Members of a burglary ring fearing recriminations from dealings with the unpredictable DeStefano were also mentioned as possible suspects. The list went on and on. Most accurate, perhaps, was the feeling that DeStefano, with a life of treachery behind him, in dubious health mentally and physically, with a wild brain and a flapping tongue, simply had no one left to keep him alive.

By late 1973, though Cain had accompanied Giancana all over the world, the relationship grew strained. Again it came down to the basic nature of the two men. Both were aggressive, domineering individuals, Cain even more so at this time because of his youth and the fact that he was anxious to get somewhere in the outfit, and also because he desperately wanted to make some money. Giancana, on the other hand, was winding down his endeavors, finding resistance to his foreign gambling efforts, satisfied to live off his investments and the concessions he'd established. Cain, however, was so strapped for cash while working with Giancana that he wired Jack Mabley for a loan.

Cain saw the potential of a gambling junket, and he became determined, with or without Giancana's blessing, to organize one. He became obsessed with the scheme, drawing plans around a boatload of gamblers bound for casinos in Malta, Cyprus, and Greece. He would organize and oversee the entire operation, receiving backing from legitimate businessmen and hoods with the understanding that a cut of the profits would go to the outfit. His plans also included his twin daughters, for by 1973 he was increasingly concerned about their drug dealings. He discovered that they were involved with heroin, both were users, and their habits were growing out of control. He said that when he got the gambling junket together, he would put them to work on the boat, and in one of the few times in his life that he actually wanted to come through as a father, he vowed to fulfill his promise.

Cain's junket, however, met resistance from Giancana and the mob. Increased federal attention to gambling concessions brought pressure that had caused the outfit to abandon some of its lucrative enterprises in Chicago. They refused to permit new ventures. In October, when Cain and Giancana left Montego Bay, Jamaica, and flew to New Orleans, the two men came to an impasse over the issue. Without Giancana's backing, Cain returned to Chicago to pursue the venture. Giancana, still afraid of federal surveillance, slipped off to California and Carolyn Morris.

In Chicago, Cain attempted to play on two developments in the mob. First, he appealed to younger hoods who had long been reported as dissatisfied with their power and the portions of outfit action given them. His appeal was simple: if the old guard won't give you more of a cut, take it. He suggested starting with his junket. Second, he attempted to play upon the disgruntlement of Marshall Caifano. The feisty little enforcer had recently been released from prison after serving a long term for extortion, and he was angry because the outfit had not taken care of him upon his release. Caifano also appealed to younger members of the mob and threatened to cause severe problems. Joey Aiuppa, the operating boss at the time, was quite ill, so Accardo called Gus Alex to settle things. But Cain still felt Caifano was a man to contact.

Regardless of how persuasive Cain and his plans may have been to a hood like Caifano or any of the disgruntled junior members of the outfit, the fact of who Cain was and what he had pulled in his career immediately dampened the appeal. Perhaps nobody brought on more suspicion than the ambitious ex-cop, and few hoods were unaware of the fact that Cain held most of them in low esteem, that he had more sense and cunning than all of them put together. He even went so far as to suggest that one day he might be the man to call all the shots, to take over. That kind of talk scared a lot of people, especially since Cain in the late fall of 1973 was no longer operating under the blessings of Giancana. The word was passed that Cain was to back off.

It meant nothing to Cain. He continued to maneuver behind the scenes, to make his contacts, to finalize his plans. He also continued to see some of his old friends, some of the Rush Street crowd, a prominent newspaperwoman and her friends. His eyesight was failing (he'd lost one eye as a result of a childhood accident and the tissue in the other was deteriorated) so he took cabs or had friends drive him around. Part of that was for his personal safety, for Cain realized by December of 1973 that he was in some danger, that he was being followed on occasion. As a precaution he traveled with a cousin, a mob heavy he called "Vinnie the Thief," who did little around Cain but nod.

But Vinnie was not with Cain the afternoon of December 20, when he left the apartment of a girlfriend and headed for Rose's Sandwich Shop at 1117 West Grand Avenue in the old Sicilian neighborhood on the Near Northwest Side. The shop was operated by Sammy Cozzo, who, with his brother Jimmy, were acquaintances of Marshall Caifano. Cain was still actively working on Caifano, having met and conferred with him on several occasions in the past few days. Caifano himself was in Rose's at noon that day, though he left before Cain arrived at 1:30.

At a table in the small, sparsely furnished diner, Cain sat down with four men. He talked with them briefly, the five of them drawing little notice from Cozzo, a waitress, and a woman patron. Shortly, the four men got up and left, two going out the front door, two out the back. Cain then sat alone until a young brown-haired woman came into the shop and walked over to him. She stood next to his table and spoke with him, again drawing little notice. But, as she talked, two men wearing ski masks, both carrying shotguns, walked swiftly into the shop. They motioned everyone over to a wall.

One of the men carried a walkie-talkie in his left hand. He blurted into it, "Who's got the package? Who's got the package?"

He waited for a reply. Then he repeated himself. "Who's got the package?"

A response crackled over his set. "Here comes a guy now. Maybe he's got the package."

The second gunman, wearing a black leather glove on his left hand and a white cloth glove on his right, then stepped close behind Cain and pointed a 12-gauge shotgun at the back of his head. Two explosions shook the sandwich shop. Cain flopped to the floor; the gunman momentarily reached inside his coat pockets but took nothing from them. Then he and his accomplice walked out of the shop. The woman who had come in before them and briefly talked to Cain had slipped unseen out of the shop just before the shooting, leaving Sammy Cozzo, his horrified waitress and customer to stare at the corpse of Richard Cain, and the spent, spotless, double-0 shot shells lying near him.

All that remained were the headlines and the eulogies. Hosts of people knew Cain and the countless sides of his personality. Each had an anecdote, an illustration of his wit, his intellect, his duplicity. Some talked of his love of literature and his voracious reading. He was such an admirer of novelist Lawrence Durrell that he once got on a plane to Paris and had lunch with the writer. Others called him a phony, a whoremonger, a fop. All, however, agreed on his unlimited intelligence, and that it was inexorably attached to his ingenious ability to lie.

But little of it counted on that cold, barren Chicago afternoon when the man with the overwhelming intelligence quotient, who said he always hated the mob for what it had done to his grandfather 45 years before, met his contract with an unsentimental shotgun. It went unnoticed that Ole Scully had also been killed in a small restaurant. Unlike the outrage that answered the murder of Ole Scully for his attempts against the scourge of Black Handers, the response to the death of his grandson Richard Cain was little more than a collective shrug of the shoulders. For all of Cain's impressive credentials, his pretensions notwithstanding, another hood had gotten his.

Giancana more and more found himself unable to maintain his globe trotting. In the first months of 1974, he spent most of his time inside San Cristóbal. His health continued to deteriorate, with stomach and abdominal problems that brought him severe discomfort. His ill-health brought on his ill-temper. He became angered even more quickly than before, over minor problems and family affairs. When he did feel good, he invited his Mexico City friends in. As much as possible, he played golf, dressing well in flared trousers and sweater shirts. He even grew a salt-and-pepper goatee, a look that pleased him and that he complemented at times with a toupee.

But none of that counted when he didn't feel well; his irascibility made him impossible to be around. He was particularly piqued by Antoinette, his oldest daughter, who upset him greatly when she filed for a divorce from her husband, Carmen Manno, after fourteen years of marriage and five children. To Giancana, who in his advanced age had become increasingly religious and tradition-bound, divorce was a grievous offense, and he all but disowned Antoinette for it. He remained close to his other daughters, particularly Francine, who had married a lawyer, Jerome

DePalma, and settled in the Chicago suburb of Schiller Park not far from Giancana's Oak Park home.

But neither his health nor his family problems were enough to encourage him to move back to Oak Park. He was convinced the government still wanted to put him in jail, and he wouldn't give them the satisfaction. His relationship with Carolyn Morris was still very much alive, but though he went to California on occasion to visit her, there was little chance of relocating there. There was nothing in his future that looked as though it would prevent him from living in semi-retirement in the sun and privacy of Cuernavaca, for the days of hustling and the nights of clubbing were behind him.

As long as Giancana was denied resident alien status he maintained and relied on his relationship with Jorge Castillio. All seemed to be in order that early evening, July 18, 1974. Giancana padded around his backyard, attending to his flowers and shrubs, the well-kept garden that he prized. He was wearing slippers and a bathrobe, a stub of a cigar in one hand. Suddenly two men jumped out on either side of him. They had made their way past the walls and waited for the chance when Giancana was alone. At first he resisted, not knowing who or what was happening, but his instincts quickly told him that the men were not hoods or even small-time thieves, but government immigration agents.

Without explanations of any sort, they whisked him from the grounds and to the local jail. In spite of his rantings, his attempts to intimidate the agents, he was kept there overnight. The next day, again without permitting him to contact anyone, they brought him a rumpled blue shirt and a pair of cotton pants that he had difficulty keeping up. They then served him a breakfast of two slices of bread and a lump of rice. Moments later he was taken from his cell and driven to Mexico City.

There he still had no idea what was going on or who was behind it. Jorge Castillio never appeared. Unknown to Giancana, a call was put through to the American consulate in Mexico City to verify his citizenship. That began a flurry of action in the consulate, for they were very aware of Giancana and what he meant to American lawmen. They, too, had been taken by surprise, and they made quick calls to the FBI office in San Antonio, Texas. From there the word was quickly passed to Washington, then Chicago, where it came as a total surprise. The message was definite: Giancana was being deported as an unwanted visitor.

Chicago agents moved fast to keep from losing Giancana once he crossed the border. They arranged for San Antonio agents to serve him with a subpoena to appear before a Chicago grand jury the following Tuesday. It was served when Giancana arrived there from Mexico. The Bureau even threw in a plane ticket to Chicago, for Giancana told them he had nothing but the clothing on his back. That afternoon he was put on an American Airlines flight to Chicago O'Hare. He was still wearing his slippers, his bathrobe over his arm.

22

BILL ROEMER WOULDN'T have missed it for anything. When the word came through that Giancana was coming back to town, he headed for the airport. He joined a handful of other lawmen, agents who would assume the Giancana file after him, and the usual delegation of Chicago intelligence detectives and sheriff's police. Most of them were younger than Roemer and had never seen Giancana before. But they had read the files and heard the stories, and Roemer would readily fill in the blanks.

When Giancana emerged from the plane, he spotted Roemer immediately. He tightened his expression, fixing the malevolent look so familiar to Roemer, now more distinctive because Giancana's face had become craggy and furrowed with age. But there was little else, none of the ebullience he'd flaunted in the past, none of the smooth, menacing self-assurance he'd thrown at agents through the years along with the flaps of his silk suits. For as he walked into the glare of the terminal lights he was noticeably tired, unshaven, carrying his bathrobe and wearing the ridiculous pants-and-shirt combination given him by the Mexicans.

It was an outfit hardly befitting Giancana, and one that made it unlikely that he'd break into an abusive outburst Roemer half expected. As shabby and unkempt as he was, he did little but cause airline employees to wonder at how a man looking as he did could attract such attention. He made no fuss. He looked slack-eyed at the officers when they asked him to accompany them.

"Should I go?" he asked Roemer.

The agent was startled at Giancana's meekness. "It's up to you," he replied.

Giancana complied, something he never would have done in years past. As he lingered with the officers, he approached Roemer and began an exchange. He said that he wanted to forget what had happened between them through the years, that he had no hard feelings. He apologized for the threats and epithets he'd leveled at Roemer and other agents in the past.

"Look," he said. "I'm not back here because I wanna be. Them Mexicans were a bunch of bums who didn't have change for the right time. But let's forget it, huh? I ain't gonna do anything anymore. I've hung it up. I'm retired."

Roemer replied that if such indeed was the case, he thought Giancana and the Bureau would get along well. He wondered if age and Giancana's bad stomach had taken their toll, if the Mooney of old, the vicious, rat-smart organizer, the 42, had actually mellowed. This was the first show of humility he'd seen in the man in the 15 years he'd kept track of him. Yet before Roemer bought Giancana's new posture, he'd wait to see if, with the boss back in his old turf, it was anything but a new maneuver.

When Giancana reached police headquarters downtown, the press were ready and waiting. They crowded in like old times, snapping photos at any glimpse of him. Inside the interrogation room he gave Chicago police vague answers to what few relevant questions they asked. They had not dealt with him for eight years, and had done so cursorily before that, so they picked at him, inquiring about his movements, his consorts, his businesses. They learned nothing, and quickly went into direct questions about the murder of Richard Cain. Giancana said he was ignorant of it, out of the country at the time. What he did want to talk about was his ouster from Mexico. He claimed that the U.S. State Department had been pressuring the Mexican government to evict him, and they had pulled a "sneak attack" when they finally came after him. "They bought me this beautiful outfit," he continued, again exhibiting his wrinkled shirt. "I'm lucky I didn't lose my pants."

But he was back, the most flamboyant don Chicago had known since Capone, and the cops wanted to give him the impression they were on top of his case, even if at the time they had no case at all. FBI agents, Roemer's understudies, made sure Giancana got the impression that they would start up where the government had left off eight years ago. They would greet him again a few days later when he answered his federal subpoena. But first he paid more dues to the photographers who were waiting, and they captured his thin, bedraggled silhouette as he walked away from them across a parking lot, saying nothing, the thin, long-sleeved shirt hanging over his waist, the ill-fitting baggy pants sagging around his hips.

In the following days and weeks he re-established his routine. His Oak Park home had remained exactly the way he had left it thanks to the meticulous care of Joe DiPersio and his wife, and the Pernos, who had continued to live there even though Francine had moved away after her marriage. The house retained its subdued elegance, from the lighted paintings and buffets filled with Giancana's carefully collected German figurines, to the well-preserved oak and mahogany furniture, the hand-painted porcelain lamps. DiPersio had kept the backyard putting green intact, and with the tall stockade fence on all sides, the yard and patio afforded Giancana as much privacy as had the walled-in San Cristóbal—in fact, in view of the way Mexican immigration officials had snatched him, more.

But Giancana's personal life was very much unsettled. He was not in good health and he continued to argue with friends and relatives. He had a violent falling-out with the Pernos and they shortly moved out of the house. He refused to reconcile his differences with his daughter Tony over her divorce proceedings. They continued to bicker to the degree that Antoinette was not always welcome at the house. Only Francine remained close, and with her husband and daughter regularly visited Giancana and had dinner with him.

His most important task as far as he was concerned, however, was to re-establish himself with the outfit. It was a delicate proposition, for the times and the personnel had changed much since he had left. He no longer had his base at the Armory Lounge, so his business was conducted from a car, again chauffeured by

Butch Blasi, and in phone booths and luncheonettes. On most days he left his house in the morning, waved at police units who again tailed him, then got into the back seat of the car and rode around to pay phones in the area. He was still the Giancana the police and FBI agents knew, again wearing the expensive suits and appropriate accessories, only now looking older, his hair curling around his ears and at the nape of his neck, a slight beard and mustache filling out the hollows of his face.

At a leisurely pace, Blasi drove him around, never to the same pay phone twice in a row. He made his calls and set up his liaisons. He met often with Chuck English, and got in his usual golf games. He sat down with Joey Aiuppa, the ranking operating boss, but also with Tony Spilotro, perhaps the toughest of the younger hoods, a one-time lieutenant of Phil Alderisio and now a mob representative in Las Vegas. It was meetings such as those that made lawmen wonder, for the tension between the young and the old guard of the mob was very much an issue, and a power like Giancana had to fit in somewhere. Yet he also made contact with Tony Accardo, the god on earth to the outfit, and the two of them, old dons who'd spanned the century, talked long and hard.

When he was not out, Giancana stayed around the house, putted endlessly in the backyard, or sat on lawn chairs on the grass. Couriers came and went, the ever-attentive Blasi, Spilotro, even Spilotro's wife, who walked over from her home only blocks away. Otherwise, Giancana tilled his garden, or took walks with Joe DiPersio. He saw a Chicago woman, a tall, dark-haired Indian in her early thirties who lived on Rush Street in Chicago but often came out to the house in Oak Park. She was another of his paramours that amazed those who observed them, a man of his age and his health who seemed unable to quit. He also traveled to other cities, seldom out of the country, mostly to Santa Monica and Carolyn Morris.

By the fall of that year, the federal grand jury began pressing him again. Giancana appeared as dictated by his subpoena, even though he told them nothing. His status was still a curiosity to many of the FBI agents who had dealt with him in the past, especially Ralph Hill, Roemer's one-time partner who had left the Giancana detail in 1963. Hill took the time one day in late 1974 to catch Giancana as he stood outside the jury chambers in the

Federal Building. Giancana recognized him, and as he had been with Roemer months back, he was amiable and somewhat talkative. Hill brought up the old times, and in his loquacious, assured manner, managed even to get a smile out of Giancana. He asked if he still saw Phyllis McGuire and Giancana shook his head.

"She was quite a girl," Hill remarked.

"Yeah, quite a girl," Giancana repeated.

"Quite a musician," Hill said.

"Quite a musician," Giancana said.

"Played a lot of instruments," Hill said.

"Yeah," Giancana said, eyed the agent, then cut it off.

Hill changed course. He was curious about Mexico and the circumstances surrounding Giancana's deportation.

"Tell me, Mo, what in hell happened down there?" he said.

Giancana looked at him, raised his eyebrows and shrugged his shoulders. It was a moment, as far as Hill was concerned, in which Giancana seemed to be leveling with him, a moment that revealed his frustration with the events in Mexico and what had followed.

Giancana's response held with what federal agents learned when they went down to Mexico to investigate his dealings there, the depositories of mob funds he may have set up, and particularly the reason for his ouster. They found only the earmarks of a political scandal that had never materialized. When Giancana was thrown out of the country, President Echeverría was also out of the country. The President's friend, Giancana's lawyer Jorge Castillio, appeared helpless, either by accident or design, to do anything. It is not known exactly why Giancana was evicted from Mexico. It was believed that Giancana had funneled sizable payments to Mexican officials in order to stay in the country as he had. Those payments had either stopped and incensed Giancana's patrons, or they were discovered and became a source of potentially damaging political scandal. In any case, to friends or enemies of his political backers, he became a liability.

What the government agents also discovered, however, was that Giancana was thrown out with little more than what he carried with him on the plane. His layered financial arrangements, holdings not in his name because of Mexican law, made him unable to recover his money or business assets. Because it was believed Castillio figured prominently in those finances, the grand jury in Chicago desired to have him testify. Castillio at first agreed, but later, when Giancana's financial intrigues became more of a jury target, he reneged. And Giancana, in a position totally unfamiliar to him throughout most of his life, seemed apparently unable to retrieve his money. Hence, when he lifted his palms to Ralph Hill in the Federal Building hallway, he wasn't being coy.

Inside the jury room, Giancana wasn't nearly as forthright. As part of a revised strategy toward grand juries, he talked but said nothing. The idea was to tell the prosecutors what they already knew but without supplying hard testimony or incriminating evidence against other hoods. Hence, Giancana hedged and dodged, offering what Organized Crime Strike Force leader Peter Vaira termed "garbage." And, without extensive data like that supplied ten years before when Giancana was functioning as boss on all levels, the government had little to go on and little to question him about. At one time they asked him about his golf game in Mexico. "What's your handicap?" asked a government lawyer. "Nine," Giancana replied. It was a slight exaggeration, the prosecutors knew from long surveillance of his game, and they wondered if a man could be prosecuted for perjuring himself on his golf scores.

Vaira and other government attorneys, however, began to consider indicting Giancana on other perjury counts, but they admitted it would have been a flimsy prosecution in view of what they had heard in the grand jury hearings. It certainly was not the indictment they wanted. They then immunized Giancana as they had ten years before, but again the mob's reaction to immunity had changed. As Murray Humphreys had advocated, they decided to talk under immunity but say only so much. With the absence of federal microphones, they felt confident they could bluff their way through, risking perjury charges but not contempt. They were also confident that, without corroborating witnesses, the government wouldn't be able to build strong cases. It was a sensitive, risky approach, but when dealing with federal grand juries, the mob found it their only viable strategy.

As the months of the grand jury proceedings passed, with Giancana's health affecting him more than most people knew, a question of whether or not he would crack became an issue in the mob. He told confidants that he would do anything to keep "from rotting in jail," a statement that made people who considered him a "stand-up guy," one who had nicely sat out a year in jail in 1965, have second thoughts.

It added a degree of tenseness to his relations with Accardo and Aiuppa. For even though Giancana came back wounded and relatively powerless, he wasn't without the will and the cunning to make a move. He told Accardo that he wasn't anyone's guinea pig, that if the outfit was worth anything it would get the federal monkey off his back, or at least make a stab at it. That meant sending out the word in Washington. If it could be done in the old days when Murray Humphreys took to extraordinary measures on behalf of Paul Ricca, it could be done now in the days of Watergate.

He even went further. There was no reason in his mind why he shouldn't be given the same authority he had when he left, why he shouldn't get the same percentages of the same concessions he ran back then. It was a sensitive point with Accardo, a man who had taken the mob out of the headlines as much as he could, immersed its funds in money laundries and legitimate businesses, even stopped lucrative gambling enterprises if there was a hint of a federal crackdown. Times had changed, Accardo had shown, and no longer could an abrasive boss like Giancana get by the way he had ten and twenty years ago.

Rather than forcing a confrontation, Accardo hoped Giancana in time would come back to reality. Times had changed, Accardo repeated. Besides, Giancana's bargaining power had diminished not only because of his present grand jury problems, but because most of his enforcers, the old guard, were gone. Buccieri and Alderisio, his personal executioners, were dead; Willie Daddano was in prison; Marshall Caifano was around but out of standing; Ross Prio, Frank La Porte, Sam and Tony Battaglia, Paul Ricca —all were dead, all were unable to reinforce the claim of mob clout that Giancana pursued. If Giancana thought he could retake his old piece without them, if he thought he could move out Accardo in the year 1974 after eight years on the lam, he was literally out of his mind.

As much as Giancana maneuvered, feeling out allegiances and suggesting deals, he failed to realize that, as far as most of the Chicago outfit was concerned, he was bad credit, a memory of things gone sour. He was remembered as the surly, alienating influence who had wasted a lot of mob contacts and run a lot of concessions into the ground. Under him, the outfit's takes had declined, its clout with politicians and judges had diminished. He was a garrulous, aggressive son of a bitch à la Capone and Nitti. Most hoods could have cared less about that if it hadn't been for the fact that Giancana was generally blamed for the present-day problems that plagued them all. People, even mobsters, had to eat.

The outfit, instead, turned the tables. Accardo was the one confronted Giancana with the fact that money was becoming increasingly scarce for the outfit. Revenues from gambling were way down, and it was harder to take care of the rank-and-file hoods on the street. What the outfit wanted was what Giancana still had. Though he hadn't been able to get his personal fortune out of Mexico, he was still deriving handy profits from Caribbean gambling junkets he had set up. Five gambling boats in particular were gold mines for Giancana, and Accardo said the mob had to share in them. He said they weren't asking, they were telling.

Giancana resisted, in fact, flatly refused. He instead trained his attempts on galvanizing new support and a new base of strength. He used every lever he had, including the threat to talk to the grand jury still on his heels. Nothing mattered to him apart from his vow not to give in, no matter how much the outfit pressed or what Accardo said the rules were.

But the outfit's demand held. Finally, it became an ultimatum.

Giancana, cavalier, snarling, still lethal, still very much a smart head of the 42's, told them to shove it.

The killer was dispatched in total secrecy, moving at his own speed, awaiting the opportune moment. Only he and his sponsor knew his deed, and neither would breathe any mention of it even to their intimates. They were pledged to the certainty of it, the unremitting intent, knowing finally that it preserved their very way of life.

In May, 1975, Giancana was in California with Carolyn Morris when he sustained the attack, a pain in his stomach that was worse than any before. He insisted on being taken to Methodist Hospital in Houston, Texas, and on the 13th he underwent acute gall-bladder surgery, a cholecystectomy, at the hands of the renowned surgeon Dr. Michael E. DeBakey. The operation was a difficult one, and he emerged a desperately sick man. He remained bedridden for three weeks, his presence in the city unknown to the press there until early June. When reporters finally did discover him, they were told that he was too sick to have visitors. His condition, however, did not keep his daughter Bonnie, Carolyn Morris, and Butch Blasi from attending to him regularly.

He was finally well enough to return to Oak Park to recuperate. He was weak and thin, his weight around 150 pounds, too sick to do anything but pad around the house, occasionally sitting outside but unable even to practice his putting. Blasi and English visited him often, as did Francine and her family. But he was in no condition to entertain anyone satisfactorily, and not well enough to pursue much business.

Still, the killer had his mission. It was a matter of time before he would kill or be killed. It mattered not that nature was coming close to beating him to it.

In mid-June Giancana suffered a relapse, a blood clot in his middle, and he went back down to Houston for treatment. Again DeBakey relieved the condition, breaking up the clot and prescribing the proper drugs. After a week there, Giancana's condition improved significantly, and though DeBakey had ordered him to stay in bed, he made arrangements with his son-in-law, Jerome DePalma, who had come down to Houston, to get him out of the hospital. By then he was being watched by the Houston police, and they provided yet another obstacle. On Tuesday, the 17th, he made his break. He dressed in a white doctor's gown and walked out a back door of the hospital. DePalma paid hospital expenses with his own American Express Card in front. Giancana then used a hospital supply van to get away unnoticed.

Houston detectives discovered he had left Methodist and rushed to his hotel, the Warwick, where they learned that he had already checked out. They caught him standing in the lobby waiting for a cab. Playing innocent, apologetic, Giancana assured police that he would return to the hospital. When they went outside to follow his cab, Giancana went out the back way once again and was gone.

Two days later, Wednesday, June 18, he was met at O'Hare Airport by Butch Blasi. He was still in bad shape, walking slowly and finding it difficult to climb steps. He still carried the deep wounds from DeBakey's incisions, and his insides gave him constant pain. Blasi drove him home.

At the house he did little but rest. The next morning he watched as Joe DiPersio fought with a leaky water pipe that had caused water damage to the basement ceiling. It was no minor affair as far as the basement was concerned, for Giancana spent much of his time down there. Some years back he had extensively remodeled the basement, paneling the walls and sectioning it into elaborately furnished den and dining-room areas, with a fully equipped kitchen. A large, rectangular oak table with ten high-backed chairs dominated the den, the table giving rise to the belief that it was the meeting place for the Giancana "cell" of the mob. Though the room may have served that purpose in the early days of his rise (its door had a jimmy-proof lock), it did not when he became operating boss, for then he did most of his business outside of the house, at the Armory or Schneider's.

The den, however, reflected Giancana's tastes and his luxuries. It was dotted with glass and porcelain ashtrays, steins, bowls, pitchers, sterling silverware and salt shakers, and an elaborate, valuable sterling silver tea and coffee service. A gothic-style hutch and matching tables completed the room, along with paintings, a fully stocked liquor cabinet, more than nine dozen glasses, a stereo cabinet, a Louis XV-style desk, sofa, armchairs, and a wine dispenser.

It was a place that told more about the private side of Giancana than almost anything else in the house. He kept his wooden pipe stand and the 29 pipes there, his wooden cigar humidor with the initial "G" on the lid. He kept his golf equipment and the usual golf novelties there, a wastebasket shaped like a golf bag, a print of a clown golfing. A closet held his putting-green flags, cups, and his clubs. The kitchen portion of the basement led into a tiled stairway out to the backyard green. Giancana had had a carpenter install a thick steel fire door with a peephole in it at the base of the stairs. Though he often left the door open to the backyard on hot summer evenings and freely went back and forth, the entryway was equipped with an electric-eye burglar alarm.

He also stored his voluminous camera equipment down there, the Minox cameras and flash attachments, Sony videotape unit and recorder, the movie and Polaroid cameras, even a 16-millimeter projector and screen, a film editor, and splicer. His love of photography was matched only by his love of a couple of his favorite full-length features. Along with copies of *Rin Tin Tin, Death Goes North,* and *The Irish Isle and Hindenburg Sports,* he had a print of a 1942 Walter Huston movie called *Always in My Heart,* a melodrama about a man who returns home after an unjust prison sentence to win back his daughter's love, a plot remarkably appropriate. Yet his favorites were copies of *The Manchurian Candidate* and *The Man with the Golden Arm,* both starring his friend Frank Sinatra.

That Thursday afternoon, however, he paid little attention to his hobbies, preferring to sit and attend to his stomach. In late afternoon, Chuck English came over and the two of them sat and talked as they had for years, the conversation centering mostly on Giancana's health and his operation. They were joined at around 7 P.M. by his daughter Francine, her husband and daughter, and Butch Blasi. The six of them sat down to a casual dinner of chicken, baked potatoes, mixed vegetables, and a salad of lettuce and tomato. Again, the chatter concerned Giancana's health and the cause of his relapse. The evening, generally, was little more than an informal get-together, and they lingered around the table undisturbed. Earlier that day an unmarked police car had parked in front of the house and a call had been made to the Oak Park police complaining of a "suspicious" car. Village police checked it and found it belonged to Chicago intelligence detectives. Later, the car left.

The hours passed. It was a quiet, dull summer night, the beginning of a heat wave that called for the use of the air conditioners in the windows of the home. Shortly, English and Blasi got up and left. Their exit was noted by the detectives who'd returned outside. Near 10 P.M., the DePalmas decided to leave, since it was getting close to the bedtime of their daughter. As they did, Giancana thanked Francine for the Italian sausage, escarole, and *ceci* beans she had brought him. It was a favorite meal of Giancana's, and since the removal of his gall bladder permitted him a more liberal diet, he looked forward to it.

The DePalmas got into their auto and backed out of the driveway. They had hardly pulled away from the house when they spotted a familiar car coming at them. It was a small yellow auto belonging to Blasi's daughter, which Blasi himself often drove.

They slowed briefly as the two cars passed and exchanged informal greetings, then drove on. Blasi pulled his car into Giancana's driveway and walked into the house.

A few minutes later the car was observed still parked in the driveway by the team of Chicago detectives keeping surveillance over the house. Their assignment was to keep a random watch on Giancana's house as well as activities around the homes of the many other hoods who lived in the vicinity: Tony Spilotro, Chuck English in River Forest, Tony Accardo in the same suburb, among others. It was a loosely structured and tedious assignment, which consisted of little more than trying to identify faces and copy license numbers. The team, in fact, was not even certain that night if Giancana was back in town. When they saw the yellow car in his driveway, they recorded its license number and paid it little attention.

They were more interested in a car that pulled out of the alley on the other side of the house. They followed it, the tail was something to relieve the monotony of the night, but before they were able to get a complete license number they lost the vehicle in traffic. They then headed over to English's place in River Forest, and when they saw nothing there they checked out an equally somnolent Accardo residence. With nothing else to go on (they later discovered the auto they had tailed belonged to a landscaper who had done some work that day at Giancana's and who had returned to get his car) they nonchalantly headed back to the Giancana house.

At just after 10:30, Joe DiPersio got up in his upstairs bedroom apartment and yelled down the stairs to see if Giancana needed anything. Giancana said not, that he'd call if he did. With that, DiPersio shut his bedroom door so as not to lose cool air from the window air conditioner he'd turned on. Then, with his wife Ann, he settled in to watch "The Tonight Show."

The killer sat across from him in the basement kitchen. He was a friend, or an associate trusted enough to sit face to face with Giancana at that time of night in his own home and discuss things. It was cool in the basement and there was no need to open the steel door leading to the backyard. Giancana, casual in a blue-and-white-checked sport shirt, brown pants, and his usual slippers, brought down the snack Francine had brought over. He got out a couple of pans. In one he began to cook the sausage; in the other he boiled the escarole and beans. Later he would sauté the two in the sausage grease for a tasty, Old Country snack, one he would offer to the killer.

Shortly after, the killer felt the outline of his gun. It was a ten-shot High-Standard Duromatic .22 target pistol, but its four-inch barrel had been tooled down to where it was no more than an elongated nipple. To it a six-inch threaded tube had been attached as a silencer. It was the crudest sort, not intricately baffled like manufactured models, but with 43 holes drilled diagonally through it to diffuse the gun's gases into a packing of glass wool. It would muffle the sound, but not to the commonly known cough of most silencers, only from an explosion to a loud crack. In the snug surroundings of the basement, with the doors closed and the air conditioning on in rooms upstairs, the killer wasn't worried about sound.

Giancana concentrated on his fixings, his attention turned away from the killer. Then, as he cooked, he felt the muzzle of the silencer tickle the hairs of the back of his head—*pop!*—and he fell to the floor with the crush of a bullet coursing upward, forward, and mildly leftward through his skull to where it lodged in the front left portion of his brain. He landed in a heap on his back, breathing his last, and the killer put the muzzle of the silencer in his mouth—*pop!*—and a bullet slashed straight backward into his cervical vertebra. Finally, the killer shoved the gun under Giancana's chin, Sam now lifeless, and aimed upward—*pop! pop! pop! pop! pop!*—bullets that shattered his lower jaw, ripped through his tongue and settled in the back of his skull; five shells, seven in all.

It was over. Giancana lay on his back, his legs crossed at the ankles, his left arm curled around, with the left hand just above his head, his right arm crooked at his side. As blood poured from the gaping throat wounds, and a small stream of blood-tinged fluid ran from Giancana's mouth and nose, the killer riffled through his pockets and pulled out his wallet. He checked through it for papers and notes, left behind the credit cards and $1,458 in cash.

Then the killer left, the wallet thrown five feet from the body and the seven shell casings. He went through the steel door, up the tiled stairway and out into the night. He checked the neighborhood, then hurried away unseen, unheard, unknown.

He headed into the upper section of Oak Park, then over to River Forest. On North Avenue he spotted flashing lights coming east. An emergency call about a burglary in River Forest had sent squad cars from three villages into motion. It was a call unrelated to what had gone on at the Giancana house, but the flurry of police cars made the killer fear that one of them might notice him. He turned onto Thatcher, a road bordering a forest preserve, and pulled over to the shoulder. Rolling down a window, he tossed the gun into the grass next to the road. He could have walked into the forest and tossed it into the deep underbrush or a creek, but apparently spotting a nearby road, a spot where teenagers liked to park, he was satisfied simply to get the gun out of his possession. It buried itself in five-inch grass. The killer drove on.

Back at the Giancana house, Joe DiPersio called down one last time before he turned in. He got no response and decided to go down to check. He found the food still cooking nicely on the stove. Then DiPersio, who in his long life had seen his share of violence and had once been taken in for questioning after a mob killing, saw the blood and the corpse. It was almost midnight. Before he called for an ambulance, Joe turned off the burners.

In minutes the house swarmed with police and firemen from the village. Giancana's daughters were contacted and they rushed to the scene. Antoinette, who had to make the long trip from her home in St. Charles, ran into the basement and became hysterical when she saw the body. "He's gone! He's dead! My father is dead!" she screamed. A relative had to restrain her, finally slapping her to calm her down. Her screams carried through the neighborhood and, along with the rush of police vehicles, awakened most of the neighbors.

Oak Park police filled the house, many of them there to get a look at the inside of the place. Detectives attempted to piece together the events leading to the killing, and present some kind of scenario for the dozens of reporters who had hurried out to the house from their desks at police headquarters in Chicago. But, aside from the media, village police did not contact any other agencies until early the next morning, giving the trail of the

murderer six hours to cool. They even spread the story that Giancana had been the center of a "welcome home" party that night,
a tale that gained credence from the many cigarette butts in the
ashtrays. Investigators later found the cigarettes to have come
from village police themselves.

That weekend Lou Graham won the U.S. Open Golf Championship at Medinah Country Club just a few miles away from Giancana's home. It was a win that Giancana would have closely
followed, as closely, perhaps, as he was following a Senate committee's hearings in Washington. Only days after his assassination, Giancana's old Las Vegas and Miami associate Johnny
Roselli told a Senate committee probing the government's intelligence agencies about the 1960 CIA attempts on Castro. He corroborated testimony given earlier by Robert Maheu, and then
made headlines by detailing the entire story, including the role
of Giancana, of the CIA's efforts with poison cigars and pills and
depilatories.

Giancana was also scheduled to appear before the committee,
a fact that gave rise to speculation that he had been silenced by
a CIA hit squad. Senator Frank Church, the head of the committee, even called for a probe into the matter. But local homicide
investigators almost immediately discounted the theory, pointing not only to conditions in Chicago that were reason enough for
the murder, but also to the fact that Roselli and Maheu had
testified at length with information severely damaging to the
CIA. They had not been touched (though a year later Roselli was
found murdered in Biscayne Bay near Miami, Florida), and it
was safe to say that Giancana had little of significance to add.

The CIA connection, however, was convenient to many close to
Giancana, who refused to believe he had been killed for being a
gangster. One of his daughters adamantly insisted that her father had been killed by the same people responsible for killing
the Kennedys. She also said she was severely disappointed that
President Gerald Ford had not sent the family a message of con-
dolence as he had to other survivors of CIA operatives killed in
action.

Instead, investigators found after piecing the evidence together, after talking with agents who had lived with the man for
years and knew him intimately, that his was a hit whose time

had come. His departure in 1965 had been a blessing in disguise for the outfit. Accardo had moved in and pulled things back under control. They stayed that way with few ruffles until Giancana came back in 1974. If he'd known better he'd have let things lie, assessed his strengths and compromised. But in years past that was something he had never done well, and wouldn't ever learn.

They had hit the don in his own home, a hit they wanted all the world to see. It still has an element of pride, the outfit, and they knew that would strip it from Giancana. The rules were and still are.

In the days following the murder and the funeral, the story refused to fade from view. Cook County state's attorney investigators removed Giancana's personal desk, filing cabinet, and safe from the home immediately after the killing, insisting they were crucial to their investigation. Giancana's daughters were furious and protested that it was their father who had had the crime committed against him, and detectives had no right to treat him like a criminal. They pursued legal action, but before they could secure an injunction the state's attorney's police opened the desk and went through its contents.

They found a microcosm of Giancana's world, slips of paper with names and notations of transactions, a record of race-track tickets and bets, a partnership agreement between him and Chuck English involving income from betting. There were personal items, hosts of pictures taken on vacations and at special events, most of them awkward family shots in color or black and white taken around the table or at resorts. Some showed them with entertainers Giancana had befriended, others relived a trip to the Vatican. There was a yellowed wedding photo, and others of Angeline. And with the pictures were religious items, rosaries, St. Christopher medals, all objects that surprised investigators familiar with Giancana's nonreligious life. There were also coins, not collectors' items, but half dollars and Eisenhower dollars. And there was the signed portrait of Phyllis McGuire.

The daughters' attorneys finally secured an injunction against investigators from Circuit Court Judge Daniel Covelli. But that too proved an acute embarrassment. It was learned that among the contents of the desk was an eleven-page wedding-guest list left over from Antoinette's 1959 marriage. On it were the names of the city's prominent hoods, and next to each was penciled in the amount given the wedding couple. A $500 gift was mandatory; most exceeded that, to a total nearing $100,000. And on the list, with a $500 notation next to his name, was Judge Daniel Covelli.

Covelli vehemently denied ever having attended the wedding or given the money. But his objections were overshadowed by the fact that he was the half-brother of Fred Morelli, one of the juke-box powers of the notorious First Ward organization in the 1940's.

The proceedings continued, with Covelli's ruling finally being reversed. In the presence of the daughters and their lawyers, investigators were finally able to empty the desk and filing cabinet, and inventory their contents.

Only the necessary proceedings remained. Giancana left no will, and the handling of the estate presented problems and conflicts. The Perno family were embittered because they were not a part of it as they had been promised. The daughters, with Francine as the executor, attempted to patch up differences and settle things. Bonnie made frequent trips up from Tucson, where she was a championship golfer, an interest she inherited from her father. The daughters even met for lunch, something they had not done for years.

The estate was filed in probate court, and Giancana's holdings were exposed for all to see. Claims came from lawyers and the undertaker, and a $750 bill for surgery was submitted by Dr. DeBakey. They were to be taken from an estate valued at $132,583.16. It was a modest amount by most standards, one that hardly reflected the wealth of a man who at one time controlled millions of dollars in cash. But it was true to the individual, one who had laundered most of his money, or put it in a bigger pot, lost it, squandered it, or simply was unable to retrieve it.

Apart from the $1,428 found in his wallet the night he was killed, another $300 was found in the home. Three accounts in the St. Paul Federal Savings and Loan Association in Chicago held $14,314.55, $20,000, and $20,000 respectively. He also held 375 shares of stock in Northwest Industries, 500 shares of Advanced Ross Corporation, 500 Central National Financial Corporation,

2,000 Utah Shale Land Corporation, 2,000 Utah Shale, Land, and Mineral Corporation, 6,000 Baltimore Transit Corporation, 1,500 shares of Quintas San Cristóbal, his home in Mexico, and a U.S. savings bond in his wife's name for $50.

The home in Oak Park was appraised at $40,000 and the goods inside it put at $55,184.21, a fraction of what they would have brought on the open market. The accompanying list of items, all appraised by a professional art dealer, gave some evidence of the quality and taste of it, and provided another look at what Giancana enjoyed, how he lived, and how far he had come.

Boxes of jewelry included pairs of gold cufflinks, a pair of jade stone with ruby eyes, gold money clips, one with sapphire chips and the initial "S," another with an affectionate, engraved message, a gold golf-ball marker, a number of gold cigarette lighters. There were an amber cigar holder, rings, one sculpted in a likeness of St. Christopher, medals, an engraved medallion from his three daughters. There were antique jewelry boxes of bronze and onyx, ashtrays, clothes trees, a wardrobe of silk suits, silk ties, silk handkerchiefs.

The house was filled with fine furniture, much of it in French provincial style, all of it in polished oak, mahogany, or maple. Rooms were furnished with paintings, porcelain lamps, urns, crystal candelsticks, and the countless groupings, the beloved porcelain that Giancana had spent years collecting.

In the entryway stood an exquisite 44-inch-high porcelain and onyx pedestal, and on it a valuable Unschuld Vienna porcelain urn. In the living room, with its porcelain lamps, end tables, plaques, and paintings, stood the Louis XV mahogany piano with its needlepoint seat. Amidst the carved, tufted chairs, loveseats, sofas, and carved, inlaid tables, was more porcelain. Again, it had been bought by Giancana himself, most after World War II, when he developed an obsession for German porcelain at its finest. He had put most objects in two wall cases on the east and west sides of the room. Close to fifty objects in all, all of significant value, perhaps to Giancana himself, priceless.

The other rooms filled out the home's elaborate furnishings: a well-preserved Romweber dining-room set, paintings, mantel clocks, chandeliers, one with three tiers of crystal and 27 lights, cabinets full of still more figurines, knick-knacks, and curios, hundreds of pieces of dinner and serving ware, an English bitters set, a gold Middle Eastern hookah inlaid with small rubies, and a hinged globe engraved, "Poor Sam—the World Is Yours," worth $3.

There was the basement, which held the trappings of Sam's hobbies, his cameras, golf equipment, the long meeting table, the well-equipped bar, the humidor.

In all, it was a well-endowed, casually elegant home, which only moderately impressed art dealers and antique connoisseurs, but which provided another side to the image of the snarling, cold-blooded don. To those who knew what it could have been, the final tally of goods was minuscule. Even those closest to him couldn't help feeling some disillusionment. The daughters faced delicate probate proceedings, then an embarrassing, publicity-filled public estate auction, another issue in lives spent hiding their surnames, marrying and moving to suburban areas where they told their neighbors nothing and demanded their children do the same. One said simply, truthfully, "You know, he didn't leave much."

In the months that followed, the name was to appear intermittently. A village worker in River Forest spotted a steel object while mowing grass along Thatcher Road, and he found it to be a gun and silencer. It turned out to be the murder weapon. Investigators made noises about the murder probe, maintaining that they were very close to the killer, but they arrested no suspect. Most went to other cases; agents kept surveillance over other houses. The home on the corner of Wenonah and Fillmore became little more than a curiosity. Neighbor kids occasionally rode their bikes into the driveway and told stories to friends. The more daring went over to the door to the basement and pointed down the steps. If he saw them, Joe DiPersio waved them away.

But he too fell ill and no longer was able to keep up the house and the grounds the way he always had. Until it was sold, the house would have to rely on the passage of time to keep out the curious. That and a rubber mat in front of the garage patio that gave evidence of what had gone on years before. Instead of welcome, it read, "Go Away." Yet in those vacant months following his murder and burial in a white marble tomb in the cemetery of his wife and parents, the mat seemed strangely inappropriate. For, in a house occupied only by an aging, ill caretaker and his wife, there was simply no one around to shoo.

Index

Abbreviation SG and nickname Mooney are for Sam Giancana.